Prehistory of the Americas

When and how did people first colonize the Americas? How did village life and agriculture arise? Why did complex societies develop in certain regions? These are some of the questions discussed in this wide-ranging book, which explores the development of the prehistoric cultures of North, Central, and South America from about 10,000 BC to AD 1530.

Beginning with an examination of the archaeological evidence for the earliest human migration from Asia to the New World, Stuart Fiedel traces the rapid expansion of Paleo-Indian hunters; the adaptations of Archaic hunter–gatherers to post-Ice Age environments; the origins and spread of farming and village life; and the rise and fall of chiefdoms and states. He shows how technological innovations, population growth, environmental constraints, climate change and social and ideological factors influenced the varying trajectories of cultural evolution that characterize different regions of the New World. He stresses the significance of New World prehistory as an essentially independent case of cultural evolution, displaying striking parallels to, yet also important differences from, the evolution of Old World cultures. He also includes a discussion of the development of American archaeology, from the early European encounters with native Americans to the "new" archaeology.

Written from a balanced theoretical stance, the book covers a vast literature in a clear and accessible way, presenting up-to-date material and highlighting current debates. It will be invaluable for students of New World prehistory, as well as appealing to general readers interested in the archaeology of the Americas.

Prehistory of the Americas

STUART J. FIEDEL

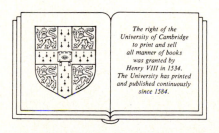

The right of the
University of Cambridge
to print and sell
all manner of books
was granted by
Henry VIII in 1534.
The University has printed
and published continuously
since 1584.

Cambridge University Press

CAMBRIDGE

LONDON   NEW YORK   NEW ROCHELLE

MELBOURNE   SYDNEY

Published by the Press Syndicate of the University of Cambridge
The Pitt Building, Trumpington Street, Cambridge CB2 1RP
32 East 57th Street, New York, NY 10022, USA
10 Stamford Road, Oakleigh, Melbourne 3166, Australia

First published 1987

Printed in Great Britain at the University Press, Cambridge

British Library cataloguing in publication data
Fiedel, Stuart J.
Prehistory of the Americas.
1. Indians – Social life and customs
I. Title
306′.097   E59.5

Library of Congress cataloguing in publication data
Fiedel, Stuart J.
Prehistory of the Americas.
Bibliography.
Includes index.
1. Indians – Antiquities. 2. America – Antiquities.
I. Title.
E61.F52 1987   970.01   86–24421

ISBN 0 521 32773 3 hard covers
ISBN 0 521 33979 0 paperback

Contents

List of illustrations   *page* vi

Preface   ix

1 The development of American archaeology: a brief review   1

2 From Africa to Siberia: early human migrations in the old world   22

3 The Paleo-Indians   39

4 The Archaic: post-Pleistocene foragers   82

5 The origins of agriculture and village life   160

6 Chiefdoms and states: the emergence of complex societies   223

7 Parallel worlds   340

References   358

Author index   379

Subject index   381

Illustrations

1	Seriation graph	*page* 9
2	C14 calibration curve	13
3	A prehistoric Anasazi kiva	20
4	Old World Paleolithic sites	24
5	Siberian Paleolithic sites	34
6	Chipped stone artifacts from Dyuktai Cave	37
7	Fluted point found at Folsom, New Mexico	48
8	Paleo-Indian sites	50
9	Clovis fluted points	57
10	Clovis artifacts	63
11	Use of the spearthrower, depicted on a Mochica gold ear-spool	66
12	Wooden mask from Spiro Mound, Oklahoma	72
13	Lindenmeier: shape and flaking of points	74
14	Plano points from the Olsen-Chubbuck site	76
15	Paleo-Indian sites in Central and South America	78
16	Fishtail points	80
17	Vegetation zones of North America, ca. 18,000 B.P.	83
18	Modern vegetation, North America	84
19	Modern vegetation, South America	85
20	Eastern Archaic sites and regions	88
21	Early Archaic points	89
22	Middle Archaic points	92
23	The L'Anse Amour burial mound	93
24	Laurentian ground-stone artifacts (New York)	102
25	Copper artifacts from the Great Lakes region	103
26	Late Archaic points from the Ossining Rockshelter	103
27	Artifacts from the Port au Choix cemetery	105
28	Steatite, fiber-tempered and Vinette I pottery	107
29	Susquehanna broad point (New York)	108
30	Poverty Point, Louisiana: mounds and concentric embankments	111
31	Western Archaic sites and regions	113
32	Crescent-shaped knife, San Dieguito complex, California	117
33	Elko corner-notched point (1500 B.C.–A.D. 500), Nevada	123
34	Pinto point, southern California	123
35	Desert side-notched point (after A.D. 1300), Nevada	124

36 Fremont clay figurine 126
37 Zoomorphic stone bowl, Marpole phase 131
38 Steatite whale figurine, Canaliño culture 133
39 Charm-stones, central California, ca. 2500–1000 B.C. 134
40 Arctic and Subarctic regions and sites 140
41 Paleo-arctic micro-blade and core 143
42 Northern Archaic point 144
43 Denbigh Flint end-blade (point) 145
44 Miniature ivory mask, Dorset culture 148
45 Ivory carvings from Ipiutak 150
46 Carved bone harpoon head, Old Bering Sea culture 151
47 Winged object (harpoon shaft weight), Old Bering Sea culture 151
48 Archaic sites in South America 156
49 Archaic points from western South America 157
50 Point types of the Magellan sequence, Patagonia 159
51 El Riego phase settlement pattern in the Tehuacan Valley 168
52 Coxcatlan maize (reconstructed) and teosinte 170
53 Colima ceramic dog 175
54 Dog figurine on wheels, Veracruz, Mexico, Classic period 176
55 Valdivia porsherds compared with Jomon potsherds 181
56 Female figurine from Valdivia 183
57 Textile from Huaca Prieta, with design showing stylized crabs and
    snakes 188
58 Central and South American sites representative of prehistoric farming
    tribes and chiefdoms 194
59 Prehistoric ceramic styles of the South American lowlands 196
60 Santarém vessel 200
61 Southwestern sites and culture areas 202
62 Early Hohokam artifacts 203
63 Pueblo Bonito 211
64 Anasazi pottery 212
65 Classic Mimbres bowl 214
66 Cliff Palace, Mesa Verde 218
67 Adena, Hopewell and Mississippian sites and regions 230
68 Adena artifacts 233
69 Hopewell earthworks at Newark, Ohio 237
70 Ohio Hopewell clay figurines 238
71 Hopewell platform pipe, in form of hawk 240
72 Hopewellian pottery with stylized bird motifs 242
73 Weeden Island vessel, "killed" before firing 245
74 Pipe in form of ocelot or jaguar, from Moundville, Alabama 246
75 Stone effigy pipe from Spiro Mount, Oklahoma 248
76 Artifacts from Tennessee, Spiro Mound, Oklahoma, and Etowah,
    Georgia 253
77 Mississippian pottery 254
78 Plains Village pot, Nebraska phase; Mississippian pot, Langston phase 258

79   Mesoamerican civilizations   261
80   A giant stone head from La Venta   262
81   Olmec jade celt   263
82   La Venta: fluted mound and associated structures   264
83   Stone relief in Olmec style, Chalcatzingo, Morelos   266
84   A "danzante' from Monte Albán   268
85   Tlatilco figurines   271
86   Teotihuacán, ca. A.D. 400: perspective view down the central avenue
     (Street of the Dead)   274
87   Stone mask from Teotihuacán   276
88   Tripod vessel from Teotihuacán   277
89   Kaminaljuyú, Guatemala: pyramid with talud-tablero facade   277
90   Stela marking twentiety year of the reign of Stormy Sky, Tikal,
     ca. A.D. 445   279
91   Olmec, Izapan, and Maya treatments of the same theme (a mask with
     toothless jaw)   284
92   Uaxactún: platform facade with stucco masks   285
93   A typical Maya pyramid: Temple I at Tikal   288
94   The lid of Pacal's sarcophagus   290
95   A section of the Bonampak murals   291
96   Scene on vase from Altar de Sacrificios   292
97   Stone column in form of a warrior, Pyramid B, Tula   297
98   Gold plate depicting human sacrifice, from the sacred cenote at
     Chichén Itzá   299
99   Stone with relief of the goddess Coyolxauhqui, found in Mexico City in
     1978   304
100 Stone figure, San Agustín culture   311
101 Coclé polychrome painted vessel   312
102 Stone belt with carved face of a zemi, from Puerto Rico   314
103 Andean civilizations   316
104 One of the buildings at Chuquitanta (El Paraíso)   317
105 A stela from Cerro Sechín   320
106 The Lanzón stela, Chavín de Huantăr   322
107 Mochica pottery   325
108 Aerial view of giant monkey, Nazca   327
109 Staff God, Gateway of the Sun, Tiahuancco   330
110 Chimu funerary mask   333
111 Maximum extent of the Inca empire   336
112 Walls of the "fortress" (possibly a religious structure) at Sacsahuaman,
     near Cuzco   339
113 Split representation in the art of the Northwest Coast and early China   348

Preface

The rather grandiose idea of writing a summary book on American pre-history first occurred to me in 1980. I was then teaching an introductory course on this subject for undergraduates, and neither I nor the students were satisfied with the few books that were available for their use. Despite the fact that I had begun my academic career as a specialist in Old World, not New World archaeology, I thought I would be able to write a concise, accurate, and readable book that would trace the development of prehistoric cultures in the Americas. The work I envisioned would focus on several questions concerning cultural processes, e.g., when and how did people first colonize the Americas? How did village life and agriculture arise? Why did complex societies develop in certain regions? Within this overall framework, I would present detailed descriptions of important and relevant sites, cultures, and artifacts. As my work progressed, I realized that in such a synthesis, the author must always strive for a balance between general theoretical discussions on one hand, and descriptive minutiae on the other. I fear that I may not have struck the ideal balance in every instance. Some readers will wish that more pages had been devoted to a theoretical issue, or to some specific data, that they regard as particularly interesting. I can only point out that the literature is vast, and I do not pretend to have written the last word on any subject. If the reader is stimulated to pursue some matter more intensively, so much the better.

It has taken five years to complete this book. During this time, new data and interpretations have continued to appear. I have tried my best to revise or supplement the text in those places where it has been rendered obsolete by new finds. I note with particular pleasure that my skeptical view of pre-Clovis occupation, regarded by some reviewers a few years ago as overly conservative, has been bolstered by the new, late dates obtained for allegedly early California skulls and for the bone tools from Old Crow. On the other hand, if pre-10,000 B.C. dates for such South American sites as Monte Verde keep appearing and ultimately form a consistent pattern, some pre-Clovis occupation will have to be admitted. We should probably expect many chronological surprises in the near future as the newly developed mass accelerator C14 dating process comes into wider use.

I want to thank a number of people for their assistance. Bernard Wailes, Shirley Gorenstein, Thomas Lynch, Herb Kraft and Judith Friedlander were kind enough to read the first draft of the manuscript. Some of their suggestions, and those of several anonymous reviewers, were incorporated in the final version. Sydne Marshall made available unpublished material from the Shawnee-Minisink site. Geary Zern provided me with many important references. Jacqueline Reilly contributed several excellent illustrations. Finally, thanks to Susan Allen-Mills, the editor for Cambridge, without whose cooperation this project could not have been brought to fruition.

1

The development of American archaeology: a brief review

America and its inhabitants suddenly emerged from prehistory into history, that is, the period in which events have been recorded in written documents, when Christopher Columbus landed on Samana Cay, in the Bahamas, in 1492. Columbus was not the first European to reach American shores; archaeological finds in Newfoundland have confirmed accounts in the Norse sagas of Viking expeditions to North America around A.D. 1000. However, the Vikings did not succeed in establishing permanent settlements on the American mainland. Even their initially prosperous colony in Greenland had perished by the mid-fifteenth century, unable to cope with climatic changes brought on by the Little Ice Age. As a legacy of their brief American venture, the Vikings left us the first description of native Americans, whom they called "Skraelings". These people, whose encounters with the Vikings were hostile, were probably Eskimos, and Algonquian-speaking Indians. Vikings who dug into the ruins of an Eskimo house in search of imagined treasures were the first Europeans known to have excavated an American archaeological site (Rowlett 1982). Even though white falcons, furs, and other items that the Vikings obtained in Greenland or farther west were traded southward into Europe, no one seems to have been very inquisitive about their point of origin. Several hundred years later, Columbus' reports of his discoveries evoked quite a different response from Europeans who had by then become acquainted with, and greedy for, the silks of China and the spices of the Indies. As is well known, the Spanish crown had financed Columbus' expedition in the hope that, by sailing west, he might find a shorter route to the Orient. Columbus himself was stubbornly convinced that he had succeeded in this mission. If the islands he had discovered were indeed the Indies, then the inhabitants must be "Indians". Thus was coined the totally inappropriate name by which the native Americans have been collectively known ever since. Actually, "Native Americans", which has recently become fashionable, is not much of an improvement, because "America" commemorates the Florentine navigator, Amerigo Vespucci, who explored the South American coast some years after Columbus' voyages. Having duly noted the inappropriateness of both

1

labels, I will proceed to use them interchangeably throughout this book, because there is no good alternative to them.

Before long, the European sea pilots who followed in Columbus' wake realized, as he had not, that he had stumbled upon a hitherto unknown "New World". America would not yield the coveted Oriental luxuries, but it possessed riches of its own. The gold of Mexico attracted Cortes and his small army, who managed, with the backing of rebellious subject peoples, to destroy the Aztec empire in 1521. The ruthless tactics of Pizarro toppled the empire of the Incas in 1532, allowing Spain to plunder the gold and silver of the Andes.

The Catholic Church enthusiastically supported these conquests of the heathens and aided in the destruction of their civilizations, melting down idols, burning sacred books, and razing temples. However, there were some priests, like Bartolomé de la Casas, who sympathized with the plight of the enslaved Indians. On the other hand, there were some churchmen who argued that the Indians were mere brutes, who should not even be offered salvation. They were not mentioned in the Biblical list of the descendants of Adam; from this, one could conclude that they were not really human, and thus had no souls to be saved. This matter was resolved by the issuance in 1537 of a papal bull affirming the Indians' humanity.

But if the Indians were human, who were they, and how had they come to live in America? Finding apparent similarities in Indian customs or languages to those that were known, or imaginatively attributed to, peoples of the Old World, theorists variously identified the Indians as lost Israelites, Phoenicians, Greeks, Scythians, Hindus, Tartars, Welshmen, etc. The theory of their origin which is unanimously accepted today by archaeologists and anthropologists was first proposed in 1590 by Fray Jose de Acosta, a Spanish priest. He suggested that the Indians were descended from hunters who had crossed into America from northern Asia. Considering how little was then known of the geography of northern Asia, this was a remarkably insightful speculation.

The natives encountered by the English and French colonists in eastern North America were not as highly organized as the Aztecs or Incas. Ironically, the absence of a centralized political hierarchy made these Indians more difficult to subdue; it also proved impossible to make profitable use of them as slaves. As late as the 1770's, the Iroquois of western New York were still a military power to be reckoned with; but they allied themselves with the British, the losing side in the Revolutionary War. The British had sought to mollify the Indians by forbidding white settlement west of the Appalachians. After the war, however, whites pushed through the mountains into the Ohio territory. They were astonished to find there large numbers of geometric earthworks and mounds, often containing skeletons. Such mounds were also present, but not so numerous, in some of the original areas of white colonization east of the mountains. One burial mound in Virginia was investigated by that all-around Enlightenment genius, Thomas Jefferson, in 1784. His aim was to determine whether the burials had all been deposited at once, or in stages. Jefferson's use of excavation to solve a problem rather than hunt for treasure, his careful excavation technique, and his cautious interpretation of the evidence, mark this as the first scientific archaeological research project in the Americas (Jefferson 1801). It was not to be equalled until more than a century had passed.

Jefferson tentatively concluded that the Indians' ancestors had raised the mounds and buried their dead in them. However, others attributed the mounds to a vanished civilized race, who had been exterminated by the Indians. The discovery of mounds in the Ohio and Mississippi valleys which were larger and more complex than those previously known in the east intensified the debate over the mound-builders' identity, and the mounds became the focus of a wildly imaginative literature in the early nineteenth century (Silverberg 1968). One avid reader of mound-builder fantasies was Joseph Smith, whose Book of Mormon, with its account of Israelite migrations to North America, seems to reflect his familiarity with this literature.

Why were nineteenth-century Americans so enthralled by the idea of a vanished race, and so reluctant to credit the mounds to the Indians? In part, this was a reasonable position to take; after all, at the time, there were no Indians building mounds. Those who attributed the mounds to a vanished race were apparently unaware of sixteenth- and seventeenth-century accounts, by French and Spanish explorers, of mound construction by Southeastern Indians. There was also a strong element of racism in the mound-builder myths. The westward expansion of whites entailed the displacement and annihilation of Indians. Any feelings of guilt or moral indignation that this process aroused might be assuaged if it were proven that the Indians themselves had violently wrested the land from its original inhabitants, the more civilized, and presumably white-skinned, mound-builders. White Americans, so acutely aware of their recent arrival from overseas, derived a peculiar psychological satisfaction from imagining the ancient landscape populated with heroic white men. The same feeling still exists today, as shown by the popular success of recent books that advance far-fetched claims that Libyans, Iberians, Celts, etc., wandered about in America 3,000 years ago.

In 1820, the first comparative study of the Ohio mounds, by Caleb Atwater, postmaster of Circleville, was published by the American Antiquarian Society, which had been founded in Boston eight years earlier. Atwater provided accurate descriptions of many sites, but he also lapsed into groundless speculation, suggesting that "Hindoos" had built the mounds. In 1848, the Smithsonian Institution published "Ancient Monuments of the Mississippi Valley", by E. G. Squier and E. H. Davis. Squier, a newspaperman and politician, and Davis, a physician, had carefully mapped and accurately drawn many Ohio mounds, and had also done some excavation. They had explicitly set out to avoid speculation; nevertheless, they theorized that the mounds were the work of a civilized, pre-Indian race, which had migrated southward under "incessant attack" by "hostile savage hordes".

In 1881, Congress forced John Wesley Powell, who preferred to spend the limited funds of his recently-created Bureau of Ethnology on studies of living Indians, to devote $5,000 a year to research on the mounds. Powell chose Cyrus Thomas, a naturalist from Illinois, to organize a project which, it was hoped, would finally resolve the question of the mound-builders' identity. In the Bureau's 12th Annual Report (1894), Thomas presented, in 730 pages, the results of his team's excavations. He interpreted the evidence as showing that a number of different cultures were responsible for the mounds in different areas, and that these mound-building groups were the immediate ancestors of historic Indian tribes. Archaeologists now realize that Thomas went too far in his attempt to link the prehistoric cultures to historic groups. For example, his suggestion that the Cherokees had built not only the mounds of Tennessee and North Carolina, but also some of the Ohio earthworks, is no longer accepted. Nevertheless, Thomas had succeeded in establishing that the Indians, not a mythical lost race, had built the mounds.

Thomas' project was symptomatic of a major organizational change in American archaeology that occurred toward the end of the nineteenth century. Archaeology was no longer solely the pastime of amateurs. Increasingly, the field was dominated by professionals, working out of museums, such as the Smithsonian and Peabody, and the universities. The involvement of the Bureau of Ethnology in research on the mounds is also an example of the close linkage that has developed in the United States between cultural anthropology and archaeology, a situation which contrasts with the separate development of these disciplines in most European countries.

THE INFLUENCE OF EVOLUTIONARY THEORY

The year of 1859 was a major turning point in the study of human origins. In his *Origin of Species*, Darwin presented his theory of evolution by natural selection. He only implied in this book that humans had evolved like other organisms, but in 1871 he offered a more extensive discussion of human evolution in *The Descent of Man*. Also in 1859, a commission of English scholars visited France to examine the stone tools that Boucher de

Perthes, a customs official, had collected from gravel deposits in the valley of the Somme. The Englishmen concluded that Boucher de Perthes was right; his discovery of these man-made artifacts in association with fossils of extinct animals showed that man had been on the earth for a very long time, much longer than the mere 6,000 years allowed by the traditional Bible-based chronology. The Neanderthal skull, discovered in Germany in 1856, was now recognized as a pre-*sapiens* human, and other examples of the same primitive-looking species began to turn up in French cave excavations.

The intellectual excitement generated by the radical new perspective on human origins spread to America, where it sparked the search for "Early Man". Crudely chipped, primitive-looking stone tools, such as those found in the Trenton Gravels of New Jersey in 1876, seemed comparable in form and age to European Paleolithic handaxes. Claims of great antiquity were also advanced for human skeletal remains, such as those found at Lagoa Santa in Brazil, which seemed to be contemporaneous with Ice Age mammals. Although the idea of very ancient occupation of the Americas was initially supported by prestigious scholars such as Frederic W. Putnam, the curator of the Peabody Museum, it had fallen into disrepute by the turn of the century. William Henry Holmes demonstrated in 1892 that the supposed Paleolithic tools were actually rejected rough-outs, left at quarries by comparatively recent Indians. Aleš Hrdlička, the Czech-born physical anthropologist at the U.S. National Museum, so effectively discredited alleged early man finds that archaeologists were reluctant to attribute ages greater than a few thousand years to their finds, lest they be subjected to his withering criticism. It was not until 1926, when fluted points were found embedded within the skeletons of extinct giant bison near Folsom, New Mexico, that the coexistence of man with Ice Age mammals in America was proven, thus pushing man's arrival back to at least 10,000 years ago.

CULTURAL EVOLUTION

At about the same time that Darwin was publishing his theories on biological evolution, other scholars were generating ideas about the evolution of human societies. The discovery of the Americas played a major part in the development of the concept of progressive stages of social evolution. As early as 1590, Indians were being viewed by European scholars as representatives of a developmental stage through which ancestral Europeans had once passed. In that year, engravings based on paintings by John White were appended to Thomas Hariot's *A Briefe and True Report of the New Found Land of Virginia*. White's imaginative portrayals of ancient Britons showed them naked and tattooed, just like the Virginia

Indians depicted in the book. The accompanying caption noted that "the inhabitants of the great Bretanne have been in times past as sauvage as those of Virginia". By the 1830's, it had been suggested that mankind had risen from hunting and gathering, first to agriculture and pastoralism, then to urban civilization. In 1877, Lewis Henry Morgan published *Ancient Society*, in which he proposed that mankind had progressed through three stages: savagery, barbarism, and civilization. Lower, middle, and upper phases of savagery and barbarism were separated by technological, economic, and social innovations, such as the bow and arrow, stock-raising, pottery, and the patriarchal family. Morgan and the other evolutionist anthropologists of the late nineteenth century believed that "primitive" peoples had somehow become fixed at developmental stages through which the more advanced cultures had passed. Thus, the Australian aborigine represented a living ancestor of the Victorian in much the same way that the platypus was a living fossil that illuminated the ancestry of the placental mammals. It should be noted that the evolutionists' stages were based primarily on ethnological comparison of still-extant societies, rather than on archaeological evidence. The difference between the approach of the cultural evolutionists and that of Darwin should also be stressed. Darwin's great achievement was not merely to postulate the gradual evolution of life forms – this had already been proposed by Lamarck, among others – but to suggest a mechanism, a process by which change had occurred, i.e., natural selection of those organisms best adapted to their environment. In contrast, the evolutionist anthropologists ranked societies along an evolutionary scale of complexity, but they could offer no convincing explanation of the apparent tendency of societies to become larger and more complex over time.

THE BOASIAN REACTION

By the early 1900s, as more ethnographic and archaeological data accumulated, it had become obvious that no amount of contortion could make them fit neatly into evolutionist schemes. Franz Boas, who had emerged through his work at the American Museum of Natural History and at Columbia University as America's foremost anthropologist, condemned evolutionism as unproductive speculation. He advised his students, who in their turn were to dominate American anthropology until the 1960s, to turn away from grand evolutionary schemes, and to concentrate instead on intensive collection of information on particular societies. Only after this phase of empirical research might it become possible to formulate general theories of cultural development.

Boas and his followers were interested in reconstructing regional prehistories, by tracing the spread of cultural traits, including technological devices, artistic motifs, myths and rituals. By revealing similarities and differences in items of past material culture, archaeology could contribute to this research program. However, its role, as perceived by the Boas school, was secondary to that of ethnology, which seemed to them to be just as effective a way of reconstructing the Indians' past. Hrdlička's and Holmes' discrediting of early man finds had resulted in a foreshortening of time perspective, so that it was widely believed that the Indians had arrived in America as recently as 5,000 years ago. Archaeologists tended to regard prehistoric artifacts as remnants from a brief, culturally static period preceding contact with whites. To take one illustrative example, a 1909 publication of the Museum of Natural History (Wissler 1909) contains photographic plates of artifacts excavated in New York City and Westchester County. They are grouped according to their presumed functions: knives, arrows, drills, pots, etc. All are referred to as "Algonquian", on the assumption that they were made by the same people who were encountered by the first Europeans in the area. Today we can recognize some of the pictured artifacts as belonging to the period of contact or a few hundred years earlier, but others are now known to be as old as 8,000 years.

CREATING A CHRONOLOGICAL FRAMEWORK

Of course, in 1909 there was no way to obtain accurate dates for these finds. Early investigators of the Ohio mounds had noted that very old trees had taken root atop some of the mounds; by counting the annual growth rings of the trees, minimum ages could be assigned to the mounds themselves. Another technique, which today we would call "cross-dating", had been applied by Cyrus Thomas, who found objects of glass and brass in some mounds. These items, of European manufacture, must have been brought into the Southeast by Spanish or French explorers, so that the mounds in which they had been placed could not be earlier than the sixteenth century. Obviously, cross-dating with Europe was not applicable to pre-Columbian sites. The only other way to approach the very basic problem of dating was the slow construction of a relative chronology; however, little progress could be made in this direction until archaeologists realized the significance of stratigraphic superposition. Simply put, where layers or "strata", whether of geological or cultural origin, lie superimposed on one another, the lower strata are earlier, and the upper ones are later; so the lower you dig down, the farther back you are going in time. This principle had been recognized by geologists at the end of the eighteenth century, and was employed by European archaeologists by the 1860s, but except for a few excavations of stratified shell mounds on the Southeastern coast, the Aleutian Islands, and California, it was not incorporated into American archaeology until 1911. American archaeologists had neglected stratigraphic studies, in part because sites with clearly superimposed layers were rarely encountered, and in part because of the general assumption that Indian cultures were not very old.

In 1911, Franz Boas encouraged one of his students, Manuel Gamio, to attempt to determine the relative ages of three different pottery styles which were represented among sherds collected from the surface of sites in the Valley of Mexico. One style was known to have been produced by the Aztecs, a second by the earlier Teotihuacan civilization; the age of the third was unknown. Bu digging a 7 m- (23 ft-) deep trench at Azcapotzalco, Gamio discovered that the third style was the earliest, for sherds of this type lay stratified below Teotihuacan potsherds which, as expected, occurred in the levels underlying those in which Aztec pottery was present. The earliest pottery is known today as "Formative".

In 1913, Nels Nelson, who had observed stratigraphic excavations in Europe, began to use stratigraphic techniques at sites in the Galisteo Basin of New Mexico. At Pueblo San Cristobal, he dug into a 3 m- (10 ft-) deep deposit, in which all the pottery types of the region were present in a vertical sequence. As there were no obvious layers in the soil, Nelson dug by arbitrary levels, bagging together all artifacts found within one-foot intervals. This arbitrary level method is still occasionally used today, particularly in situations where there are no discernible differences in soil color or consistency. However, arbitrary levels are likely to cut across natural layers; the result is mixing of material from different periods. Therefore, archaeologists today consider it preferable to excavate according to natural strata wherever these are apparent. An early example of such an excavation was carried out by Alfred Kidder at Pecos Pueblo, where he began to dig while Nelson was working at San Cristobal (Kidder 1924). Stratigraphic excavations were conducted at other Southwestern sites in the 1920s, and had become common elsewhere in the Americas by the end of the 1930s.

Both Nelson and Kidder made numerical tabulations of the potsherds of each recognized type that were recovered from each stratigraphic level; Kidder also noted the relative percentage frequencies of the pottery types. At both San Cristobal and Pecos, this procedure revealed small changes in relative frequencies of different types from level to level; these were best explained as the result of gradual change in the local culture through time, rather than abrupt replacement of one population by another. Nelson further observed that, while the quantities of some types remained about the same throughout his sequence, other types seemed to follow a sort of life cycle. Sherds of these types appeared in small numbers in lower levels, increased to maximum numbers in middle levels, then decreased toward the top of the stratigraphic sequence.

8

The life cycle of styles was the basis of another relating dating technique, seriation. Pioneering studies of pottery seriation were conducted in the Southwest by Alfred Kroeber (another Boas student) in 1915 and by Leslie Spier in 1916. They observed that the relative frequencies of surface-collected sherds of distinct types varied from site to site. This variation allowed the sites to be dated, relative to one another. Seriation was further developed by James A. Ford, who began to apply the method to Southeastern sites in the 1930s.

Seriation dating is based on the observation that particular styles of pottery, and other artifacts, are made and used by only a few people at first. Later, they are adopted by increasing numbers of people, and alternative, competing styles become correspondingly less popular. After a time, the popularity of the new style wanes as others displace it, and ultimately it is no longer produced. Drawn on a graph, where time is the vertical axis and percentage frequency is the horizontal axis, the lifespan of a style will approximate to a lens or "battleship" shape. Seriation is most useful in comparing ceramic assemblages from sites that were occupied for brief periods and are close enough to one another to permit the assumption that they belonged to the same culture. The relative age of the sites can be determined by arranging paper strips, whose lengths correspond to the percentages of each pottery type in the total assemblage, so that the strips representing each type form either a complete or truncated vertical lens shape. In the example shown here, sites A through H have been arranged chronologically. Notice, however, that it is quite possible to invert the sequence, making A the earliest site instead of the latest. In order to fix the beginning and end of the seriated sequence, it is necessary either to find a stratified site, where two or more types are present in superimposed levels, or to cross-date recognizable artifacts found in association with the ceramics at one of the unstratified sites. In

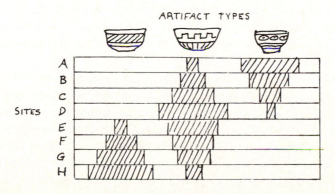

Fig. 1. Seriation graph.

the Southeast, Ford was able to fix one end of his ceramic sequence by association with historic European trade goods.

Stratigraphy and seriation could provide only relative dates; but in 1929, absolute year by year dating became possible, though only in the Southwest. For this, archaeologists could thank A. E. Douglass, an astronomer whose interest in the effects of sunspot activity on the earth's climate had led him, in 1913, to the study of tree rings. In the Southwest, fluctuations in rainfall caused variations in the thickness of the annual growth rings of coniferous trees. Each year, a pine tree adds another growth ring to the concentric pattern of rings, of varying width, which represent a year by year record of the tree's previous growth. In the arid conditions of the Southwest, wood was sometimes preserved for hundreds, even thousands, of years. Starting with trees that were still living, Douglass was able to push ever farther back in time, to about A.D. 1300, by matching up distinctive overlapping series of wide and thin growth rings. The prehistoric inhabitants of the Southwest had often used pine beams for the roofs of their houses, and Douglass applied the same counting method to build a "floating" chronology for these ancient samples. After some years of searching by archaeologists, in 1929 beams were found at Showlow Pueblo that allowed the floating chronology to be tied in to the established chronology, which was anchored to modern trees of known age. Today, archaeological dates based on tree rings extend as far back as 59 B.C. Tree ring dating of very old bristlecone pines in southern California has recently allowed the correction or "calibration" of carbon 14 dates (see below). Unfortunately, tree ring dating (dendrochronology) has not been feasible outside the Southwest, in regions where rainfall is more regular and growth rings are consequently less variable, and where a more humid climate causes wood to decay rapidly.

DEFINING ARCHAEOLOGICAL UNITS

It is easy to understand why, in the absence of absolute dating methods, archaeologists of the twenties and thirties were primarily concerned with the development of a chronological framework into which their material could be fitted. Another preoccupation of archaeologists of that period was the definition of archaeological entities. Their ethnologist colleagues had taken the "culture" as their unit of study. A culture was represented by a group of people with distinctive patterns of behavior and thought, a group conscious of their own separate identity, who usually spoke a language different from those of their neighbors. In some cases, the boundaries of the culture might correspond to those of a political entity, e.g. the Iroquois Confederacy. In other cases, e.g. the California Indians, a single culture might comprise numerous small, independent tribelets.

Ethnologists noted that cultures in the same broad region shared certain basic similarities in their material culture, evidently as the result of their adaptation to the same natural environment and their close contact with one another. These similar cultures could be grouped together for analytical purposes as larger units, known as culture areas, e.g., Plains, Northeast Woodlands, Sub-Arctic, etc.

What were the archaeological equivalents of the ethnologists' cultures? How could these units be recognized? One approach to this problem was to link archaeological assemblages to the historic cultures that produced them. Stylistically similar, but earlier, assemblages in the same area could then be identified as ancestral cultures. This is known as the direct historical approach, and it was pioneered by W. D. Strong in the early 1930s, in his study of sites in Nebraska that could be linked to the historic Pawnee.

Another way of dealing with archaeological material was to ignore ethnological categories and create an independent system of archaeological classification, based entirely on artifact similarities. Such a system was devised in the 1930s by archaeologists working mostly with museum collections in the eastern and midwestern states. The basic unit of this "Midwestern Taxnonomic Method" was the "component" – generally the assemblage of artifacts and features from one site, or, less often, the assemblage from one level of a stratified site. Very similar components were grouped together as "foci"; somewhat less similar components constituted "aspects". With decreasing similarity, components were classified as belonging to a "phase", then as part of a "pattern".

W.P.A. ARCHAEOLOGY

An important practical development of the 1930s was government-sponsored archaeology. The Works Progress Administration and other New Deal agencies provided funds and workers for large-scale archaeological projects, many of which were salvage operations in advance of the flooding caused by hydroelectric dams. Salvage work prior to construction of dams and roadways continued in the years after World War II, and archaeologists today are still working to mitigate the disastrous effects of development on the archaeological record, through Cultural Resource Management projects which are mandated and funded by the Federal Government.

CARBON 14

The most significant contribution to archaeological methodology after World War II was made by the physicist Willard F. Libby, who perfected the technique of carbon 14 dating in 1949. Carbon 14 is a radioactive isotope that is produced in the upper atmosphere when nitrogen atoms are bombarded by cosmic radiation. C14 behaves chemically just like normal non-radioactive C12. It is incorporated into carbon dioxide molecules which are absorbed from the air by green plants. When the plants are ingested by herbivorous animals, C14 passes into their tissues as well, and so on through the whole trophic chain of life forms. When a plant or animal dies, it takes in no more C14, and the slow breakdown of the radioactive atoms within it begins. Libby discovered that this breakdown by the emission of beta particles proceeded at a constant rate. Half of the radioactive carbon atoms remained after 5,568 years; half of these would decay in the next 5,568 years, and so on. The "half-life" figure was later corrected to 5,730 years, but by convention dates are still based on the original calculation.

By converting a sample of organic, once-living material into a gas, and counting the beta particles emitted over the course of a few days, the amount of C14 remaining in the sample can be determined. The difference in the ratio of C14 to C12 from that which normally exists indicates the amount of radioactive decay that has occurred, and therefore the length of time that has passed since the death of the organism.

Anything that was once alive can be dated by this method – wood, bone, seeds, wool, linen or cotton textiles, etc. – but the most reliable dates come from charcoal. If organic remains have perished in acid soils, no date can be obtained. C14 dating has other limitations. Not enough C14 remains in samples older than 50,000 years to permit dating; this is a major problem for early man studies in the Old World, but it is less significant in the Americas, where there are no credible traces of human activity at such an early date. Radiocarbon dates are not precise; because of the possibility that the particle emissions recorded during the brief time that the sample is in the laboratory counting chamber are not representative of its actual C14 content, there is a statistical margin of error that is expressed by the standard deviation figure (e.g. ± 150) that always accompanies a C14 date. In this case, there is a 66.6% probability that the real date lies somewhere within 150 years of the stated age, and a 95% probability that it lies within two standard deviations, i.e. in a range of 600 years. Another potential problem is contamination of the sample, either by recent carbon (e.g. from invasive rootlets) or by old carbon (as in calcium carbonate, absorbed by shellfish).

Suspicions about a possible systematic error in the radiocarbon method began to arise when C14 dates for objects from the First Dynasty of Egypt came out at about 2600 B.C., five or six hundred years later than expected on the basis of calendrical dates. In the late 1960s, C14 testing of ring dated bristlecone pines showed that there was indeed a serious problem.

Libby had assumed that the rate of cosmic radiation, and therefore the creation of C14, was constant; but in fact, there have evidently been fluctuations through time, probably caused by periodic changes in the strength of the earth's magnetic field. Organisms that lived when there was more C14 in the atmosphere than there is today will seem younger than they really are. Thus, an object with a C14 date of 3500 B.C. dates from 4375 B.C. in real years. The margin of error becomes less significant after about 1500 B.C. in radiocarbon years. Several laboratories have published charts which allow C14 dates to be corrected or "calibrated" on the basis of tree ring dates. Trees older than about 6300 B.C. in real years have yet to be found; but the shape of the calibration curve constructed so far hints that C14 and real dates may become less divergent as one moves farther back in time. Today, many archaeologists continue to report C14 dates in their uncorrected form, while others have begun to publish calibrated dates, sometimes unfortunately without explicit statements that they are doing so. This can create false impressions of the relative ages of different sites and cultures. In this book, I will follow the practice of stating calibrated dates in parentheses.

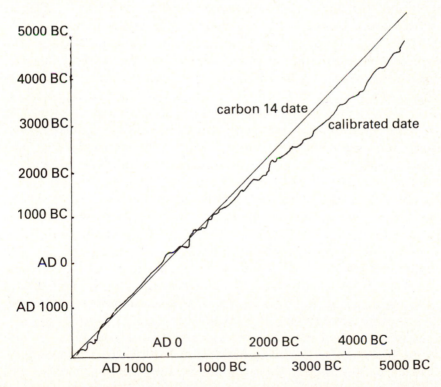

Fig. 2. C14 calibration curve. Example: a radiocarbon date of 4750 BP (2800 BC) is equivalent to 5530 B.P. (3580 B.C.) in real years.

The relatively minor problems that have complicated C14 dating should not obscure the fundamental, revolutionary significance of this technique for archaeological research. It allowed archaeologists to transcend their former obsession with chronology. Given a framework of absolute dates, they could move on to compare the cultural sequences in different areas, to investigate the causes of variation in the rates of cultural development. In short, they could now ask not only "When?" but also "Why?"

FUNCTIONALISM IN ARCHAEOLOGY

In the late forties and the fifties, changes occurred in the theoretical perspectives of American archaeology, largely in response to trends in cultural anthropology. In the 1930s, American anthropologists began to absorb the ideas of the British structural-functionalists, Malinowski, Radcliffe-Brown, and their disciples. Like Boas, these British scholars eschewed the speculations of the evolutionists. They assumed that each of the different aspects of a society – its economic, social, and political systems – had a role or function in satisfying basic human needs and in maintaining the social order, just as the organs of a living organism had their own appropriate functions. It was the task of the anthropologist to demonstrate the functional inter-relationship of institutions and patterns of behavior as parts of an integrated whole.

The impact of functionalism on archaeology was evident in the increasing attention devoted in the late 1940s and afterward, to the spatial associations of artifacts and features. Artifacts that are found close together, at the same horizontal level, may usually be assumed to have been deposited at about the same time. Where the context is clearly delineated, the relationship of the artifacts and other nearby objects may be functional or behavioral as well as temporal. For example, stone points and knives excavated amongst the disarticulated and broken bones of bison can be interpreted as a killing and butchering tool kit. Similarly, clay pots and grinding stones found in the vicinity of a hearth, within a structure, may be the remnants of a food preparation kit. Moving up a step in scale, house foundations clustered within an acre or two, and containing artifacts of the same period, obviously constitute the remains of a village. The number and arrangement of the houses may permit inferences about the social and political organization of the community. Is there a centrally located structure, larger and more elaborate than the others and filled with more items of exotic origin? Perhaps this was a chief's dwelling, or possibly the village shrine. Is the settlement internally subdivided into smaller clusters of houses? This may indicate a society composed of several separate lineages or clans. On a still larger scale, the distribution of contemporaneous settlements within an entire region may indicate the political and economic relationships among communities that were linked in a complex system; or it may show how the human inhabitants differentially exploited the resources available in their natural environment.

In the 1930s and 1940s, archaeologists developed better techniques for the excavation of structures, learning how to recognize and follow living floors; such horizontal excavation increased the likelihood that close associations of artifacts and features would be recognized. In 1946, Gordon Willey conducted a survey of sites in the Viru Valley in Peru. This was the first research project to concentrate on the recognition and analysis of settlement patterns.

CULTURAL ECOLOGY
AND THE REVIVAL OF EVOLUTIONISM

As archaeologists of the 1950s turned their attention to settlement patterns, they realized that even in complex, stratified societies, settlement patterns reflected not only social and political relationships but also systematic adaptations to features of the natural environment. Most obvious was the clustering of sites of the early civilizations, such as Egypt and Mesopotamia, in river valleys. This pattern suggested to Karl Wittfogel, a specialist in Chinese history, that irrigation and flood control systems, which were required for survival in river valleys, had caused centralization of political power, thus giving rise to the early states (Wittfogel 1957). The similar adaptations and courses of development of the riverine civilizations had also attracted the attention of Julian Steward. In the 1930s, Steward had studied the lifeways of the Shoshoni Indians of Nevada, and had observed that their social organization and settlement pattern were dictated by the sparse and fluctuating resources of their arid environment. Apparently, both simple and complex societies were shaped to some extent by their natural environments. Steward theorized that each culture was constructed around a set of "core" features which were environmentally determined. The study of the interaction of culture and environment, which Steward advocated, he termed "cultural ecology". As we shall see, this approach was to have a profound effect on archaeological research strategies and theories.

The parallel developmental trajectories followed by the riverine civilizations suggested to Steward that recurrent processes of culture change had driven societies occupying similar environments through the same stages of development (e.g., Formative, Regional Florescent, Initial Empire, Dark Ages, Cyclical Conquests). These developments had occurred only in particular environmental contexts; elsewhere, societies

15

had followed different trajectories. In advancing these ideas, Steward was reviving the theory of cultural evolution, which had lain dormant in American anthropology since Boas' reaction against it. However, Steward was careful to distinguish his approach, which he called "multilinear evolution", from that of the nineteenth-century evolutionists and of his own contemporaries, V. Gordon Childe, the Australian archaeologist, and Leslie White, the American anthropologist. Steward dismissed their "unilineal" conceptions of the cultural evolution of mankind as a whole, without regard to ecological factors, as too general to be of any use as a strategy for anthropological research (Steward 1955).

The renewed anthropological interest in cultural evolution, sparked by Steward, continued to be expressed in the late fifties and sixties in the work of such scholars as Elman Service (1965) and Morton Fried (1967). Service and Fried each devised evolutionary schemes by which existing societies could be classified according to their level of socio-political development. Service differentiated bands, tribes, chiefdoms, and states; Fried's roughly equivalent stages were egalitarian, ranked, stratified, and state. Transitions from one stage to the next were explained as resulting from techno-economic change (e.g., the introduction of agriculture) and population growth.

The work of Steward and his successors contributed to archaeologists' formulation, in the 1960s, of a new agenda for their own research. The long sequences of prehistoric cultural development that they were now able to construct, with the aid of radiocarbon dates, could be examined and compared to discover recurrent processes. This could conceivably lead to the formulation of general laws of culture change, comparable to the laws of the physical sciences. A renewed interest in stages of cultural evolution was evident in a 1958 synthesis by Gordon Willey and Philip Phillips, in which they outlined five sequential stages to describe the process of culture change in the Americas: Lithic, Archaic, Formative, Classic, and Post-Classic.

Cultural ecology had several repercussions in archaeology. Archaeologists began to devote more effort to the recovery and analysis of non-artifactual material – animal bones, pollen, carbonized seeds and nutshells, etc. – which would aid them in reconstructing prehistoric environments and the subsistence practices by which societies adapted to them. One new technique that was introduced in the 1960s was flotation. Soil samples are floated in water or a chemical mixture, and carbonized bits of plants are skimmed off the top. Recently, advances have been made in the recovery and analysis of microscopic silica skeletons, or phytoliths, which allow plants to be identified with some accuracy. Phytoliths are long-lasting and quite resilient; they have even been found adhering to the surfaces of stone tools. These are among the many new techniques that have led to more detailed reconstructions of prehistoric environments and subsistence strategies.

Archaeologists were encouraged by the realization that Steward's culture "core" – the basic technological and ecological adaptations of a society – was accessible to study. Social institutions and ideological forms were not so easily reconstructed, but if, as Steward implied, these were secondary phenomena whose characteristics were largely determined by the core features, this did not appear to be an insurmountable difficulty.

The idea of a determinant techno-economic core was very similar to, and undoubtedly influenced by, Karl Marx's conception of society as composed of a technological and economic infrastructure, underlying and ultimately determining the shape of the social and political institutions and ideology that comprise the superstructure. Marx saw changes in the superstructure as mere secondary reactions to and reflections of more basic changes that occurred in the technological and economic domain. This was the essence of his materialist view of history. A slightly modified version of Marx's model has been promulgated in recent years by anthropologist Marvin Harris, who describes himself as a "cultural materialist" (Harris 1968, 1979). For Harris, the infrastructure is the techno-environmental base, which is the society's means of adaptation to its environment. The secondary level of social and political institutions, and the tertiary level of ideology, are determined by the base, which shifts over time in response to environmental change and demographic pressure. In view of the inherent limitations of their data, it is obvious why archaeologists have almost unanimously adopted a materialist approach to the explanation of cultural processes.

The "New Archaeology" that emerged in the late sixties was ideologically committed to multilineal evolutionism, cultural ecology, and materialism. "New" archaeologists, whose most prominent spokesman was Lewis Binford, saw the ultimate goal of archaeology as the explanation of culture change. They sought to discover general laws, or at least to make law-like probabilistic statements about culture change. They contended that this goal would only be achieved through a deductive research procedure, modelled on that used in the physical sciences. This involved the testing of alternative hypotheses against the data collected; one of these would be confirmed through the rejection of the others. This procedure required unbiased data; to ensure their availability, much attention was focussed on the development of appropriate sampling techniques to be used in surveys and excavations. Hypothesis testing often took the form of statistical manipulation of numerical data, frequently accomplished with the aid of a computer. The new archaeologists took functionalist assumptions, cultural ecology, and the Marxist base–superstructure model a step further, viewing each culture as an open system, externally interacting with its ecosystem, and internally composed of sub-systems – economic, political, social, ideological – all linked by feedback mechanisms. There has been some tension between this systems approach, most eloquently presented in the writings of Kent Flannery, and the law-seeking (or "nomothetic") strategy; the feedback loops of systematic models can become so complicated that simple cause and effect relationships may be obscured.

After some overly optimistic early pronouncements that our knowledge of the past is limited only by our theoretical and methodological shortcomings, Binford and others have come to realize that the archaeological record is itself incomplete, material remains having been destroyed, modified, or displaced by natural and cultural processes. This realization has led to recent studies of the decomposition of dead animals, the accumulation of garbage, and other processes, observable today, that replicate those which presumably shaped the archaeological record. Ethno-archaeologists have gone to live in extant "primitive" communities, to observe the operation of simple technologies which are comparable to those known archaeologically. For example, Binford (1978) has done an exhaustive study of butchering, cooking, and consumption of caribou by the Nunamiut Eskimo. Such studies, it is hoped, will ultimately sustain a set of "middle range' theories, or bridging arguments that will allow archaeologists to connect material remains to the behavior patterns that produced them.

The evolutionary perspective of contemporary archaeology is reflected in the structure and content of this book. While there is a chronological progression in the overall treatment of the material, I have occasionally cut across temporal boundaries to compare cultures at the same level of development. From an evolutionary vantage point, we can recognize four or five broad levels or stages of economic, social, and political development of prehistoric American cultures:

1 Paleo-Indian: intensive big game hunting, band organization.
2 Archaic: scheduled nomadic foraging; band organization.
3a) Developed or Sedentary Archaic: intensive collection, villages, tribes or small-scale chiefdoms.
 b) Formative: agriculture, villages, tribes and chiefdoms.
4 Civilizations: intensive agriculture, cities, states.

It is clearly the subdivided third stage that is most ambiguous, and that departs from traditional schemes. By subdividing this stage, I have given explicit recognition to the fact, which recent archaeological and ethnological work has clarified, that in certain favorable environments, e.g., the Northwest coast, California, the Ohio valley, and possibly the Peruvian coast, hunter–gatherers lived in stable villages and established socio-political systems as complex as those of early agricultural societies.

In this survey of American prehistory, apart from providing simple descriptions of the distinctive traits of various archaeological cultures, I will ask questions about cultural processes, such as: How did the first hunting peoples make their way through the Americas? How and why did permanent settlements and food production begin? Why did complex societies emerge where they did? How did ecological opportunities or constraints influence the differing developmental trajectories of cultures in various environments? We will be looking for archaeological indications of those factors which may have induced culture change, e.g. population growth, environmental shifts, and technological innovations.

From time to time, I will refer to ethnographic analogies, drawn from historically observed American Indians or other cultures, which may help to reconstruct the behavioral contexts of prehistoric sites and artifacts. Use of analogies implies acceptance of the materialist assumption that the technological and economic domains or sub-systems, which are those most adequately represented by archaeological remains, have a determining influence on other cultural domains.

For eixample, take the case of the Paleo-Indian hunters. We know from the kill sites that have been excavated that they pursued big game. Their artifactual assemblages are dominated by hunting weapons and butchering tools, whose functions can be identified on the basis of comparison with similar artifacts from later cultures, distinctive use-wear on the tools' edges, and experimental replication. More recent, ethnographically known hunting peoples, such as the Eskimos and the Ona of Tierra del Fuego, usually move about frequently, in groups of 25 to 50 people. The need for mobility, and an ethical emphasis on cooperation and sharing within the band, discourage accumulation of personal wealth, so there is little inequality. The inference, based primarily on their mode of subsistence, that Paleo-Indians were band-organized, like recent hunters, seems to be supported by the small size of most excavated campsites. In the realm of ideology, which is generally even more difficult to infer from material remains than is socio-political organization, analogy with modern hunters can suggest at least the general outlines of the prehistoric ideological system. Hunting peoples, in the Americas and elsewhere, generally ascribe curative and divinatory powers to shamans, who are believed to communicate with spirits and deities. So widespread is shamanism that we can be reasonably confident in attributing some variety of it to the Paleo-Indians.

In other archaeological cases, analogies may be more precisely drawn, especially where there is evidence of historical continuity. For example, the use of certain rooms in ancient Southwestern villages as ceremonial chambers is indicated by the correspondence of their internal features to those found in the kivas of modern Pueblo Indian villages. Or, to cite another good example of direct historical analogy, the worship of Tlaloc, Quetzalcoatl, and other gods in the ancient Mexican city of Teotihuacán can be inferred from the presence there of symbols which the later Aztecs used to designate those same gods.

DIFFUSION VS. INDEPENDENT DEVELOPMENT

The "new" archaeologists, reacting against earlier interpretations of prehistory, have tried wherever possible to explain cultural change by reference to internal, systemic factors. Diffusion, the transfer of items or ideas from one culture to another, has been rejected as an inadequate explanation by itself. It must be shown why the imported innovations were acceptable to an existing culture, by what mechanisms they could be transmitted, and how they could be absorbed without disrupting the ongoing cultural system. Not very long ago, archaeologists speculated unabashedly about the diffusion of such cultural traits or trait-complexes as pottery, farming, metal-working, and mound-building, from the Old

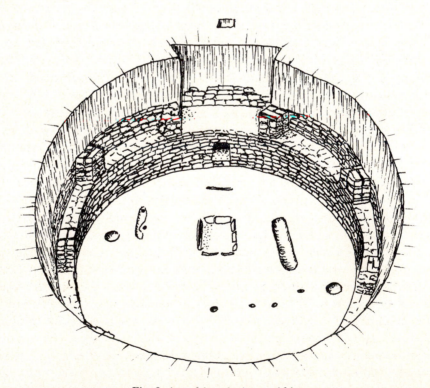

Fig. 3. A prehistoric Anasazi kiva.

World to the New. However, as research has progressed, independent, indigenous development of all these traits has been convincingly demonstrated. Today, only a few marginal theorists, such as Thor Heyerdahl, persist in explaining Old World–New World similarities as the results of trans-oceanic voyages. Heyerdahl (1971) has sailed papyrus boats across the Atlantic, to demonstrate that ancient Egyptians could have done the same, carrying with them pyramid-building, sun worship, and mummification, which they introduced to the less advanced peoples of Mesoamerica. Heyerdahl's theory is the same one that was proposed by the British diffusionists, Smith and Perry, in the 1920s. Like Barry Fell's (1976) "America B.C." fantasies about Bronze Age Celts and Libyans wandering throughout North America, the Egyptian theory is not taken seriously by contemporary archaeologists.

Even less grandiose diffusion theories, which postulate transmission over shorter land routes, are regarded with skepticism today. A good example is the controversy over the causes of the sudden burst of building and craft production in Chaco Canyon, in northern New Mexico, early in the eleventh century. Most Southwestern archaeologists attribute this to an internal process – centralization of political and economic control, either as the outcome of differential access to irrigation water, or as a means of facilitating redistribution of essential resources in an arid environment. However, another group of scholars sees Chaco Canyon as a northern outpost of Mexican civilization, its inhabitants drawing upon the knowledge and techniques brought to them by itinerant merchants from the south. As we shall see, chronological difficulties preclude a simple diffusionist explanation of the Chaco phenomenon. Nevertheless, there can be no question that, at a much earlier date, the staple crops of Southwestern farmers – maize and squash – had been carried northward from their point of origin in Mexico. Whether this was accomplished by diffusion or by colonization has yet to be determined. It is noteworthy that squash, and the techniques for its cultivation, had been transmitted as far as Kentucky by about 2500 B.C.; yet some 3,000 years elapsed before the peoples of the eastern woodlands began to rely to any significant extent on cultivated crops. Similarly, cultivation of Mesoamerican crops was never adopted by the hunter–gatherers of California. These differing reactions to the introduction of Mesoamerican plants show, on the one hand, the significant cultural change that can result from the borrowing of diffused traits, but on the other hand, how items exotic to a culture may be rejected or under-utilized until internal factors – perhaps, in the case of the eastern woodlands, the growth of population beyond the number that could be supported by traditionally exploited wild resources – permit or require their acceptance.

2

From Africa to Siberia: early human migrations in the Old World

The journey of the ancestral Paleo-Indians across the land bridge between Siberia and Alaska, more than 12,000 years ago, was the final stage of a process of migration and colonization that had begun 1½ million years earlier. Continual northward and eastward movements of hunter–gatherer bands had resulted in the extension of the range of human habitation from the tropical savannas of southern and eastern Africa to the cold, dry tundra-steppes of northern Asia. In adapting to the diverse environments of this vast region, humans had changed both physically and culturally. In this chapter we will briefly review the major evolutionary developments that occurred prior to the arrival of early humans at the threshold of the New World. Some familiarity with the pre-history of Eurasia is necessary, both to see the Paleo-Indian migration in a broader perspective, and in order intelligently to evaluate arguments concerning the date and nature of the initial colonization of the Americas.

EARLY HOMINIDS OF AFRICA

On the basis of recent fossil discoveries and comparative studies of proteins and DNA, a consensus has been reached among most anthro-pologists that the ancestral human line diverged from that of the chim-panzee in Africa, some time between 10 and 5 million years ago. The earliest hominid species that is well-represented by fossil remains is *Australopithecus afarensis*, which dates from about 3.5 million years ago. Fossils found in Ethiopia and Tanzania show that *A. afarensis* walked bipedally, like later humans. However, their brains were still ape-sized, and there is no evidence that they hunted or used tools. Between 3 and 2 million years ago, probable descendants of *A. afarensis* lived in eastern and southern Africa. At least two, and probably three species of Australopithecines are represented by fossils of this period: a smaller, gracile type, *A. africanus*, and two larger types, *A. robustus* in southern Africa and *A. boisei* in eastern Africa. The larger varieties are thought to have ulti-mately become extinct; but whether *A. africanus* suffered the same fate, or was ancestral to later humans, is not yet clear. In any case, a larger-brained hominid, *Homo habilis*, appeared in Africa about 2 million years ago. The growth of the brain, from the 450 cc of *A. africanus* to the 600–800 cc of *Homo habilis*, seems to have been causally related to the first use of stone tools and to the eating of hunted or scavenged meat. At 2 million year-old sites in Olduvai Gorge and near Lake Turkana, close to the find-spots of *Homo habilis* specimens, broken bones of elephants, hippo-potamus, antelopes, and other animals have been found, in association with stone tools. These Oldowan, or "pebble" tools, include both simple choppers (or cores) and sharp flakes, which were probably used as knives and scrapers. The hominids, with their small canines and clawless fingers, needed such tools to slice through the tough hides of animal carcasses. The habit of meat-eating seems to have distinguished the early members of the genus *Homo* from their Australopithecine cousins, whose huge molars imply an almost exclusively vegetarian diet of fibrous fruits, roots, and seeds.

A lower jaw found on the island of Java, in deposits which may be as old as 1.8 million years, resembles *Homo habilis* specimens from Olduvai Gorge. Recently, Chinese archaeologists have reported their discovery of Oldowan-like cores and flakes, along with animal bones, at the Hsihoutu site in Shangsi province; this site may also be about 1.8 million years old (Gowlett 1984). If further research confirms the early dating of these finds, we will have evidence that bands of *Homo habilis* had migrated into Asia, reaching its easternmost regions almost 2 million years ago.

Back in eastern Africa, there is evidence of the appearance of a more advanced hominid about 1.5 million years ago. This hominid, *Homo erectus*, is generally assumed to have evolved from *Homo habilis*. A more highly developed stone tool industry, the Acheulian, seems to have been intro-duced by *Homo erectus*. Acheulian tools appeared at sites in eastern and southern Africa about 1.5 million years ago, and the industry later spread to Europe and western Asia. The most typical Acheulian artifact was the handaxe. These large, teardrop-shaped, bifacially chipped tools may have served a variety of functions, but a recent study of edge wear on some English specimens has shown that they were used to skin and butcher animals. This is not surprising, because archaeologists have excavated a number of sites where *Homo erectus* killed and butchered animals, such as giant baboons at Olorgesailie (Kenya), elephants at Torralba and Ambrona (Spain), and cattle-like *Pelorovis* at Olduvai.

HOMO ERECTUS IN EASTERN ASIA

Skeletal remains of *Homo erectus* have been found at several sites in eastern Asia. Fossils recovered from the Trinil beds of Java are probably 700,000–800,000 years old, and a skull from Lantien, China, is of comparable age.

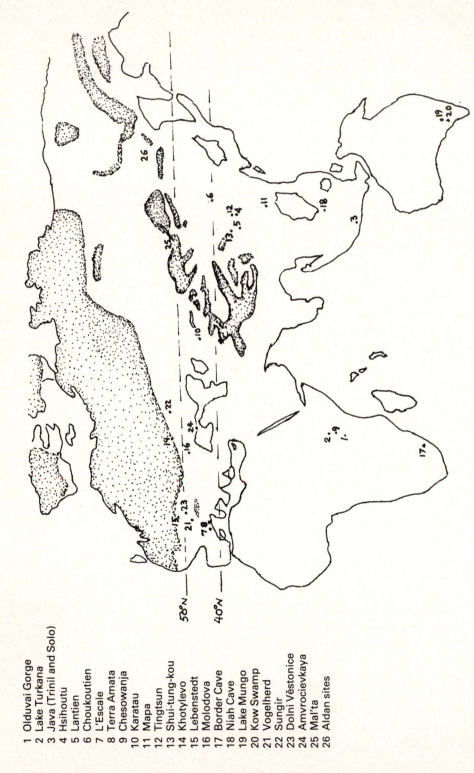

1 Olduvai Gorge
2 Lake Turkana
3 Java (Trinil and Solo)
4 Hsihoutu
5 Lantien
6 Choukoutien
7 L'Escale
8 Terra Amata
9 Chesowanja
10 Karatau
11 Mapa
12 Tingtsun
13 Shui-tung-kou
14 Khotylevo
15 Lebenstedt
16 Molodova
17 Border Cave
18 Niah Cave
19 Lake Mungo
20 Kow Swamp
21 Vogelherd
22 Sungir
23 Dolní Věstonice
24 Amvrocievkaya
25 Mal'ta
26 Aldan sites

Fig. 4. Old World Paleolithic sites. Glaciated areas are indicated by stippling. Note the extended coastlines resulting from lower sea level.

Another famous Chinese site, where remains of 40 individuals were discovered, is Choukoutien, southwest of Peking. Unfortunately, the original specimens, excavated in the 1930s, were lost in the chaos caused by the Japanese invasion of China, but well-made casts survived, permitting further scientific analysis of the finds. Studies of the skulls and casts revealed several intriguing similarities between the Choukoutien *erectus* skulls and those of modern Mongoloids and native Americans. These features include: the mid-line ridge or "keel" along the top of the skull; the mandibular torus, an overgrowth of the lower jaw which is particularly common among Eskimos; molars with large pulp cavities (taurodont), and shovel-shaped incisors (upper front teeth with concave inner surfaces) (Laughlin 1966). Although many of the dozen Mongoloid-like traits discerned in the Choukoutien fossils occur in some individuals in modern populations in other parts of the world, these traits nevertheless strongly suggest that Chinese *Homo erectus* contributed some genes to later Asian and native American *Homo sapiens*.

Besides fossil hominids, the Choukoutien caves also yielded evidence of early human lifeways about 400,000–350,000 years ago. The inhabitants of Choukoutien were efficient hunters, preying upon giant sheep, horses, pigs, buffalo, rhinoceros, and – most often – deer. Excavators of the cave sites found many charred bones of these animals, showing that *Homo erectus* used fire not only for warmth but also for cooking. Deep charcoal deposits marked the locations of the ancient hearths, which had apparently been kept burning continuously.

Controlled use of fire was essential if hominids were to succeed in occupying regions with temperate (or colder) climates; without its artificial warmth, furless, tropics-adapted humans could not have survived the winter months. There is a good possibility that *Homo erectus* may already have known how to use fire when he arrived in northern areas. At the 1.5 million year-old campsite of Chesowanja, in Kenya, burnt clay and stones seem to be the remnants of ancient hearths. Fire may have been used more than 1 million years ago at a few other sites in eastern Africa (Gowlett 1984). Later, indubitable traces of fire have been found at two French sites, L'Escale, dated to about 700,000 years ago, and the 400,000 year-old campsite at Terra Amata, on the Riviera. We cannot tell whether *Homo erectus* knew how to start fires, or only preserved naturally occurring flames; the earliest known fire-starting tools come from Upper Paleolithic sites.

The faunal remains from Choukoutien indicate that *Homo erectus* lived there during an interglacial episode in the Middle Pleistocene. The Pleistocene, or "Ice Age", began about 1.7 million years ago (actually, there were previous glacial advances as early as 2.5 million years ago, but the Pliocene–Pleistocene boundary has been arbitrarily defined on the basis of marked changes in marine sediments). It used to be thought that there had been only four periods of glaciation during the Pleistocene, but geologists now realize that there have been 17 glacial–interglacial cycles, with maximum southward extension of ice sheets occurring every 100,000 years. The intervening warm periods (interglacials) have been quite brief, usually lasting only 10,000 years.

Despite the fact that Choukoutien was inhabited during an interglacial, the winters must have posed some difficulty for *Homo erectus*; the site lies close to the apparent northern limit of human occupation of Middle Pleistocene (700,000–130,000 B.P.) Eurasia. There are probable sites of this age a little farther east, at about the same latitude (40°N), in Korea and Japan (which was occasionally connected to the Asian mainland). A Middle Pleistocene site is also reported to have been found northwest of Choukoutien, in Mongolia. At the opposite end of Eurasia, *Homo erectus* populations seem to have ventured north into Germany and even into the British Isles (above 50°N) during interglacials, only to retreat southward as the ice advanced again. There is evidence at the site of Karatau of similar north–south fluctuations of populations in central Asia, about 250,000 years ago. The apparent absence of Middle Pleistocene sites, except in western Europe, north of about 45°N latitude, suggests that *Homo erectus* lacked the cultural equipment necessary to survive in the snow climates that prevail farther north, where, even today, winter temperatures often fall below freezing.

The thousands of stone tools made by *Homo erectus* at Choukoutien were simple choppers and sharp-edged flakes of quartz, which resembled the much earlier Oldowan tools of eastern Africa. Handaxes have been recovered from a few Middle Pleistocene sites in Mongolia and Korea, but they are absent from the great majority of Far Eastern assemblages of this period. These contain instead simple "chopper-chopping tools", similar to those found at Choukoutien. The near total absence of handaxes in eastern Asia, when they were so common in contemporary Europe, Africa, and western Asia, has yet to be satisfactorily explained.

It should be clear from the foregoing discussion that the handaxe-like artifacts occasionally found in surface collections in the Americas are most unlikely to have been made by *Homo erectus*. Any hypothetical Middle Pleistocene immigrants would probably have used only chopper-chopping tools. However, in view of the absence of early sites in far northern Eurasia, the possibility that Asian *Homo erectus* bands could have survived long treks through Siberia, even during an interglacial, is very remote.

THE ORIGIN AND EXPANSION OF *HOMO SAPIENS*

By about 300,000–200,000 years ago, some *Homo erectus* populations had evolved into a larger-brained, higher-browed, smaller-faced species, *Homo sapiens*. After the last interglacial, about 130,000–120,000 B.P., Europe was occupied by a distinctive sub-species of archaic *sapiens*, *Homo sapiens neanderthalensis*. Neanderthals were stockier and more heavily muscled than modern humans, with long faces, heavy brow ridges, and chinless jaws. They were nevertheless intelligent, resourceful people who adapted successfully to the deteriorating climate and environments of the last glaciation (known as Würm or Weichsel in Europe, Wisconsin in America).

Outside Europe and North Africa, contemporary populations of archaic *sapiens* represent a comparable evolutionary stage. In eastern Asia, Neanderthal-like fossils have been found at Mapa and Tingtsun in China, and at Solo in Java. These Asian specimens have brains in the size range of modern *sapiens*, yet also display primitive features that demonstrate their descent from earlier *erectus* populations.

In Europe, North Africa, and western Asia, Neanderthals made and used some 60 types of stone tools – scrapers, cutting tools, and points – which are referred to collectively as the Mousterian industry (after the site of Le Moustier in France). Acheulian handaxes had tended to become smaller and to be replaced by retouched flake knives and scrapers as early as 200,000–150,000 years ago, and this trend continued in the Mousterian assemblages, which were produced from about 100,000–40,000 B.P. Some Mousterian tool-makers continued to turn out Acheulian-style handaxes, but most Mousterian tools were flakes, carefully detached from prepared cores and then retouched into the desired forms. A common core preparation technique, which produced large flakes and remnant cores shaped like tortoise shells, is called Levallois. Middle Paleolithic assemblages that contain numerous tools made in this way are called Levallois–Mousterian.

Among the Mousterian flake tools were the first haftable spearheads; before this, Acheulian hunters had used wooden spears, with whittled and fire-hardened tips. Late Mousterian assemblages in central and eastern Europe, dated at about 40,000–35,000 B.P., include particularly well-chipped spearpoints. Some archaeologists have speculated that these bifacially thinned, leaf-shaped points might represent the ultimate source of the point-making tradition that was carried into the Americas by the first immigrants (Müller-Beck 1967).

Flake tools resembling the Mousterian artifacts of the West have been found at several sites in China and Inner Mongolia. At the Mongolian site of Shui-tung-kou, Levallois–Mousterian scrapers and saw-toothed flakes (denticulates) were present, along with blade tools of Upper Paleolithic type. The presence of blades suggests that this might be a late Mousterian site, perhaps 30,000 years old, although an earlier date, closer to 70,000 B.P., has also been proposed. Makers of Mousterian tools probably entered Mongolia from Central Asia. They do not seem to have stayed in the region very long, perhaps because the climate worsened. Following their departure, Mongolia was occupied by makers of chopper-chopping tools, who probably came from China. As we shall soon see, Levallois–Mousterian tools are reported to have been found at several sites in Siberia, which may have been colonized briefly during a relatively warm interstadial episode, around 45,000–35,000 B.P.

It was somewhat cooler and wetter than today from about 115,000 to 80,000 years ago. Then, the earth was plunged into a long cold period, the Würm–Weichsel–Wisconsin glaciation, which lasted until 10,000 B.P. The final northward retreat of the ice sheets at that time is taken to mark the end of the Pleistocene and the start of a new climatic epoch, the Holocene (in all probability, however, we are now living near the end of an interglacial period, which we may have artificially prolonged by burning fossil fuels, creating a greenhouse effect that raises temperatures). During the coldest periods of ice advance (stadials), annual average temperatures may have been 14° to 20°F (8° to 11°C) lower than at present. It was some-what warmer during several episodes of glacial retreat (interstadials); Mousterian groups probably moved northward during these warmer phases.

The northernmost site in Europe where Mousterian artifacts have been found is Khotylevo in Russia, at a latitude of 53′15′N. At Lebenstedt in Germany, faunal remains show that Neanderthals occupied the tundra during the summer months. They hunted reindeer, mammoth, bison, horse, and woolly rhinoceros, and also ate fish, waterfowl, and freshwater mollusks. During the winter, the site's inhabitants seem to have retreated southward, to the shelter of the taiga forest. A thousand miles to the east, at Molodova in the Ukraine, the remains of a Mousterian dwelling have been excavated (Klein 1974). An oval ring of mammoth bones and tusks, 9 meters in diameter, enclosed 15 fireplaces and thousands of flint tools. The roof had probably been made of hides, stretched over saplings and weighed down by the bones. A C14 date places the construction of this shelter earlier than 44,000 B.P. These sites show that the Mousterians were capable of surviving in the cold, arid tundra at the edge of the ice sheets; however, the Lebenstedt evidence suggests that occupation may have been limited to the warmest months. Very few Mousterian sites occur north of 50°, and none have been discovered above 54°. In contrast, later Upper Paleolithic sites in Russia occur as far north as 65°, above the Arctic Circle.

Mousterian industries were replaced by Upper Paleolithic tool kits in western Asia, North Africa, and Europe about 40,000 to 33,000 years ago. Characteristic Upper Paleolithic stone tools were retouched blades, that is, flakes two or more times as long as they were wide. These blades were struck off a cylindrical or conical core, probably by using a bone punch and hammer. The flintworker would proceed around the core in a spiral manner, using the ridge left by each detached blade to guide the force of the next blow. This technique enabled the Upper Paleolithic flint-worker to produce a much greater length of sharp edge from a given volume of flint than could his Mousterian (Middle Paleolithic) predecessor. It should be noted that Mousterian tool-makers were capable of producing blades; they are present in most Mousterian assemblages, but always as a small percentage.

The Aurignacian is the earliest widespread tradition of blade tool manufacture. It seems to have originated in the Near East and eastern Europe about 40,000–35,000 B.P., and spread into western Europe a few thousand years later. Aurignacian assemblages include several kinds of retouched blade tools: burins, endscrapers, edge-retouched blades, and thick-bodied nosed scrapers. Thin bone points, with split or bevelled bases, were also typical of the Aurignacian. Few Middle Paleolithic artifacts had been made of bone, but bone, antler and ivory were frequently worked during the Upper Paleolithic. The tool used for this purpose was the burin, which was made by striking off a long flake at the corner of a blade, parallel to the blade's axis. This created a strong point that could be used to incise bone or wood.

The appearance of Aurignacian tool-kits in Europe coincided with the replacement of the western European "classic" Neanderthals by anatomically modern *Homo sapiens sapiens*. The modern type may have first evolved in southern Africa; a modern-looking skull from Border Cave is at least 39,000 years old, and perhaps 90,000. *Homo sapiens sapiens* skeletons, which retain fairly strong brow ridges and some other archaic features, have been found in the caves of Skhul and Qafzeh in Israel; they were buried about 40,000–35,000 years ago. Modern-looking humans appeared at approximately the same time in southeast Asia. A *Homo sapiens sapiens* skeleton excavated in Niah Cave, Borneo dates to about 38,000 B.P., according to a single C14 determination. At some time before 32,000 B.P., people had rafted across the 100 km of water that separated Asia from Sahul, the then connected islands of New Guinea, Australia, and Tasmania. A modern-looking woman was cremated near Lake Mungo, in southeastern Australia, about 25,000 years ago. More than 40 very archaic-looking skeletons were found at another site, to the southwest of Lake Mungo, called Kow Swamp. These people had heavy brow ridges, sloping foreheads, and skulls that were constricted behind the eyes. In view of these *erectus*-like traits, the age of these skeletons is surprising – only 9,000–10,000 years. This population seems to have descended from southeast Asian *Homo erectus* and the locally evolved archaic *sapiens* population represented by the Solo skulls from Java. The Lake Mungo people seem to have been derived from another, intrusive population.

Physical anthropologists have not yet reached agreement on the process by which modern *sapiens* replaced archaic *sapiens*. Because recent genetic studies confirm that all living humans are descended from a common ancestor who probably lived some time between 300,000 and 50,000 years ago, totally independent, parallel evolution by regional archaic populations is out of the question. Both gene flow between populations, and actual migrations, probably occurred. It is now clear that in Europe, the classic Neanderthals evolved no further, but were rapidly replaced within a period of 2,000 or 3,000 years by modern *sapiens*, who came from the east, bearing the Aurignacian tool-kit. Some genetic exchange may have occurred, but for the most part the intruders probably pushed the Neanderthals out of their former habitats, and thus to extinction. The presence of both modern- and archaic-looking populations in Australia suggests that the modern-type intruders could not dislodge the local population as easily as their counterparts did in Europe.

In northeastern Asia, the evolution or arrival of modern *sapiens* is, at present, poorly documented. As noted above, the *erectus* skulls from Choukoutien exhibit certain traits that suggest an ancestral relationship to modern Mongoloids. Several Chinese sites have yielded human skulls or teeth dating to the late Pleistocene, but the earliest well-preserved *sapiens* skeletons were found at Choukoutien. Three skeletons were discovered in the Upper Cave, which is located above the much earlier *erectus* site. Stone choppers and flakes, ornaments of bone, shell, and stone, and a bone needle, were associated with the skeletons. The precise date of these finds is uncertain, but they are probably 10,000–20,000 years old. Surprisingly, the Upper Cave skeletons are said to display few classic Mongoloid features, such as characterize the modern Chinese population (Laughlin 1966). This observation has interesting implications, which we shall examine later in detail, for the origin of the native Americans.

In Europe, the appearance of modern *sapiens* was accompanied not only by the introduction of a more sophisticated tool-kit, but by the first appearance of works of art and items of personal adornment. Beautifully carved bone figures of a lion and horse, found at Vogelherd in Germany, are 30,000 years old. During the ensuing millennia, Upper Paleolithic artists carved bone and ivory into "Venus" figurines – naked, usually obese women whose faces and feet were not modelled. Such figurines, found at sites from Spain to Russia, are strikingly similar; this implies that there must have been communication of ideas and styles between the hunting bands that occupied this great expanse.

We can infer from the sudden appearance of artwork and ornaments in the Upper Paleolithic that some mental threshold had been crossed. The brain of *Homo sapiens sapiens* was no bigger than the Neanderthals', but it must have undergone some internal reorganization, which was reflected in the altered shape of the skull, which became higher, shorter, and rounder. There may also have been a change in the shape of the vocal tract, which, by allowing more rapid production of more varied sounds, led to a much greater elaboration of language in Upper Paleolithic cultures. The enhanced linguistic and symbolic capabilities of modern humans may account for their replacement of the physically formidable Neanderthals. These capabilities may also have permitted more rapid creation and transmission of innovative technologies and new behavioral patterns, so that the pace of cultural evolution became much more rapid after 30,000 B.P.

These intangible mental and behavioral factors may in part explain the success of *Homo sapiens sapiens*, where precursors had failed, in colonizing the far northern tundras. In any case, the technological innovation that made possible the northern expansion of the Upper Paleolithic was probably tailored skin clothing, similar to the modern Eskimo parka. Such garments were sewn together using bone needles, which have been dated as far back as 17,000 B.C. at European sites. There is even earlier evidence of tailored clothing at Sungir, 210 km (130 miles) northeast of Moscow. Here, burials of an adult and two boys were excavated; they dated from about 20,000 B.C. The dead had been buried wearing skin clothing, which had disintegrated over time. However, the decorative rows of mammoth ivory beads that had been sewn on to the garments remained in place, allowing archaeologists to reconstruct with some confidence the caps, shirts, jackets, trousers, and moccasins that these people had worn (Bader 1970).

One of the best-known Upper Paleolithic sites in the tundra-steppe zone of eastern Europe is Dolni Věstonice, in Czechoslovakia. The stone tools found there resemble those of the Perigordian industry of France, which appeared after the Aurignacian, and differed from the latter mainly in the absence of chunky scrapers. Dolni Věstonice is C14 dated to about 23,500 B.C., and was a campsite that consisted of five large huts. Alongside these dwellings lay heaps of mammoth bones, most of them from young animals. At contemporary sites in the Ukraine, huts resembling the earlier Mousterian dwelling at Molodova were built. There can be little doubt that the inhabitants of these sites were mammoth-hunters,

31

but some of the very numerous bones may have been collected expressly for building the huts, or for use as fuel during the winter. Elsewhere in Russia, evidence of drive-hunting of bison has been found at Amvrocievkaya, north of the Sea of Azov. Farther to the north, Upper Paleolithic hunters seem to have preyed most often on reindeer and horse.

POPULATION PRESSURE AND MIGRATION

Simply by having demonstrated that Upper Paleolithic people were technologically and behaviorally prepared to cope with the rigors of life on the northern tundras, we have not really explained why they undertook the colonization of this environment. The northward movements of earlier human populations, such as occurred during interglacials, also require explanation. Why would any hunting band have packed up their spears and huts and left their traditional territory, only to take their chances in an unfamiliar and comparatively inhospitable environment? They probably would not have done so unless compelled by a shortage of food or inability to cope with hostile neighbors. Migration may have offered a safety valve to hunting and gathering populations whose ecological balance was threatened by population pressure. The hunting and gathering way of life required maintenance of a very low population density. Modern hunter–gatherer densities range from 0.4 to 9.6 persons per 100 square km (one to 25 persons per 100 square miles); in the richer environments available to Pleistocene hunters, higher densities, of about 0.4 persons per square km (one person per square mile), may have been common. If a prehistoric population exceeded this density, pressure on resources probably resulted. If this situation was not relieved, the population would exceed the carrying capacity of the environment, and mass starvation would cause a catastrophic decline in numbers, back to an acceptable level. Recent hunter–gatherers have avoided such a vicious cycle of unchecked growth followed by decimation by practicing various population control measures, including infanticide, abortion, and birth-spacing induced by prolonged breast-feeding and post-partum sex taboos. Another way in which population pressure might be alleviated would be to increase the food supply, either by devising a more efficient collecting and processing technology, or by trying new foodstuffs, previously ignored or disdained. However, we have no evidence of such innovations until the end of the Pleistocene. The solution that was probably most often resorted to during earlier periods was migration. Part of a band might split off and move into a previously uninhabited territory, but remain tied to the parent band by kinship and marriage relationships, renewed over successive generations. Such individual "budding" episodes, seen cumulatively on a region-wide, long-term scale, would appear to constitute a directional wave of migration. When the front of a migration wave encountered a border between environmental zones, such as forest and tundra, it would probably halt, perhaps for centuries, until people developed an effective cultural adaptation to the unfamiliar environment. Once this was accomplished, an explosive burst of rapid migration into the new territory would occur.

This model offers a framework for interpretation of archaeological evidence from the Upper Paleolithic. In both western and eastern Europe, Upper Paleolithic sites are often bigger than Middle Paleolithic sites, and there are more of them. Although hunting techniques were probably more efficient (both the spear-thrower and drive-hunting are attested by 13,000 B.C.), and there was more selective predation on one or two species, such as horse and mammoth, the meat-based diet did not change significantly. Thus, human population seems to have grown markedly, while the resource base remained about the same. Population pressure must have resulted, leading to migration. At first, the Upper Paleolithic hunters, like their predecessors, may have ventured onto the tundra-steppe only seasonally; but once they had devised tailored clothing and effectively insulated and heated shelters, permanent occupation of the tundra became possible. The environmental barrier to migration having thus been removed, big game-hunting Upper Paleolithic bands moved rapidly northward and eastward, carrying their blade tool technology from Russia into Siberia.

PALEOLITHIC CULTURES OF SIBERIA

During the Pleistocene, Siberia was largely free of glacial ice. There does not seem to have been enough snow for the accumulation of ice sheets. However, during periods of glacial advance elsewhere, early man was unable to cope with the severe cold of northern Siberia. During warmer interglacial or interstadial periods, the prevailing environment of Siberia was coniferous forest (taiga) which supported relatively few animals and was therefore probably unattractive to human hunters. During colder glacial or stadial periods, a band of grassy tundra-steppe extended into Siberia from the west. This game-rich environment would have drawn human hunters, provided that they could withstand the cold.

It is possible that *Homo erectus* groups, using pebble tools, entered southwestern Siberia at a very early date. Quartzite pebble tools found at the site of Ulalinka have recently been dated to some time earlier than 690,000 B.P., based on the reversed magnetic polarity of the geological layer from which the tools were reportedly derived. Another possibly early site is Filimoshki, located in the Amur River basin in southeastern Siberia (Michael 1984). Various Soviet scholars have assigned widely differing

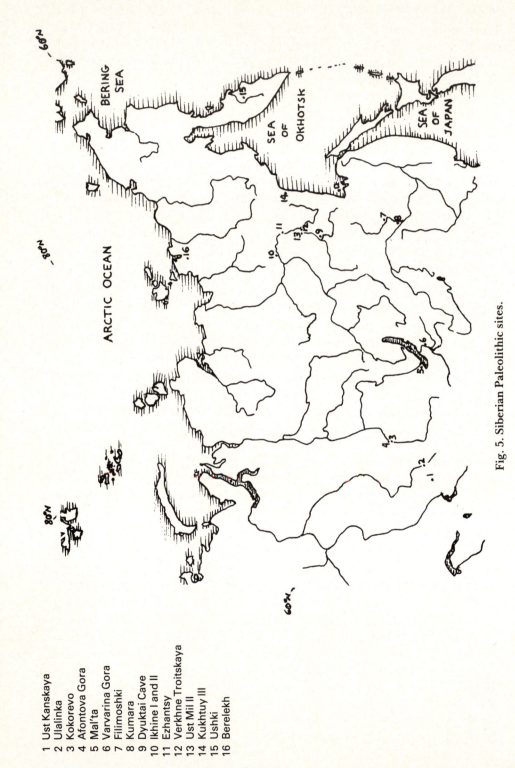

Fig. 5. Siberian Paleolithic sites.

1 Ust Kanskaya
2 Ulalinka
3 Kokorevo
4 Afontova Gora
5 Mal'ta
6 Varvarina Gora
7 Filimoshki
8 Kumara
9 Dyuktai Cave
10 Ikhine I and II
11 Ezhantsy
12 Verkhne Troitskaya
13 Ust Mil II
14 Kukhtuy III
15 Ushki
16 Berelekh

dates to this site, ranging from Middle Pleistocene (ca. 700,000–130,000 B.P.) to less than 30,000 years ago. There is also some question as to whether these stones were really modified by humans, or were instead shaped by natural forces (Yi and Clark 1983). The alleged presence of very early humans in Siberia must therefore be regarded as unproven, at present.

To the south of Siberia, in Mongolia, there is evidence of an eastward incursion of Levallois–Mousterian industries (see p. 28). The age of these Mongolian finds, which come from unstratified and undated contexts, is not certain; but judging from the technological attributes of the stone tools, an age in the order of 60,000 to 30,000 years is plausible (Chard 1974; Yi and Clark 1983). In Siberia, too, cores and flakes of Levallois–Mousterian appearance have been found at a number of sites, including Ust Kan (in western Siberia), Varvarina Gora (south of Lake Baikal), and Kumara (in the Amur basin). Soviet geologists believe that the climate of Siberia was relatively warm from 43,000 to 33,000 B.P. Based on artifact types, geological context, and associated faunal remains, the afore-mentioned sites are assigned to this interstadial period (Michael 1984).

Carbon 14 dates from several sites located near the Aldan River, in far eastern Siberia, suggest that this area may have been occupied as early as 35,000 B.P. (Mochanov 1977, 1980). At Ust Mil II, stone bifaces, cores, and flakes, found along with bones of mammoth, horse, bison, and woolly rhinoceros, were dated by C14 to between 31,500 and 35,000 B.P. Stone artifacts from Ikhine II seem to be somewhat older than 26,000 to 35,000 years, based on C14 dating of wood found in overlying deposits. Ezhantsy, another Aldan site that is estimated to date from around 25,000–35,000 B.P., yielded a bifacially chipped knife, numerous burins, and other tools, in association with horse and mammoth bones. The major problem that renders these dates dubious is the anachronistic character of the stone tool assemblages. These artifacts are not Levallois–Mousterian, nor do they resemble the Aurignacian tools that began to be made in western Eurasia around 40,000–35,000 B.P. Instead, the supposedly early tools include micro-cores and bifaces of the same types that are found in the Dyuktai culture, which flourished in the Aldan area only after 18,000 B.P. While it is not inconceivable that the micro-core technique of blade manufacture was invented in eastern Siberia or north-ern China by 35,000 B.P. and the tool-kit then remained unchanged for 20,000 years, this seems very unlikely. There is reason to suspect that the C14 dates for the Aldan sites are too early, perhaps because the wood samples used for dating came from well-preserved old pieces that had been eroded from older contexts and redeposited at the sites (Yi and Clark 1985).

A blade industry, similar in a general way to the Upper Paleolithic industries of Europe, had arrived in southern Siberia by 13,000 B.C. Backed blades, end scrapers, and burins were manufactured at the site of Mal'ta, west of Lake Baikal (Coles and Higgs 1969). Mal'ta has been C14 dated to about 12,800 B.C., although some scholars suspect that the real age of the site is more like 20,000–25,000 B.C. (Michael 1984). Alongside the tools of Upper Paleolithic type were found others of a Mousterian appearance, including points, scrapers, and disc-cores. Like the Upper Paleolithic peoples of Europe, the inhabitants of Mal'ta made points and needles of bone; they also carved bone and mammoth ivory into bracelets and figurines of birds and women. Three of the women were depicted wearing hooded garments that resembled the Eskimo parka. Some writers have claimed to see Mongoloid eye-folds in these figurines, but the modelling of the faces is not really detailed enough to support this racial identification. In addition to the figurines, a tusk bearing an engraving of a mammoth was found at Mal'ta. These art objects are reminiscent of the figurines and engravings of Upper Paleolithic Europe. The remains of dwellings excavated at Malta point in the same direction. These semi-subterranean huts, their (presumed) skin walls secured by mammoth and rhinoceros bones and reindeer antlers, resemble structures found in the Ukraine and Czechoslovakia (see p. 31). Taken together, the stone tools, the artwork, and the dwellings indicate that the Mal'ta culture was an eastward extension of the tundra-adapted Upper Paleolithic cultures of the East European plains.

Northwest of Mal'ta, in the Yenisei Valley, hunters using blades and bone tools may have occupied the site of Afontova Gora II as early as 19,000 B.C. They preyed upon the animals of the tundra-steppe, including mammoth, reindeer, hare, ptarmigan, and arctic fox, as well as other species. Stone tools from later occupation levels are typically Upper Paleolithic: blades, end scrapers, backed blades, bifacial leaf-shaped points, and microliths (Coles and Higgs 1969). At another Yenisei Valley site, Kokorevo, a bone point was found imbedded in the lower jaw of a bison. This site dates to 11,300 B.C. (Michael 1984).

Sites in the Aldan region, dating from roughly 16,000 B.C. to 8000 B.C., have yielded artifacts of the distinctive Dyuktai culture, named after Dyuktai Cave (Mochanov 1977, 1980; Michael 1984). The three occupation levels (7 a, b and c) at this rockshelter were C14 dated to between 12,000 and 10,000 B.C. Artifacts found here, and at other sites of the Dyuktai culture, include Levallois and discoid cores, which hint at Mousterian roots; but the Upper Palaeolithic is well-represented by end scrapers, burins, large blades, and bladelets struck off wedge-shaped cores. The tool-kit also included choppers and pebble cores, mammoth ivory spearheads and bone needles. The most interesting artifacts of the Dyuktai culture, from the perspective of New World origins, are well-made, bifacially chipped knives and spearheads. Two thin knife-like bifaces from the site of Verkhne–Troitskaya are somewhat older than 16,000 B.C.; a biface from Dyuktai layer 7b dates to about 11,000 B.C. The significance of these artifacts is that they are plausible prototypes for the finely-chipped bifaces which, as we shall see, were characteristic of early Paleo-Indian cultures in the Americas. However, we cannot leap to the inviting conclusion that the Dyuktai culture was directly ancestral to the Paleo-Indian cultures, even though it was in the right place, at the right time. One cause for hesitation is the absence of fluting in the Dyuktai bifaces; this is a distinctive and ubiquitous characteristic of Paleo-Indian spearheads (see p. 56). Furthermore, the wedge-shaped bladelet cores which are common at Dyuktai sites are not found in Paleo-Indian assemblages. Similar cores are common at early Alaskan sites, where their presence testifies to Siberian influence; but these Paleo-Arctic sites are no earlier than 9,000 B.C. (Dumond 1980), and therefore post-date the migration of the ancestral Paleo-Indians through Alaska.

We must bear in mind that the ancestral Paleo-Indians had to traverse a considerable expanse of territory, north and east of the Aldan region, as they made their way across the land bridge, known as Beringia, that then connected Siberia to Alaska. As groups dispersed over such an extensive area, the process of cultural drift probably resulted in the appearance of distinctive local tool-making traditions. There are marked differences between the Upper Paleolithic assemblages of Russia and France; if we consider that the distance from the Aldan region to the Bering Strait is even greater than that which separates Russia from France, it becomes

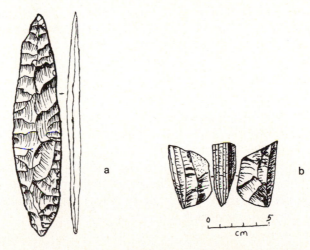

Fig. 6. Chipped stone artifacts from Dyuktai Cave: (A) biface (level 7b), length 13 cm; (B) micro-blade core (level 7a), length ca. 5.5 cm.

clear that we should not expect the cultures of easternmost Siberia to have been identical in every respect to the Dyuktai culture.

In fact, very few sites have been located to date in areas north and east of the Aldan region. To the east, on the Kamchatka Peninsula, the site of Ushki was first occupied at about 12,000 B.C. Excavation of the lowest layer (VII) at Ushki revealed a settlement composed of large (100 m²), oval semi-subterranean houses, resembling those found in the Ukraine. Associated with these dwellings were 30 stemmed dart points, burins, one leaf-shaped point, and stone beads. Notably absent from this assemblage were the typical Dyuktai wedge-shaped cores; but these were present, along with Dyuktai-style leaf-shaped points, in the overlying layer VI, which dates to about 8800 B.C. Although there has been some suspicion that the stemmed points of layer VII might be intrusive from uppper layers of the site, this layer seems to have been well sealed by an overlying sterile deposit (Dikov and Titov 1984). The stemmed points of Ushki offer no better prototype for American fluted points than do Duyktai bifaces; nevertheless, Uskhi is significant because it demonstrates the presence in northeastern Siberia of cultures that were contemporaneous with Dyuktai, but did not use micro-blades. Only a Siberian culture with well made bifaces but without micro-cores would be a credible ancestor of Paleo-Indian cultures. It is noteworthy that a site near the western shore of the Sea of Okhotsk, Kukhtuy III, is reported to contain Dyuktai-like bifaces, but no wedge-shaped cores (Michael 1984). Unfortunately, this site has not been dated; it might represent a local variant of the Dyuktai cultural tradition that lacked the micro-core technique.

The site of Berelekh lies north of the Aldan sites, near the present-day shoreline of the Arctic Ocean. C14 dates put the occupation here between 11,500 and 8500 B.C. More than 7,000 bones were recovered from the site, most of them from mammoths. These may be the remains of dwellings like those found in the Ukraine. Artifacts found at Berelekh include broken bifaces, stone beads, and an engraving, on a mammoth tusk, of an exaggeratedly long-legged mammoth (Mochanov 1977, Michael 1984). Berelekh lies on or near the route probably taken by the ancestral Paleo-Indians, and it seems to have been inhabited at about the time that their migration occurred. No other sites older than 9,000 B.C. have yet been discovered in the still-exposed areas of northeastern Siberia that, during the Ice Age, formed part of the land bridge; nor have unequivocal habitation sites, dating from between 30,000 and 9000 B.C., been found on the Alaskan side of Beringia. Nevertheless, as we shall see in the next chapter, archaeological evidence from the New World shows that the ancestors of the Paleo-Indians must have crossed the land bridge at some time during that period.

3

The Paleo-Indians

In the preceding chapter, we have traced the physical and cultural evolution of the hominids, from their emergence in East Africa to their penetration of the frigid tundra of Siberia. We have thus brought man to the very threshold of the New World.

You may recall that, as early as 1590, Fray Jose de Acosta suggested that the ancestors of the American Indians had come from Northern Asia. Today, there is virtually unanimous support for this theory among anthropologists. However, the date of the arrival of the earliest Asian immigrants remains a matter of heated dispute. The most convincing evidence for the Asian origin of the native Americans comes not from archaeology but from physical anthropology and geology.

THE EVIDENCE OF PHYSICAL ANTHROPOLOGY

When we compare native Americans with the other living races of mankind, we find them to be most similar to the Mongoloid peoples of Asia. Among the visible physical characteristics which these groups share are coarse, straight black hair, relatively hairless faces and bodies, light brown skin, brown eyes, epicanthic eye-folds (only occasionally present in American populations), high cheek bones, and a high frequency of shovel-shaped incisor teeth. Both in Asia and the Americas, infants sometimes develop a purplish discoloration of the lower back, known as a "Mongoloid spot". The distribution patterns of invisible, genetically-determined traits offer less clear-cut evidence of relationship. In the Americas, blood type O is predominant; in South and Central American populations, no other blood type exists. But Asian populations are characterized by the world's highest frequencies of type B (11–25%). In the Americas, the highest frequency of type B, and the most classically Mongoloid physical appearance, are found among the Eskimos, who probably represent the most recent migration from Asia. The difference in blood type frequencies of the more southerly native Americans from those found in Asia has been explained as resulting from either a disproportionate sampling of Asian genes in the small population that left Asia

39

("founder effect"), or from micro-evolutionary changes that occurred as populations adapted to different New World environments.

Although the similarities we have noted are sufficient to establish a relationship between native Americans and Asian Mongoloids, significant physical differences do exist, which may have some bearing on the question of the date of the first Americans' departure from Asia. Native Americans often have more prominent noses than Asians. Eye-folds do occur in the Americas, but in only a small proportion of the population. And some native American groups, particularly in California and the Great Basin, exhibit an unusual amount of facial hair. These characteristics seem to indicate some connection with the Caucasoid or "white" racial stock, prevalent in southwest Asia, Europe and North Africa. How can these features be explained?

Both skeletal evidence and recent racial distributions suggest that the Mongoloids developed at a relatively late date, and replaced or absorbed earlier Asian populations, some of whom were Caucasoids. On the margins of Asia may still be found remnants of these earlier inhabitants: the "hairy" Ainu of Japan, and the Australian aborigines.

It has been argued that the distinctive features of the Mongoloids, such as their flat faces and folded eyelids, evolved as adaptations to a cold climate. If so, their probable homeland would have been in northern Asia; but the prevalence of Mongoloid populations in Southeast Asia today shows that the supposed cold-adapted traits posed no hindrance to the spread of the Mongoloids, even into tropical environments.

Analysis of the skeletal remains from the Upper Cave at Choukoutien has shed some light on the racial affinities of the early inhabitants of China, but the evidence is ambiguous. One problem is the lack of a precise date for this material; the bones could be anywhere from 30,000 to 10,000 years old. Apart from this, the differences among the three individuals from the Upper Cave are surprising. The renowned anatomist who studied the Choukoutien finds, Franz Weidenreich, saw one female's skull as resembling that of an Eskimo, a second female's skull as similar to that of a Melanesian, while a rugged male skull seemed comparable to those of Europeans. More recently, it has been suggested that these skulls show only a mixture of Caucasoid and Mongoloid features (Birdsell 1951). Thus, the Upper Cave remains indicate that, late in the Pleistocene, China was not yet exclusively occupied by Mongoloids. Instead, here and probably elsewhere in eastern Asia, there existed a highly variable population with some Caucasoid features. Such a population could well have included the ancestors of the native Americans.

Before we proceed to examine the skeletal evidence for early American populations, a few words of caution are in order. There is a tradition of skull measurement in physical anthropology, going back to the eighteenth century. Early anthropologists divided mankind into four or five major races, in each of which they recognized several geographic sub-races. A sample of skulls collected from each racial group was measured extensively, and thus an ideal type of that race was defined. Thereafter, whenever a new skull turned up, one had only to take the standard measurements and compare them to those of the "typical" skulls, in order confidently to assign the new specimen to its appropriate racial slot. As an example of this approach, consider the analysis of skeletons from Pecos Pueblo, completed in 1930 by Earnest Hooton of Harvard. He distinguished among the residents of a single prehistoric village no fewer than seven skull types. These included, in addition to three native American types, a "Pseudo-Australoid", a "Pseudo-Negroid", a "Pseudo-Alpine", and a "Long-faced European" (MacGowan and Hester 1962).

The significance of such types based on skull measurements was called into question as early as 1911 by Franz Boas, who demonstrated that the skulls of Jewish and Italian youths born in New York differed markedly from those of their immigrant parents. Clearly, environmental and nutritional factors could affect head shape. Furthermore, Boas showed that head and body form varied more widely within than between populations, and that there was often considerable overlap in the measurements of different races (Boas 1940). Nevertheless, racial classification by head form continued as an anthropological obsession until World War II, when the Nazis used skull types (among other criteria) to determine who should be sent to the gas chambers. Revulsion at this practice contributed to the post-war decline in skull measurement studies. Today, physical anthropologists have a much greater awareness of the range of variability within populations, and of the effects of nutrition and environment on human morphology. However, skull measurements are not without their uses, for specific problems. A recent statistical analysis of skull measurements, aided by a computer, has indicated that it is possible to distinguish consistently skulls belonging to different geographic races (Howells 1973); but the uncertainties involved in the use of skulls for racial classification should be kept in mind as we consider the American evidence.

The remains of early man in the Americas fall into two broad categories: 1) skeletal remains that have been scientifically excavated in secure, datable archaeological contexts, and 2) allegedly ancient finds, often collected by amateurs and removed from their original contexts, or found in circumstances that allow some doubt as to their real age.

The first category includes only a few finds of undoubted antiquity. One whose age is generally accepted is the skull of a woman from Midland, Texas. This skull, which lacks facial bones, was found protruding from the sand in a windblown depression. Its stratigraphic position, underlying a layer from which Folsom-style artifacts were recovered, implies that the skull dates to some time before 8000 B.C. Somewhat dubious C14 and uranium dates suggest an age of about 20,000 years, but snail shells from a layer *below* the grey sand in which the skull was found yielded a C14 date of only about 13,000 B.P. (11,000 B.C.). The skull probably dates to 9,000–10,000 B.C. The Midland skull is long and narrow (dolichocephalic), like other American skulls from relatively early contexts. Later American populations were predominantly broad-headed (brachycephalic), as are Asian Mongoloid populations. The significance of this shift from long to broad heads is unclear. This seems to be a general evolutionary tendency; modern man is markedly broad-headed in comparison to the Neanderthals. The trend toward broad-headedness may be part of the increasing neotenization of *Homo sapiens*, that is, the retention by adults of fetal or infantile physical characteristics. Broad-headedness may also have been selected for, if round-headed infants and their mothers were less prone to mishaps at birth. The high frequency of skeletons of women in their twenties, in many prehistoric cemeteries, attests to the hazards of childbirth. Any genetic change affecting head shape that enhanced survival by easing the infant's passage would have become predominant in the whole population in the course of time. Head shape might also have been affected in some way by changes in diet or child care habits. Finally, we cannot rule out the racial explanation that was proposed by earlier anthropologists, who postulated successive migrations from Asia. The first wave was composed of long-headed people, similar to the Australian aborigines; these people were later genetically swamped by an incoming wave of round-headed Mongoloids. There is some evidence that Mongoloid phenotypic (i.e. visible) traits tend to become dominant when inter-breeding of Mongoloids and Australoids occurs (Birdsell 1981). Thus, the Mongoloid appearance of modern native Americans could conceivably mask the genetic contributions of early Australoid or "proto-Caucasoid" ancestors. Hypothetically, isolated populations in marginal, out-of-the-way areas might have retained pre-Mongoloid physical characteristics down to a relatively late date. In fact, it has been claimed that late prehistoric skulls from the Gulf Coast of Texas show long-headedness, heavy brow ridges and bulging at the back of the head, traits indicative of the persistence of an early Ainu or Australoid strain. On the other hand, one would expect the earliest inhabitants of the Americas to have been pushed gradually southward by later immigrants from Asia. Logically, therefore, the highest concentration of pre-Mongoloid traits should be found at the tip of South America. In fact, however, the natives of Tierra del Fuego are not noticeably less Mongoloid in appearance than are populations living farther to the north. So the present distribution of physical traits does not confirm the theory of a pre-Mongoloid migration.

Apart from the Midland skull, the most widely accepted early man finds are those from Tepexpan in the Valley of Mexico and from the Marmes site in Washington. However, there are questions about the age of each of these finds. The skeleton of Tepexpan man was found in late Pleistocene sediments, dated to 8000–9000 B.C. But the excavation of this skeleton was poorly reported, and there is some suspicion that it may be an intrusive burial from a later period. This suspicion is heightened by analysis of the skull, which is not significantly different from those of modern native Americans. Nevertheless, chemical tests of the bone indicated that the Tepexpan skeleton was of the same age as the bones of extinct animals found in the same geological formation.

The Marmes find consists of remains of three skulls, discovered in salvage excavations preceding the flooding of a reservoir. An overlying layer yielded shells, C14 dated at 8700–9000 B.C.; however, such shell-based dates are often unreliable. Artifacts associated with the skulls suggest that they may be 2,000 or more years younger than indicated by this C14 date. Like the Tepexpan skull, those found in the Marmes rock-shelter are broad-headed.

There are a few skeletons from South American sites that have been reliably dated to between 9000 and 8000 B.C. In the 1930s, Junius Bird excavated the cremated skeletons of two adults and a child in Palli Aike Cave, in Patagonia (Bird 1938). An early date for these remains is indicated by Bird's discovery of sloth and horse bones in an overlying deposit, and of a fishtail point in an underlying lava deposit. C14 dates for nearby Fell's Cave place such points at about 9000 to 8700 B.C. The Palli Aike people were long-headed and they had shovel-shaped incisors, as one would expect to find in a population of North Asian origin. A site in Peru known as PV 22–13 has yielded the skeleton of a young woman (Lynch 1983). Charcoal found directly beneath this burial produced a C14 date of 8250 ± 180 B.C. Like the Palli Aike individuals and other well-attested early Americans, this young woman was long-headed. Rather surprisingly, her teeth are reported to display wear suggestive of a plant-dominated diet; one would have supposed that hunting was still the main subsistence activity for such an early population.

Many other skeletal finds from North and South America have been claimed to be of late Pleistocene age, on the basis of the mineralized condition of the bones, or skull characteristics, particularly long-headedness and heavy brow ridges, or apparent geological context. Archaeologists have generally regarded these specimens with great skepticism, because they have been removed from their find-spots by non-professionals, and there are usually no clear associations with bones of extinct animals or artifacts of known date.

Recently, astonishing claims of great antiquity have been made for some North American skeletal finds. An age of 18,000 or even 60,000 years has been suggested for the Taber child, a fragmentary infant's skeleton found beneath apparently undisturbed glacial deposits in Alberta. Several skulls and skull fragments, which had been collecting dust for years in California museums, were subjected to dating tests in the 1970s. Bone collagen was radiocarbon dated, and other bone samples were tested for amino acid racemization. A skull from Laguna Beach, California yielded a collagen-based date of 17,150 ± 1450 B.P. Another skull, from Del Mar, was dated by the amino acid technique at about 48,000 B.P. Although this date was widely accepted, some scholars remained skeptical. The Del Mar skull is entirely modern-looking; but in the Old World, skulls 10,000 or 15,000 years younger than this still retain some Neanderthal features.

The skeptics were vindicated when samples from the Taber, Laguna Beach, and Del Mar skulls, along with other allegedly very old human remains, were re-dated in 1984. The samples were dated using the newly developed C14 accelerator mass spectrometry process, which yields more accurate dates for small samples than could previously be obtained. The results confirm doubts about the supposed great age of these finds. The Taber infant turns out to be only 3,550 years old; the Del Mar skull is 4,900 years old, and the Laguna Beach skull is 5,100 years old. None of the other tested skeletal samples is older than 11,000 years (Taylor et al. 1985).

One point to emphasize as we conclude this excursion into physical anthropology is that, despite the occasional appearance of heavy brows, large teeth, and occipital "buns" (angular protrusions at the back of the skull, often found in Neanderthals) in early American skulls, not one specimen has ever been found that could be assigned to the more primitive human varieties, *Homo erectus* or *Homo sapiens neanderthalensis*. Now, a human migration into the Americas as early as 300,000 or 400,000 years ago is not entirely inconceivable; after all, by this time Peking man was an efficient hunter, successfully coping with the cold winters of northern China through the use of fire and, perhaps, clothing. Why should these rugged people have been deterred by the rigors of Siberia and the Bering landbridge (of which more shortly)? Similarly, the European archaeological record attests to the Neanderthals' efficient adaptation to environments on the margins of the Pleistocene ice sheets. Why should they not have adapted to Siberia, and then crossed into North America? Siberia was not heavily glaciated during the Pleistocene, so it would appear that ice did not seal off the route to the Americas for pre-*sapiens* hunters. Perhaps it was the cold that deterred them. Tailored skin clothing, like that of the modern Eskimo, might have been indispensable for life in Siberia and Beringia; and the earliest evidence of such clothing comes from a 25,000 year-old burial at Sungir in Russia. In any event, if any pre-

sapiens hominids had made it to the Americas, one would expect that, with all the professional and amateur archaeology that has been done in North America, at least a few fossil scraps of them would have turned up by now. No such remains have been found, nor is there convincing evidence of the presence in the Americas of the stone industries that are associated with these early hominids in the Old World.

In summary, native Americans are clearly derived from an Asian population with affinities to the Mongoloids. However, the native Americans retain certain non-Mongoloid features. These might represent the genetic legacy of a pre-Mongoloid, Australoid–Caucasoid population, swamped by a later Mongoloid immigration; more likely, they reflect the broad range of physical variation found in early northern Asian populations, before Mongoloid traits became predominant. Such diversity is well represented by the late Pleistocene fossils from the Upper Cave at Choukoutien. It is almost certain that the first immigrants from Asia were of the modern human variety, *Homo sapiens sapiens*. This implies an initial entry date no earlier than 35,000–40,000 B.P., when modern man seems to have replaced the Neanderthals throughout Eurasia.

A recently conducted comparative study of the teeth of native American skeletons (Turner 1983, 1986) provides additional evidence for the North Asian origin of the ancestral Paleo-Indians. Peculiarities of the crowns and roots, collectively forming a "Sinodont" pattern, suggest that native Americans are more closely related to northern than to southern Asians. The dental evidence indicates only a very distant relationship to the Caucasoids of Europe. Turner concludes that the separation of North Asian and American populations occurred about 15,000 years ago.

GEOLOGICAL EVIDENCE – THE LAND BRIDGE AND THE CORRIDOR

The present geographic proximity of the Asian and American land masses is itself suggestive of an Asian origin for the first Americans. Even today, Siberia and Alaska are separated, at the narrowest part of the Bering Strait, by only 90 km (56 miles) of water. In winter the strait freezes over, and it is sometimes possible to walk across on the ice. But geological evidence indicates that, before about 8000 B.C., it was often easier to go from Siberia to Alaska; one could walk across dry land. At present, the floor of the Bering Strait is at a depth of about 37 m (120 ft) below the water's surface, but during the stadial periods of the Wisconsin glaciation, great quantities of water were frozen into the massive ice sheets that spread over much of the northern hemisphere. This had the effect of lowering sea levels, worldwide, by as much as 100 m (300 ft). Thus, what is now the bottom of the Bering Strait was, during those glacial episodes, comfort-

45

Table 1

1 (B.P. dates)		2	3	4	
75,000–65,000 open	or	75,000–58,000 open	75,000–62,000 open	110,000(?)–90,000(?)	open
65,000–60,000 submerged		58,000–55,000 submerged	62,000–55,000 submerged	75,000 –65,000	open
60,000–50,000 open		55,000–48,000 open	55,000–48,000 open	50,000 –45,000	open
50,000–44,000 submerged		48,000–44,000 submerged	48,000–44,000 submerged	40,000 –30,000	narrow or submerged
44,000–41,000 open		44,000–35,000 open	44,000–10,000 open	30,000 –15,500	open
41,000–33,000 submerged		35,000–31,000 submerged		after 15,500	narrow or submerged
33,000–29,000 open		31,000–12,000 open			
29,000–23,000 submerged					
23,000–12,800 open					
12,800–11,500 submerged					
11,500–10,000 open					
after 10,000 submerged					

1: from Butzer 1974.
2: after Street; in Sherratt 1980.
3: Gowlett 1984.
4: Hopkins et al. 1982.

ably above sea level. Siberia and Alaska formed a continuous land mass, about a thousand miles across from north to south, which geologists have named "Beringia" (Hopkins et al. 1982). Beringia offered a broad highway to the Americas, not only to early man but also to the animals that he was accustomed to hunting. Despite its northern location, Beringia was largely free of ice. It was covered by a grassy tundra-steppe, an extension of the environment found just south of the ice sheets farther west in Eurasia. Pleistocene mammals that thrived in that environment, such as mammoth, horse and bison, doubtless roamed across Beringia in substantial numbers. Their presence would have been inviting to human hunters.

The land bridge of Beringia may have emerged as early as 75,000 years ago, at the onset of the Wisconsin glaciation. It probably remained open during stadial periods of glacial advance, but was submerged during warmer interstadials (see Table 1). Geologists are obviously not in complete agreement on the details of this sequence, but it is clear that Asian hunters had several opportunities between 75,000 and 10,000 years ago to cross the land bridge to Alaska. However, once in Alaska they would have encountered a formidable barrier to their southward progress. The same glacial advances that caused a lowering of sea level also covered Canada and the northern border of the United States with two massive ice sheets. The western sheet is known as the Cordilleran, and the eastern sheet is called the Laurentide. At certain times during the Wisconsin glacial, the Cordilleran and Laurentide sheets met, forming an impenetrable mass of ice. However, at other times they were separated by a narrow unglaciated corridor, stretching southward from Alaska to the vicinity of Edmonton, Alberta, where it opened on to the northern Plains. There has been much disagreement among geologists concerning the opening and closing of the ice-free corridor. It was thought until recently that the corridor would have been open only during the Sangamon interglacial, prior to 75,000

B.P., again during the interstadial of 41,000–33,000 B.P., and finally as the ice began to retreat around 12,000 B.P. At present, some geologists believe that the corridor was open more often during the Wisconsin, and opened permanently after about 15,000 B.P. But even when it was free of ice, the passage between the glaciers was probably inhospitable; it was very cold, and possibly often interrupted by melt-water lakes and swamps.

The land bridge and corridor route would have been the most practicable one for a cold-adapted, inland-dwelling hunting population. However, we must note that early humans were not necessarily restricted to this route. When the land bridge was submerged, they could have walked across pack ice in the strait in winter, or paddled boats across in summer. Once on the Alaskan side, they could have continued by boat along the coast (Fladmark 1979). The coastline was probably cut across in places by tongues of ice extending from the Cordilleran sheet; these would have blocked movement south by land. However, there is no reason to question the ability of early man to build boats that could circumvent these obstacles. On the other side of the Pacific, man seems to have reached Australia as early as 40,000 years ago. As Australia was apparently not connected to the Asian mainland during the Pleistocene, humans must have reached it by floating over on some kind of water-craft. Unfortunately, most of the Pleistocene coastal shelf of North America has been submerged under the rising post-glacial seas. Consequently, there is no direct archaeological support for a hypothetical coastal migration route. The evidence we do have suggests that coastal adaptations developed at a relatively late date in the Americas, and that the first immigrants were inland-adapted hunters of big game.

ARCHAEOLOGICAL EVIDENCE OF THE FIRST AMERICANS

In the latter part of the nineteenth century, American scholars and amateurs, inspired by Darwin's theories and the Stone Age discoveries made in Europe, sought evidence of early man in the New World. Sure enough, they turned up a great many stone tools. The crudeness of some of these suggested that they were very ancient, belonging either to the Pleistocene or even to some earlier epoch. In addition, human remains were found, and for these too great antiquity was claimed. However, the eminent Czech-born physical anthropologist, Aleš Hrdlička, ruthlessly demolished these claims, demonstrating that all the American skeletal finds represented humans of modern type. On the basis of this conclusion, Hrdlička asserted that Ice Age man had not lived in the Americas; he set the initial entry at about 3000 B.C. No one seems to have pointed out at the time that humans of modern type had lived during late glacial times in Europe, where their remains had been found at Cro-Magnon and elsewhere; so the absence of pre-*sapiens* fossils in the Americas did not preclude a Pleistocene occupation. Hrdlička's conservative view prevailed in scholarly circles until an astonishing discovery in 1927 rendered it untenable.

A black cowhand had noticed some bones protruding from the side of a gulley near Folsom, New Mexico. This find was brought to the attention of J. D. Figgins of the Denver Museum of Natural History, who excavated the site. The bones turned out to belong to a large, long-horned species of bison (*Bison antiquus*) which became extinct at the end of the Pleistocene. In 1926, Figgins found a stone spear point embedded in clay near the bones. This point was initially dismissed by other archaeologists as intrusive. But in 1927, Figgins came upon another point, this time lying between two bison ribs. He left the point in place, and invited several prestigious archaeologists to examine the new find. They agreed that the Folsom site presented an indisputable association of man-made artifacts with the remains of extinct Pleistocene animals. Initially, archaeologists could only guess the age of the Folsom remains; but, since 1950, a series of C14 dates for sites where stone points of the same type have been excavated place the Folsom culture at about 9000 to 8000 B.C.

Many more Folsom sites have been discovered since 1927. At a few of them, artifacts were recovered from geological strata lying *below* those that yielded Folsom points. The distinctive artifact type of these earlier assemblages is the Clovis point. Clovis points were first excavated at the Blackwater Draw site near Clovis, New Mexico; here, and at several other sites, they were found in association with the remains of mammoths. The Clovis or "Llano" culture of the western U.S. has been dated to about 9500 to 9000 B.C. Clovis-like fluted points have a very wide geographic distribution, having been found throughout the United States and in Canada and Central America. The striking similarity of these points,

Fig. 7. One of the fluted points found in association with bones of *Bison antiquus* at Folsom, New Mexico (actual size).

found over such a vast area, has led many archaeologists to conclude that the points were made and used by closely related hunting bands.

We can envision one or several ancestral bands entering the northern Plains through the ice-free corridor, thus stumbling upon a hunter's paradise, teeming with game that had never experienced the terrible cunning and tenacity of the human predator. In such a favorable situation, the original human population would have grown rapidly: where growth is not constrained by food or space limitations, population can double or even triple in each successive generation. We can estimate, using some speculative yet reasonable calculations, the minimum length of time necessary for the Americas to have been filled to capacity with hunting bands. We start with figures derived from ethnographic studies of extant hunting and gathering groups. These studies indicate that, irrespective of environmental differences, the typical hunting band consists of 25 to 50 people. These studies also reveal a range of population densities, from 0.4 to 9.6 persons per 100 square km (one to 25 persons per 100 square miles) (Lee and DeVore 1968). Pleistocene densities may have exceeded the upper end of this range; we can use a figure of 0.4 persons per square km (one person per square mile). North and South America, south of the glacial margins at 10,000 B.C., contained roughly 26 million square km (10 million square miles). Ignoring for the moment environmental differences which made areas more or less suitable for human habitation, and applying the 0.4 per square km (one per square mile) density figure, we get 10,000,000 as the potential hunting population of the Americas. If we assume that a band of 25 people passed through the corridor into North America, and that this population doubled in each successive generation (every 30 years or so), we reach the 10,000,000 figure in about 500 years.

This hypothetical figure assumes greater significance in the light of the archaeological evidence, which shows that man had reached the southernmost tip of South America by about 9000 B.C. That is the implication of C14 dates of 9050 ± 180 and 8770 ± 300 B.C. for cultural and faunal remains from Fell's Cave in Patagonia. It has sometimes been assumed that thousands of years must have elapsed between the initial entry of humans into North America and their arrival at Fell's Cave; however, our calculations have shown how rapidly population expansion could have occurred. The distance from the base of the corridor to Tierra del Fuego is about 13,000 km (8,000 miles). If the expansion of human population to the limits of the continents took as little as 500 years, we would have to assume that the rate of migration was about 26 km (16 miles) a year, or 780 km (480 miles) per generation. Such movement is quite feasible, particularly in light of evidence that Paleo-Indians sometimes made tools of flint that they had carried from sources located several

1 Marmes
2 Folsom
3 Blackwater Draw
4 Lewisville
5 Santa Rosa Island
6 Old Crow and Bluefish Cave
7 Selby-Dutton
8 Meadowcroft
9 Valsequillo
10 Tlapacoya, Tequixquiac
11 Wilson Butte Cave
12 Fort Rock Cave
13 Dent
14 Debert
15 Vail
16 Bull Brook
17 Shawnee-Minisink
18 Plenge
19 Flint Run (Thunderbird)
20 Batza Tena
   (obsidian fluted points)
21 Olsen-Chubbuck
22 Dutchess Quarry Cave
23 Kimmswick
24 Whipple
25 Little Salt Spring
26 Wacissa River

27 Lehner, Naco, Murray Springs
28 Williamson
29 Shoop
30 Wapanucket 8
31 West Athens Hill
32 Anzick
33 Jones-Miller
34 Bonfire Shelter
35 Lindenmeier
36 Quad
37 Hell Gap
38 Casper
39 Lime Creek
40 Medicine Lodge Creek
41 Levi

Fig. 8. Paleo-Indian sites. Ice sheets are represented by stippled area; note shrinkage by 12,000 B.P. Broken line indicates late Pleistocene coastline.

hundred kilometers away (as, for example, at the Shoop site in Pennsylvania and the Wapanucket site in Massachusetts). The southward movement was probably wave-like, constantly widening on its southern front. The impact of this human wave on the herd animals of the Americas may well have contributed to their extinction (see below).

So, we see that the presence of man at "the end of the road", Tierra del Fuego, by about 9000 B.C., is consistent with an initial entry through the ice-free corridor as late as 9500 B.C. However, the widespread and easily recognized Clovis culture was not necessarily the earliest in the Americas. The archaeological record offers tantalizing hints of earlier occupation.

Over the years, thousands of crude stone tools have been found in North America. These closely resemble the chopper-chopping tools of East Asia; as you may recall, the latter were produced from hundreds of thousands of years ago until quite recently. Some archaeologists have suggested that the American choppers must be older than the Clovis points, that they in fact represent a "pre-projectile point horizon" (Krieger 1964). The absence of points in the supposedly pre-Clovis industries has been interpreted as evidence of a subsistence pattern involving less specialized hunting of large mammals and greater reliance on small game and plant foods.

However, claims for a pre-projectile horizon must be regarded with skepticism. Most of the crude choppers have been surface finds, whose age cannot be determined. Others have been found in datable geological contexts, but they are so formless that they are almost certainly not artifacts at all. Still other choppers are definitely man-made, but are associated with relatively late, more delicate artifacts. Such choppers were probably used for tasks that did not require more finely made tools. Some crudely retouched bifaces found in North America superficially resemble the Acheulian handaxes of Europe and Africa; but the American pieces have been shown to be "blanks", stones retouched into rough form at a quarry site with a view toward later, finer modification into a desired tool.

One of the most famous sites which has been thought to belong to a pre-projectile stage is Lewisville, in Texas. Here, choppers were found in proximity to hearths that were C14 dated at about 36,000 B.C. However, a Clovis point was also found, lying within a hearth; it could not possibly be as old as the radiocarbon date implied. It was suspected that some prankster had put the point in the fireplace, but was afraid to admit his foolish act. But the situation has been clarified by a recent re-excavation, which has shown that Lewisville is in fact a Clovis campsite; the C14 dates must have been erratic.

Among the other sites often pointed to by advocates of a pre-projectile stage are Santa Rosa Island, off the California coast, and Pikimachay, or

Flea Cave, in the Peruvian highlands. It has been claimed that dwarf mammoths, native to Santa Rosa, were slaughtered by man about 30,000 years ago, as indicated by C14 dates on seemingly charred bones. However, there is no clear association of the mammoth bones with artifacts, and thus no certainty that the dates obtained pertain to human activity.

At Pikimachay, Richard MacNeish has excavated a deep, stratified cultural sequence; the lowest artifact-bearing layer has been C14 dated to somewhere in the range of 19,000 to 11,000 B.C. (MacNeish 1971). However, the so-called "artifacts" appear to be small chunks fallen from the roof of the cave; such stone would have been an unlikely choice as raw material for the manufacture of tools (Lynch 1983). The next level has yielded about 200 artifacts, made of exotic stone and therefore much less dubious as examples of human workmanship. These artifacts were associated with the bones of extinct giant sloth and horse, as well as modern animals. A single C14 date on sloth bone from this level is 12,200 ± 180 B.C. But cultural material from the layer above this one can be dated, by comparison with similar artifacts from other sites in the Peruvian highlands, at about 7000 B.C. It seems unlikely that these deposits are really separated by a 5,000-year interval; the single bone-derived date may be unreliable. For these reasons, Pikimachay is not yet acceptable as positive proof of the occupation of South America before 10,000 B.C.

Recently, the arguments for a pre-projectile stage have taken a new turn. Archaeologists such as Dennis Stanford and Richard Morlan have suggested that the pre-Clovis immigrants may have worked almost exclusively in bone rather than stone. This view is based primarily on recent discoveries in the Canadian Yukon, where thousands of ancient bones have been recovered from the mudflats of the Old Crow River (Morlan and Cinq-Mars 1982). Some of the broken and polished bones seem to have been modified by man; one indisputable artifact is a caribou legbone with a neatly serrated edge, that was probably used in scraping the flesh from hides. This piece was C14 dated, some years ago, to about 25,000 B.C.; but a more recent and more accurate determination has shown it to be only 1,350 years old (Nelson et al. 1986). Most of the other Old Crow bones are simply jagged fragments. It has been claimed that the kind of breakage seen in these cases, known as spiral fracture, could only have been caused by human activity. However, spiral fractures have recently been recognized in collections of animal bones that certainly antedate man's presence in the Americas (Myers, Voorhies, and Corner 1980). Therefore, spirally fractured bones found, in the absence of stone tools, at a few sites in the western United States (e.g. the Selby-Dutton sites in Colorado) are not convincing as evidence of pre-Clovis human occupation. In any case, there is no known Old World parallel for the hypothetical all-bone tool-kit. It does not seem probable that Asian emigrants gave up flint-working *en route* to the Americas, only to re-invent sophisticated techniques such as blade manufacture and pressure retouch many generations later. It is more likely that the first Americans brought with them, from Siberia, an Upper Paleolithic technology.

The most convincing evidence of pre-Clovis occupation in North America, south of the Pleistocene ice margins, comes from the Meadowcroft rockshelter in western Pennsylvania (Adovasio et al. 1977, 1978, 1980). Here, stone tools and waste flakes from the earliest culture-bearing layer (Stratum IIa) have been dated, by eight radiocarbon determinations, between 17,000 and 11,000 B.C. C14 dates for the overlying strata form a consistent sequence, and are appropriate for the Archaic and Woodland period cultural material with which they are associated. However, the geologist C. Vance Haynes has suggested that the early dates from the lowest level might be the result of contamination by old carbon from coal deposits in the vicinity of the site (Haynes 1980). This attempt to explain away the early dates has been vigorously disputed by the excavator of Meadowcroft, James Adovasio, and his colleagues. But there is other evidence that casts doubt on the dates for Stratum IIa. Flotation of soil samples from this layer yielded abundant remains of plants – pits, nutshells, and carbonized fragments. These remains clearly indicate that the prevailing environment at the time of the Stratum IIa occupation was the same as that which existed during later periods – a deciduous forest including oak, walnut and hickory trees (Carlisle and Adovasio 1982). But at the time indicated by the C14 dates for Stratum IIa, the front of the Laurentide ice sheet was only 83 km (50 miles) to the north of the rock shelter. It is almost certain that Meadowcroft lay within a band of tundra, bordered by forests of spruce and pine, at about 15,000 B.C. It was not until about 8500 B.C. that the tundra and boreal forest was replaced by deciduous forest, spreading up from the south. An earlier presence of deciduous forest around Meadowcroft at the height of the Wisconsin glaciation would be very surprising (Mead 1980). The few animal bones from Stratum IIa do not resolve the apparent contradiction between the radiocarbon dates and the paleo-botanical evidence. Among the highly fragmented bones, only a piece of antler could be assigned to a particular species. It came from a white-tailed deer – usually an inhabitant of deciduous forests. No remains of extinct Pleistocene mammals such as horse, mastodon, or mammoth, nor remains of tundra-dwelling caribou, have been found at Meadowcroft.

The stone tools from the lowest levels of Meadowcroft rock shelter do not appear to be typical of eastern Paleo-Indian assemblages, but neither do they represent a pre-projectile horizon. Small blades are common. Also found were a bifacially retouched flake knife (called "Mungai" by Adovasio) and a projectile point. This point is lanceolate in shape like a

Clovis point, but it is neither fluted like Clovis points nor as finely retouched as they usually are. Haynes, who questions the pre-Clovis dating of this material, suggests that the point is basically similar to unfluted, post-Clovis Plano points. Adovasio, on the other hand, sees similarities to points from a few western sites, such as Fort Rock Cave, which may be earlier than 10,000 B.C. He suggests that the Meadowcroft point might represent the prototype from which Clovis and Plano points were derived.

The Upper Paleolithic character of the Meadowcroft lithic assemblage is obvious. This is not the first discovery of blades in an early context in North America; well-made blades were reported in 1963 from the Clovis site of Blackwater Draw in New Mexico (Green 1963). These had been detached from a cone-shaped core by striking a bone or antler punch, resting on the core's basal rim, with a stone hammer. The small blades from Meadowcroft were made in the same way. In the Old World, this technique probably developed out of Middle Paleolithic Levallois flaking from prepared cores; but blades, retouched into numerous tool types, first became dominant in Upper Paleolithic assemblages. But, as we have seen, some archaeologists have argued that the first Americans were exclusively users of crude chopper-chopping tools and broken bones; according to this view, they made neither bifacially flaked points nor blades. The development from these simple Lower Paleolithic tools to the elegantly made Clovis point would have been an indigenous process, unrelated to cultural developments in Eurasia. This seems to me a very unlikely course of events. Even if Clovis points were an American innovation – and to date, nothing like them has turned up in Asia – they were products of an Upper Paleolithic technological tradition, incorporating methods of blade production and retouching which were developed in Eurasia.

Among the other sites that are most frequently referred to as possible pre-Clovis occupations, particular notice should be taken of several sites in Mexico. In the vicinity of the Valsequillo Reservoir, near Puebla, apparent associations of artifacts and fossils were observed at four sites. One of these, Hueyatlaco, was excavated, revealing a stratified sequence of stream-laid deposits (Irwin-Williams 1968). In several of these strata, stone artifacts were found, apparently in close association with bones of horse, camel, and mastodon. The remains of other extinct species were also recovered from these deposits. Among the half-dozen artifacts from the lowest culture-bearing level were three points – one made on a flake, the others on blades. Stone tools found four layers above the first include a bifacially retouched, bipointed projectile point. A still higher level yielded a few scrapers, some retouched flakes and blades, a leaf-shaped point and another point which was shouldered and stemmed. Thinning flakes had been removed from the base of the stem of the latter point, which is called "pseudo-fluted" by the excavator, Cynthia Irwin-Williams.

A C14 date on shell puts the Valsequillo material in the area of 20,000 B.C. However, shell-based dates are often unreliable. Another estimate, based on the local geology, is in the order of 200,000 years and is quite unbelievable. The artifacts seem to imply a much later date for Hueyat-laco. The bipointed and leaf-shaped points resemble Lerma points, found in Mexico and Texas and probably to be dated considerably later than 9000 B.C. The pseudo-fluted, stemmed point is rather similar to points from El Inga, Ecuador, which are also later than 9000 B.C. To summarize, the Hueyatlaco evidence is tantalizing, but firmer dating is necessary before it can be accepted unequivocally. As in the case of Meadowcroft, this may be a pre-Clovis site but it is *not* a pre-projectile site; points and blades are present at all levels.

Some 130 km (80 miles) north of Valsequillo, at Tlapacoya in the Valley of Mexico, there are indications that man may have been present as early as 22,000 B.C. Several C14 assays on charcoal from an apparent hearth point to that date. In addition, a log found on top of an obsidian blade has been C14 dated at about 22,000–20,000 B.C. However, the charcoal is not necessarily man-made, and the blade could be intrusive from a much later period.

At another site in the Valley of Mexico, Tequixquiac, in 1870, a work-man digging a canal came upon an animal's head, carved in bone taken from the base of the spine of a camel. Other bones of extinct animals were uncovered in the same area. The carved head was found some 12 m (40 ft) below the surface. More recently, chipped stone tools have been recovered from fossil-bearing deposits in this locality, which date to about 7000 to 14,000 B.C. Since the artifacts reportedly come from the base of these deposits, they could be more than 12,000 years old, and therefore pre-Clovis.

Two caves in the western United States may have been occupied before 10,000 B.C. In a deep level of a stratified sequence in Wilson Butte Cave, in southern Idaho, a bifacially worked, bipointed point and a blade have been C14 dated, using samples of associated bones, at about 12,500 B.C. It is conceivable that the dated bone was contaminated by older carbon in the surrounding soil, or that it was brought in from earlier deposits by rodents. At Fort Rock Cave in south-central Oregon, a charcoal concentration lying on Pleistocene lake gravels has been C14 dated at 11,200 B.C. Nearby were two projectile points, several scrapers and gravers, and some flakes, as well as a milling stone and a hand stone fragment. These ground stone artifacts are suggestive of the processing of collected seeds, a subsistence activity that is well attested in the Desert Archaic culture of this region after about 8000 B.C. However, grinding stones do not occur at Paleo-Indian sites that are earlier than 8000 B.C. Therefore, some doubt exists as to the association of the dated charcoal and the lithic finds. But since an overlying level was C14 dated at 8200 B.C., it seems indisputable that the artifacts are at least that old.

CLOVIS

It is only after about 9500 B.C. that we find entirely convincing evidence of human occupation in North America. The distinctive artifact of the period 9500–9000 B.C. is the Clovis point, named after a town in eastern New Mexico. Near Clovis, in the 1930s, points of this type were excavated at kill sites, where they were associated with the remains of butchered mammoths. Similar points had been found in 1932 at a mammoth kill site near Dent, Colorado. The Clovis culture is also referred to as "Llano", after the Llano Estacado, the region of New Mexico in which the kill sites were discovered.

Clovis points are lanceolate in shape, 7 to 15 cm (3 to 6 ins) long, bifacially thinned by skillful percussion flaking; most distinctively, they are fluted at the base, usually on both faces. Fluting was produced by the removal of a long flake, parallel to the edges of the point. The longer fluting flakes of later Folsom points may have been removed by pressing down on the point's base with a crutch-like device, propped against the flint-worker's chest. Such devices are known to have been used in Mexico, at the time of the Spanish conquest, to make obsidian blades. Experiments by modern flint-workers suggest that fluting flakes were detached either by this method or by indirect percussion (i.e., striking a bone or antler punch, resting on the point's base, with a hammer made of wood or antler) (Flenniken 1978). The shorter Clovis fluting flakes may have been struck off by direct blows with such "soft" hammers. The purpose of fluting was probably to allow the point to be more firmly fastened to a spear-shaft. The grinding that is usually evident on the base and lower edges of Clovis points supports this interpretation of fluting; the ground edges would have been less likely to cut through the thongs that tied the points to the spearshaft.

Clovis points have been found throughout the continental United States, in southern Canada and in Central America. Although the well-known kill sites in New Mexico, Colorado, Arizona, Wyoming and Oklahoma may give the impression that the culture that produced Clovis points had a primarily western distribution, the fact is that a greater number of Clovis or Clovis-like points have been found in the eastern U.S. Fluted point finds are particularly numerous in Kentucky and Tennessee and the states surrounding them. Most of the eastern points are surface finds, but there are also excavated Clovis sites in the east, such as Debert in Nova Scotia, Vail in Maine, Bull Brook in Massachusetts, Shawnee-Minisink and Plenge in New Jersey, and the Flint Run sites in Virginia.

Only a few Clovis-like points have been found in Alaska (Clark and Clark 1980); none of these has been in a securely datable context. Their scarcity poses a major problem for interpretations of the evidence found farther south. The striking similarity of fluted points and associated artifacts across the whole expanse of North America suggests that the continent was rapidly filled by Paleo-Indian hunting bands, each retaining for several centuries the tool-making traditions of an ancestral population that originally entered through the ice-free corridor around 10,000–9500 B.C. But the only place from which this hypothetical ancestral group could have come is Alaska, where there is hardly any existing evidence of Clovis occupation. The earliest Alaskan cultures, which date to the period

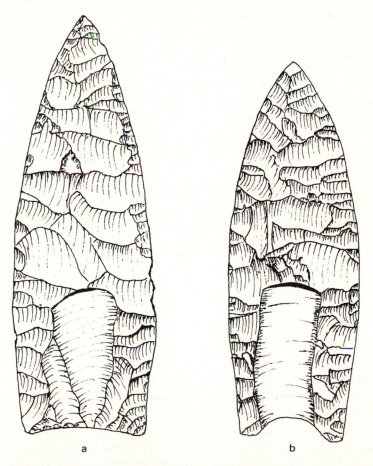

a   b

Fig. 9. Clovis fluted points: (A) Blackwater Draw, New Mexico (actual size); (B) Vail site, Maine (actual size).

from 9000 to 6000 B.C., are characterized by small-blade tools, derived from wedge-shaped cores (Dumond 1980). This "Paleo-arctic" tradition has clear ties to northeast Asia, where similar lithic industries have been found in Japan and Siberia. It is quite apparent that this small-blade tradition is not ancestral to the Clovis culture. Unfortunately, there is no convincing evidence of a substantial human presence in Alaska before 9000 B.C. Most of the broken bones from Old Crow are probably non-artifactual; the few that are indisputably man-made are now known to be only 1,350 years old. Recently, a stratified cave (Bluefish Cave 1), not far from Old Crow, has yielded a few flint chips indicative of human activity, in association with broken animal bones, in deposits thought to date to about 12,000 B.C. (Morlan and Cinq-Mars 1982); however, these finds are too meager to support any conclusions about the cultural affinities of this site. Evidence of Clovis ancestors may yet turn up as archaeological exploration of Alaska intensifies, but as of now it does not exist.

The next logical place to look for Clovis ancestors is on the other side of Beringia, in Siberia. Although much work has still to be done there, recent research by Soviet archaeologists has begun to clarify the prehistory of Siberia. One thing seems clear: there are no Clovis points in Siberia – at least, none have yet been found there. So we must look for more general similarities between the early American and Siberian assemblages. Among the resemblances we do find are: hunting of mammoth, bison and other big game; bifacially chipped projectile points (found in Siberia at Dyuktai); Upper Paleolithic-style endscrapers and blades, in association with Mousterian-style flake scrapers and knives, and crude choppers of Lower Paleolithic appearance; bone points and needles. But, apart from the absence of fluted points in Siberia, there are other important differences. Burins are common at most Siberian sites, but they are rare or absent in Paleo-Indian assemblages, where their place is taken by functionally equivalent gravers. No human figurines like those from Mal'ta have been found in the few excavated Clovis campsites; nor do the semi-subterranean huts of Mal'ta have any Paleo-Indian counterpart.

The Clovis culture therefore appears distinctive in several important respects from known Siberian Paleolithic cultures. Cultural change and innovation must have occurred during the migration of the ancestral Paleo-Indians across Beringia and through the corridor. It seems, on present evidence, that the fluted point was invented in North America.

If we accept the evidence from Valsequillo, Meadowcroft, and the few other sites that indicate that man was present in the Americas as early as 20,000 B.C., the rapid spread of Clovis-style lithic industries around 9500–9000 B.C. becomes more difficult to explain. We must choose among several plausible models for Clovis expansion:

1) Pre-Clovis occupation was ultimately unsuccessful; earlier inhabitants vanished or were restricted to a few isolated areas before the Clovis point-makers arrived.

2) Pre-Clovis occupation was widespread and successful. Somewhere in North America, fluted points began to be made. Then, a) this new technology spread quickly as it was adopted by local hunting groups, who found it useful in hunting big game, or b) the fluted point gave its inventors such an adaptive advantage that they rapidly expanded, encroaching upon and replacing the original inhabitants of other areas.

Model 2(a) seems the least likely explanation. There are no significant regional distinctions among Clovis tool-kits, such as would indicate the addition of point-making to ongoing local flint-working traditions. The known distribution of Clovis points causes problems for model 2(b). It seems unlikely that fluted points would have been decisively advantageous in all of the diverse environments – tundra, grassland, boreal and deciduous forests – that Paleo-Indians occupied at the end of the Pleistocene. Model 1 poses an obvious problem: why should hunters equipped with a sophisticated Upper Paleolithic technology, including effective stone projectile points (found at most of the convincing pre-Clovis sites), and resourceful enough to have endured a trek through Beringia and the glacial corridor, have been any less successful than the Clovis hunters? The paleontologist Paul S. Martin has wryly suggested an answer to this problem: "Given the biology of the species, I can envision only one circumstance under which an ephemeral discovery of America might have occurred. It is that, sometime before 12,000 years ago, the earliest early man came over the Bering Strait without early woman" (Martin 1973: 973).

Martin (1973) has proposed an elegant model of Paleo-Indian migration. His theory would account at once for the rapidity of occupation of North and South America, the uniformity of Clovis tool-kits, and the extinction of many species of large mammals at the end of the Pleistocene. Discounting claims of earlier sites, Martin assumes that the makers of Clovis points were the first humans to pass through the ice-free corridor into North America. Here they encountered herds of animals that had no experience of human predation, and so had developed neither defensive nor reproductive strategies to deal with this new threat. Taking advantage of the seemingly limitless supply of game, the Clovis hunters multiplied rapidly, their numbers doubling with each generation. As their numbers grew, the hunters also pushed southward, their movement taking the form of a great wave of advance, with the greatest density of population at its front. After a brief bottleneck in Central America, the same sort of expansion occurred in South America. Martin calculates that the descendants of an original band of 100 people who emerged from the ice-free corridor could have finished off the large Pleistocene mammals in North America. He estimates that the maximum total animal biomass for unglaciated North America at the end of the Pleistocene was some 230 million metric tons. Human population in North America could have reached a maximum of 600,000, at a density of 0.4 per square km (one per square mile), in about 250 years. If, at the front of the wave of advance, one person did all of the hunting for himself and three others (as might the adult male in a small nuclear family), and if this hunter killed only one animal weighing 450 kilograms (or 992 pounds – about the weight of a young modern bison) per week, the animals at the front would have been wiped out in less than ten years. At this rate, all of the large mammals in the Americas could have been slaughtered in about 500 to 1,000 years – as long as it took for the Paleo-Indians to reach Tierra del Fuego (see p. 49).

Numerous objections have been raised against Martin's "overkill" hypothesis. However, scientists agree that there is a basic fact that requires explanation: at the end of the Pleistocene, some 32 genera of American mammals became extinct (Martin and Wright 1967). These included the mammoth, the mastodon, the giant sloth, the armadillo-like glyptodon, the camel, the horse, the saber-toothed "tiger" and the dire wolf. Clearly, these extinctions must be connected in some way with the major environmental and climatic changes that were caused by the retreat of the Wisconsin ice sheets. However, the ice sheets had retreated before, in previous interglacial episodes, but these events had not resulted in the extinction of so many species. As Martin points out, the unique factor present during the last glacial retreat was human hunting.

Several unique aspects of the late Pleistocene extinctions seem to support Martin's overkill theory. In previous cases of extinction, better-adapted competitive species took over the ecological niches vacated by the extinct animals; but the large American mammals disappeared without replacement. It was primarily large mammals (weighing over 50 kg) and the carnivores, scavengers, and parasites that depended on them that died out. Few small mammals disappeared, and there was no significant increase in extinctions of marine animals or of plants. The climate changes accompanying the glacial retreat caused environmental stress for some animals, but actually led to expansion of the preferred habitats of others; yet these mammals also became extinct. For these reasons, the changes in climate at the end of the Pleistocene do not seem sufficient to account for the rapid extinction of so many large mammals, at least some of which are known to have been hunted by man.

However, critics of the overkill theory point out that there is little or no archaeological evidence that Paleo-Indians hunted many of the species that became extinct. It is possible that some of these animals, such as the saber-tooth, may already have become extinct several thousand years before the Clovis hunters arrived. On the other hand, some genera of large mammals that Paleo-Indians are known to have hunted (bison and caribou) or that were eminently huntable (moose, elk, musk-ox) survived into the Holocene. The survival of the bison is a particularly interesting case. There is evidence of a little bison-hunting at Clovis sites, but it was the makers of the Folsom points who began to specialize in bison-hunting. The later hunters (ca. 8000–6000 B.C.) of the western Plains, who used unfluted Plano points, developed the strategy of driving whole bison herds over cliffs, or into arroyos where the animals trampled upon one another. At one such Plano kill site, the Olsen-Chubbuck site in Colorado, the wastefulness of this hunting method is apparent. Bison lying at the bottom of the pile-up in the arroyo had been left intact; their meat was evidently superfluous to the hunters' needs, so it had not been worth the effort to butcher them. Despite such large-scale and wasteful hunting, the bison did not become extinct: instead, they evolved into the smaller modern species. At the time of European contact, there were probably 30 to 40 million bison in North America. It has been estimated that Indian hunters killed about 2 million a year; but this number was probably less than the annual increase of the herds. Records for the period 1872–4 indicate that Indian hunters, even though equipped with horses and firearms, killed only 405,000 bison per year. The bison was driven to the verge of extinction, but by white commercial hunters, not the Plains Indians. As critics of the Pleistocene overkill theory point out, modern hunting peoples, such as the Kalahari Bushmen, have not wiped out the animals on which they depend. Why should Pleistocene hunters, with a similar technology, have had so much more devastating an impact?

Paleontologists have proposed several alternative explanations for the late Pleistocene extinctions (Martin and Wright 1967). Most have seen climate change as the primary cause. Dramatic shifts in temperature and rainfall patterns led to contraction of the habitats of at least some Pleistocene mammals. Over-specialized animals could not adjust to the new environments, and large animals, with their greater food and space requirements, could not compete with smaller species for which readaptation was easier. But this theory does not account for the extinction of those mammals whose habitats changed very little as the ice sheets retreated. Another theory emphasizes the inability of the large mammals to adjust their reproductive cycles to the increased seasonal temperature differences in the post-glacial climate. These mammals tended to have long, seasonally fixed gestation periods, timed so that the young would be born in the spring, when food was most abundant. But if winters suddenly became longer by two months, calving would have occurred at a time of scarcity, and many of the young would have perished. However, the extinction of animals in tropical latitudes cannot be attributed to this cause.

It has also been suggested that the late Pleistocene opening of the glacial corridor permitted not only human hunters but also an assortment of new parasites and disease organisms to invade North America. But epidemics did not cause widespread extinction during previous inter-glacials. Generally, after initial high fatality rates, populations became resistant, and more stable disease–host relationships set in before extinction of the host. So diseases are unlikely to have been the critical factor in the Pleistocene extinctions.

The problem of Pleistocene extinctions is a challenging one, and none of the suggested solutions is entirely satisfactory. Many scientists would probably grant that Paleo-Indian hunters might have delivered the *coup de grâce* to several species, but would also emphasize that these and other mammals were already seriously weakened by climatic and environmental stress.

PALEO-INDIAN LIFEWAYS

As we have seen, the characteristic artifact of the Paleo-Indians was the fluted projectile point. Even in the absence of associated animal remains, these points would indicate the importance of hunting in the Paleo-Indian subsistence pattern. At excavated sites, points are often associated with other tools that were used for the processing of meat, hides, and bones: flake knives, endscrapers, sidescrapers and gravers. In addition to these stone tools, the Paleo-Indians made tools of bone: spear points and fore-shafts, shaft-straighteners, and needles.

The tool-kits' implication of a hunting-dominated way of life has been graphically verified in the western United States, Mexico and South America, by the excavation of Paleo-Indian kill sites. In the western U.S. and Mexico, the hunters seem to have had a pronounced taste for mammoth. It is possible, of course, that the apparent concentration on mammoth-hunting is the illusory result of inadequate sampling of the archaeological record, which is probably biased in favor of the preservation of bones of bigger animals. However, there is a consistent distinction between Clovis kill sites, where mammoths are exclusively or pre-dominantly represented, and later Folsom and Plano sites, where no mammoths at all are found, and the most common animal is the bison. In addition to mammoth remains, bones of bison, camel, horse, and tapir have been found at western Clovis sites.

Until recently, no kill sites were known in the eastern or central United States; furthermore, bone preservation at the few excavated Clovis camp-

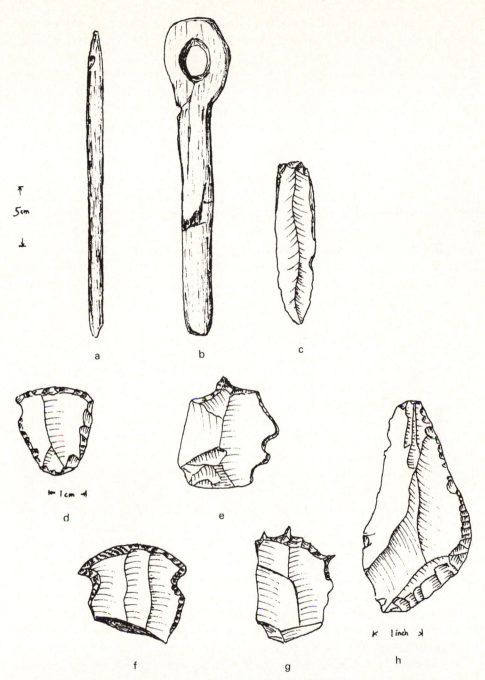

5cm

a b c

1 cm

d e

f g h

Fig. 10. Clovis artifacts: (A) bone point, Blackwater Draw, New Mexico; (B) bone shaft straighter, Murray Springs, Arizona; (C) blade, Blackwater Draw; (D) spurred endscraper, Bull Brook, Massachusetts; (E) graver, Bull Brook; (F) spurred end scraper, Quad site, Alabama; (G) graver, Quad site; (H) sidescraper, Lehner, Arizona. (A–C after Gorenstein 1975; F and G after Griffin 1960).

sites was poor, so we could only speculate about the game preferences of the eastern hunters. The skeletal remains of large Pleistocene mammals, including mammoth, mastodon, and moose-elk, had been found at many locations in the eastern United States, but there was no convincing evidence that they had been butchered by Paleo-Indians. As of 1976, the only faunal evidence relating to eastern Paleo-Indians consisted of a few caribou bones from Dutchess Quarry Cave in southeastern New York, which were C14 dated at 10,850 ± 370 B.C. (Funk 1976). A fluted point was recovered from the same layer of the cave, but it is of the Cumberland type – generally believed to be a relatively late Paleo-Indian type (ca. 8500–8000 B.C.). Assuming that the association of the point and the bones is significant, the C14 date, which is the earliest for any Clovis site, is probably inaccurate.

More evidence has become available in the last few years. A few caribou bones have been found in association with fluted points at the Whipple site in New Hampshire (Curran 1984) and at Bull Brook in Massachusetts (Grimes et al. 1984). In northern Florida, the skull of a *Bison antiquus* was recovered from the bottom of the Wacissa River in 1981 (Webb et al. 1984). The tip of a broken chert point was embedded in the skull, which has been dated by C14 to approximately 9000 B.C. Another Florida find is the shell of a tortoise, with a wooden stake driven into it. Divers discovered this evidence on a submerged ledge within the Little Salt Spring sinkhole. The tortoise seems to have been killed as early as 10,000 B.C. (Canby 1979).

A probable kill site was found in western Maine in 1980, when part of the bed of artificial Aziscohos Lake was exposed. Ten whole or broken fluted points were discovered in one area; no chipping debris was associated with them. Four of the finds were tips which could be fitted precisely to bases that were found at the habitation site, located 250 meters to the east. Charcoal samples taken from the same hearth at the campsite but sent to different laboratories have yielded slightly discrepant dates of 11,120 ± 180 B.P. (9170 B.C.) and 10,300 ± 90 B.P. (8350 B.C.); recently obtained accelerator dates indicate an age of about 8600 B.C. for this site, known as the Vail site (Gramly 1982, 1984; Haynes et al. 1984).

The recent discovery (Graham et al. 1981) at the Kimmswick site, about 30 km (20 miles) south of St Louis, of Clovis points in apparent association with mastodon bones, has provided the first North American evidence of the hunting of this creature (there are a few Paleo-Indian sites in Mexico and South America where mastodon remains were already known). The environment of the site around 9000 B.C. is reconstructed as a deciduous woodland with open grassy areas. This is particularly interesting, because it implies that mastodons were thriving, at least for a while, in the environment that spread throughout eastern North America when the Pleistocene ended. If that was the case, we must question whether environmental change is an adequate explanation of the mastodon's extinction; perhaps, following Martin's suggestion, we must ascribe a decisive role to human predation. A further implication of the Kimmswick site is that, if Paleo-Indians were hunting mastodons in Missouri, they were probably also hunting them in the woodlands that stretched eastward from there. Finally, the striking uniformity of the Clovis culture over a vast area is underlined by the obvious similarity of one of the Kimmswick points to the type-specimens of Clovis points from Blackwater Draw, New Mexico. The latter site lies almost 1,600 km (1,000 miles) southwest of Kimmswick. For that matter, the similarity of fluted points from Vail to the Blackwater Draw points is equally striking, and these two sites are separated by more than 3,200 km (2,000 miles).

Some archaeologists have suggested that the mammoth kill sites give a mistaken impression of the normal Paleo-Indian subsistence pattern. In the Tehuacan Valley, in the arid highlands of Mexico, Paleo-Indians sometimes hunted horse and now-extinct species of antelope, but most of their meat came from jackrabbits, gophers, rats and other small mammals, turtles, and birds. Richard MacNeish, the excavator of the Tehuacan sites, comments wryly: "They probably found one mammoth in a lifetime and never got over talking about it" (MacNeish 1964: 533). The hunters of Tehuacan did not make Clovis-like points, but they did make Lerma points, like those found associated with mammoth remains at Iztapan.

The ubiquitous Clovis points of North America do not seem to have been designed with small animals in mind. The fluting of the base, and the grinding of the lower edges of the typical point, were probably intended to insure that the spearhead would remain securely fastened to the shaft, even when subjected to great stress. One gets the impression that Clovis points may have been affixed to stabbing-spears, which were repeatedly plunged into the bodies of large mammals. On the other hand, it has been suggested that fluted points were often lashed to bone foreshafts, which would easily become detached when the point lodged in an animal's flesh. The main shaft could then be retrieved and another foreshaft assembly fitted into place, ready for the next thrust or throw of the spear (Lahren and Bonnichsen 1974). We have no definite proof that the Paleo-Indians used spearthrowers. These devices, which add force and distance to thrown spears without added effort, were still in use in Mexico at the time of the Spanish conquest; in the Nahuatl language, they were called *atlatls*. Antler spearthrowers have been found at Magdalenian sites in France, dating to 13,000–11,000 B.C. A somewhat earlier depiction of what seems to be a spearthrower, with its butt carved in the form of a bird, occurs at the famous French cave, Lascaux. In North America, bone atlatl spurs dating to 8500–5500 B.C. are reported from sites of the Windust phase, located near the lower Snake River in southeastern Washington. A ground stone "bannerstone", probably once attached to an atlatl as a balancing weight, indicates that the spearthrower was in use in New England by 6000–5000 B.C. (Dincauze 1976); atlatl weights of the same period have also been found in the Carolinas (Coe 1964). Independent invention cannot be ruled out, but it seems more likely that the ancestral Paleo-Indians brought spearthrowers with them from Asia.

It has been suggested that not only small animals, but also plants, were more important in the Paleo-Indian diet than one would infer on the basis of big-game kill sites alone. Steep-edged stone scrapers, found at a few eastern Clovis sites (e.g. Shoop and Shawnee-Minisink), have been interpreted by some archaeologists as plant-processing tools. The apparent concentration of eastern Paleo-Indian finds in river valleys might indicate some reliance on the dense stands of vegetation to be found in those areas. However, these areas might also have been preferred by animals, and the abundance of game might have been the prime attraction of the river valleys. It is also possible that the observed concentration of Paleo-Indian finds in the eastern river valleys simply reflects the greater density of recent habitation in these areas.

There is clear evidence that the inhabitants of Meadowcroft rock shelter in Pennsylvania collected plant foods: fragments of walnuts,

Fig. 11. Use of the spearthrower, depicted on a Mochica gold ear-spool (coastal Peru, ca. 200 B.C.–A.D. 600), diameter ca. 7.5 cm.

hickory nuts, acorns, black cherries, and other nuts and fruits were recovered by flotation of soil samples from Stratum IIa (Carlisle and Adovasio 1982). As we have see (p. 53 ff.), this level has been C14 dated at 17,000–10,000 B.C. If these dates are accurate, we may be dealing here with a pre-Clovis occupation; in any case, the small blade-dominated assemblage does not appear to be typical of the Clovis culture as it is known from other sites. In fact, a major difference in subsistence patterns has been postulated by some archaeologists to explain why the Clovis culture expanded so widely and rapidly while its alleged predecessors remained only isolated local manifestations. According to this interpretation, pre-Clovis groups practiced a more generalized hunting and plant-collecting strategy, while Clovis hunters specialized in the pursuit of big game. If Meadowcroft is really representative of the supposed generalized adaptation, we obviously cannot extrapolate from the evidence for plant-eating at this site to Clovis adaptations elsewhere. At present, the floral remains at Meadowcroft cannot be reconciled with the C14 dates; this situation must be clarified before too much is made of this evidence.

There is evidence of Clovis utilization of plant foods at another recently excavated site in Pennsylvania. The Shawnee-Minisink site, like many other eastern Paleo-Indian sites, lies in a river valley – in this case, the Delaware. Among the finds from Shawnee-Minisink are a typical Clovis fluted point, four knife-like bifaces, and many scrapers (McNett et al. 1975, 1977). These artifacts were recovered from a level that has been C14 dated to about 8800 B.C. Flotation of soil samples from this level yielded seeds and nuts of a variety of plants, including hackberry, wild plum, grape, blackberry, ground cherry, and chenopodium (goosefoot) (Kauffman 1977). Some fish bones were also found. Edge-wear on the chipped stone tools suggests that some were used to work soft materials such as meat and hides, while others were applied to hard substances such as bone or wood (Marshall 1986). Assuming that there was minimal contamination from overlying Archaic deposits, the floral remains indicate that the Paleo-indians who camped at Shawnee-Minisink collected and ate berries, seeds, and nuts that were abundant in the area from May to November. However, no mortars, pestles, or milling-stones were found at this site; indeed, such seed-processing tools are conspicuously absent from most Paleo-Indian assemblages. Grinding slabs first appear around 8000–7000 B.C., in Plano sites in the Plains, and in Desert Archaic sites in the Great Basin and Plateau. The absence of ground stone tools at earlier Paleo-Indian sites suggests that the inhabitants did not eat many seeds. However, they may have eaten plant foods that did not require grinding; nuts could be cracked open with unworked stones, and berries could be eaten as they were picked. Nevertheless, it is hard to avoid the conclusion that the Paleo-Indians were more dependent on hunted meat, and less reliant on gathered plants, than later Archaic populations. We can hypothesize that the Paleo-Indians were forced to broaden their diet to include more small game and plants (and in some regions, fish and shellfish) after the sudden disappearance of the large Pleistocene mammals.

SETTLEMENT PATTERNS AND SOCIAL ORGANIZATION

On the basis of relative frequencies of artifact types and varying environmental settings, archaeologists have distinguished several kinds of Paleo-Indian sites. These include kill sites, quarry sites, hunting camps, and base camps.

Almost all kill sites, as we have already noted, are found in the western states. At these sites, bones of from one to 12 mammoths are usually associated with Clovis points, and occasionally butchering tools are also present. The kill sites are generally located near ancient ponds or streams, and in some cases at least, the area where the kill occurred is reconstructed as a bog or marsh. It is possible that the mammoths were driven into these areas, where they were speared as they struggled to free themselves from the muck. Another possibility, based on observations of the behavior of African elephants, is that the animals, after being wounded by the hunters, would run toward the nearest water-hole, only to drop there from exhaustion and loss of blood. It has been suggested, again on the basis of the African elephant's behavior, that the Clovis hunters may have waited quietly until one animal strayed off from a small herd, then attacked it without alarming the others. If the rest of the herd (perhaps, as among African elephants, a matriarch-dominated family comprising about a dozen animals) became aware of the attack, they might turn on the hunters, who would be forced to kill the whole herd, just to protect themselves. This scenario may explain the presence of 12 mammoth skeletons at the Dent and Lehner sites.

In spite of the size of elephants, African Pygmies hunt them single-handedly, armed only with short stabbing-spears. In view of this ethnographic analogy, we need not assume that Clovis mammoth hunters always operated in large groups. On the other hand, the presence at Dent and Lehner of so many animals, apparently slaughtered at the same time, and the association, in several cases (Lehner, Naco, El Llano), of six to eight points with a single skeleton, point to cooperative hunting by a group. Stylistic variations among the points recovered from each kill site are not so pronounced as to indicate that hunting groups were formed by coalescence of several normally separate bands (Gorman 1972). It is just as likely that all of the hunters were members of the same band.

The Paleo-Indians seem to have quickly discovered sources of high quality flint, jasper, and chalcedony from which to manufacture their points and other tools. Paleo-Indian quarries and stone-working sites have been found near Flint Mine Hill, in eastern New York, and at Williamson and Flint Run in Virginia. Bands apparently travelled long distances, sometimes more than 160 km (100 miles) to gather stone from such sources. At the Shoop site in eastern Pennsylvania, most of the artifacts were made of Onondaga flint from western New York, and a few pieces came from eastern New York. All of the flint at the Wapanucket 8 site in the southeastern part of Massachusetts came from the Hudson Valley, about 240 km (150 miles) away. At other eastern Paleo-Indian sites, locally available stone predominates, but a small amount of exotic material is usually present. Some of the exotic stone may have been obtained by trade, but this is an unlikely explanation of the concentrations of material from distant sources found at Shoop and Wapanucket 8. Nor is it probable that the Paleo-Indians would have gone so far just to quarry flint, since there were equally good stones available at less distant sources. It seems most likely that the exotic stones were collected in the course of the bands' habitual movements through their hunting territories. On the basis of the distribution of stones, we can guess that Paleo-Indian bands may have established roughly circular territories, each with a radius of about 160 km (100 miles).

Hunting camps were probably occupied by small groups of men, who made and repaired their tools and weapons as they waited for animals to pass nearby. Generally, such camps were situated on high ground, overlooking lake shores where animals would come to drink, or valleys through which they would pass in their seasonal migrations.

Successful hunters would bring their game back to the base camp, to be shared with other band members. Several probable base camps have been found in the eastern states and Canada. Among these sites are Debert in Nova Scotia, Bull Brook in Massachusetts, the Thunderbird site in Virginia, and possibly the Shoop site in Pennsylvania and West Athens Hill in New York. These sites are distinguished by their large size and, usually, by a diversity of stone artifacts suggestive of a wide range of activities, such as flint-chipping, hide-working, meat-cutting, bone-working and wood-working. At the Thunderbird site, post-holes may mark the locations of the only Paleo-Indian structures known; but recent ploughing has confused the stratigraphy of the site, so the house remains might really belong to a later Archaic occupation. At the other sites, there is no remaining evidence of structures, only concentrations of debris, which are often associated with hearths or burnt earth. At Debert, 11 such concentrations were present; they ranged in size from 70 to 205 square m (750 to 2,200 square ft). These living floors may represent successive seasonal occupations, each lasting for a few weeks, by the same band. The extents of the living floors at Debert are consistent with a band size on the order of 15 to 50 people. Bands of this size have been observed among recent hunting peoples of the Arctic and sub-Arctic, such as the Nunamiut Eskimo. Paleo-Indian dwellings may have resembled the simple structures of branches, moss and skins found in Nunamiut camps.

A Nunamiut band of about 50 people, such as the Tuluaqmiut, would live in one large camp of 10 or 12 dwellings in the spring and summer. In the fall and winter, when game, particularly caribou, was scarce, the band broke up into groups of one or two families, living in smaller camps in sheltered areas (Campbell 1968). Similar patterns of seasonal aggregation and dispersion have been observed among most extant hunting and gathering peoples. Bands generally come together to take advantage of seasonally abundant resources (in the Nunamiut case, migrating caribou). But these gatherings also have important non-economic functions. They are occasions for gambling and dancing, trading, performing initiation rites and arranging marriages. The duration of such gatherings is limited, because the food supplies which support them begin to diminish after a while, and because there is no established authority to deal with the occasional disputes that are usually settled by the departure of the people involved. Clovis settlement patterns are not well enough known for us to be sure that they reflect cyclical aggregation and dispersion of bands. However, as we shall see, there are hints of such a pattern at a few Folsom and Plano sites.

Based upon studies of existing hunter–gatherers (Lee and DeVore 1968), we can indulge in plausible speculation about aspects of Paleo-Indian society that are difficult or impossible to reconstruct from archaeological data. Bands were probably patrilocal; men remained attached to the group in which they were born, hunting in cooperation with their fathers, uncles, brothers, and sons. Bands were exogamous; women born in the group were sent off to marry men in neighboring bands, and wives were obtained from these bands in exchange. Thus a network of kinship ties was formed between bands, which encouraged rapid settlement of conflicts, and allowed people to move in with their relatives if food became scarce in their own territory. A band's ownership of its territory was recognized by others, but boundaries were rarely defended (however, the Ona of Tierra del Fuego are reported to have killed trespassers) and outsiders were usually permitted to use the band's resources. Within the band, decisions were reached by consensus, but the opinions of the older men carried most weight. One man of exceptional wisdom, experience and persuasiveness might be recognized as a leader, but he had no formal authority to enforce compliance with decisions or to punish wrongdoers. The economy of the band was based upon sharing and reciprocity. A few individuals might excel in particular activities, such as flint-knapping, but they did not become full-time specialists. Clothing, tools, weapons and ornaments were probably regarded as personal property, but the need for mobility prohibited the accumulation of goods, as did social norms which encouraged gift-giving and condemned hoarding. This description would be applicable to any recent hunting and gathering societies (with a few exceptions, such as the complex societies of the Northwest Coast). The common features of these societies are independent of environmental and cultural differences, and therefore it is likely that they also characterized Paleo-Indian hunting bands.

IDEOLOGY

The religious beliefs and world-views of prehistoric cultures are reconstructed primarily on the basis of artistic representations and mortuary remains. In the case of the Paleo-Indians, there is hardly any evidence of either kind.

As we have seen, carvings and engravings in bone, antler and ivory have been found in Upper Paleolithic sites from Spain to Siberia. It is therefore surprising that so few examples of Paleo-Indian art have been discovered. Only two pieces are probably authentic; both come from Mexico, and neither has been securely dated. One is the coyote-like animal head, carved out of a camel vertebra, which was dug up at Tequixquiac in 1870 (see p. 55). The other is part of a mastodon's pelvis, which was incised with lines which seem to depict several animals, possibly a tapir, two mastodons, and a bison (Canby 1979). Associated with these animals are straight lines and small triangles of unknown significance. This incised bone was found at Valsequillo; we have already discussed the problematic dating of the artifacts and bones from this area (p. 55). Recently, a few archaeologists have suggested that an engraved depiction of a mammoth, on a whelk shell, found near Holly Oak, Delaware, in the late nineteenth century and long dismissed as a forgery, might be genuine. However, the style of this piece is suspiciously similar to that of Upper Paleolithic art objects from western Europe. A recent geological survey of the area where the engraved shell was reportedly found indicated that it must have come from deposits that were more than 40,000 years old (Newman and Salwen 1977). It is most improbable that the Holly Oak piece is really that old; even those who believe it is genuine concede that it must somehow have intruded into so ancient a context.

The only known Clovis burial site is the Anzick site, near Wilsall, Montana (Lahren and Bonnichsen 1974). It was discovered as a result of earth-moving activity, which unfortunately badly disturbed the remains. Two children were buried there, their bodies covered with red ochre and accompanied by more than 100 artifacts, including Clovis points, knives, and carved bone points or foreshafts. Red ochre is a frequent feature of Upper Paleolithic burials in Eurasia. The application of a blood-colored pigment to the corpse may have been a symbolic restoration of life. The placing of hunting weapons in children's graves is known in both earlier Old World burials (e.g. Sungir) and later New World burials (e.g. at Port au Choix, Newfoundland). Since the children can hardly have been full-fledged hunters, we are obviously not dealing with provision of the deceased with their former belongings. The points and other items were instead gifts from adult kinsmen, who gave them to the children for use in the afterlife. The quantity of grave goods accompanying the Anzick burials incidentally suggests that more than one or two nuclear families were involved in the mortuary ritual; this is consistent with our reconstruction of Paleo-Indian bands.

On the basis of ethnographic and archaeological data, we can suggest that each Paleo-Indian band included one or more *shamans*. This term, which comes from the language of the Tungus of Siberia, refers to individuals who exercise supernatural power by virtue of their communication with spirits. The shaman enters the spirit world by falling into trance. His spirit contacts are generally animals, who may speak through him while he is in trance. While thus possessed, the shaman may dance, sing, or play an instrument. His primary social function is to use his supernatural powers to cure the sick, which he generally claims to do by sucking out from the body a small object which is blamed for the illness. Shamans

Fig. 12. Wooden mask from Spiro Mound, Oklahoma(Mississippian, ca. A.D. 1250), height 29 cm.

are sometimes thought to be able to predict and even influence the weather. They can also ensure success in hunting, by exercising their power over animal spirits. This may be done directly, as in the case of Shoshoni antelope shamans who lured the antelope into ambush. A more indirect approach was taken by Eskimo shamans, who had to travel (spiritually) to the bottom of the sea to appease a female spirit, Sedna, so that she would release the seals that she was withholding from the hunters. Supernatural beings like Sedna, who exercise a kind of parental control over all animals or those of a particular species, are found in the belief systems of many hunting peoples; another American example is the "Master of Caribou" of the Montagnais-Naskapi.

The classic ethnographic examples of shamanism come from Siberia and North America, but similar beliefs and practices existed throughout the Old and New Worlds (LaBarre 1972). French cave paintings of dancing and instrument-playing men in animal costumes, and another which may depict a shaman falling into trance, suggest that shamans were present in Upper Paleolithic societies of western Europe by about 15,000 B.C. or earlier. The deer antlers worn by the dancing "sorcerer" of Trois Frères are echoed by the reindeer antler headdresses of eighteenth-century Tungus shamans, and by the carved antlers of a wooden mask found in Spiro Mound, Oklahoma, and dated to about A.D. 1250.

The earliest possible evidence of shamanic activity in the Americas comes from the recently excavated Jones-Miller site in eastern Colorado (Stanford 1979). At this Plano kill site, dating to about 8000 B.C., bison herds were slaughtered, apparently by driving them between ice-glazed snow banks. A post-hole was discerned by the excavator, and near it were found an antler flute, a miniature point, and other objects which might have belonged to a shaman. The post-hole may mark the location of a pole, upon which perched a shaman, who magically lured bison into the trap. The same shamanic role in bison-hunting was observed among historic Plains Indians; it seems that this hunting strategy persisted for an astonishing 10,000 years.

FOLSOM AND PLANO

About 400 years after the makers of Clovis points entered the Plains, their descendants began to produce a slightly different style of fluted point – the Folsom point. These were generally smaller than Clovis points, their bases were concave, with pointed "ears" at the corners, and deep flutes ran from their bases almost to their tips. Folsom points are only found in the west; they are contemporaneous with the eastern Clovis variants found at Debert (8600 B.C.) and Bull Brook.

In addition to this change in point style, there is evidence of new hunting strategies after 9000 B.C. The mammoth, which had been preyed upon by Clovis hunters, was now extinct, and the Folsom hunters turned their attention to the bison. Sometimes, one or a few hunters would stalk and spear a single animal. But on other occasions, large numbers of hunters would collaborate in driving whole herds into natural traps such as box canyons, or over cliffs. At the Folsom site itself, where Folsom points were first discovered in 1926, the remains of 23 bison were excavated, in association with 19 points. A recent re-analysis of the bones suggests that all of the animals were probably killed at the same time, in the early winter (Frison 1978). The bison seem to have been driven into an arroyo, where they were speared. At Bonfire Shelter in Texas, bison were stampeded over the edge of a 21 m- (70 ft)-cliff. Three such "jumps" are thought to have occurred, resulting in the accumulation of the bones of about 120 animals at the base of the cliff. Found in association with these bones were both Folsom and unfluted Plainview points. The site has been dated to about 8300 B.C. by C14.

Folsom campsites have been located by surveys, and a few have been excavated. In the central Rio Grande Valley of New Mexico, 33 Folsom and Plano campsites were discovered. The Folsom camps were always situated on ridges, northeast of and overlooking broad flat expanses of land, and close to *playas*, which are now dry but would have been ponds at the time of occupation. The Folsom hunters apparently intended to surprise animals as they came to drink at these water-holes.

An extensive campsite, repeatedly visited by Folsom bands, was excavated at Lindenmeier in northern Colorado in the 1930s. The site reports and artifact collections have been re-analyzed recently by Edwin Wilmsen (1974). An assortment of points, knives, scrapers, and gravers, as well as flint-knapping debris and cut and broken bones of extinct bison, pronghorn antelope, jackrabbits, wolf, fox, and coyote, indicate that Lindenmeier was a base camp where many different activities were carried out. Wilmsen recognized consistent differences in shape and retouching technique between points excavated in the eastern and west-

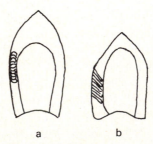

Fig. 13. Lindenmeier: shape and flaking typical of points from areas I (A) and II (B) (after Wilmsen 1974).

ern parts of the site. The raw material used for stone artifacts in the eastern area included obsidian from Yellowstone Park, which is about 560 km (350 miles) northwest of Lindenmeier; but obsidian found in the western area of the site came from sources in central New Mexico, located about as far to the south of Lindenmeier as Yellowstone is to the north. Taken together with the stylistic differences between the points, the distribution of obsidian suggests that two Folsom bands that usually wandered far to the north and south of Lindenmeier rendezvoused occasionally at this site on the border of their territories. The economic purpose of these periodic gatherings may have been communal bison-hunting, but they also served important social functions (see p. 70). Lindenmeier dates to about 8800 B.C.

We have already noted the occurrence of unfluted Plainview points alongside Folsom points at Bonfire Shelter. At Hell Gap in eastern Wyoming, a stratigraphic sequence suggests that Plainview points, which resemble unfluted Clovis points, may actually be earlier than Folsom points. In any case, some time before 8000 B.C. Plains hunters stopped fluting their spear-points, thinning them instead by careful pressure retouch. Unfluted points made between 9000 and 6000 B.C. have been divided into numerous types, on the basis of size, shape and other attributes. Collectively, however, they have been referred to as Plano points. Plano points, like Folsom points, have been found only in the Plains, with the exception of a few stray finds in other regions.

The Plano hunters continued to prey upon bison, using tactics similar to those of the Folsom hunters. At the Casper site in Wyoming, about 100 bison were driven into a U-shaped sand dune where, unable to climb the steep slope, they were killed. At the Jones-Miller site in eastern Colorado, 300 bison were slaughtered in the course of several winter hunts. The animals may have been driven between ice-covered snow embankments, too slippery for them to climb over. We have already noted the possibility that a shaman participated in the Jones-Miller drives (see p. 73).

The best-known Plano kill site is the Olsen-Chubbuck site in eastern Colorado (Wheat 1972). Like the Casper and Jones-Miller sites, it dates to about 8000 B.C. Skeletal remains of 190 bison were found in an ancient arroyo, in association with 27 Plano points, a few scrapers, and other artifacts. A whole herd was apparently surrounded and driven into the steep, narrow arroyo. The animals struggled vainly to escape as others fell on top of them. Those that lay on top of the pile were finished off by the hunters, while the bison trapped beneath them were crushed to death. On the basis of studies of the tooth eruption of the calves, the season in which the kill occurred can be determined; it was summer or early fall. It has been estimated, based on the recorded behavior of historic Plains Indians, that each person who participated in the Olsen-Chubbuck hunt may have consumed about 4.5 kg (10 lb) of meat per day. Even at this rate of consumption, there was more meat than the hunters could use; they did not butcher 10% of the dead animals at all, and another 16% were only partially butchered. The animals that were butchered yielded about 31,000 kg (69,000 lb) of meat; one-half to two-thirds may have been eaten fresh, while the rest was preserved by sun-drying. The excavator of the Olsen-Chubbuck site, Joe Ben Wheat, after weighing several alternatives, has suggested that the number of people involved in butchering and consumption was probably 150–200. Such a large group might have been formed by the coalescence of a few bands. The presence of at least two bands of hunters with somewhat divergent traditions of tool-making is suggested by Wheat's recognition of two different types of spear-points among the 27 found at the site; he has referred to these as Firstview and San Jon points. Olsen-Chubbuck may therefore be another example of the seasonally-scheduled aggregation of Paleo-Indian regional bands into "macro-bands".

At a few sites, there is evidence that the Plano hunters preyed on other animals besides bison. Bones of pronghorn antelope, a now extinct

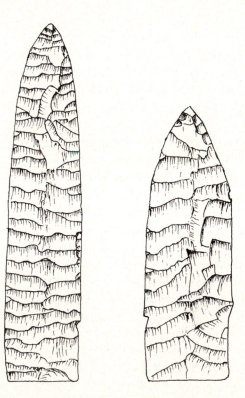

Fig. 14. Plano points from the Olsen-Chubbuck site: (A) length 8.2 cm. (B) length 6.2 cm.

species of giant beaver, elk, deer, rodents, raccoon, and coyote, in addition to bison, were found in association with Plainview and other types of points at Lime Creek, in southern Nebraska. In levels dating to 7300–5400 B.C. at Levi rock shelter in Texas, remains of bison, deer, rodents, rabbits and carnivores were excavated. At this site, there was also evidence of the collection of seeds, in the form of grinding stones. Grinding stones were also used at Medicine Lodge Creek in northern Wyoming, as early as 7500 B.C. (Frison 1978). Besides bones of rodents, rabbits, carnivores and elk, a large number of fish bones were present in late Paleo-Indian levels at this site. Medicine Lodge Creek provides evidence that after 8000 B.C. some Plano groups were developing a more broad-based hunting and gathering strategy as an adaptation to the mountainous and hilly areas that border the Plains. Similar "broad spectrum" subsistence strategies, involving hunting of small game and collection of plants, appeared at about the same time in the eastern woodlands and in the arid regions of the far west. These new adaptations mark the beginning of the Archaic stage, which we will examine more closely in the next chapter.

PALEO-INDIANS IN SOUTH AMERICA

Carbon dates from Fell's Cave in Patagonia indicate that man had reached the southernmost tip of South America by about 9000 or 8700 B.C. As we have seen (p. 49), these dates are not inconsistent with an initial entry into South America only a few hundred years earlier. However, there have been claims that a few sites demonstrate occupation of the continent before 10,000 B.C. Clearly, if it can be proven that any South American sites are really that old, claims of pre-Clovis habitation of North America will gain credibility.

The most controversial of these supposedly early sites is Pikimachay. Richard MacNeish, who excavated this stratified cave in the Peruvian highlands, contends that it was occupied as early as 19,000 B.C. by a group with a crude, pre-projectile technology. But, as we have already seen (p. 52), it is doubtful that the crude tools of the "Pacaicasa complex" are artifacts at all; and the unquestionable artifacts of the "Ayacucho complex", which come from the next level above, are not securely dated by a single C14 determination, based on sloth bone, of 12,200 ± 180 B.C. Other South American sites which have produced material yielding pre-10,000 B.C. radiocarbon dates include: Los Toldos, Cave 3, in Argentina (10,650 ± 600 B.C.); Taima Taima (more than six dates, from 7700 ± 80 to 12,060 ± 140; Bryan et al. 1978) and Muaco (four dates, 7080 ± 240 to 14,415 ± 400 B.C.) in Venezuela; and Guitarrero Cave in the highlands of Peru, where one date from the lowest level is 10,610 ± 360 B.C. (Lynch 1980). The Venezuelan dates are regarded

1 Fell's Cave
2 Pikimachay
3 Los Toldos
4 Taima Taima and Muaco
5 Guitarrero Cave
6 Monte Verde
7 El Inga
8 Madden Lake
9 Turrialba
10 El Jobo
11 Tagua Tagua

Fig. 15. Paleo-Indian sites in Central and South America.

skeptically by many archaeologists, and other dates for level I at Guitarrero suggest that the cave was first occupied around 9000–8000 B.C. On the other hand, the date from Los Toldos has not yet been seriously questioned; but it is always unwise to draw conclusions from single radiocarbon dates.

A recently reported series of C14 dates from a stratified rockshelter in northeastern Brazil, called Toca do Boqueirao do Sitio da Pedra Furada, makes a strong case for occupation of South America long before 10,000 B.C. Dates ranging from 32,160 ± 1000 to 23,500 ± 390 B.P. were obtained for samples of charcoal taken from hearths in the lowest layers of the site (Guidon and Delibrias 1986). Simple tools made from quartz and quartzite pebbles – flakes, notched pieces, denticulates and burins – were associated with the dated hearths. Rock spalls bearing traces of painting were also found in the lower levels of the shelter. C14 dates for the 1.5 m- (4 ft)-thick middle layer of the site indicate a very long interruption in occupation, from ca. 15,000 to 6400 B.C., that is apparently not reflected in the site's natural stratigraphy. This puzzling hiatus must be explained to allay the suspicion that the earliest dates are unreliable. The seeming absence of remains of Pleistocene fauna is also disquieting. However, if these dates withstand further scrutiny, not only will pre-Clovis occupation of the Americas be demonstrated, but the rock art tradition of northeastern Brazil will be shown to be among the oldest in the world.

According to preliminary reports of an extraordinarily well-preserved campsite at Monte Verde, in south central Chile, 12 wooden structures, abundant plant remains, and bones of butchered mastodon and guanaco have been C14 dated at 11,500 to 10,500 B.C. (Dillehay 1984). The houses, made of planks and small tree trunks, are thought to have been covered with hides. Clay-lined hearths had been excavated outside the houses. Wooden mortars and grinding stones were used to process plant food. Actual plant remains include wild potatoes, medicinal plants, and salt-rich plants which must have been brought from the coast, 30 km distant from the site. The stone tool kit is reported to be a very simple one, consisting mostly of split pebble choppers and flakes. Some roughened stones may have been tied together with leather thongs and used as bolas. Hunting devices of this sort would seem to have been a necessity, if stone spear-points were indeed unknown to this culture. However, a few examples of bifacially flaked stone have been found at Monte Verde, and points and knives may yet turn up at kill sites or hunting camps of this culture. At present, too little is known about the Monte Verde culture to compare it with any others. Apart from the mastodon remains, the lifeway represented seems more Archaic than Paleo-Indian. Nevertheless, if the C14 dates are verified by further research, Monte Verde will have provided irrefutable evidence of a human presence in the Americas about 1,000 years before the Clovis migration (or diffusion). If Monte Verde and other South American sites really do pre-date 10,000 B.C., archaeologists will have to explain the puzzling absence of proven sites of comparable antiquity in North America.

South America was occupied around 9000 B.C. by Paleo-Indians who made fluted points, stylistically distinctive from, yet obviously related to, the Clovis points of North America. In the 1930s, Junius Bird found "fishtail" points, many of them fluted, at Fell's Cave. Similar points have been discovered at El Inga, in the highlands of Ecuador. Unlike North American fluted points, these broad-bodied points taper to markedly thinner stems, which take up more than a third of the points' length. However, some Clovis-like points from the southeastern U.S. have very similar fishtail-shaped bases, and are constricted just above the base so that they almost appear to have stems. A link between these northern and southern points is provided by several surface finds from Central America. Short, broad fishtail points, of the type found at Fell's Cave, are known from Panama (Madden Lake) and Costa Rica (Turrialba) (Snarskis 1979). Somewhat thinner fishtail points, more similar to the Clovis-like points of eastern North America, have been found at the same sites, and also in western Costa Rica, Guatemala, and Durango, Mexico. Recently, a Clovis point like those found in the southwestern U.S. was collected from a site in the Quiche Basin, in the highlands of Guatemala (Brown 1980); similar points are reported from recently excavated sites in Belize. Lacking firm chronological controls, we cannot be sure that the more slender of the Central American points represent a transitional phase in the stylistic evolution of fishtail points from North American Clovis prototypes; but

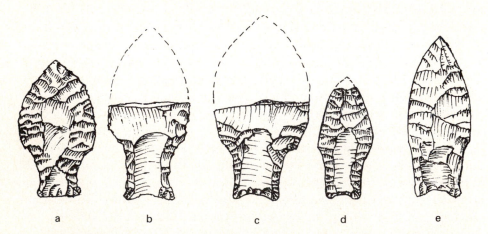

Fig. 16. Fishtail points: (A) and (B), Fell's Cave, approx ⅔ actual size; (C) and (D), El Inga (Ecuador), ¾ actual size; (E) Turrialba (Costa Rica), actual size 6 cm. (A–D after Willey 1971; E from a photograph in Snarskis 1979).

this seems to be the best explanation of the existing evidence. The close resemblance of fishtail points from sites in Costa Rica and Patagonia, separated by more than 6,400 km (4,000 miles), implies a very rapid migration of Paleo-Indians along the mountainous spine of western South America. As in North America, such a rapid migration seems to imply that there was no previous human occupation of the region; alternatively, if the pre-10,000 B.C. dates are valid, the earlier population must have been so small and scattered that they could be easily replaced or absorbed by the makers of fluted points.

It should be noted that there have been finds in South America of leaf-shaped and lanceolate points that seem to be as old as the fishtail points. Some archaeologists argue that such points, of which the best known examples are the El Jobo points from Venezuela, may in fact be older than the fishtail type (Bryan 1978, Bryan et al. 1978); however, this argument rests primarily on a few dubious radiocarbon dates. The closest North American parallels to the leaf-shaped points are the Lerma points of Texas and Mexico, and the San Dieguito points of California and the Great Basin; these types are dated to between 9000 and 6000 B.C.

Apart from fluted points, other items in the tool-kit of the South American Paleo-Indians – scrapers, gravers and knives – suggest a derivation from North American forms. The probable use of these tools in the processing of meat and hides further implies a continuation of the ancestral North American Paleo-Indians' pursuit of big game.

The South American Paleo-Indians' big game-hunting orientation is confirmed by associations of artifacts with remains of extinct Pleistocene mammals at several sites. There is evidence of the hunting of horse, mastodon, and giant ground sloth. The Paleo-Indians also hunted animals of modern species – deer and guanaco, various rodents, rabbits, and birds, particularly the ground-dwelling tinamou. The Paleo-Indians probably turned increasingly to such small game as the Pleistocene mega-fauna disappeared. Bones found at Los Toldos, Argentina, and Tagua Tagua in Chile hint at the early domestication of the dog, which would have been helpful in hunting the tinamou. In addition to small animals, plants became more important as a food source after 9000 B.C. There is evidence at Guitarrero Cave that beans and peppers were cultivated, and various tubers and fruits were collected, perhaps as early as 8500 B.C. and certainly before 7000 B.C. (Lynch 1980, 1983). This dietary diversification in the Andean highlands is comparable to the broad spectrum adaptations that developed after the extinction of the Pleistocene mega-fauna in North America and Mesoamerica.

4

The Archaic: post-Pleistocene foragers

When the Paleo-Indian hunters entered the New World, the last ice age was nearing its end. The ice sheets reached their maximum extent around 16,000 B.C.; they began to melt and recede northward 4,000 years later. The glacial retreat was interrupted by several episodes of minor re-advance, but by about 8000 B.C., the ice caps were restricted to the far north, and warmer interglacial temperatures prevailed. Average annual temperatures in northern areas were now as much as 16°C higher than they had been during the glacial maximum. After 11,000 B.C., as vast quantities of water were released from the melting ice sheets, sea levels rose around the world. The Bering land bridge was severed by water about 8000 B.C., and the coastal shelves of North America were inundated. Post-glacial changes in temperature and rainfall patterns had major effects on vegetation. Some Pleistocene environments, such as the game-rich tundra-steppe, disappeared. Other environments spread into new areas, like the deciduous forest of southeastern North America, which now extended its range into the Northeast. In South America, tropical forest may have replaced previously widespread grasslands in Amazonia. These and other changes in vegetation in turn affected animal populations. We have already examined the possible role of human predation in the extinction of the Pleistocene megafauna. However, the impact of Paleo-Indian hunting on large mammals probably would not have been so devastating if the animal populations had not already been weakened by stressful readjustment to changing and shifting habitats. A few anomalous C14 dates raise the possibility that some species of Pleistocene megafauna may have lingered on in isolated areas after 8000 B.C., but most were extinct by that time.

As the mammals they had hunted became scarce and (in some cases) disappeared entirely, the Paleo-Indians had to alter their subsistence patterns, depending more heavily on smaller mammals, birds, fish, shellfish, and plants. With the continents now filled to capacity with hunters, migration into adjacent territories no longer offered an easy outlet for excess population. Restricted movement and the emergence of social (and, perhaps, linguistic) barriers to communication seem to be reflected

ICE	ice sheets
T	tundra
DS	desert scrub
TS	tundra steppe
DF	temperate deciduous forest
BF	boreal forest
MW	Mediterranean-type woodland
TW	thorn woodland
CF	western coniferous forest
F	tropical wet forest
ME	montane evergreen woodland
EF	montane evergreen forest
ST	subtropical and tropical deciduous forest
SW	subtropical and tropical deciduous woodland or savanna
EW	evergreen woodland
P	grasslands (prairie)
S	shrub steppe
A	high Andean vegetation
SA	subantarctic forest (mostly beech)

Fig. 17. Vegetation zones of North America, ca. 18,000 B.P. (based on Canby 1979).

in the greater regional diversity of Archaic artifact styles. In order to maintain a stable balance of population and wild resources within a bounded region, either population growth had to be slowed by cultural measures such as birth-spacing, abortion or infanticide, or new sources of locally available food had to be exploited with increasing efficiency. Post-Pleistocene hunting–gathering bands learned to schedule their movements through their territories so as to take advantage of the seasonal abundances of various plants and animals. In certain areas, such as the Arctic and the Great Basin, food sources were widely dispersed and undependable, and frequent shifting of camps was necessary. But in other environments, where resources were more predictable and more densely clustered, subsistence needs could be met with little or no movement of base camps. Provided that social mechanisms were developed to prevent disruptive conflicts, permanent villages could and did arise in such set-

Fig. 18. Modern vegetation, North America.

Fig. 19. Modern vegetation, South America. Paleoclimatic data are inadequate for detailed reconstruction of late Pleistocene environments. However, the expansion of tropical wet forest in northern South America, replacing deciduous woodland and savanna, appears to be a post-Pleistocene development.

tings. On the Northwest Coast and California, permanent villages with hundreds of inhabitants, subsisting by fishing, gathering, and hunting, existed at the time of European contact. There is archaeological evidence of much earlier Archaic villages based on foraging, in eastern North America and coastal Peru.

As patterns of movement became cyclical and scheduled instead of randomly nomadic, and as gatherers became familiar with the life cycles and reproductive mechanisms of the various plant species they collected, human manipulation of plants became feasible. Seeds or root cuttings could be planted in a clearing, and the band could return months later to harvest the crop. Certain plant species responded to such human attention with genetic changes that produced, over many generations, characteristics such as larger seeds and the loss of hard seed-casings, which made these plants increasingly attractive to human collectors. As crop yields increased over time, so did the labor and time invested in harvesting, and this investment took place at the expense of other subsistence tasks which had comprised the seasonal round. As storage techniques were devised which allowed surplus crops to be used for extended periods, there arose a strong incentive to establish permanent villages, close to cultivated fields and storage facilities. There is clear archaeological evidence, from the Tehuacan Valley in Mexico and Guitarrero Cave and the Ayacucho Valley in Peru, that cultivation of plants long preceded the appearance of permanent agriculture-based settlements in these areas.

In recent years, archaeologists have become increasingly aware that foraging could be the basis of quite complex societies, as exemplified by the chiefdoms of the Northwest Coast. It is probable that the cultures which raised the impressive burial mounds of the eastern U.S. were supported not by agriculture but by intensive collecting and hunting. Nevertheless, the highest level of socio-cultural complexity, which we label "civilization", has been reached only by agricultural societies. The reason is obvious: agriculture can support much denser and larger human populations than foraging. The development of agriculture in the highlands of Mexico and Peru thus laid the foundation for the later emergence of high civilizations in those regions, and therefore we will look more closely, later on, at the transition from foraging to agriculture. But for now, we should realize that this transition was accomplished by hunter–gatherers whose way of life was basically similar to that of Archaic peoples elsewhere.

THE CONCEPT OF THE "ARCHAIC"

The term "Archaic" was introduced into American archaeology in 1932 by William Ritchie, who used it to describe the Lamoka phase of central

New York (now dated to ca. 2500 B.C.). Recognition of similarities between this material and excavated material from Alabama, Kentucky and Georgia led to the extension of the "Archaic" designation to include Southeastern cultures, particularly those associated with coastal shell middens. There were even suggestions that sites as far away as California were somehow connected with these eastern "Archaic" cultures. In the early 1950s, the term was still used by some archaeologists to refer to a period, but Willey and Phillips (1958) argued that it should be applied to a developmental stage, and that is the meaning which it will usually have in this book. However, we should bear in mind that "Archaic" still denotes a chronological period in the prehistory of eastern North America. Willey and Phillips defined the Archaic succinctly as "the stage of migratory hunting and gathering cultures continuing into environmental conditions approximating those of the present" (1958: 107). They listed as characteristics of this stage:

1) dependence on smaller, more varied fauna following extinction of Pleistocene megafauna;
2) an increase in gathering;
3) large numbers of stone implements and utensils, apparently used to prepare wild vegetable foods;
4) ground-stone wood-working tools, atlatl weights, and ornaments;
5) greater stability of occupation, based on specialized subsistence economies (e.g. fishing, seed-gathering);
6) in chipped stone, a greater variety of points (stemmed, corner-notched and side-notched), generally not as well-made as Lithic (Paleo-Indian) points; use of an increased variety of lithic materials; drills;
7) artifacts of bone, horn, ivory, shell, copper, asphalt, clay; some of these used in basketry, fishing and marine hunting;
8) burials.

Since the concept of an Archaic stage originated in the study of eastern North America, it is appropriate that we begin our survey with the Archaic cultures of that region.

ARCHAIC CULTURES OF THE EASTERN WOODLANDS

In the eastern United States, the outstanding post-Pleistocene environmental development was the northward expansion of the oak-dominated deciduous forest, replacing the spruce and pine forests of the Northeast. The Southeastern Paleo-Indians, who had encountered this deciduous forest upon their arrival in the area, would already have begun to adapt to it while their northern contemporaries were still living on the tundra-steppe and in the boreal forests. Thus, they would have been less hard-hit

by the environmental shifts following the glaciers' retreat. As the deciduous vegetation and the animals that fed upon it – deer, raccoon, opossum,
turkey, etc. – spread north, so too, probably, did the Early Archaic foragers who had become dependent on these food sources. It is not clear to
what extent Southeastern immigrants may have physically replaced
earlier Northeastern populations, and to what extent the local inhabitants
simply adopted new technologies and subsistence strategies.

In the Southeast and the southern Midwest, Clovis points were
replaced after about 8500 B.C. by Dalton points (Goodyear 1982).
Though obviously derived from the earlier fluted points, Daltons are
generally smaller; they taper markedly toward the tip, and their concave
bases have pairs of pointed ears that sometimes flare outward. Of the
same age, and apparently stylistically related to the Dalton type, are

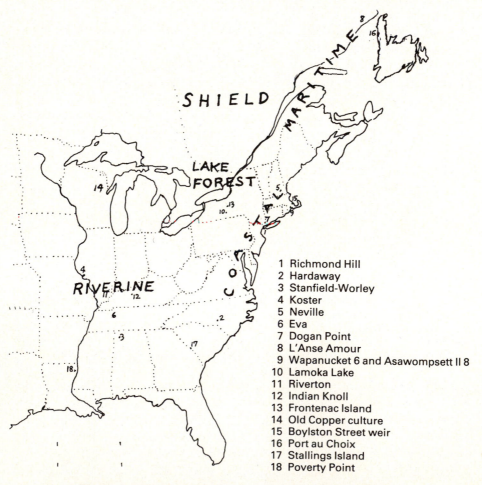

1 Richmond Hill
2 Hardaway
3 Stanfield-Worley
4 Koster
5 Neville
6 Eva
7 Dogan Point
8 L'Anse Amour
9 Wapanucket 6 and Asawompsett II 8
10 Lamoka Lake
11 Riverton
12 Indian Knoll
13 Frontenac Island
14 Old Copper culture
15 Boylston Street weir
16 Port au Choix
17 Stallings Island
18 Poverty Point

Fig. 20. Eastern Archaic sites and regions (same scale as 67).

Hardaway points. These triangular-bladed, fluted points, with side notches and flaring ears, are best-known from North Carolina, but specimens have also been found in Illinois, Alabama and other eastern states. They are very rare in New England, but examples have been recovered from Richmond Hill on Staten Island and from the Harrisena site in eastern New York.

By about 7900 B.C., the popularity of the Dalton-Hardaway style was waning, and eastern hunters began to make and use corner-notched points of the Palmer and Charleston types. Side-notched and corner-notched Kirk and St Albans points were made for several hundred years after 7500 B.C. Another style change occurred around 6800 B.C., with the appearance of the LeCroy and Kanawha types; these points featured distinctive bifurcated bases. C14 dates from sites in West Virginia, Tennessee, and Alabama place points of these types in the range of 6800–

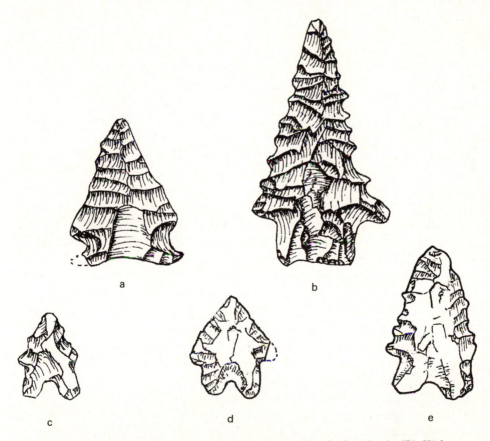

Fig. 21. Early Archaic points: (A) Hardaway (North Carolina); (B) Kirk stemmed (Kentucky); (C) Bifurcate (Alabama); (D) Bifurcate (West Virginia); (E) Bifurcate (New York). (A, B after Snow 1980; C after Walthall, 1980; all actual size.)

6000 B.C. However, a few dates associated with Kirk, LeCroy, and Kanawha-like points in the Northeast suggest that these types may have lingered in that area until about 5500–5000 B.C. In addition to these southern-related types, points that indicate cultural contacts with the Plano bison-hunters of the western plains have been found as far east as Massachusetts.

Until quite recently, archaeologists did not even recognize the traces of Early Archaic (8000–6000 B.C.) occupation in the Northeast. Now that the significance of the bifurcated base points is apparent, it is still true that very few Early Archaic artifacts or sites are known, in comparison to finds from later periods. Some archaeologists have theorized that there was a sharp decline in population from Paleo-Indian to Early Archaic times, because after 8000 B.C. the pine-dominated boreal forest supported much less game than had the late Pleistocene tundra-steppe. However, recent detailed pollen studies show that there were areas in the Northeast, particularly southern New England, that were more hospitable after 8000 B.C. than was formerly suspected. An alternative explanation is that Early Archaic sites have been obscured by later deposition of silt in river valleys, or engulfed by the rising ocean. In fact, the problem which these hypotheses address may be illusory, because the number of Early Archaic finds in the Northeast is actually somewhat greater than the number of Paleo-Indian finds (Snow 1980). Since both periods lasted for about the same length of time, the evidence does not indicate a major population decline; but population evidently did increase dramatically later in the Archaic period, probably due both to the onset of milder climatic conditions and the development of more efficient adaptations.

Very few well-preserved Early Archaic campsites have been excavated, so we do not know very much about the hunting–gathering adaptations and settlement patterns during this period. Level D of the Stanfield-Worley Bluff Shelter in Alabama yielded, in addition to Dalton and Hardaway points, knives, scrapers, and gravers, fragmented bones of hunted animals: mostly white-tailed deer, plus turtle, turkey and squirrel. No tools which might have been used to prepare vegetable foods were found.

At the Koster site in southern Illinois, 14 stratified occupation levels (horizons) have been exposed, sandwiched between sterile rainwater-laid deposits. These horizons present a rare cultural sequence, stretching from 7500 B.C. to A.D. 1200 (Struever and Holton 1979). The earliest well-investigated horizon is 11, dated at about 6500 B.C. The C14 dating is corroborated by the discovery of a St Albans-style point at this level. The campsite of this period covered about 0.3 hectares (three-quarters of an acre), and was probably occupied repeatedly, at certain seasons, by a band of about 25 people. As at the Stanfield-Worley site, bone fragments show that deer and small mammals were hunted. The Koster diet also included fish, freshwater mussels, and pecan and hickory nuts. The predominance of pecan nuts may indicate occupation of the site in the late fall, since today they are best collected in November. There is also evidence of the preparation of seeds and other vegetable foods; near some of the many fireplaces were found metates (lower grinding slabs) and matching manos (handstones). Two complete ground and polished stone adzes as well as fragments of such tools, show that wood was being worked. Bone awls were probably used in making baskets, and bone needles in sewing leather.

Seven human burials have been uncovered in Horizon 11 – four adults and three infants. The dead had been buried in tightly flexed positions (knees drawn to the chest), in oval pits. Some of the pits had been covered with logs or limestone slabs. The skeleton of one infant was sprinkled with red ochre, a practice we have seen earlier in the Paleo-Indian children's burial at Anzick. Three dog burials were also found in Horizon 11, in shallow pits at the western edge of the site. This ceremonial treatment is a clear indication that dogs had been domesticated in this area by 6500 B.C.

Early Archaic people seem to have had less access than their Paleo-Indian predecessors to distant sources of fine grade lithic material. They sometimes made do with less easily worked, but locally available, stones such as quartz and quartzite. This reliance on local sources may be related to the adoption of less wide-ranging patterns of movement, as bands concentrated less on migratory game and more on intensive harvesting of animals and plants available in their immediate vicinities.

THE MIDDLE ARCHAIC

During the Middle Archaic, 6000–4000 B.C., there were still strong similarities among cultures occupying the eastern woodlands, from the Carolinas as far north as Labrador. Projectile points of the same styles were made throughout this region. At the Neville site, near the Merrimack River in New Hampshire, Neville points, characterized by triangular blades and tapering stems, are dated to 6000–4500 B.C. (Dincauze 1976). Around 5000 B.C., Stark points, with less definite shoulders and more pointed stems, began to be made here; they persisted until 4000 B.C. The Neville and Stark points closely resemble those of the Stanly and Morrow Mountain types that have been found in the Carolinas. Points of the Morrow type were also present in Strata IV and V, the lowest levels of the Eva site in western Tennessee. These levels date to about 5200–3500 B.C.

At the Neville site, high mercury levels in the soil seem to indicate that large numbers of fish were caught. At other sites in the Merrimack drainage, located near lakes and streams, Neville and Stark points were associated with stone objects that were probably used as net sinkers. Also found were a variety of wood-working tools made of ground stone: grooved axes, "celts", and gouges. These may have been used in the making of canoes for river travel. Semi-lunar ground slate knives, resembling the *ulus* used in more recent times by the Eskimo, are also present in these sites. At the Neville site, in association with Stark points, were found winged atlatl weights of ground and polished stone. Such objects were once called "bannerstones" in the belief that they had ceremonial or status significance; but it is now thought that they were slipped on to thin, flexible wooden spearthrowers to accentuate the snapping motion as the spear was released. These atlatl weights from the Neville site are among the earliest excavated examples from the eastern woodlands.

In view of the evidence for fishing in lakes and rivers, we would expect to find evidence of Middle Archaic exploitation of marine resources at coastal sites. In fact, such evidence is scarce, probably because coastal sites of this period (as well as any Early Archaic coastal sites) have been covered by rising seas. Sea level at 6000 B.C., though it was much higher than Pleistocene levels, was still about 9 m (30 ft) lower than it is today. Most of the mounds of clam and oyster shell that dot the Atlantic coast date to some time after 3000 B.C. The oyster shell mounds located in the lower Hudson River valley are an exception to this general rule. Sea level fluctuations caused changes in the Hudson's salinity and also affected the river's height; but the campsites of early shellfish collectors were generally situated on steep bluffs, well above the water-line. Therefore Archaic shell middens remained high and dry, while similar early sites on the sea-

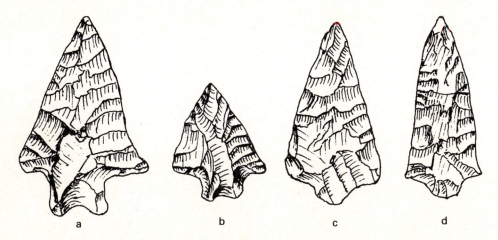

Fig. 22. Middle Archaic points: (A) Stanly (North Carolina); (B) Stanly or Neville-like point (lower Hudson Valley, New York); (C) and (D) Morrow Mountain (North Carolina). (All actual size.)

coast were submerged. This would explain the C14 date of 5000 ± 100 B.C. for oyster shell from the base of a mound at Dogan Point (Brennan 1974). However, at several other C14-dated shell mounds along the lower Hudson, there is an apparent discrepancy of some 2,000 years between the radiocarbon ages and the later dates that were expected on the basis of point types found in association with the dated material (Snow 1980). Either these points have somehow intruded into earlier deposits, or, perhaps, there is a systematic error in shell-based C14 dates from this area. At Dogan Point and Kettle Rock, another lower Hudson shell mound, levels containing giant oyster shells are dated at about 4000–3500 B.C. These giant 20-cm (8-in) shells may reflect optimal temperature and salinity, conducive to oysters' growth, but they could also mark the beginning of oyster harvesting by Late Archaic groups. Once this practice was established, oysters would normally have been collected before they could reach their full size. This would account for the smaller size of shells in later mounds.

Whatever the date of the earliest shellfish-collecting in coastal New England, we have surprising evidence of very early coastal adaptations farther north, in Labrador. Early sites in this region have remained above sea level because of rebounding of the land following the glaciers' retreat. At L'Anse Amour, the burial of a 12 year-old child under a low artificial mound has been dated at 5580 ± 140 B.C. (Tuck 1975). This C14 date, which has not been seriously questioned, is astonishing not only because of the associated remains of a specialized marine-adapted technology, but because this mound pre-dates other North American burial mounds by more than 4,000 years. The child's body had been laid out, face down, in a three-foot-deep pit. Earth and stones had then been piled on top, forming a mound 7.6 m (25 ft) in diameter and about 50 cm (1 ft 6 ins) high. Accompanying the body were: a walrus tusk, two large quartzite knives and an oval knife of the same material, graphite pebbles, a caribou antler pestle, a bone pendant, a bird-bone whistle, a harpool line holder of antler, an antler head for toggling harpoon, stemmed and socketed bone points, and six points of chipped stone. Several of the objects bore traces

Fig. 23. The L'Anse Amour burial mound (after Tuck and McGhee 1976).

of red ochre. Some of the chipped stone points resembled the Neville points of New England, which tends to confirm the C14 date for the burial. The toggling harpoon, a complex weapon fitted with a detachable fore-shaft and a head designed to swivel so as to embed the point in the prey, was used in hunting seals and other marine mammals. Prior to the L'Anse Amour find, it had been thought to be a much later invention of the Esikmo. The L'Anse Amour harpoon head is evidence of the importance of coastal resources to these early Maritime Archaic people. On the other hand, the use of antler aw a raw material shows that inland caribou hunting was also practiced. Like some recent Eskimo bands, the Archaic hunters probably moved seasonally between the coast and the interior, in accordance with the breeding and migration cycles of their prey species.

The adaptations and settlement patterns of inland-dwelling Middle Archaic hunter–gatherers have been illuminated by surprising recent discoveries at the Koster site in southern Illinois (Struever and Holton 1979). In Horizon 8, dated to 5600–5000 B.C., remains of substantial structures were found. Wooden posts, 20 to 25 cm (8 to 10 ins) in diameter, had been set into foundation trenches to form the long walls of houses, 6–7.5 by 3.5–4.5 m (20–35 by 12–15 ft). The 2.4- to 3-m (8- to 10-ft) spaces between the posts were presumably filled with branches covered with clay ("daub"); pieces of this clay have been recovered. Computer-aided analysis of Horizon 8 indicates that there were four successive occupations during this period; the house remains come from the earliest of these occupations, so they probably date to about 5500 B.C. These houses are probably the earliest known in North America; they pre-date by 1,500 years the earth lodges found in Surprise Valley in northeastern California (however, remains of dwellings at the Thunderbird site in Virginia may be even older).

The impression of permanence given by these substantial houses is supported by analyses of the plant and animal remains from Horizon 8. These include hickory nuts, marsh elder seeds, mussels and fish, and suggest that the site was occupied throughout the year, except possibly during the winter. The population was apparently larger than that of the earlier Horizon 11 encampment, as the site now covered 0.7 hectares (one-and-three-quarter acres).

In the Southeast, the Eva site in western Tennessee provides evidence of continued reliance on hunting, but there are also indications of the growing importance of aquatic and vegetable foods. In Strata IV and V, dating to 5200–3500 B.C., about 90% of the bone debris came from deer. Bones of bear, raccoon, opossum, turkey and fish were also present. Atlatl weights were used in hunting with spears, and fish were caught with bone hooks. Although plant remains were not preserved, there is indirect evidence that plants were collected. Anvil stones were probably used to crack nuts, and grinding stones were used to crush seeds. Numerous bone awls were probably used in weaving baskets, which would have served to store and cook vegetable foods.

THE LATE ARCHAIC (4000–1700 B.C.)

The great number of sites and surface finds attributable to the Late Archaic attests to a marked growth in population after 4000 B.C. There are several possible explanations for this development. Some archaeologists (e.g. Cohen 1977a) contend that it is the natural tendency of human populations to grow until they reach the carrying capacities of their environments. As they begin to feel the effects of the resultant population pressure, people start to experiment with previously untapped food resources, and refine their technological equipment so that food can be collected and processed more efficiently. The new foods may not be as palatable as the traditional ones, and they may require more laborious preparation, but their addition to the diet averts a crisis and permits population growth to resume its inexorable course.

Applying this model to the eastern Archaic, we would expect to find in the archaeological record a gradual increase in the number and size of sites, from Early to Middle to Late Archaic, punctuated by occasional appearances of new foodstuffs and new and improved weapons and tools. We could interpret the increasing importance of fish, shellfish, nuts and seeds, as we move from the Middle to Late Archaic, as a response to population pressure. The various kinds of atlatl weights, net sinkers, fish hooks, wood-working tools (perhaps used to make canoes), nutstones, manos and metates, all of which occur in Early or Middle Archaic contexts, could be similarly explained. However, in view of the early appearance of these additions to the diet and tool-kit (fish, mussels, nuts, grinding stones and wood-working tools were present at 6500 B.C. at the Koster site), we must ask why the seemingly abrupt and rapid take-off in population occurred so long afterward.

Simple population pressure models of culture change have been criticized by archaeologists (e.g. Cowgill 1975, Hassan 1980) who regard population growth as dependent upon other factors, such as environment, technology, and social structure. According to this point of view, one would expect rapid population growth to occur only when permitted by certain special circumstances. In the case of the Late Archaic, rapid growth could have been a response to changes in environment, technology, subsistence strategies and settlement patterns.

By 4000 B.C., the various component species of the deciduous forest that had been spreading north in the wake of the glaciers had coalesced into a stable ecosystem. About this time, the climate of North America reached its post-glacial optimum; average temperatures seem to have been slightly higher than those of the present day. Flooding of the Atlantic coast by rising ocean waters created a new environment of tidal marshes and estuaries, which teemed with fish, shellfish and migratory birds. When exploited with appropriate tools and foraging strategies, the new inland and coastal environments could support larger human populations.

Increasing sedentism may also have played a role in stimulating population growth. As we have seen, Middle Archaic house remains and food debris at the Koster site suggest that the inhabitants stayed there through most of the year. Perhaps, as we learn more about the Middle Archaic, this near-permanent settlement may turn out to be but one representative example of a widespread tendency toward sedentism. In any case, several Late Archaic sites have yielded evidence of lengthy occupation; either structures, as at Wapanucket 6, Lamoka Lake and Riverton, or large accumulations of debris and numerous burials, as at Eva and Indian Knoll.

How would sedentary life encourage population growth? If camps were less frequently moved, women would not have to carry their dependent infants about with them; so, there would be less reason to avoid overlapping of newborn and unweaned infants. The birth rate would increase as the time between births decreased. Contrary to what we might expect, sedentary living did not significantly lengthen women's lives. Analysis of the skeletons from the Eva site shows that almost half the women died before reaching the age of 30. It is likely that complications arising from childbearing were the principal cause of death for young women. Men, on the other hand, enjoyed a decreased mortality rate; 18% of the men buried at Eva had lived more than 60 years (Jennings 1974). This is quite a high survival rate, compared to the average adult life expectancy of Upper Paleolithic and modern hunter–gatherers (about 35 and 41 years respectively). Perhaps the Archaic shift to smaller, less dangerous game, hunted with weapons that were effective at greater distances, contributed to the reduction in male mortality. But a longer lifespan for men would not have had much effect on population growth. Only a lengthening of the reproductive period of women would lead to population expansion; and since present evidence does not indicate that Archaic women were living any longer than before, we must conclude that if sedentism did have any effect on the rate of population growth, it was through the reduction of spacing between births.

We must also consider the possible effects on population of economic and social motivations. As bands established settlements of longer duration, their mobility decreased. Items such as flint, red ochre, or shells, which they might formerly have collected in the course of their seasonal wanderings, now had to be sought by special expeditions, or by trade with groups living closer to the sources. The establishment of trading relationships would encourage the collection and storage of surplus food, which would be exchanged for valuables. Given this incentive for intensive food collection, the need would arise for a larger labor force, which could be supported using stored food. This situation could lead to population growth. Furthermore, social ranking could begin to develop in this setting. Stored food surpluses would occasionally have to be doled out, or "redistributed". Typically, in ethnographically described cases, this is accomplished by periodic feasting, often organized by chiefs or "big men", whose prestige derives in part from their ability to provide generous quantities drawn from their own stores and those of their kinsmen and followers. As we shall see, Late Archaic mortuary remains provide evidence of extensive trade networks, and hint at the emergence of ranking in some Archaic societies (Bender 1985).

REGIONAL VARIANTS OF THE LATE ARCHAIC

During the Late Archaic, cultures east of the Mississippi developed regionally distinctive characteristics, reflecting their adaptations to different environmental zones. These regional variants were: 1) Central Riverine, 2) Lake Forest, 3) Coastal, Piedmont or Mast Forest, 4) Maritime, 5) Shield (Dragoo 1976b).

The Central Riverine Archaic is represented by sites in and near the valleys of the Mississippi, Ohio, Cumberland and Tennessee rivers. The roots of this cultural tradition are already evident in the Early and Middle Archaic occupations at Koster and Eva. Riverine Archaic peoples took advantage of the wide range of resources offered by the deciduous forests and the many rivers and streams of this region. They hunted and trapped deer, small mammals, turkey and water-fowl; they took turtles, fish and mussels from the rivers, and gathered many kinds of nuts and seeds.

The efficiency of the Riverine Archaic adaptation is well illustrated by Horizon 6 at the Koster site, which dates to 3900–2800 B.C. The village of this period covered 2 hectares (5 acres), and was occupied by about 100 to 150 people. Traces of six houses have been recognized; the floors had been dug about 45 cm (1 ft 6 ins) into the ground, and the walls were made of wooden posts, set into trenches. These posts may have been connected by plaited branches that were smeared with clay ("wattle and daub"). The floor space of each house was about 12–15 square m (96–140 square ft), an appropriate size for a nuclear family.

This seems to have been a year-round settlement, made possible by systematic harvesting of the local wild resources. Vast numbers of fish (bass, buffalo fish, bowfin, catfish and sunfish) were caught in sluggish backwater lakes. Some of the fish were evidently smoked and stored, to be eaten during the winter. The local waters also yielded mussels. The main game animal was the white-tailed deer; but the villagers ate meat from raccoons, woodchucks, beavers, muskrats, cotton-tail rabbits, squirrels and domesticated dogs. Additional meat was provided by birds: ducks, geese, swans, prairie chickens and turkeys. The main source of plant food was hickory nuts; black walnuts, acorns, pecans, and hazelnuts were also collected. Seeds of plants such as the marsh elder and pigweed (amaranth) were gathered and ground in metates into whose surfaces basins and channels had been carved, but seeds do not seem to have been as important as nuts in the diet.

Neither baskets nor leather items have been preserved at Koster, but bone awls, which were found, were probably used to produce them. Bone hairpins engraved with geometric designs resemble pins found in Indiana, Missouri and Kentucky.

A small cemetery, containing only eight skeletons, was located at the edge of the Horizon 6 village. Most of those buried here were elderly males, more than 40 years old. Their skeletons reveal that, prior to death, they were incapacitated by unhealed injuries or arthritis. The bodies had been laid in the grave pits on their backs, with their legs flexed and their heads turned to the right. Other graves held the remains of adolescents, under 13 years of age, who had been buried lying on their right sides. Accompanying both young and old were utilitarian artifacts: grinding stones, stone points and drills, bone needles and punches. The corpses had been sprinkled with red ochre. Obviously, this cemetery held only a fraction of the village's population. The excavator of the Koster site, Stuart Struever, suggests that only those who had no productive role in society, because of their disabilities or immaturity, were buried here (Struever and Holton 1979). Struever's team has found another contemporaneous Archaic cemetery, underlying a much later Woodland period burial mound, across the Illinois River from Koster. The burials at this site were of healthy men and women, 18 to 40 years old, with no injuries or ailments that would have impaired their work. Judging from the associated grave goods, they seem to have been people of higher social status than those buried at Koster.

More light is shed on Late Riverine Archaic burial customs and socio-economic organization by the remains excavated at Indian Knoll, in western Kentucky (Webb 1964). This site, which probably dates to about 2500–2000 B.C., was a five-foot-deep mound composed of mussel shell, other debris, and earth, two acres in extent. More than 1,100 burials were excavated at Indian Knoll. These included individuals of all age groups, from newborn infants to old adults. Of the 503 burials whose sex could be confidently determined, 283 (56%) were males, 220 (44%) females. This deviation from the expected sex ratio of about 50:50 could be the result of mistaken identification of some females as males. However, there were some ostensibly female individuals whose association with normally male-related items – projectile points and spearthrower parts – renders their sexual identification rather suspect. So, if errors were made in sexing the skeletons, they may not all have been in the same direction. If the sexual imbalance is not an illusion created by faulty skeletal analysis, it may point to the practice of selective female infanticide as a means of population control. However, there was probably a strong economic incentive for Riverine Archaic groups to keep such infanticide to a minimum. Women's work most likely included collection of the nuts, seeds, and shellfish which were such important components of the Archaic diet, and this crucial economic role of women probably enhanced their social status. We can infer from the frequent presence of items of social or ceremonial significance in women's graves that some women were accorded high status, either because of their personal accomplishments or because of their membership of high-ranking kinship groups.

The differing economic roles of the two sexes are reflected in the grave goods that accompanied male and female skeletons. Objects found only in male burials include: axes and groundhog incisors, for wood-working; fishhooks; antler flint-retouchers; cannon bone awls, perhaps for leather-working; and animal bones and jaws, which may have been the contents of sacred medicine bags. Items found mostly in males' graves, but occasionally associated with females, were: projectile points and atlatl parts; knives, scrapers, drills, bone awls and pins, and bone hairpins. Associated exclusively with females were nut-cracking stones, bone beads, and stone gravers. Most pestles were also found with female skeletons.

Objects that may have been used in shamanic curing ceremonies – bones from medicine bags, turtle shell rattles, and bone flutes – were about as frequently associated with females as with males. Females were provided with grave goods as often as males, and a greater proportion of female than male skeletons were sprinkled with red ochre.

About one-third of the dead at Indian Knoll were accompanied by tools or ornaments. A small minority (about 4% of the population) were buried with objects that had come from distant sources. These exotic grave goods included copper ornaments, present in only five burials, and ornaments made from marine shells – conch, *Marginella* and *Olivella* – which accompanied 42 skeletons. The copper came from the Great Lakes region; the marine shells must have been imported from the shores of the Gulf of Mexico or the South Atlantic. These imported – and, therefore, probably highly valued – objects were found in association with both males and females, and both juveniles and adults. Ornaments of exotic shell were somewhat more frequently associated with males (14 of 283, or 4.9%) than with females (5 of 220, or 2.3%). Another pointer to the higher status of males is the fact that the largest shell objects – gorgets and cups – were usually found with males. However, the greatest quantity of shell – 38 tubular beads, a conch cup, and a whole conch shell – was associated with a young woman.

It is quite possible that male and female adults could have accumulated valuable imports as a consequence of their own actions. It is much less likely that infants and children could have acquired such wealth by virtue of their personal achievements; but at Indian Knoll and related sites in the same region (Carlson Annis, Chiggerville, Barrett, Ward and Read), some 40% of the conch shell ornaments and 50% of the copper objects were found in the graves of infants and children (Winters 1968). At Indian Knoll, juveniles were frequently provided with disc-shell beads, which were probably made from imported shells; in fact infants, children and adolescents account for 65% of the 18,378 beads recovered from 143 burials. It is likely that these youngsters were buried with valuable imported goods because of their relationship to adults of high status and wealth. Whether access to such items was the inherited perquisite of the members of a high-ranking lineage, or could be acquired through free competition among individuals of each generation for prestige and wealth, remains uncertain (Rothschild 1979).

Exactly how the exotic shells got from the southeastern coasts to Indian Knoll is also uncertain. It seems improbable that the inhabitants regularly travelled as a group more than 1,200 km (750 miles) to Florida to collect shells – trade is a more likely mechanism. But was this "down the line" exchange of goods, passing from partner to partner along a string of villages, or did bands of traders meet at a central redistribution point somewhere in the Southeast? Might Indian Knoll itself have been such a center, where Great Lakes copper could be exchanged for Gulf Coast shells?

Evidently, some sites of the Lake Forest Archaic were hooked into the same trade network that brought shells from the southern coasts to western Kentucky. Twelve pendants made of conch shell were found in burials at the Frontenac Island site in central New York. These shell ornaments were present in the graves of women and children only. One child of five years wore six neck ornaments of conch shell. Adult males, on the other hand, were more frequently accompanied by tools and weapons for fishing and hunting. As at Indian Knoll, only a small percentage of the dead were provided with any grave goods at all; this suggests that status differences may have been recognized. There was clear evidence on Frontenac Island of Late Archaic warfare. In several cases, the deaths of adult males appear to have been caused by flint points, which were found embedded in the skull or ribs, or lying within the rib-cage (Ritchie 1965).

The tradition represented at Frontenac Island is the Lake Forest Archaic, which developed in the northern hardwood and pine forests that stretched eastward from the Great Lakes into New York and the St Lawrence Valley. Because of the scarcity in this region of the nut-bearing trees that provided staple foods for the inhabitants of the Riverine area, the Lake Forest people were more dependent on hunting and fishing. They hunted deer, elk, moose, beaver, bear, and a variety of small mammals. The social units of the Lake Forest Archaic seem to have been smaller than those of the Riverine Archaic, and the population was probably less dense – an adaptation to the less abundant resources of the northern forests (Snow 1980).

The large, side-notched Otter Creek points are the earliest type in the Late Archaic sequence of this region, dating to about 4500 to 2600 B.C. They may be related to point types known from the Middle West and South, such as the Big Sandy points found at the Eva site in Tennessee. Other artifacts, associated with Otter Creek and later point types in assemblages which have been called "Laurentian", seem to have been derived from prototypes in the Maritime Archaic tradition of the northern Atlantic coastal region. These artifacts include ground slate points, knives and ulus, and barbed bone points. Also characteristic of the Laurentian are polished "bannerstones" (atlatl weights), chipped stone gouges and adzes for wood-working, and stone weights for fishing lines or nets. Local stylistic variants which developed in the Laurentian tradition over time include Vergennes, Frontenac, Moorehead, Brewerton, and Vosburg "complexes".

In the Great Lakes region, Late Archaic peoples quarried chunks of native copper from the shores of Lake Superior. They hammered and heated it to make socketed and tanged spear-heads and knives, barbed harpoons, chisels, awls, and ulus. These tools have counterparts made of ground slate in Laurentian assemblages. The craftsmen of the so-called "Old Copper Culture" treated copper much as they would have stone, which was sometimes heated prior to chipping. They did not smelt or cast copper, so their techniques cannot properly be called metallurgy. True metal-working was only developed many centuries later, in the centers of civilization in the Andes and Mexico.

Southeast of the Lake Forest region, along the Mid-Atlantic coast, Late Archaic assemblages were characterized by narrow, side-notched or stemmed points. Recognized types include Sylvan Lake, Taconic, Wading River, Bare Island, Squibnocket, and Lamoka points. This areal tradition has been referred to as the Coastal or Piedmont Archaic.

Recently, the term "Mast Forest Archaic" has been proposed (Snow 1980). This usage emphasizes the environmental difference between this region and the Lake Forest zone to the north. The mast forest contained more oak trees, and the assemblages in this zone include more milling stones and pestles, which were used to make acorn meal.

Fish and shellfish accounted for a significant part of the diet of coastal groups. Late Archaic shell mounds, composed mostly of oysters and clams, are known from the lower Hudson, the north shore of Long Island, and Martha's Vineyard. Fishtraps (weirs) made of rows of thousands of wooden stakes, were built on tidal flats and at river mouths; the fish were stranded at low tide. An example of such a trap was preserved in silt deposits in Boston's Back Bay, where it was accidentally discovered in 1913. The Boylston Street weir dates from about 2500 B.C. The clay layer into which the stakes had been driven lies some 5 m (16 ft) below present-day sea level. We are forcibly reminded once again that coastal areas which may have supported the densest Archaic populations in this region now lie underwater.

Coastal Archaic groups probably spent the summer at the shore, then moved inland to their winter camps. Farther inland, fish were taken with

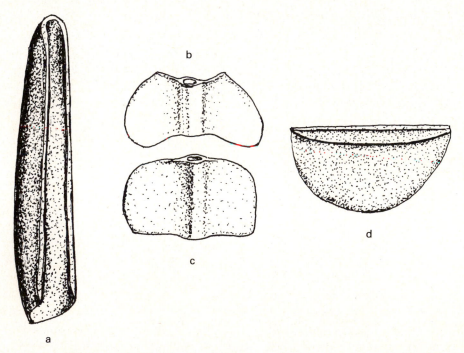

Fig. 24. Laurentian ground-stone artifacts (New York): (a(gouge (length 28 cm); (B) and (C) spearthrower weights ("bannerstones"; length 11 cm and 10.5 cm)); (D) crescentic knife resembling Eskimo ulu (length 12.5 cm). (After Willey 1966.)

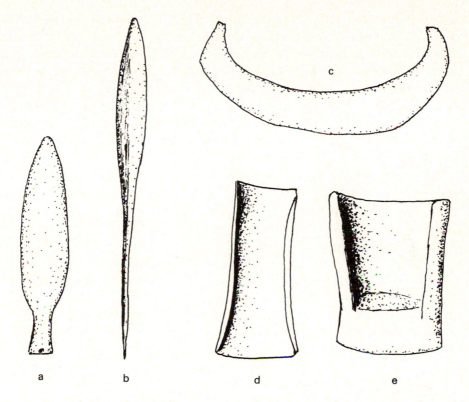

Fig. 25. Copper artifacts from the Great Lakes region: (A) socketed spearhead; (B) tanged spearhead; (C) crescentic knife; (D); gouge; (E) socketed axe (Length of C 11 cm, others to same scale; after Willey 1966.)

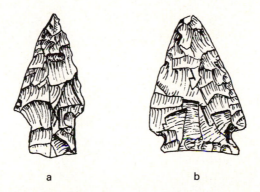

Fig. 26. Late Archaic points from the Ossining Rockshelter, lower Hudson Valley, New York: (A) Narrow stemmed point ("Sylvan Lake" or "Taconic" type), typical of Mast Forest (Coastal) cultures ca. 2500–1500 B.C.; (B) Vosburg point, ca. 2500 B.C. (both actual size). Occurrences at stratified sites indicate that the corner-notched Vosburg type is somewhat earlier than the stemmed points. It may represent a southward extension of Lake Forest-adapted cultures.

nets or bone hooks from rivers and streams. The narrow stemmed points were used to hunt deer and other mammals.

Traces of a settlement dating to 2300 B.C. have been excavated at Wapanucket 6, in southeastern Massachusetts. Post molds revealed the outlines of six circular dwellings, with diameters of 9 to 14 m (30 to 45 ft). The posts had probably been covered with bark. A seventh structure was 20 m (66 ft) in diameter, and may have had ceremonial functions. The size of the Wapanucket houses implies that each was occupied by several related families.

Not far from this village, at the site of Assawompsett II 8, burials of the same period have been found. These were cremations in pits, some of which contained red ochre. Grave goods included stone slabs, gouges, sharpening stones, plummets, fire-starting kits, atlatl weights, bone beads and awls, choppers, points and scrapers.

Dwelling floors, marked by post-holes, were recognized at the site of Lamoka Lake, in central New York. The houses were rectangular, measuring about 4.9 by 4 m (16 by 13 ft). Judging from the extent of the most heavily occupied part of the site – about one acre – there might have been 27 dwellings standing at any one time; this leads to a population estimate of 150–200 people. However, the actual group size may have been much smaller: the horizontal extent of the site may be the result of overlapping of successive small, temporary camps.

A few burials found at Lamoka Lake attest to the occurrence of warfare (Ritchie 1965). Two adult males, whose heads, hands and feet had been cut off, were buried with dart points embedded in their backbones. A third young male was found with a point lying inside his rib-cage. There is also evidence that hints at the practice of cannibalism. Disarticulated human bones, broken and split in the same fashion as the animal bones among which they lay, were found scattered in the occupational debris. In view of the apparent abundance of game and fish available to the Lamoka Lake people, it is very doubtful that they were driven to cannibalism by desperate hunger. Instead, cannibalism probably had a ritual aspect. It is noteworthy that much later, post-contact European accounts refer to warfare-related cannibalism practiced by the Iroquois, who lived in central New York. These accounts have been dismissed by some anthropologists as propagandistic; but they become more credible in light of the evidence of cannibalism by much earlier inhabitants of the same region.

Farther north along the Atlantic coast, from Maine to Labrador, Maritime Archaic peoples pursued a sea-oriented lifeway that had developed before 5000 B.C., in the Middle Archaic (see p. 93). The distinctive tool types of this tradition were bayonet-like points and wood-working tools made of ground and polished slate. The ground stone tools of the Lake Forest Archaic were probably derived, by diffusion or migration, from these Maritime Archaic prototypes. Maritime Archaic craftsmen also produced a variety of polished bone artifacts. Such artifacts have perished in the acidic sands of most coastal sites, but they were extraordinarily well-preserved in a Late Archaic cemetery discovered in 1967 at Port au Choix, Newfoundland.

The cemetery has been dated by C14 to about 2400 B.C. More than 100 people were buried at Port au Choix. Males and females were equally represented, and there were many neonates and infants. The bodies had been coated with red ochre, and were provided with tools and ornaments. Among the grave offerings were ground slate "bayonet" points, which may have been used, like similar Alaskan points, for whale-hunting. There were bone toggling harpoons, barbed bone fishing spears, and slate tools for heavy wood-working, perhaps used in the creation of large ocean-going dugout canoes. The dead were also provided with daggers made of walrus ivory, caribou bone and antler, and with bone awls, needles, tubes, combs, hairpins, whistles, and pendants. Shell beads, made from locally available species, had probably been sewn on to skin garments. Seal claws, bird beaks, and other animal parts may have been worn as amulets, to ensure hunting success. Bird figurines and two killer whales, carved from stone, hint at totemistic identification, or shamanistic communication with certain animal species. Tools and ornaments accompanied children as well as adults. Such treatment clearly implies a belief in an afterlife.

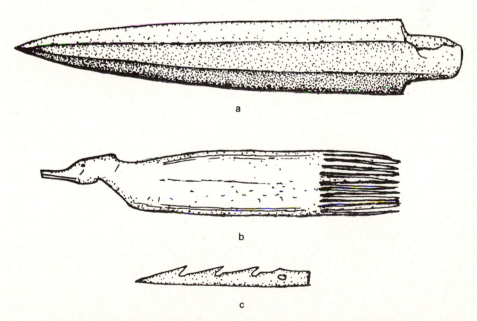

a

b

c

Fig. 27. Artifacts from the Port au Choix cemetery: (A) ground slate point; (B) bone comb in form of merganser; (C) bone harpoon point.

Since grave goods apparently were not reserved for a privileged minority of the dead at Port au Choix, we seem to be dealing here with an egalitarian society (Tuck 1970, 1976a).

Farther west, in the interior boreal forest around Hudson's Bay, small bands hunted caribou and moose and trapped smaller animals in the winter; in the summer, they ate mostly fish. The cultures of these "Shield Archaic" peoples are not well-known. They may have been descendants of Paleo-Indians who followed the ice sheets as they retreated northward; they were probably ancestral to the Algonquian-speaking Indians of this region, whose lifeways were still much the same when whites arrived in the area in the sixteenth century.

The end of the Archaic period in the eastern woodlands is demarcated by technological, economic, and social innovations. However, it is not easy to decide where to draw an arbitrary line dividing the Archaic from the succeeding Woodland period, nor is it clear that these innovations really transformed Archaic societies in any significant way. This ambiguity is manifest in the way archaeologists have referred to the final centuries of the Archaic period (ca. 1700–1000 B.C.). Some scholars (e.g. Ritchie 1965) see evidence of sufficient innovation to warrant designation of a full-fledged period, called "Transitional"; others, stressing continuity of lifeways, regard this period as the "Terminal" phase of the Archaic (Snow 1980).

The technological division between Archaic and Woodland is marked by the appearance of pottery. Fiber-tempered pottery, dating from about 2000 to 1000 B.C., is known from Stallings Island in the Savannah River and from other Late Archaic sites, mostly in Georgia and northern Florida but also in Alabama and the Carolinas. The shape of the open bowls, and the technique of tempering them with grass or rootlet fibers, are reminiscent of the much earlier ceramics from Puerto Hormiga on the coast of Colombia, which date to about 3000 B.C. There, as in the Georgia and Florida sites, the fiber-tempered potsherds occur amid the refuse in ring-shaped shell middens. These similarities have given rise to suggestions that the North American ceramics were introduced from northern South America, by means of migration or diffusion (Ford 1969). However, the absence of similar sites in the Caribbean and on the Gulf Coast, the presence of fiber-tempered pottery at interior sites in the Southeast, and the pottery's occurrence as an additional element in assemblages that otherwise represent continuation of local Southeastern Archaic cultural traditions, argue against a migrationary explanation (Peterson 1980). On the other hand, it is difficult to believe that it is purely coincidental that pottery began to be made in Mexico around 2300 B.C. Cultivated plants of Mexican origin had arrived in Kentucky and Missouri by 2000 B.C.

(Chomko and Crawford 1978), and it is quite plausible that the basic idea of ceramic manufacture reached the Southeast at the same time, *via* the same route of transmission. Inspired by the new concept, innovative Southeastern potters (probably women) might have experimented with various materials and techniques, thus discovering that vegetal fibers made an effective temper. This kind of "stimulus diffusion" seems more probable than a completely independent re-invention of pottery in the southeastern U.S.

At about the same time that fiber-tempered pottery began to be made in the Southeast, durable vessels were being carved from a soft stone, steatite (also called soapstone), in several parts of the eastern woodlands. Steatite pots were used in northern Alabama (Lauderdale phase), Georgia and the Carolinas (Savannah River phase) prior to 2000 B.C. Fragments of stone vessels have also been found at Wapanucket 6 in Massachusetts,

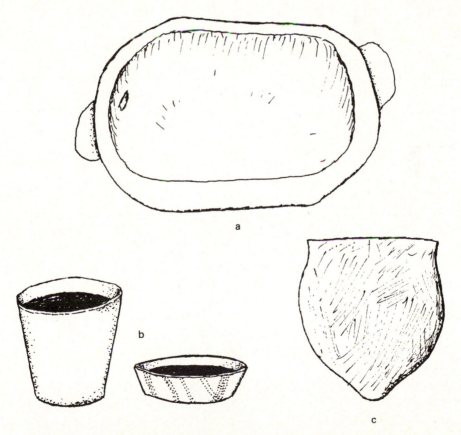

Fig. 28. (A) Steatite vessel, with lug handles (New England), length 27 cm; (B) fiber-tempered pottery (Alabama); (C) Vinette I pot, with conoidal base (New England), height 24 cm. (A and C after Snow 1980; B after Walthall 1980.)

in a context with a C14 date of 2300 B.C. However, steatite vessels seem to have become widely distributed in the Mid-Atlantic and Northeast only around 1700–1300 B.C.; this diffusion appears to have been related to the appearance, in these regions, of very distinctive broad-bladed, small-stemmed points, which are referred to as the Lehigh, Koens-Crispin, Perkiomen, Susquehanna, and Snook Kill types (Snow 1980). These points were probably derived from slightly earlier point types of the Southeast, such as the Savannah River points of the Carolina Piedmont, dated to ca. 1900 B.C., and the Cotaco Creek points of Alabama (Coe 1964, Walthall 1980). It seems clear that in some areas, such as northern New England, broad spear-points were introduced by an intrusive population that replaced the indigenous Late Archaic people. The newcomers also introduced the custom of cremation of the dead. In other areas, it is not clear to what extent the spread of broad points reflects migration and population replacement, adoption of a new technology by indigenous groups, establishment of an inter-regional exchange network, or some combination of these developments.

The round or flat-bottomed and lug-handled steatite pots seem to imitate the shape of no longer extant wooden vessels, which were probably still used for many purposes. However, steatite, unlike wood, could be heated to a high temperature and used to cook food; this unique property was also discovered by the California Indians (at a rather late date) and by the Eskimos, who continued to use steatite vessels even after they had abandoned the use of pottery. In the eastern woodlands, however, steatite could only be obtained at a few quarry sites. When one considers

Fig. 29. Susquehanna broad point (New York), actual size. (After Ritchie 1971.)

that Eastern Archaic people had been cooking by means of stone-boiling, and serving and storing food in containers of wood, bark or basketry, for several thousand years, it is not apparent why they should have begun to rely on steatite vessels, which were not only hard to come by but so heavy that they were not easily carried from one campsite to the next. The use of stone vessels seems to imply that Terminal Archaic groups may have been more sedentary than their predecessors, shifting camp less frequently. The increasing use of durable pots, first of stone, later of baked clay, after 2000 B.C., was perhaps related to some change of diet, such as the consumption of more small seeds. Social considerations may also have prompted the use of stone vessels; individuals who fed guests from stone pots might thereby have enhanced their own prestige. Certainly, the inclusion of steatite vessels in Terminal Archaic burials in New England (Snow 1980), Long Island (Ritchie 1965) and Alabama (Walthall 1980) suggests that they were highly valued items. In order to obtain steatite, Terminal Archaic groups would have had to create or strengthen exchange relationships with neighboring bands, thus forming a network that might also have facilitated the diffusion of broad points.

By about 1300 B.C., women in the mid-Atlantic region had learned how to make vessels of baked clay. Just as the steatite pots had been carved in imitation of wooden prototypes, the earliest clay vessels, of the Marcey Creek Plain type, resembled steatite pots in shape, and were even tempered with bits of crushed steatite. We seem to be dealing here with another example of stimulus diffusion. Familiarity with the fiber-tempered (and later sand-tempered) pottery of the Southeast probably stimulated creation of the early steatite-tempered pottery of the mid-Atlantic region. Then more northern groups became aware of this new technology, and started to experiment with other materials and techniques. The result was the earliest pottery style of New York and New England, known as Vinette I, which dates to about 1000 B.C. Vinette pots had conoidal bottoms, were tempered with grit, and were beaten, inside and out, with cord-wrapped wooden paddles.

The economic innovation that separates the Archaic from the ensuing Woodland period is the beginning of agriculture, or more precisely horticulture, or gardening. However, gardening does not seem to have had any immediate, dramatic effect on Late Archaic lifeways. Recent finds show that pumpkins and gourds, which were originally cultivated in Mexico, were being grown in Missouri and Kentucky by 2500 B.C. Prior to these discoveries, many archaeologists had thought that cultivation of several plants, indigenous to North America, had occurred independently, without external influence. However, it now appears that intensive collecting and purposeful re-seeding of these local plants – sunflower, sumpweed (marsh elder), goosefoot, knotweed, and maygrass – began only *after* the introduction of Mexican cultigens, so stimulus diffusion was probably involved (Chomko and Crawford 1978, Kay, King, and Robinson 1980). Many seeds of sumpweed were found in levels of the Koster site dated to 3800–2900 B.C., but judging from their size, they seem to have been harvested from wild stands (Asch, Farnsworth and Asch 1979). The large size of sumpweed seeds found in human feces from two sites in Kentucky, Salts Cave and Newt Kash Hollow, indicates that cultivation had begun by about 600 B.C., perhaps as early as 1000 B.C. (Yarnell 1977). A single sunflower seed recovered from the Riverton site in Illinois and dated to about 1250 B.C. shows that this plant was being grown, but had not yet changed in form because of human manipulation (i.e. it had not yet been domesticated). Sunflower seeds from the Higgs site in Tennessee, dated at about 800 B.C., were still rather small, but the seeds found in the Salts Cave feces (ca. 600–250 B.C.) were large enough to indicate domestication. The starchy seeds of goosefoot (chenopod) and maygrass were present in feces from Newt Kash Hollow (600 B.C.), and they were collected, along with knotweed seeds, in large numbers in the Illinois Valley after 150 B.C. These seeds do not differ significantly from those of wild plants, but their presence at sites that probably lay outside their native habitats suggests human transplantation and cultivation.

Another plant that may have been cultivated at an early date in tobacco. Tobacco seeds, which are so small that they are difficult to recover archaeologically, have not been found in late Archaic or early Woodland contexts (Haberman 1984). However, smoking-pipes made of stone begin to appear in Archaic sites in Illinois around 2000 B.C., and pipes became a common artifact type in the eastern woodlands by 500 B.C. It is possible that these were used to smoke native plants, but it is more likely that tobacco was smoked. Tobacco was native to South America, so it must have been carried into North America in the same way that squash and gourds were.

Maize, a Mexican cultigen that might have served as a dietary staple, was not as rapidly adopted as the other tropical plants. It was grown in the Ohio Valley by 300 B.C. (Carlisle and Adovasio 1982), and in the Illinois Valley by 200 B.C. (Struever and Vickery 1973), but was not relied on heavily in these or other areas until A.D. 700 or 800.

It is important to note that none of the native or introduced cultivated plants served as a dietary staple: in fact, available evidence indicates that even in Middle Woodland times (100 B.C.–A.D. 400), the Hopewell mound-builders of Ohio and Illinois relied much more on nuts, particularly hickory, than on gathered or cultivated seeds (Ford 1979). Early and Middle Woodland people probably tended gardens, in which they planted tobacco, gourds, and edible seeds. The latter only supplemented a diet consisting largely of hunted and gathered foods; the seeds could

provide a relatively secure food source to fall back on whenever wild foods
became scarce.

The emergence of a more complex social organization in some parts of
the eastern woodlands is reflected in the appearance of burial mounds and
other earthworks. In the Northeast, the first such mounds were raised by
the Adena culture, after about 500 B.C. However, considerably earlier
earthworks, on a massive scale, had been built in the Southeast, at Poverty
Point, Louisiana (Webb 1968, Gibson 1974a, Muller 1983). The complex
of earthworks at this site included several mounds, the largest of which
was almost 21 m (70 ft) high and 183 m (600 ft) across, as well as 6 concentric embankments. Averaging of available radiocarbon dates places
this site and related sites in the same region at about 1200 B.C. It has been
estimated that almost three million man-hours of labor were needed to
build just the embankments at Poverty Point. Clearly, a large labor force
was involved, which must have been mobilized and organized by some
central authority. Poverty Point may have been the central settlement of
a chiefdom, perhaps similar to the Natchez chiefdom which the Europeans encountered in Louisiana 3,000 years later.

Some archaeologists have suggested that the building activity of the
Poverty Point culture was stimulated by contact with the Olmec civiliz-
ation, which was emerging on the Gulf Coast of Mexico at the same time.
However, there is little evidence to support this idea. Squash, of Mexican
origin, was present at sites of the Poverty Point culture; but it had also
reached Kentucky a thousand years earlier, so its presence at Poverty
Point does not imply that this culture was more strongly influenced by
Mexico than were other Archaic cultures of the Southeast. The fiber-

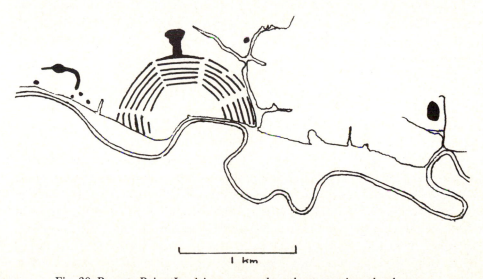

Fig. 30. Poverty Point, Louisiana: mounds and concentric embankments.

tempered pottery and steatite vessels that are found in small quantities at Poverty Point sites are similar to vessels from earlier Southeastern Archaic sites; they are not derived from Mexican types. Crude ceramic figurines from Poverty Point bear no specific resemblance to Olmec pieces. In short, apart from the huge earthworks complex, the Poverty Point culture is essentially similar to other Late Archaic cultures of the Southeast; but it does seem to represent the attainment of a new level of complexity of socio-political organization. However, the florescence of this culture seems to have been followed by a relapse of Southeastern cultures to a strictly Archaic level of subsistence, settlement, and social organization. When mound construction resumed in the Southeast, around A.D. 1, it was under the influence of the Hopewell cultures of the Northeast.

There are obvious problems in attempting to use mound construction, or the more complex forms of social organization that mounds presumably betoken, as criteria of a new cultural stage, succeeding the Archaic. In the case of Poverty Point, complexity was achieved only briefly. In the case of Adena and Hopewell, mound-building did not catch on in some areas, such as eastern New York and New England. However, the trade network that extended outward from the Hopewell centers in Ohio as far west as Yellowstone Park and as far south as the Gulf Coast, must also have incorporated the peripheral cultures of the east to some degree. This linkage is our justification for placing these comparatively backward societies in the same stage as the more highly developed contemporary societies of the Ohio and Mississippi valleys. Used in this sense, the term "Woodland" does appear to have some cultural validity, aside from its chronological convenience. Nevertheless, strictly speaking, many Northeastern groups, particularly those living in Canada who never adopted agriculture, continued to live at an Archaic level right down to the time of European contact.

THE WESTERN OR "DESERT" ARCHAIC

In western North America, the adaptations of post-Pleistocene hunter–gatherers paralleled those of the eastern woodlands. To replace the now extinct Pleistocene megafauna, western Archaic peoples turned to smaller mammals, birds and fish; they also collected a wide variety of seeds, nuts and roots. They devised an appropriate technology for the processing of these foods, most notably grinding stones and baskets. Archaic adaptations in the west varied according to the environmental setting. In the arid Great Basin, small groups moved seasonally between hills and valleys, to take advantage of temporary resource abundances. Their material culture was relatively simple, as required by this high

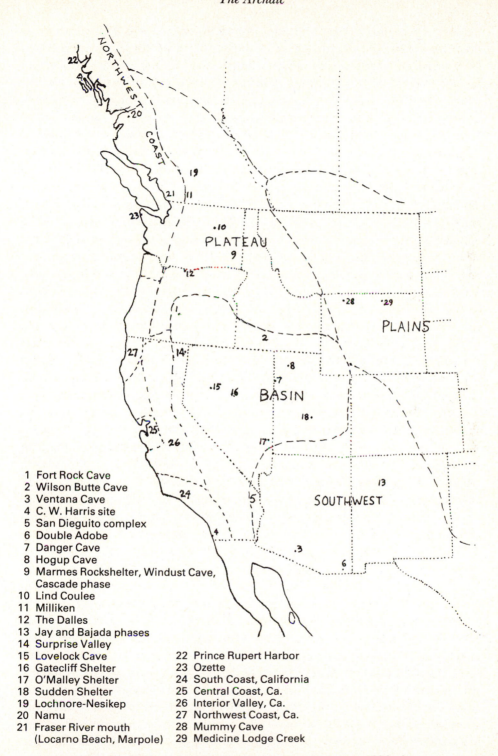

1 Fort Rock Cave
2 Wilson Butte Cave
3 Ventana Cave
4 C. W. Harris site
5 San Dieguito complex
6 Double Adobe
7 Danger Cave
8 Hogup Cave
9 Marmes Rockshelter, Windust Cave,
   Cascade phase
10 Lind Coulee
11 Milliken
12 The Dalles
13 Jay and Bajada phases
14 Surprise Valley
15 Lovelock Cave
16 Gatecliff Shelter   22 Prince Rupert Harbor
17 O'Malley Shelter   23 Ozette
18 Sudden Shelter   24 South Coast, California
19 Lochnore-Nesikep   25 Central Coast, Ca.
20 Namu   26 Interior Valley, Ca.
21 Fraser River mouth   27 Northwest Coast, Ca.
   (Locarno Beach, Marpole) 28 Mummy Cave
                       29 Medicine Lodge Creek

Fig. 31. Western Archaic sites and regions (1.1 cm = 200 km).

degree of mobility. To the north of the Basin, in the Plateau region, riverine fishing became the primary means of subsistence, supplemented by hunting and gathering. Emigrants from the Plateau followed the rivers to the Pacific coast, where they could catch large numbers of migrating salmon and other fish. At the time of European contact, this rich resource base supported a dense population, living in large villages with several hundred inhabitants each. Northwest Coast societies were ranked according to inherited status, and they produced elaborate artwork in a distinctive style. The full-blown development of these coastal cultures can be traced back to about A.D. 1000; status-ranking may have begun as early as 500 B.C. (Ames 1981). In California, hunter–gatherers came to depend on a mix of acorns, fish, and game. The relative contribution of each element to the diet varied from tribe to tribe according to ecological zone, whether coast, central valley, or hills. As on the Northwest Coast, the reliable and abundant wild resources of California supported dense populations, in some areas dwelling in large permanent villages.

The western Archaic cultures can be described in greater detail than those of the eastern Archaic, primarily because of the extraordinary preservation of normally perishable materials in the arid caves of the Basin and Southwest. Besides the expected stone and bone tools, objects of wood, leather, fur, cordage, basketry, even human feces have survived. Another factor which aids in interpretation of the archaeological remains is the availability of relevant ethnographic data. For example, when whites entered the Great Basin in the nineteenth century, they found it occupied by Shoshoni Indians, who were still living by gathering and hunting. By the time anthropologist Julian Steward arrived in the 1930s, this way of life had disappeared, but there were still some Shoshoni left who remembered the old ways and described them for Steward. Archaeologists analyzing the finds from Danger Cave and other Basin sites referred to Steward's (1938) ethnographic account to help flesh out their reconstruction of the prehistoric "Desert Culture".

Despite the apparent continuity in many aspects of culture from 7000 B.C. to the period of white contact, we must be cautious about simply projecting Shoshoni lifeways into the past. Linguistic evidence indicates that the Shoshoni migrated northward from the southwestern Great Basin after A.D. 1000. This conclusion is supported by archaeological evidence of the northward expansion, from A.D. 1000 to 1300, of a distinctive type of pottery that was presumably made by the Shoshoni. As the Shoshoni moved into the eastern Basin, they replaced a culture known as Fremont, which had relied on a subsistence base of maize agriculture and bison-hunting. Thus, the Shoshoni were not descendants of the original inhabitants; they were relatively recent immigrants into the Basin. The expansion of the Shoshoni confronts us with a problem similar to that raised by the spread of the broadpoint cultures in the Terminal Archaic of the Northeast. What was the distinctive feature of the Shoshoni adaptation that gave them an edge in competition with other similar hunting and gathering peoples, and enabled them to compete successfully even against agricultural groups? Whatever the answer, we have to suspect that the ecological adaptation of the Shoshoni's predecessors may have been significantly different from theirs, as described by Steward.

However, in a surface survey of the Reese River Valley in central Nevada, David Thomas concluded that the distributions of several functional types of artifacts within riverine, sagebrush, and pinyon microenvironmental zones tended to confirm the applicability of Steward's Shoshoni model to the lifeways of the prehistoric inhabitants, from about 2500 B.C. onward (Thomas 1973). According to Steward's ethnographic data, semi-permanent villages were established during the winter, close to the pinyon forests on the mountain flanks. Pinyon nuts were the staple food of the 15 or 20 families that camped together in the winter village. While the families were thus aggregated, they cooperated in drive-hunting of jackrabbits and antelopes. In the summer, each family went its separate way, collecting Indian ricegrass and other seeds and roots in the sagebrush flats. Steward contended that it was the scarcity of summer resources that forced the Shoshoni to spend most of the year in dispersed nuclear families. However, Elman Service (1975) has suggested that the Shoshoni lived in multi-family bands, like those found among most other hunter–gatherers, prior to contact with Europeans. Their dispersal into smaller units, Service argues, was an evasive response to slave-raiding by neighboring Indians, who pursued the Basin Shoshoni on horseback. Thomas' findings tend to support Steward's ecological explanation, by suggesting that the adaptive pattern he described originated long before the contact period.

However, there is some evidence that the ecological adaptation just outlined was not characteristic of Basin groups before about 1000 B.C. According to pollen sequences from various parts of the Basin, it was only then that pinyon pines became numerous in the forests on the mountain flanks (Madsen and Berry 1975). Clearly, multi-family villages could not have subsisted on pinyon nuts until this relatively late date. Instead, earlier Desert Archaic groups in the northeastern Basin tended to congregate by the shores of the Great Salt Lake. The size of the lake fluctuated in response to rainfall variations during the Holocene. As lake waters receded, saline marshes formed in which pickleweed and other usable plants could thrive. At two of the best known Desert Archaic sites, Danger Cave and Hogup Cave, much of the fill in the early occupation levels was composed of chaff from threshed pickleweed, the seeds of which had been ground and eaten. Both sites also yielded bones of marsh-dwelling birds. Increased rainfall and consequent rise of the lake level at about 1500 B.C. may have caused the decline of lake-edge resources, forcing a shift of Archaic population to upland sites.

EARLY ARCHAIC CULTURES, 8000–6000 B.C.

In late Pleistocene and early Holocene times, the lakes, grassland and woodlands of the Great Basin and Southwest must have been attractive to both animals and humans. Claims of great antiquity, in the order of 40,000 years, have been advanced for crude choppers, scrapers, and handaxe-like artifacts, found on the surface near dried up lake beds in southern California. However, such tools have been shown to be rough pre-forms or heavy duty tools belonging to post-Clovis industries. Two sites in Nevada, Gypsum Cave and Tule Springs, were formerly thought to be more than 20,000 years old; but the C14 dates for these sites have been proven to be erroneous. There may have been pre-Clovis occupations at Fort Rock Cave in Oregon, where a small assemblage, including unfluted points, was C14 dated to 11,200 B.C., and at Wilson Butte Cave, Idaho, where a few artifacts came from a level dated at 12,500 B.C. Neither of these early dates has yet been conclusively established as valid.

While claims of a "pre-projectile" occupation of the West remain unproven, evidence has accumulated in recent years of a Clovis presence in this region. Fluted points have been picked up from 11 surface sites in California, 15 in Nevada, seven in Oregon, eight in Idaho, and three in Utah (Aikens 1983). There are no C14 dates for such points in a sealed context, but they presumably date to around 9500–9000 B.C., like the similar points excavated in the Plains. In the light of this evidence of Clovis hunters in the Far West, we need no longer postulate, as some archaeologists have in the past, an independent, contemporaneous evolution of the Desert Archaic from ancient, pre-projectile roots. Instead, as in the case of the Eastern Archaic, it can be seen as a re-adaptation of a Clovis point-using, big game-hunting population to a rapidly changing post-Pleistocene environment. As rainfall decreased, the vast lakes of the Great Basin shrank and the coniferous forests of the region were replaced by desert scrub. The megafauna on which the Paleo-Indian hunters had preyed died out, although their extinction does not seem to have been complete until about 7000 B.C. As in the East, the early Archaic people continued to hunt the remaining large mammals, such as bison, deer, antelope and mountain sheep, but also added smaller mammals, birds, and, eventually, large quantities of seeds, nuts, roots and other vegetal foods to their diet.

The earliest post-Clovis assemblages in the West have been found in a few stratified cave sites, and at more numerous surface sites. At Ventana

Cave in south-central Arizona, the lowest level, which contained stone tools in association with bones of extinct animals such as horse, tapir, and ground sloth, as well as modern species, was C14 dated at 9300 ± 1200 B.C. One of the artifacts was a lanceolate point, resembling the Clovis type in shape but crudely worked and unfluted. The assemblage also included scrapers, choppers and knives, all crudely flaked from coarse-grained basalt. A single disc-shaped mano was also found, suggesting that some seed-grinding might have been done. However, grinding stones do not appear in significant numbers at Ventana Cave until well after 5000 B.C.

The Ventana assemblage resembles other lithic assemblages from southern California, southwestern Nevada and western Arizona, which have been referred to collectively as the San Dieguito complex. San Dieguito artifacts, excavated at the stratified C. W. Harris site in San Diego, have been C14 dated at about 7000 B.C. The typical tools are leaf-shaped bifacial points, crescent-shaped knives, and various heavy scrapers, choppers, and hammer-stones. San Dieguito artifacts have often been found by the shores of now dry lakes, the same setting in which most surface finds of fluted points have also occurred. This implies that the San Dieguito people were still following essentially the same subsistence and settlement patterns as the Clovis hunters. A continued emphasis on hunting would account for the conspicuous absence of grinding stones among the San Dieguito assemblages.

However, not far to the southeast of Ventana Cave, some Desert Archaic people were using grinding stones, and presumably collecting seeds, at a very early date. Grinding stones are known from sites of the first stage of the Cochise culture, called the Sulphur Springs stage. At the Double Adobe site, grinding stones and other tools of this stage were found stratified below a layer that contained mammoth bones. C14 dates put the Sulphur Springs stage between 7300 and 6000 B.C. These dates indicate that some of the large Pleistocene mammals (mammoth, horse, camel, dire wolf) whose remains occur at Sulphur Springs sites, may have survived in the Southwest for several thousand years after the end of the last glacial.

Possibly the earliest ground stone tools of the Western Archaic are a mano and metate found at Fort Rock Cave in the northern Great Basin;

Fig. 32. Crescent-shaped knife, San Dieguito complex, California (length ca. 5 cm). (After Heizer and Elsasser 1980.)

these seem to pre-date 8200 B.C. In the northeastern Basin, grinding stones were recovered from Level II of Danger Cave, which dates to about 7700 B.C. This level also yielded remains of twined baskets, which were used to collect, store and cook seeds. Fragments of slab metates were also found in stratum I of Hogup Cave, C14 dated at about 6400 B.C. These metates were surely used to mill pickleweed seeds. Chaff from this plant occurred throughout the cave deposits, and its seeds and pollen were found in preserved human feces (coprolites) (Aikens 1970). Taken together, these finds show that, while the San Dieguito people were apparently still relying heavily on hunting, other Southwestern and Basin groups had devised tools for collecting and processing seeds, which were to become a dietary staple.

Ground-stone seed-processing tools were an important factor in the development of agriculture by Mexican peoples, whose lifeways closely resembled those of Desert Archaic groups. It is therefore interesting to note that manos and metates first appear in the well-known cultural sequence of the Tehuacan Valley (see next chapter) during the El Riego phase, ca. 6700 to 4800 B.C. The early Western Archaic cultures thus seem, on present evidence, to have been technologically more advanced than their Mexican contemporaries.

In the Plateau region, the 8000–6000 B.C. period is represented at the sites of Marmes Rockshelter, Windust Cave, Lind Coulee, and Milliken. As in the contemporaneous San Dieguito assemblages, the typical artifacts at these sites are leaf-shaped and stemmed lanceolate points, knives, scrapers and choppers; grinding stones are rare. At Lind Coulee, in Washington, bison-hunting was a major activity. The inhabitants of Marmes rockshelter, on the lower Palouse River, used atlatls to hunt deer, elk and pronghorn antelope. They also ate rabbits and beaver, and supplemented the game with mussels collected from the river. The Marmes finds closely resemble those from Windust Cave, and have been classified together with them as a "phase" named for the latter site. The Milliken site, which lies off the western edge of the Plateau, contains a similar lithic assemblage, C14 dated to 7500 to 6000 B.C. It is situated above rapids in the Fraser River, which in recent times teemed with salmon during their late-summer migrations. Although bones were not preserved at this site, its location suggests that fishing was already an important means of subsistence at 7000 B.C. There is more definite evidence of early salmon-fishing in the rapids of the Columbia River, in the region called the Dalles, between Washington and Oregon. In a level of the Roadcut site, C14 dated as earlier than 5800 B.C., many thousands of salmon vertebrae were found. Also present were bones of various small mammals and of birds of prey (Aikens 1983).

6000–3000 B.C.

In the Great Basin, lake-side encampments of small bands, subsisting on collected seeds and large and small game, continued through this period. Levels IV through VII at Hogup Cave, and levels III and IV at Danger Cave, date from this time. Apart from the usual projectile points and other chipped and ground stone tools, the artifacts made of normally perishable materials, which survived intact in the aridity of these caves, are worthy of note. These included: baskets, now often made by coiling as well as twining; hemp cordage and nets; hide thongs; bone awls, flakers, tubes, and pipes; sheep-horn wrenches; rabbit-fur robes. Among the wooden artifacts were atlatl fragments, dart shafts and foreshafts, fire drills, digging sticks, throwing sticks, and a bull roarer (a whirling noise-maker, similar to those used by Australian aborigines) (Jennings 1974).

As we have noted, pickleweed seeds were the main vegetal food at Hogup Cave (Aikens 1970); prickly pear was also eaten. Numerous other plants (33 species, in levels I to VII) were used for wood, cordage and fuel. The most important meat source was bison, which accounted for 41% of the meat weight represented by the bone remains. In descending order of importance by weight, other fauna present at Hogup were rabbits, deer, pronghorn antelope, sheep, rodents and carnivores. A single domesticated dog is represented by a mandible from Hogup level V (ca. 6100–5500 B.C.). It is noteworthy that the oldest dog remains in North America were found at another Desert Archaic site, Jaguar Cave, and dated to about 7500 B.C. Apart from mammals, the inhabitants of Hogup Cave also hunted or trapped many species of birds, which lived by the lakeshore and in the marshes below the cave. The site was probably occupied during the late summer, when pickleweed seeds could be harvested.

THE ALTITHERMAL

Although we call the climatic epoch in which we live the Holocene, and regard it as post-Pleistocene, in all probability we are living near the end of an interglacial period. Indeed, there is evidence that the peak temperature during this interglacial was reached about 7,000 years ago. For centuries thereafter, annual temperatures in the middle latitudes of the Northern Hemisphere averaged 1°C higher than today's, which is 15°C. The higher temperatures of this period were accompanied by decreased rainfall. Authorities on ancient climate do not agree on the precise beginning and ending dates of this warm, dry spell, which is known as the Altithermal or Hypsithermal (it corresponds to the "Atlantic" phase in the European climatic sequence). Higher than modern temperatures pre-

119

vailed until some time between 3000 and 1500 B.C. The onset and end of the Altithermal probably varied from region to region, due to differences in latitude, altitude and atmospheric circulation. In the eastern woodlands, as we have seen, the Altithermal may have triggered the population explosion of the Late Archaic. In contrast, archaeologists have suspected that the hot, dry conditions of the Altithermal must have had a disastrous effect on the inhabitants of the Basin, Southwest and Plains, areas that have scant rainfall even in modern times. However, as archaeological evidence has accumulated, it has become clear that the actual effects of the Altithermal varied from one locality to the next. As Hogup Cave, Danger Cave, and other sites in the northeastern Basin, there was hardly any change in the local plant and animal communities during the Altithermal (Aikens 1978, 1983). For lake-edge dwellers in the Great Basin, the Altithermal may have been the best rather than the worst of times. As Lake Bonneville dried up and shrank, it left in its wake salt marshes, rich in seed-bearing plants and aquatic birds.

In contrast, Altithermal aridity seems to have seriously affected the Cochise culture of Arizona. The Sulphur Springs stage was followed by a hiatus, from 6000 to about 3500 B.C., from which there are no dated sites. This apparent gap in occupation was followed by the Chiricahua stage, with sites dating from 3500 to 1500 B.C.

In northwestern New Mexico there is a possible indication of climatic change in the replacement, about 6000 B.C., of Plano bison-hunters by an Archaic culture whose roots seem to have been in the San Dieguito complex (Irwin-Williams 1967). However, the basic lifeway of the Jay phase (5500–4800 B.C.) people seems not to have been very different from that of their Paleo-Indian predecessors; an abundance of large-stemmed points, scrapers and knives, and the absence of grinding stones, suggest that hunting was their primary subsistence activity. The Jay phase was followed by the Bajada phase; an increased number of flake scrapers and choppers hints at a greater reliance on plant foods. The Altithermal seems to have had no deleterious effect on the inhabitants of this area, as there may have been a slight increase in population during the Bajada phase.

In the Plateau region, along the lower Snake River, the Windust phase developed into the Cascade phase (5500–3000 B.C.). The typical Cascade artifacts were well-made, leaf-shaped points, which were used to hunt deer, elk and pronghorn antelope. Riverine resources – salmon, trout and mussels – were also part of the diet, as were seeds, processed with manos and metates. By about 4000 B.C., bands living along the lower Snake were spending the winter in pit-house villages, where they probably ate preserved salmon, which had been caught during the summer spawning runs. In the spring and fall, people dispersed into the hills, where they subsisted on roots and hunted game. This was the basic Plateau subsistence and settlement pattern that continued from this period down to the time of contact with whites.

Pit-house villages of comparable age, about 4000 to 3000 B.C., have been excavated in the Surprise Valley, in the Plateau area of northeastern California (Aikens 1978). These Menlo phase sites were probably permanent villages, from which foraging groups occasionally ventured out to occupy small, temporary camps. The Menlo diet included meat of bison, deer, antelope, and mountain sheep, with lesser amounts provided by rabbits and other small mammals. The mortars and pestles that have been found were presumably used to process nuts.

CALIFORNIA

Along the southern coast of California, the various cultures that followed the San Dieguito complex after 5500 B.C. have been referred to a common tradition, called Encinitas. There are some sites where local development of this tradition out of San Dieguito seems to have occurred, but the evident increase in seed-gathering may have been spurred by the immigration of displaced gatherers from the interior who were unable to cope with Altithermal aridity. Encinitas gatherers processed plant foods using manos and metates and large, crude choppers and scrapers. Shellfish remains are abundant at Encinitas sites, but mammal and fish bones are rare, as are the crude, leaf-shaped spear-points that were used in hunting. This evidence suggests a shift away from hunting to a primary dependence on collection of seeds and shellfish. The Encinitas tradition lasted until A.D. 1000 near San Diego, but on the Santa Barbara coast, around 3000 B.C., it was followed by the Campbell tradition. An increase in the number of points, knives and scrapers suggests that hunting became more important, while the appearance of both hopper mortars and stone bowl mortars and pestles indicates some reliance on acorns.

THE GREAT BASIN – 3000 B.C.–A.D. 1800

In the northeastern Great Basin, the early Archaic lake-shore adaptation, exemplified at Hogup Cave, continued until about 1200 B.C., when the level of the Great Salt Lake rose, drowning the fringing marshes. This caused the decline of pickleweed and a sharp increase in the number of water-fowl found at the site. After this time, Hogup Cave seems to have been visited only briefly by hunting parties, who discarded bones of pronghorn antelope and bison there. Some archaeologists (Madsen and Berry 1975) would generalize from the Hogup sequence to the whole northeastern Basin, suggesting that the lake's rise so depleted the marsh resources that the people who had depended on them abandoned the area. While other specialists disagree (Aikens 1978), there is a consensus that resources found in the uplands became more important after 1500 B.C.; this would have caused changes in the pattern of seasonal movements. As previously noted, the pinyon nuts, which were a staple winter food of the historic Shoshoni, may have become available only as late as 1000 B.C.

In the western Basin, a fairly rich culture is represented by the assemblage from Lovelock Cave, which dates from about 2500 B.C. to A.D. 500. The cave was situated near a shallow pond, surrounded by tule marshes. Here the cave's inhabitants collected fish, shellfish, edible tubers, roots and seeds, and rushes with which to make baskets. Vegetal fiber cordage was used to make snares and nets in which rabbits and birds were caught. Blankets were made of bird-skins or rabbit fur, and clothing was made of shredded bark. Seed-gathering baskets, and jug and tray-shaped baskets, were made by both coiling and twining techniques. *Olivella* shells show that the Lovelock people were connected to an exchange network that reached as far as California's Pacific coast. The later levels of the site yielded bows and arrows, coiled baskets, moccasins, sandals, tubular pipes, porcupine quill work, and duck decoys. At related sites in the area, figures made of clay, wood and stone have been found; these portray humans, bears, fish, owls, grasshoppers and fantastic animals. The remains of dwellings that resembled historic Paiute wickiups were discovered at the Humboldt Lakebed site. The Lovelock lifeway seems to have been based on efficient use of lake-side resources, which permitted a sedentary existence that contrasts with the hand to mouth, nomadic image that is conjured up by the label "Desert Culture" (Aikens 1978).

In the central Basin, the results of Thomas' Reese River Valley survey (see p. 115) indicate that the pattern of seasonal movements between the hills and sagebrush flats that Steward recorded among the historic Shoshoni of the area may have been established as early as 2500 B.C. Thomas also excavated a deeply stratified site, Gatecliff Shelter, where the lowest levels date to around 6000 B.C. At O'Malley Shelter, another site in southern Nevada, which had been uninhabited since 4500 B.C., occupation resumed around 2600 B.C. and lasted until 1000 B.C. The assemblage from this period includes dart-points of the Elko, Pinto and Gypsum types. Points of these same types occurred in the eastern Basin also, for example at Sudden Shelter, where they were found in well stratified deposits dated at 5800–1300 B.C.

In Surprise Valley, California, in the northwestern corner of the Basin, the semi-subterranean earth-covered lodges of the Menlo phase were no longer built after 2500 B.C. They were replaced by less substantial dwellings – small domed brush wickiups. Whereas the earlier lodges may have held 12 to 15 people each, the Bare Creek phase wickiups probably housed nuclear families. The Bare Creek people hunted fewer bison, deer and sheep, instead relying more on the meat of rabbits and water-fowl. There were also changes in the artifact inventory; Pinto-type dart-points, and manos and metates, were introduced. A warmer and drier climate may have compelled the inhabitants to shift to a more dispersed, less sedentary settlement pattern, as an adjustment to a reduction in carrying capacity. The changes in dwelling and artifact types, and in dietary preferences, may reflect not re-adaptation by the Menlo phase population, but their replacement by Numic-speaking ancestral Paiutes who were better adapted to the drier environment. Linguistic evidence, however, suggests that the expansion of Numic speakers occurred much later, so there is some doubt about this identification of the Bare Creek people. In any case, the Bare Creek phase lasted until about 1000 B.C.; subsequent phases, up to the historic period, were essentially similar, differing only in some style changes and the introduction of the bow and arrow after A.D. 500. The Menlo phase residents who departed from Surprise Valley may have been ancestral Klamath; they may have retreated to the Klamath

Fig. 33. Elko corner-notched point (1500 B.C.–A.D. 500), Nevada (actual size).

Fig. 34. Pinto point, southern California (length ca. 3.5 cm). (After Heizer and Elsasser 1980.)

lake area of southern Oregon, where there is evidence of the continuity of Klamath culture from about 4000 B.C. until historic times (Aikens 1978).

In the southern Basin and southern California desert, the San Dieguito phase (ca. 7000–5000 B.C.) was followed by the Pinto Basin phase, which was characterized by nomadic hunting and gathering. This phase may have begun around 5000 B.C., and ended about 1900–1500 B.C. In the Mohave Desert, it was followed by the Amargosa phase, which lasted until A.D. 1000. In Owens Valley, the Rose Spring phase, with triangular stemmed and notched points and other artifacts that resemble those of Amargosa, is dated to around 1500 B.C. to A.D. 500. Both Amargosa and Rose Spring were basically continuations of the earlier lifeways. By A.D. 1000, Numic speakers were definitely present in this area; besides notched, triangular Desert and Cottonwood arrow-points, scrapers, manos and metates, and mortars and pestles, they used heavy brown pottery.

I have already alluded briefly to the archaeological problem posed by the Numic expansion. At the time of contact with whites, Numic speakers occupied the deserts of southern California, the northern Southwest, the whole Great Basin, and much of the northwestern Plains. The Numic language group was divided into three sub-branches, each of which comprised two languages: Mono and Paiute – Western branch; Panamint and Shoshoni – Central; Kawaisu and Ute – Southern. The speakers of these languages seem to have fanned out northward and eastward from their common place of origin in southeastern California; linguists estimate that their expansion occurred at about A.D. 1300 or 1500.

It has recently been suggested (Bettinger and Baumhoff 1982) that the Numic speakers' subsistence strategies differed significantly from those of their predecessors. Pre-Numic groups appear to have been solely responsible for the widespread and elaborate rock art of the Great Basin, about which the historic Numic inhabitants professed ignorance. These petroglyphs often represent mountain sheep and other animals, and hunting weapons too, suggesting that the art was executed in the context of hunting rituals. In some instances, Numic speakers seem to have intentionally defaced their predecessors' work. They also set up camps and milled seeds in places that had formerly been reserved for petroglyphs

Fig. 35. Desert side-notched point (after A.D. 1300), Nevada (actual size).

and for hunting. Whereas pre-Numic hunters set up small hunting camps away from their base camps, Numic hunters only operated out of their base camps, which were situated where plant foods could be most efficiently harvested. The earlier Archaic people had used horn sickles to collect seeds, and flat coiled basketry trays for winnowing and parching them. In contrast, the Numic people used twined, paddle-shaped seed-beaters and deep, twined triangular winnowing trays. It is not clear exactly how this different equipment enabled the Numic speakers to harvest small seeds more efficiently. In any case, these several lines of evidence suggest that the Numic speakers emphasized seed-gathering at the expense of hunting. This difference from their predecessors in subsistence strategies would probably have had demographic implications. The sex ratio of pre-Numic societies may have been imbalanced in favor of males, whose economic role as hunters was of critical importance; on the other hand, women's role as seed-gatherers may have led to a more balanced sex ratio in Numic populations. In situations where these groups competed for the same territory, the Numic advantage in the number of women would have enabled them to maintain a higher birth rate, thereby out-populating their rivals. Another factor that may have affected the outcome of this competition was the use of the bow and arrow by pre-Numic hunters after A.D. 600; this may have led to over-cropping of game, making the pre-Numic subsistence strategy less effective and thereby more susceptible to replacement by the incoming Numic speakers.

Whether or not this explanatory model is valid, the linguistic evidence of a recent and rapid expansion of Numic speakers into the Great Basin and adjacent regions seems to be incontrovertible. This poses a serious problem for archaeologists, who have generally assumed that there was an unbroken development from the Desert Archaic into the culture of the historic period. They will have to re-examine closely the various local culture sequences, in search of stylistic and adaptive discontinuities around A.D. 1300–1500.

One area where such a break is particularly clear is the eastern Basin. Here, the Fremont culture, whose subsistence was based in part on maize cultivation, had become established around A.D. 500. The styles of Fremont corner and side-notched points, and of their coiled baskets (Adovasio 1979), suggest that the Fremont folk were local hunter–gatherers who had adopted maize cultivation from the Mogollon or Anasazi. They also learned from their southern neighbors how to make brown and grey pottery. By storing maize, the Fremont people could live in villages all year round. Their villages were small, consisting of pit-houses and a few surface structures build of stone or adobe. Pueblo-like surface architecture and painted pottery were characteristic only of the southeastern Fremont area on the Colorado Plateau; this area lay closest to, and was most influenced by, the Anasazi. The more western and northern Fremont groups were less Anasazi-like, showing instead some similarities to the cultures of the western Plains. Traits that were shared by all five recognized Fremont sub-groups include unfired clay human figurines, large, broad-shouldered anthropomorphic pictographs, and a distinctive type of leather moccasin (Aikens 1983). The Fremont people never became as reliant as the Anasazi on farming; they hunted bison and other large game, and wherever marshes were accessible, they hunted water-fowl and collected cattail roots and other wild plant foods (Madsen 1979). Fremont pottery and other artifacts have been found in the upper levels of Archaic sites such as Hogup Cave; these sites were evidently visited by Fremont hunting parties.

Around A.D. 1300, the Fremont culture disappeared, and the eastern Basin was occupied by the Numic-speaking Shoshoni and Utes. Apart from the challenge posed by these nomadic intruders, the Fremont culture must have been sorely stressed by the same deteriorating climatic conditions that drove the Anasazi from the Colorado Plateau. The fate of the Fremont people after they abandoned their villages is a mystery. They do not seem to have remained in Utah as hunter–gatherers, because there are no stylistic continuities linking Fremont to the late prehistoric Shoshoni or Ute cultures. Alternatively it has been suggested that they

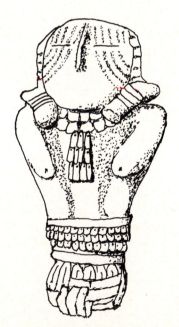

Fig. 36. Fremont clay figurine (about ½ actual size).

migrated eastward into the Plains, or southward into the Pueblo region, but neither area has yielded Fremont assemblages (Aikens 1983, Lipe 1983).

RIVERINE CULTURES OF THE PLATEAU, 3000 B.C.–A.D. 1800

Along the lower Snake River, in eastern Washington, the Cascade phase was followed, around 3000 B.C., by the Tucannon phase, which lasted until 500 B.C. Tucannon assemblages include crudely chipped corner-notched and stemmed points, some chipped knives, and edge-flaked cobbles. Hopper mortars, pestles and net sinkers were made of ground stone. Elk, deer and antelope were hunted, and salmon were taken from the river.

The Harder phase followed Tucannon around 500 B.C. Pit-house villages of this phase have been found along the river; earlier villages probably existed, but their remains have eroded away. The pit-houses were large, with diameters of 20–40 feet. There is evidence of both salmon-fishing and hunting; in addition to the species known from Tucannon sites, Harder phase faunal remains also include bones of mountain sheep. During the earlier part of the Harder phase, hunters used the atlatl; but later on, smaller corner-notched points signal the adoption of the bow and arrow. Domesticated dogs were kept in the villages.

The Harder phase ended around A.D. 1300, and was followed by a phase called Piqunin. Piqunin villages consisted of large circular pit-houses, 5.5 m (18 ft) in diameter. Small arrow-points were used to bring down deer and elk, and salmon were taken from the river. Vegetal foods were processed using mortars and pestles and pounding stones. The last archaeological phase of the lower Snake, called Numipu, is proto-historic; burials of this phase contained Euro-American trade goods and horse trappings. This phase undoubtedly represents the Nez Percé of the historic period. The ancestral line of the Nez Percé probably extends back in time at least as early as the Harder phase, if not earlier (Willey 1966, Irwin 1975).

The Nez Percé were Sahaptin-speakers, as were the Yakima, Umatilla, Tenino, and other tribes of the southern and western Plateau, as far south as the Klamath River, near the Oregon–California border. Speakers of the Chinookan languages, which were related to the Penutian languages of California, occupied the Columbia River valley, and they were also present on the Pacific coast. The northern Plateau tribes were Salishan-speakers: the Kalispel, Flathead and Wenatchi, and the Shuswap of British Columbia. The same language group was represented on the coast by the Salish of the Gulf of Georgia region, and the Bella Coola, who lived farther north. These linguistic connections between Plateau and North-west Coast tribes are echoed in the archaeological record, which shows continual interactions between these culture areas in prehistoric times.

The salmon-rich Dalles of the middle Columbia River lie in the zone of transition from the dry Plateau to the humid, forested Northwest Coast. People had been camping at the Dalles since 8000 B.C. The Late Period of this area began about 4100 B.C., and lasted until historic times. The stone points made during this long period included Cascade-like leaf-shaped points, triangular basal-notched points similar to those of the Harder phase, and small, finely chipped basal-notched and barbed points that resemble those of the Piqunin phase. At about 1000 B.C., various ground-stone artifacts were added to the assemblage, including mauls, pestles, atlatl weights, fish gorges, tubular pipes, two-holed gorgets, and animal sculptures. Stone-grinding and -polishing techniques were prob-ably adopted from the Northwest Coast, where they had been used since before 2500 B.C. However, the presence of gorgets in particular raises the suspicion that the inhabitants of the middle Columbia might have had some sort of contact with the late Archaic cultures of the Northeast (Willey 1966). There is also linguistic evidence suggestive of a Northwest–Northeast connection: the Yurok and Wiyot, who lived on the northwest-ern coast of California, spoke languages that were distantly related to the Algonquian languages of the eastern woodlands (Heizer 1978). Perhaps the inception of a new ground-stone technology in the Plateau was associ-ated with the arrival of Algonquian-speakers.

The culture sequence revealed by excavations at the Lochnore-Nesikep sites on the Fraser River, at the northernmost tip of the Plateau region, provides evidence of some interaction between early Plateau dwellers and bearers of an Arctic-derived tool kit. Leaf-shaped and large side-notched points were made at these sites between 5500 and 4000 B.C., when basal and side-notched triangular points appeared. Salmon fishing had begun by 5100 B.C., and continued through subsequent cultural phases. During the Middle Period, 3000 B.C. to A.D. 1, the notched points were joined by a stemmed type, with indented bases. Antler wedges, chisels made from rodent incisors, celts and mauls of ground stone were used for wood-working. Deep pit-houses were being built by 1700–1500 B.C. Immi-gration or cultural diffusion from the Arctic is evident in the large numbers of micro-blades and micro-cores that were included in the Middle Period assemblage; they were also present, although not as abun-dant, in the tool-kit of the preceding period. These tool appear to rep-resent a southern extension of the Paleo-arctic micro-blade industry, which had its roots in northeastern Asia. The micro-blades gradually fell out of use during the Late Period, A.D. 1 to historic times (Dumond 1983).

The way of life that was observed along the rivers of the Plateau in the nineteenth century took shape at least as early as 500 B.C. Although there are very few traces of village life prior to that time, the evidence of salmon-fishing before 5000 B.C., and the earth lodges on the lower Snake that date to 3000 B.C., indicate a much earlier origin for this pattern of subsistence and settlement. The nineteenth-century Plateau dwellers spent the winter in villages of five to ten earth lodges; these villages were situated in the sheltered canyons of the Columbia and Fraser rivers, where the temperatures averaged 5°C warmer. Here the Indians hunted deer and ate preserved salmon, which had been netted or speared during the summer spawning runs. In the spring and fall, people left the villages and set up temporary camps in the tributary canyons and uplands, where they hunted and collected camas and kous roots and berries.

THE NORTHWEST COAST

A few finds of Cascade-like points at sites on the forested Pacific coast of Oregon, Washington, and British Columbia show that early Plateau groups penetrated into this area around 6000 B.C. There they made contact with people who had migrated down the coast from Alaska, carrying with them the Paleo-arctic micro-blade and micro-core technology. The interaction of the Arctic and Plateau-derived groups is demonstrated by the occurrence of micro-blades and leaf-shaped points in the same assemblages, for example, at Namu, on the south-central coast of British Columbia, around 3500 B.C. These early coast dwellers hunted wapiti, deer, and seal, collected shellfish, and caught salmon and other fish.

By 2500 B.C., micro-blades were no longer being made in most parts of the coast between Alaska and Vancouver. Tools of polished slate and bone began to appear, and shell middens and sea mammal bones attest to a marine orientation. The prehistoric sequence of coastal cultures has been most thoroughly investigated at sites near the mouth of the Fraser River, on the eastern shores of the Strait of Georgia, which separates Vancouver Island from the mainland. In this area, the Eayam (or Charles) phase lasted from about 2500 to 1200 B.C. Sites of this period yielded both chipped stone points with stems, and chipped and partially ground slate points and knives. These ground stone tools imply some form of interaction between Northwest Coast peoples and the contemporary inhabitants of Kodiak Island. The Eayam phase was followed by the Locarno Beach stage: typical Locarno Beach assemblages included chipped basalt points, chipped slate knives, micro-blades, points and knives of polished slate, small polished nephrite adzes, lip-plugs, earspools, and assorted bone and antler tools – barbed points, wedges, foreshafts and toggling harpoons. Locarno Beach was followed after 200 B.C. by the Marpole stage. Micro-blades and chipped stone points were still made, but there was increasing use of polished slate to make large points and ulus; barbed harpoons were used to hunt sea mammals; salmon and other fish, shellfish, land mammals, and birds were also eaten.

Marpole villages were large, sometimes extending over several acres; they probably consisted of cedar-plank houses, like those built by the historic coastal Salish of the same region. The construction of dug-out boats has been inferred from the presence of many wood-working tools – adzes, mauls, and wedges. Marpole burials vary in the quantity and quality of accompanying grave goods, a probable indication that ranking by inherited status had already developed (Ames 1981). Cranial deformation, seen in some burials but not others, may also have been a sign of high rank. Farther north, in the Prince Rupert Harbor area, there is similar evidence suggestive of the inception of ranking around 500 B.C. The contents of graves from this period vary in the amounts of copper, shell beads, shell gorgets, and sea otter teeth. Violence-induced injuries have been noted in some of the skeletons, and trophy skulls had been placed in some graves; this evidence points to the increasing frequency of warfare. During Marpole times, *dentalium* shells, disk beads, native copper, and large, well chipped stone points were probably regarded as items of value, as they were in the contact period cultures of the Northwest Coast and northern California. These valued objects may have been accumulated and then given away by chiefs at ceremonial feasts, similar to the historic potlatches. Antler and steatite sculptures, including stone bowls in the form of seated humans or animals, indicate that the elaborate art of the contact period Northwest Coast cultures was taking shape during Marpole times. The preferred material of the later artists was, of course, wood, which has rarely been preserved at prehistoric sites. The culture of the Marpole stage developed, with minor changes, into that of the late prehistoric Gulf of Georgia stage, at around A.D. 500–1000. This cultural tradition was perpetuated by the coastal Salish into the early nineteenth century.

To the south, the classic Northwest Coast lifeway seems to have become established at the mouth of the Columbia around A.D. 1. However, most of the known sites in this area date to late prehistoric or protohistoric times. Most notable is the Ozette site, where part of a Makah village of cedar-plank long houses was covered by a mudslide around A.D. 1550. This resulted in the preservation of the houses themselves, and also of the many artifacts of wood and other organic materials that they contained. Among these artifacts were: wooden boxes; baskets full of tools or stored food; harpoons, lances, bows, wood-working tools, and many nicely carved objects. One of these, a whale-fin replica with shells set into it, resembled an object seen by Captain Cook in this region in 1778.

The richness and complexity of the Northwest Coast societies that

Cook and other explorers encountered offer a striking contrast to the generalized image of hunter–gatherers, which is based on observation of groups that lived in relatively inhospitable environments. Unlike most hunter–gatherers, Northwest Coast groups were not highly mobile: they spent most of the year in permanent villages composed of long houses, made of planks. In some cases, each long house held an entire lineage. Some villages were occupied by several hundred people. Intense labor by the villagers at a few critical times, when salmon and other fish spawned, provided enough food to last the whole year, if the fish were properly dried and stored. Whale, seal, and olachen (candlefish) oils played an important role in the diet, perhaps making up for the lack of plant-derived carbohydrates. Dependence on stored supplies of fish and oil was a major reason for people to stay in one place for most of the year. Northwest Coast societies were not egalitarian: individuals differed markedly in inherited social status and wealth. Social status was determined on the basis of closeness to, or distance from, the line of descent of the lineage chief. This ranking system was generally more rigid in the more northern groups – the Tlingit, Haida, Tsimshian and Haisla. The lineage system was absent, and ranking was looser, among the more southern groups, including the Salish. The ranked societies were divided, along a graduated scale, into nobles and commoners. At the bottom of the social ladder were slaves, who had been captured in war. Slaves were liable to be sacrificed by being crushed under a house-post when a new house was built, or killed for use as a "roller" for the canoe of a visiting chief. Besides

Fig. 37. Zoomorphic stone bowl, Marpole phase (height 35 cm).

131

slaves, trophy skulls or scalps were also taken in Northwest Coast wars. However, the main aim of warfare was to win control of territory, whether it be a prime fishing location or a strategic point along a trade route.

Each inherited rank came with a set of names, titles, crests, ceremonial roles, and land use rights. The display of the symbols of inherited rank was the underlying purpose of most Northwest Coast artwork. It consisted primarily of stylized representations of the supernatural beings who had either appeared to lineage ancestors in animal, monster or human form, or had themselves been transformed into ancestors. These were the beings who were depicted on the famous "totem" poles. Some poles were mortuary monuments for dead chiefs, others stood in front of houses. The carving of these massive crest-displays evidently pre-dated contact with whites, who provided iron tools that made wood-working easier. The first white visitors to the Northwest Coast, in the eighteenth century, observed poles that had been set up years before they arrived (Drucker 1963).

CALIFORNIA 3000 B.C.–A.D. 1700

California, like the Northwest Coast, was one of the few regions where abundant resources supported dense hunter–gatherer populations, until the historic period. Archaeologists have generally divided prehistoric California into three regions, corresponding to the ecological zones and culture areas that ethnologists have delineated. These are the South Coast, the Central Coast and Interior Valley, and the Northwest Coast.

In southern California, the Encinitas tradition, which had originated around 5000 B.C., lasted until A.D. 1000 in the San Diego area. On the coast, near Santa Barbara, the Campbell (or Hunting) tradition followed Encinitas, around 3000 B.C. Numerous points, knives and scrapers, and the bones of deer, elk, bear and smaller mammals, indicate that hunting was an important activity. The remains of seal, fish and shellfish show that the Campbell people also made use of coastal resources. Finds of hopper mortars, to which bottomless baskets were attached with asphalt, and stone bowl mortars and pestles, suggest that acorns, the staple plant food of later California Indians, were being processed and eaten. The climax of the southern coastal tradition in late prehistoric times is represented by the Canaliño culture, which was directly ancestral to the Chumash of the historic period. The Canaliño culture had become sea-adapted, using plank canoes for coastal travel, fishing, and hunting sea mammals. Acorn-collecting was also a very important subsistence activity, and additional meat was provided by hunting of land mammals. At the time of contact, some Chumash villages held almost 1,000 inhabitants. Their dwellings were circular, domed houses made of poles covered with reed mats; house diameters ranged from four to seven meters. Besides the dwellings, each village generally included a semi-subterranean sweat lodge, roofed with heavy timbers and earth; a beaten earth dance floor, and a stone-ringed ceremonial enclosure. The Canaliño–Chumash carved bowls out of sandstone and steatite, and they also made steatite sculptures, portraying such subjects as whales and canoes. In a Chumash cemetery at Medea Creek, which was associated with a small village of 30–60 inhabitants, the greatest quantities of shell beads tended to occur in the graves of children who had been buried in the western section of the cemetery. This has been plausibly interpreted as evidence of a ranked social organization, in which children belonging to the higher ranked and wealthier lineages were interred with richer grave goods (King 1969).

In central California, around Sacramento, the culture sequence has been defined largely on the basis of excavated burials. It comprises the Windmiller (3000–1000 B.C.), Cosumnes (1000 B.C.–A.D. 500) and Hotchkiss (A.D. 500–historic) phases (Elsasser 1978). The Windmiller assemblage includes large, heavy dart-points for hunting, antler fish-spear prongs, and manos, metates, and mortars for seed-grinding. Windmiller graves also yielded non-utilitarian items, including shell beads, rectangular stone palettes, tubular pipes and charmstones. Charmstones are long, thin, carefully shaped ground-stone objects, of phallic or spindle form. They were often perforated for suspension. Ethnographic analogy suggests that they may have been hung from branches over preferred spots in streams, either to claim ownership or to exert a magical influence. Some traits of the Windmiller culture were shared by the contemporary inhabitants of the San Francisco Bay area, but these coastal people had a different subsistence pattern, emphasizing fishing, shellfish and seed-gathering rather than hunting.

Cosumnes sites, which occur both on the central coast and in the central valley, have yielded points, fish-spear barbs, and also more mortars and pestles than occur in assemblages of the Windmiller phase; this implies a greater dependence on acorns for food. Burial ornaments

Fig. 38. Steatite whale figurine, Canaliño culture (length 18 cm).

included *Olivella* and *Haliotis* (abalone) shell beads, coyote teeth, and bear claws. Ranking has been inferred from the distribution of grave goods in a cemetery in the Tiburon Hills, on the northwestern edge of San Francisco Bay (King 1976). In this cemetery, which dates from about A.D. 1, a central area contained the cremation burials of male and female adults and children, accompanied by numerous *Olivella* and *Haliotis* beads, bone pendants and bone whistles. Around this central cluster lay a ring of male burials, without associated ornaments, and a loose outer cluster of male and female adults who were buried with few artifacts. Some Cosumnes people suffered violent deaths, as shown by the points found embedded in a number of skeletons.

Cremation became more common in burials of the next phase, called Hotchkiss. Numerous mortars and pestles show the reliance of Hotchkiss folk on acorns. Small side-notched points were probably arrow-tips; barbed bone spears were used to take fish. Charred basket fragments and bone awls attest to the making of baskets, which was a highly developed craft in California at the time of contact. Baked clay objects were probably used in place of boiling-stones in cooking acorn mush. Ornaments and beads made from *Haliotis* shell, clamshell, magnetite and steatite accompanied Hotchkiss burials. This late prehistoric tradition was ancestral to the Wintun, Miwok and Yokuts who occupied central California at the time of contact.

It is possible that the Windmiller people were Hokan-speakers, while the Cosumnes people were Penutian-speaking intruders. The distribution of native languages at the time of contact suggests that a wedge of Penutian-speakers had split the Hokan-speakers into four isolated pockets. Hokan languages were also spoken in southern California; they were separated from the northern members of the family by the intrusive Numic-speaking Shoshonians.

Prehistoric cultures with ties to both central California and the Great

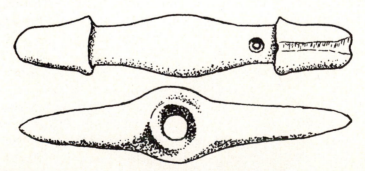

Fig. 39. Charmstones, central California, ca. 2500–1000 B.C. (length 16.5 cm. Figs 38 and 39 after Heizer and Elsasser 1980.)

Basin occupied the foothills of the Sierra Nevada. In the northern foothills, the cultural sequence begins at around 1000 B.C.; the sequence starts at around 300 B.C. in the southern foothills. Bows and arrows seem to have been introduced about A.D. 500; after A.D. 800, an increased frequency of mortars and pestles shows that acorns had become a staple food. In the Buchanan Reservoir, south of Yosemite, several cemeteries dated at about A.D. 200–800 display a clustering, in their western sections, of shell bead-ornamented individuals, including men, women and children; burials in the eastern sections contained fewer ornaments. This pattern suggests that society was divided into two classes, on the basis of inherited status distinctions (King 1976, 1978).

In the North Coast ranges, the Borax Lake phase (ca. 5000 B.C.–A.D. 500), with assemblages that contain points, burins, manos and metates, was followed at about A.D. 500 by the Houx phase, which persisted until contact and was presumably ancestral to the historic Pomo and Yuki cultures. The most significant change in the Houx tool-kit was the replacement of the mano and metate by the mortar and pestle, indicating a greater reliance on acorns.

The northwestern coast of California was inhabited at the time of contact by the Wiyot, Yurok, Karok, Hupa and Tolowa. Such features of their cultures as plank houses, heavy dietary dependence on fish, and an emphasis on wealth and prestige show that these groups formed a marginal southern extension of the Northwest Coast culture area (Heizer 1978). Linguistic evidence indicates that only the Hokan-speaking Karok were long-established residents of the region; the Wiyot and Yurok spoke Algonquian-related languages, and the Tolowa and Hupa were Athapaskan speakers, who must have come from western Canada originally. The archaeological evidence also indicates that these groups became established in the area at a relatively late date, around A.D. 900. Traces of earlier inhabitants, dated at around 300 B.C., were excavated at the Point St George site, but there is no evidence of continuity from this poorly-known early culture into the better-attested later cultures of the region. Among the distinctive traits of these late cultures were adze handles of carved stone, *dentalium* beads and large obsidian blades. In historic times, the Yurok employed *dentalia* as a form of money; the large blades were highly valued objects, as were scarlet woodpecker scalps and albino deerskins, for which there is no archaeological evidence. The late prehistoric assemblages also include artifacts that were no longer produced after contact: baked clay figurines and stone clubs carved in the form of animals. These are popularly known as "slave-killers" because of their resemblance to weapons that were used for this purpose on the Northwest Coast. It is most unlikely that the California pieces were used in this way, but their actual function is unknown.

THE "DEVELOPED ARCHAIC" STAGE

California, like the Northwest Coast, is most interesting as an example of the sedentary lifeways and complex social organization that could develop among hunter–gatherers. The inhabitants of these areas were familiar with the basic concepts of agriculture, as is shown by the cultivation of tobacco by the Yurok and by some Northwest Coast groups. Maize, beans and squash were grown only in the southeastern corner of California, by the Mohave and related Yuman-speaking groups living in the lower Colorado River Valley. Their ancestors, represented in the archaeological record by the cultural tradition called Hakataya, evidently borrowed both agriculture and pottery-making from the Hohokam of Arizona, around A.D. 500–900. Why did agriculture not catch on farther north? The California climate may have caused some difficulty in shifting to agriculture, since maize was not naturally adapted to the dry summer–wet winter pattern. Furthermore, the advantages of agriculture would not have been clear to the California Indians, who maintained fairly dense populations – as many as 2.3 people per square km (six people per square mile) in some areas – by collecting acorns and seeds, hunting and fishing.

The primary dietary dependence on acorns throughout California seems to have been a rather late development, if acorn use is accurately monitored by the varying frequency of mortars and pestles in archaeological assemblages. In all areas of California, dependence on acorns seems to have increased some time between 1000 B.C. and A.D. 1000. Acorns had to be pounded, leached with water, then boiled before eating. The increasing use of this labor-intensive resource may have been an expedient response to mounting population pressure. The evidence of violent death in Cosumnes phase (1000 B.C.–A.D. 500) burials and in the Buchanan Reservoir cemeteries, where 10% of the skeletons had embedded points or other indications of violence, suggests that another result of population pressure was more frequent warfare. The introduction of the bow and arrow, around A.D. 500, might have led to over-hunting, resulting in more acorn consumption to make up for the loss of meat from the diet. Dependence on acorns would probably have had certain social consequences. Acorns could be gathered only in oak groves, whose location was fixed, and by storing the acorns in baskets or wooden granaries, food could be made available for the whole year. The fixed location of this resource, and its storability, would have been conducive to the establishment of permanent villages. To ensure access to their oak groves, and to the streams where fish were most abundant, the native

Californians became more rigidly territorial than most other hunter–gatherers. This territoriality may account, to some extent, for the creation of the formal cemeteries of prehistoric California; they can be seen as symbolic expressions of the unbroken connection, through successive generations, of a group to its land. Exclusive territoriality, by limiting movement between areas, may also have led to the extraordinary linguistic diversity of California, where at the time of contact there were some 60 different languages, which were further divided into local dialects. Because the California Indians lacked the mobility and social fluidity enjoyed by other hunter–gatherers they required alternative mechanisms to deal with localized resource fluctuations. This may explain the development of exchange networks, in which shell beads functioned as currency (King 1978). The archaeological occurrences of *Olivella*, *Haliotis* and *dentalium* shell beads suggests that such exchange systems may have appeared as early as 2000 B.C. At the time of contact with whites, hereditary chiefs were responsible for maintaining ties with neighboring groups, by arranging alliances, ceremonial dances and feasts, and trade meetings (Bean and King 1974, Heizer 1978). The most common political unit among the native Californians was the tribelet (Kroeber 1925); a central village, where the chief resided, was surrounded by satellite communities. The average village's population was about 100. Certain types of shell beads could be amassed and exchanged only by the chiefs, so concentrated distributions of similar beads in prehistoric cemeteries such as Medea Creek may denote the graves of chiefs and their kinfolk.

The sedentism, high population density, and ranked social orders of California and the Northwest Coast stand in such sharp contrast to the generalized ethnographic model of mobile, widely dispersed, egalitarian hunter–gatherers, that some archaeologists have wondered if the later prehistoric cultures of those areas should be relegated to the same "Archaic" category as less complex hunter–gatherers. California and Northwest Coast societies were comparable in some respects to the "Formative" agriculture-based societies of other regions. However, the fact remains that they were not food-producers; dense though their populations may have become, their growth was ultimately limited by the availability of the wild foods on which they depended. We can recognize their continuity in mode of subsistence with earlier Archaic groups, yet also note the emergence of more complex social and political institutions, by regarding Northwest Coast and California cultures as "Developed Archaic". As we shall see, quite complex cultures, whose economic base was provided, for the most part, by efficient collection of wild resources, also developed in the eastern woodlands.

THE PLAINS ARCHAIC

Continuous development from the late Pleistocene hunting cultures to the cultures of the early Holocene is most evident in the Plains, where neither the tool-kit nor the basic adaptive strategy changed very much. The extinction of the mammoth, horse and camel forced the post-Clovis hunters to focus more exclusively on the largest surviving mammal of the grasslands, the bison. Well-coordinated hunting parties could stampede whole herds over cliffs or into box canyons, ravines, or corrals, where the bison could be slaughtered at will. At first, the hunters who used Plainview and Folsom points may have cut off small groups of animals from herds and pursued them. The number of animals represented at each of their kill sites in generally in the range of five to 25; for example, remains of 23 bison were found at the original Folsom site. However, as the Olsen-Chubbuck site shows clearly, whole herds were being efficiently killed and butchered by about 8000 B.C. Drive-hunting persisted in the Plains down into the historic period; the apparent continuity of some specific techniques is astonishing (see earlier discussion of the Jones-Miller site).

The most important item in the tool-kit of the early bison-hunters was still the finely-worked lanceolate spear-point. The Folsom points of ca. 8800 to 8000 B.C. were thinned for hafting by the removal of long channel flakes; they are distinguished from the earlier Clovis points mainly by their longer flutes. Fluting was abandoned by the later Plano hunters, who thinned their points by delicate pressure-flaking of the blade edges, instead of the base. Plano points of slightly varying styles occurred in stratigraphic relationship at the Hell Gap site in eastern Wyoming. On this basis, a sequence of stylistic phases has been outlined for the period from 9000 B.C. to 6350 B.C. There is some uncertainty about the chronological relationship of the first two phases, Plainview and Folsom, and the later phases cannot yet be precisely dated. These phases, which probably overlapped, are Midland (8500–8000), Agate Basin (8000–7000), Hell Gap (7500), Alberta (6500), and Cody (7000–6000). The particularly exquisite Eden and Scottsbluff points belong to the Cody phase, as does the distinctive off-angled Cody knife.

While most Plano folk maintained the big game-hunting tradition in the flat, open grasslands, other bands were developing a different way of life in the mountains, hills and stream valleys that are found here and there in the Plains region. This lifeway, which more closely resembled the Archaic adaptations of the eastern woodlands and the Great Basin, is represented by remains from several sites in Wyoming. Thirty-eight occupation levels were recognized at Mummy Cave, in northeastern Wyoming. In the lowest levels, relatively crude Plano-like points were found; they dated from before 7300 B.C. Points with side or basal notches occurred in level 17, around 5700 B.C., and in the later, upper levels. Well-preserved material from about 2400 B.C. includes tubular bone pipes, coiled baskets, cordage and nets, worked leather, and grinding stones. At Medicine Lodge Creek, a stratified site 160 km east of Mummy Cave, Plano-type points were made from 8000 to 6500 B.C. Stemmed points appeared at around 6300 B.C. The faunal remains – small mammals, fish, deer, mountain sheep and a few bison – indicate a diet that was more broad-based than that of the contemporary big game-hunters. There seems to have been little contact between these foragers and the bison hunters who left their Eden and Scottsbluff points at the Horner kill site, only 64 km away (Frison 1978).

Beginning about 6000 to 5000 B.C., the climate of the Plains became significantly drier and warmer; this was the regional aspect of the more widespread Altithermal climatic episode. The dry period lasted until about 3000 or 2500 B.C. The short grasses on which the bison herds depended probably shrivelled or died when long droughts set in. Those animals that did not starve as a result migrated to areas where they could still find enough food. It seems that the bison deserted much of the Plains; some of them may have taken refuge in stream valleys or peripheral foothill areas where the water shortage was less severe. The smaller animals, who could survive on less food, may have had a selective advantage over the bigger ones. This would explain the observed reduction in the size of bison, which, based on finds in Wyoming, is known to have occurred in the period from 4500 to 2500 B.C. The stress caused by climatic deterioration may have had an analogous effect on the human inhabitants of the Plains. The broad spectrum foragers probably fared better than the Plano bison-hunting specialists during the Altithermal. Whether the Plano hunters adopted the techniques of their neighbors, merged with them, or were replaced by them, we cannot determine from the skimpy evidence at our disposal. Only a few Altithermal sites are known; they are located in the northern, eastern, and western edges of the Plains (Wedel 1983).

When it became relatively wetter, around 2500 B.C., the bison re-occupied the Plains grasslands, and the human population also expanded. This is shown by the greater number of sites, including bison kills, fishing camps, and rock shelters, that date from 2500 B.C. to A.D. 1. Although some of the spear-tips used for bison-hunting were still lanceolate in shape, they were not as finely chipped as the earlier Plano points, and they were associated with stemmed and side-notched types. If the post-Altithermal people were lineal descendants of the earlier Plano population, which remains to be demonstrated, it is clear that they must have adopted elements of the peripheral foraging cultures. Migratory bison-hunters continued to inhabit the southern Plains until historic times, but in the major river valleys, village-dwelling collectors and culti-

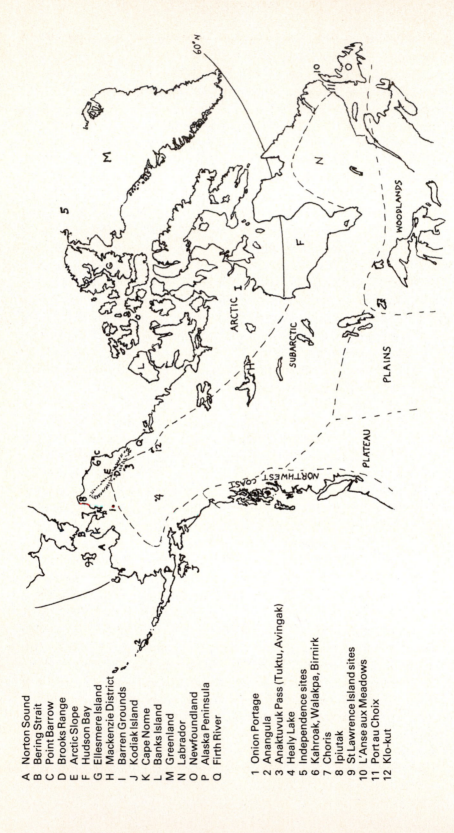

A Norton Sound
B Bering Strait
C Point Barrow
D Brooks Range
E Arctic Slope
F Hudson Bay
G Ellesmere Island
H Mackenzie District
I Barren Grounds
J Kodiak Island
K Cape Nome
L Banks Island
M Greenland
N Labrador
O Newfoundland
P Alaska Peninsula
Q Firth River

1 Onion Portage
2 Anangula
3 Anaktuvuk Pass (Tuktu, Avingak)
4 Healy Lake
5 Independence sites
6 Kahroak, Walakpa, Birnirk
7 Choris
8 Ipiutak
9 St Lawrence Island sites
10 L'Anse aux Meadows
11 Port au Choix
12 Klo-kut

Fig. 40. Arctic and Subarctic regions (letters) and sites (numbers).

vators, with ties to cultures of the eastern woodlands, became established after 250 B.C.

HUNTERS OF THE ARCTIC AND SUB-ARCTIC

Northernmost North America was still inhabited by hunting peoples when the Europeans began to explore the region in the sixteenth century; some Arctic groups were not significantly affected by contact with whites until the early twentieth century. This vast northern region comprised two environmental zones. The Arctic tundra, which extends along the northern coast from Alaska to Greenland, is treeless and bitterly cold: the winters last for eight or nine months, and temperatures sometimes drop to $-72°C$ ($-100°F$). The tundra receives little precipitation, but surface water cannot penetrate the permanently frozen ground, so there are many lakes and streams. The tundra grasses support herds of caribou. Along the ice-encrusted shore, seals and walruses can be hunted, and whales frequent the deeper offshore waters. Fish can be taken from the lakes and streams, but because they do not provide much fat, a vital nutrient for proper bodily function under Arctic conditions, they have never been a dietary staple. South of the tundra lies the sub-Arctic boreal forest, which is composed of short spruces, birches, and poplars. The forest receives more snow than the tundra, and its winters, though shorter, are equally severe. The summers are about twice as long as tundra summers; there are about 100 frost-free days in the forests. As in the tundra, a layer of permafrost causes an abundance of surface water. Both caribou and moose feed on forest vegetation. The boundary between tundra and forest is not sharply defined; there are areas of tundra within the forest zone, and in some places trees extend into the tundra. Furthermore, it is important to note that the tree-line has shifted northward and southward through the centuries, in response to climatic changes.

When the Europeans arrived, the tundra was inhabited by the Eskimos, and the boreal forest by Indians. The Indians who lived west of Hudson Bay spoke Athapaskan languages; those living to the east spoke Algonquian languages. Relations between Eskimos and Indians were generally hostile, a fact that is reflected in the very name "Eskimo", which derives from a contemptuous Indian reference to their neighbors as "eaters of raw meat". (In recent years, it has become more common to refer to the Eskimos as Inuit, as they call themselves. Here, I will retain the older term, only because it is so much more familiar from the existing literature.) The mutual exclusivity of Eskimo and Indian cultures seems to have been prevalent throughout prehistoric times also: in places such as Labrador, where prehistoric Eskimos and Indians lived in close proximity at certain times, remarkably little cultural exchange occurred

(Fitzhugh 1976). When warming climate caused the northward extension of the forest, cultures with ties to more southern Archaic Indian cultures spread northward also, only to retreat when tundra replaced the forest.

Physically, the Eskimos resemble the classic "Mongoloids" of eastern Asia more closely than other American natives do (Laughlin 1966). The Athapaskan Indians seem to fall mid-way between Eskimos and other Indians in several genetic, dental and anatomical traits. It is most likely that the first Eskimos left Asia at some time after the departure of the Indians' ancestors; by that time, the eyefold, extremely flat face, and blood types A and B had probably become characteristic of Asian populations. These traits, which are also found in Eskimos, might alternatively have resulted from continual genetic inputs from Asian populations. There is archaeological evidence of periodic infusions of Asian traits into the cultures of the American Arctic; it would be surprising if this cultural diffusion were not accompanied by some gene flow. The Athapaskans' intermediate status might indicate that they arrived after the more southern Indians but before the Eskimos; however, it more probably resulted from some degree of gene flow that occurred between Eskimos and Athapaskans, despite their mutual antipathy.

All the Eskimos who live between Alaska and Greenland speak mutually intelligible dialects of the same Inupik language. However, the Eskimos of southwestern Alaska speak languages that differ from Inupik, constituting a distinctive sub-family called Yupik. The inhabitants of the Aleutian island chain, which stretches westward from southwestern Alaska, speak a language that is rather distantly related to Inupik and Yupik. Linguists estimate that Aleut and Inuit (the family that includes Inupik and Yupik) split off from a common ancestral language around 2500 B.C., and that Yupik and Inupik diverged about A.D. 900. The greater linguistic diversity of Alaska obviously suggests that it was the original homeland of the Eskimos who now inhabit the more eastern Arctic regions; the striking uniformity of the Inupik languages, on the other hand, indicates that the eastward migration of Inupik-speaking Eskimos must have occurred quite recently. In fact, the ancestral Inupik-speakers can be confidently identified in the archaeological record as the bearers of the Thule culture, which spread rapidly eastward from the Bering Sea coast of Alaska around A.D. 1000. The Thule people somehow replaced the Dorset people, the descendants of Eskimos who had moved eastward 3,000 years earlier. Exactly how the Thule took over Dorset territory remains a mystery, although archaeologists suspect that climate change may have been an important factor.

As we noted earlier (Chapter 3), Alaska and the Yukon have yielded tantalizingly few traces of the early Paleo-Indians who must have trekked through the region *en route* to the more southern parts of America. The oddly broken fossil bones of the Old Crow basin may attest to the presence of humans 27,000 years ago or even thousands of years earlier, but this evidence is not yet entirely convincing. The stone-chipping debris recently discovered at Bluefish Cave No. 1 shows that the Yukon was probably inhabited by 12,000 B.C., but tells us very little about the cultural affiliations of the population. A number of fluted points have been found in Alaska, but not in securely dated contexts. They have turned up in seeming association with micro-blades and -cores, as well as larger blades and, at some sites, bifacially chipped disc-cores. Micro-blades are conspicuously absent from the Clovis assemblages of North America, so most archaeologists are understandably hesitant to identify the Alaskan micro-blade-makers as Clovis ancestors. In any case, radiocarbon dates place the "Paleo-arctic" Alaskan sites between about 9500 and 6000 B.C., too late for them to represent the ancestral culture from which Clovis sprang (Dumond 1980). The Paleo-arctic tradition was clearly derived from northeastern Asia, where similar micro-blades, struck from small wedge-shaped cores, were present in the Dyuktai culture of Siberia by 14,000 B.C., and were used in northern Japan by 8000 B.C. At the Onion Portage site in northwestern Alaska, the Akmak assemblage, which included micro-blades, has been dated to about 7700 B.C. (Anderson 1968). Most Paleo-arctic groups seem to have been inland-oriented hunters, but an atypical site on Anangula, an eastern Aleutian island, which yielded large blades and cores, shows that some groups must have developed an effective marine adaptation by 6000 B.C. At that time, to which the site dates, the island could only have been reached by boat.

Assemblages that contain micro-blades, and date from 6000 B.C. or possibly as early as 8000 B.C. to as late as 3000 B.C., have been found along the Pacific coast, as far south as south-central Washington. At sites that lie south of the central coast of British Columbia, the micro-blades are associated with chipped points and knives that seem to have been derived from the early cultures of the Plateau. The merging of the Arctic and Plateau traditions would ultimately culminate, millennia later, in the elaborate cultures of the Northwest Coast.

It is possible, but unproven, that the original source of both the Eskimo

Fig. 41. Paleo-arctic micro-blade and core (½ actual size). (After Anderson 1968.)

and Athapaskan cultural traditions was the Paleo-arctic tradition. However, at present there is a gap in the archaeological record of Alaska between about 6000 and 4000 B.C. (Dumond 1983). Around 4000 B.C., during the Altithermal period, warmer temperatures seem to have encouraged the northward expansion of the sub-Arctic forests. Forest-adapted people, probably Indians related to the Archaic inhabitants of the more southern and eastern temperate woodlands, occupied both interior and coastal Alaska from 4000 to 2000 B.C. Their characteristic side-notched or corner-notched dart-points have been found in the Palisades complex at the stratified Onion Portage site, at Tuktu in northern Alaska, in the "Tuktu" complex at Healy Lake, in eastern Alaska, and at other sites that are not as well dated. At Onion Portage, the side-notched points were associated with large knives and end scrapers. In the course of time, corner-notching of points became more common, and then, in the Portage complex of about 2500 B.C., leaf-shaped or lanceolate points were made. The finds from Tuktu included side-notched, corner-notched and lanceolate stone points, endscrapers, side-scrapers and knives, as well as micro-blades and micro-cores (Campbell and Cordell 1975). These small tools perhaps show that the Northern Archaic people had assimilated some cultural traits of the earlier Paleo-arctic population.

The Northern Archaic people seem to have retreated southward, along with the forest, as a colder climate set in around 2500–1500 B.C. They were replaced by a new population, which appeared in northern Alaska some time before 2000 B.C. These people, who were almost certainly ancestral Eskimos, made the small, finely-flaked stone tools of the Denbigh Flint complex: delicate end-blades (i.e., points) and side-blades, knives, scrapers, micro-blades, micro-cores, burins, and retouched burin spalls. Sites of the Denbigh complex have been discovered from Norton Sound on the west Alaskan coast, northward as far as Point Barrow, throughout the northern part of the Brooks Range, and on the Arctic

Fig. 42. Northern Archaic point (about ⅘ actual size). (After Anderson 1968.)

144

Slope, as far east as the northernmost Yukon. A few sites have also been found on the southern flanks of the Brooks Range, within the boreal forest zone. Most Denbigh sites are near the coast; they were small, temporary camps that were probably occupied during the summer. The Denbigh folk moved 50 to 250 km inland to spend the winter in square pit-houses. Typically, the house floor was dug to a depth of about half a meter, and the dwelling was entered through a sloping tunnel. This settlement pattern appears to reflect a subsistence system that was based on caribou-hunting and fishing, particularly for salmon. There is no evidence in the Denbigh complex of such key elements of later Eskimo culture as seal-hunting, dog sleds, or skin boats.

At the same time that the Denbigh complex was becoming established in northern Alaska, proto-Eskimo groups, using rather similar tool-kits composed of small blades, were moving rapidly into the coastal tundras of northern Canada. Some of them had reached northeastern Greenland by about 2000–1700 B.C. (There is some uncertainty about these and other dates for Arctic cultures, because many of the C14 assays were run using samples of preserved sea mammal fat, which is suspected of yielding erroneous dates. Some archaeologists would discard fat-based dates altogether; others think they might be salvaged by applying a correction factor. See McGhee and Tuck 1976, Arundale 1981.) These eastern Arctic immigrants are generally referred to as pre-Dorset, because of their evident ancestral relationship to the later Dorset culture of the same region. However, there are some differences between the assemblages of the early Independence I culture of Greenland and Ellesmere Island and other pre-Dorset assemblages (Maxwell 1976). It remains to be determined whether Independence I, and a possibly related early culture found in northern Labrador, are regional variants of pre-Dorset, or, as now seems more likely, represent a slightly earlier wave of migration. For that matter, the

Fig. 43. Denbigh Flint end-blade (point), slightly less than actual size (after Giddings 1954).

relationship of pre-Dorset cultures to the Denbigh Flint complex needs to be further clarified. The pre-Dorset tool-kit, which consists of micro-blades, end- and side-blades, knives, scrapers, and burins, is obviously similar to that of Denbigh, to the extent that archaeologists have classi-fied them as members of a single cultural tradition, the "Arctic Small Tool" tradition. However, pre-Dorset tools are not as finely-chipped as Denbigh tools, so it is doubtful that they were derived from the latter. More probably, both pre-Dorset and Denbigh developed from a common ancestral culture. A plausible candidate for the role of common ancestor is the culture represented by an assemblage excavated at Kahroak, near Point Barrow, Alaska, which seems to be earlier than the Denbigh com-plex (Campbell and Cordell 1975). More than one site will have to be found in order to substantiate this theory. The "Arctic Small Tools" immediately bring to mind the much earlier micro-blades of the Paleo-arctic tradition. However, in order to postulate a Paleo-arctic origin for the Small Tool tradition, one must ignore the intervening cultural hiatus of about 4,000 years. One way to evade this difficulty is to suggest that development of the Small Tool tradition from a Paleo-arctic base occurred on the Siberian side of the Bering Sea; that would imply that the proto-Eskimos who carried the small tools eastward with them were recent immigrants from Asia.

Although the dynamics of the Arctic Small Tool tradition's expansion are poorly understood, it is interesting to compare this migration of Arctic hunters into previously uninhabited territory to the analogous earlier migration of the Paleo-Indians. It apparently took the proto-Eskimos no more than two or three centuries to occupy the coastal tundras from Alaska to eastern Greenland – an expanse of more than 4,800 km (3,000 miles). Assuming for the sake of argument that the Paleo-Indians who emerged south of the ice front in southwestern Canada headed southward by the most direct route, they would have had to traverse about three times this distance to reach Tierra del Fuego. Extrapolation from the pre-Dorset migration rate suggests that the Paleo-Indians could have accomplished this within 600 to 900 years. This figure offers additional support to our earlier calculations (Chapter 3).

Non-lithic artifacts are more often preserved at pre-Dorset sites than at Denbigh sites. These finds show that the pre-Dorset folk used bone toggling harpoons to hunt seals and walrus, and both lances, tipped with antler-points or side-blades, and the short, composite bow, to hunt caribou, musk-oxen, birds and small mammals. This is the earliest certain appearance (ca. 1500 B.C.) of the bow and arrow in North America, which raises the possibility that their use was spread by diffusion from Siberia to the Arctic, and from there to the Indians farther south. The pre-Dorset folk used bone and ivory needles to make tailored clothing, which was necessary for survival in the Arctic. They kept dogs, perhaps as hunting aids or as a reserve food source, but apparently not for sled-pulling. Pre-Dorset camp sites are generally coastal, perhaps indicating the primary importance of sea mammal-hunting. The summer dwellings may have been tents, weighed down by stones placed around their edges. The remains of winter houses are of ovoid shape, with poorly-defined margins, which suggests that the houses may have been built of snow blocks, like the familiar igloos of more recent Eskimos. Heat and light were provided by soapstone lamps filled with seal fat (Harp 1983).

The cooling trend, around 2000–1000 B.C., that forced the tree line, and the forest-dependent Northern Archaic Indians, southward, opened up more tundra land for the pre-Dorset folk to exploit. Thus they expanded into areas to the south and west, about 1500 B.C. In the process, they displaced Northern or Shield Archaic Indians from the Mackenzie District and the Keewatin Barren Grounds, as far as southern Hudson Bay. The Arctic Small Tool tradition persisted in this region until as late as 200 B.C. A few centuries later, Indians who were probably ancestral Athapaskans re-entered the Barren Grounds. Yet another Eskimo penetration occurred before A.D. 1700, resulting in the occupation of the area by the Caribou Eskimo during historic times (Maxwell 1980).

The pre-Dorset culture evolved into the Dorset culture around 1000–800 B.C. Continuity is evident in the Dorset tool-kit, which consisted of micro-blades, end- and side-blades, scrapers, and burins. Unlike pre-Dorset burins, however, Dorset burins were ground. In general, Dorset assemblages include more ground and polished slate tools than are found in the earlier tool-kit. The slate points and knives were often side-notched. Stone lamps became more common, and new items in the Dorset assemblage included barbed bone fish-spear points; bone knives resembling the later ulu, or "woman's knife"; bone and ivory "ice creepers", which were attached to boot soles to prevent slipping; bone sled runners; and the ivory snow knife, which may have been used to build igloos. At later Dorset sites, many figures carved in bone, ivory, and wood have been found; they depict human beings, animals, and spirit monsters. Some of these small sculptures are realistic, while others are more stylized.

The Dorset culture reached its greatest extent – from Banks Island in the west, eastward to Greenland, and southward as far as Newfoundland – during the period from 200 B.C. to A.D. 400. Coastal sites excavated in Newfoundland show that the Dorset people hunted seals there during the spring and summer. Their warm-season camps consisted of round or rectangular semi-subterranean houses, which had roofs made of drift-wood or spruce poles, covered with hides and sod (Harp 1983, Maxwell 1980).

It is not clear what was happening in Alaska while Dorset was evolving from pre-Dorset in the eastern Arctic. Some authorities believe that there was a cultural break around 1500 B.C., while others see evidence of a continuous development from Denbigh into the various cultures that appeared between 1000 B.C. and A.D. 1. Among these cultures were the Walakpa complex, found near Point Barrow, the Choris complex, found on the peninsula of that name, in northwestern Alaska, the Avingak complex, from Anaktuvuk Pass, on the southern side of the Brooks Range, and the Norton culture.

The Walakpa complex included, besides Denbigh-like small tools, some ground-stone artifacts, and square-based, round-shouldered points that resembled those of the Choris complex. Pottery was another trait that the Walakpa and Choris complexes shared. These resemblances, along with the stratigraphic relationship of the complexes, suggest that Choris developed from Walakpa around 700 B.C.

Choris pottery was fiber-tempered and bore linear stamping on its surface. The ceramic craft presumably had diffused from Siberia to Alaska. The manufacture of pottery by these early Archaic cultures should demonstrate that its presence need not be indicative of an agricultural and sedentary way of life; this is a point to recall when we consider cultural developments in the eastern woodlands. Apart from pottery, Choris assemblages comprise stemmed stone points, arrow- or dart-points made of antler, harpoons, adzes, and oil lamps. Some tools were made of rubbed slate. Typical Arctic small tools, except for micro-cores and micro-blades, were also used. The inhabitants of the type site, on the Choris peninsula, lived in large oval winter houses.

The contemporary Avingak assemblage, found within and around several large rectangular winter houses, consisted of Arctic small tools, including micro-blades and micro-cores. Oddly, no burins were found, nor pottery, nor any ground slate tools.

The Norton culture flourished in northwestern Alaska from about 500

Fig. 44. Miniature ivory mask, Dorset culture (3.3 cm high).

B.C. to A.D. 500. By 200 B.C., Norton sites were present all along the Alaskan coast, from the Alaska Peninsula in the southwest to the Firth River in the northeast. In the Walakpa mound, a Norton assemblage was stratified above Walakpa and Choris remains. Norton's derivation from these earlier complexes is suggested by similarities in end- and side-blades and discoidal scrapers. Norton chipped stone points were somewhat cruder than those of the Arctic Small Tool tradition. Stone was also shaped by grinding, to make lip-plugs, whetstones, ulus and skinning knives, adze blades, engraving tools, lamps and dishes. Antler was used for toggling harpoon heads, arrowheads, ice picks, and the prongs of fishing spears. Flaked stone burins were absent from this complex, as were micro-blades and micro-cores. Pottery was abundant; its appearance was different from that of Choris ware, in that the Norton pottery was more often check-stamped than linear-stamped. Unlike the people of the Arctic Small Tool tradition, who had lived inland during the winter, Norton folk seem to have spent winters on the coast, hunting seals on the fast (attached) ice. Their winter houses were similar to those of the Arctic Small Tool tradition, however – squarish and semi-subterranean, with sloping entry passages.

While the middle to late stages of the Norton tradition were thriving, several distinctive Eskimo cultures appeared along the western Alaska coast. These cultures – Ipiutak, Okvik, Old Bering Sea, and Punuk – owed something to the Norton and earlier Arctic Small Tool traditions, but they also contained Asian-derived traits.

The Ipiutak culture dates to about A.D. 1 to 500. Its chipped stone tools were almost identical to those of Norton, but Ipiutak sites lack the pottery, ground slate tools, and oil lamps that occur, albeit not in great quantity, at Norton sites. At the type site of Ipiutak, on Point Hope, the ruins of more than 600 rectangular houses were found. These dwellings were clustered in four long rows, along beach ridges. Even if only the houses on one ridge were occupied simultaneously, Ipiutak would have been quite a large village, with hundreds of inhabitants. An extensive cemetery was located southeast of the village. Most of the dead had been placed in log coffins and interred in half-meter-deep pits; others seem to have been laid on the surface and covered with wooden frames or piles of logs. The special status of these people was denoted by the elaborate carved ivory pieces that accompanied them, and they have been plausibly identified as shamans. Among the associated ivory carvings were chains and swivels, which were quite probably inspired by the iron chains and swivels that have traditionally been worn by shamans in Siberia. Other carved ivory pieces included realistic and fantastic animals, human heads and skulls, snow goggles, and grotesque composite masks that were probably attached to a wood backing. Besides the ivory chains, the presence of some iron tools in the Ipiutak assemblage suggests contact with Siberian cultures. Ipiutak carving was not restricted to grave goods, but was applied to everyday objects as well. Harpoon sockets and knife handles were carved to resemble animal heads. Ivory harpoon heads, which closely resembled those of the contemporary Old Bering Sea culture, were engraved with curvilinear designs, and their basal spurs were carved to imitate the tucked feathers of birds. Such elaborate decoration of harpoon heads may indicate that the ancient hunters, like some recent Yupik Eskimos, believed that sea mammals might be displeased by ugly weapons.

The Okvik and Old Bering Sea cultures, found on the Siberian coast and on St Lawrence Island and other islands in the Bering Strait, date from about 200 B.C. to A.D. 500. It is not clear whether the Old Bering Sea culture, which had an art style that differed from that of Okvik, developed from the latter or existed at the same time. These cultures were typified by numerous polished slate tools, fiber-tempered pottery, and ornately incised ivory harpoon heads and shaft weights (the latter, also known as

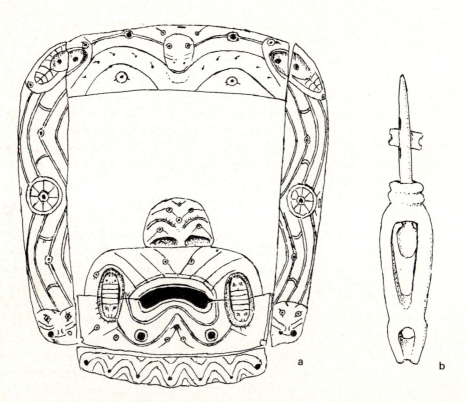

Fig. 45. Ivory carvings from Ipiutak: (A) composite mask (height 16 cm); (B) swivel (length (length 25 cm). (After Willey 1966.)

150

"winged objects", sometimes resemble wing nuts in shape). The toggling harpoons came in three different sizes, for use in hunting whales, walrus or seals. Houses were rectangular; the entrance was a tunnel that dipped lower than the house floor, thereby trapping cold air. Toy replicas of the kayak and umiak show that these skin boats, familiar from recent Eskimo culture, were used.

Around A.D. 500, the Punuk culture developed on St Lawrence Island. Punuk people may have hunted walrus and whales more often than their Okvik ancestors had, as implied by the greater frequency of large harpoon heads. They were also more sedentary, living in villages that sometimes held several hundred people. The introduction of antler plate armor, bone and ivory daggers, the dog sled and iron engraving tools shows that Punuk had been influenced by Asian cultures, by way of Siberia. Punuk harpoon heads were less elaborate than those of the Old Bering Sea culture; these and other tools became still plainer in the late prehistoric and recent Eskimo cultures of the Bering Sea region.

Fig. 46. Carved bone harpoon head, Old Bering Sea culture (length 11.5 cm).

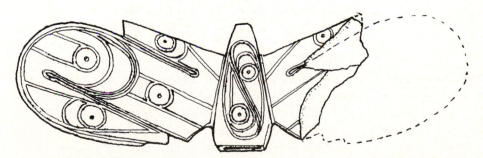

Fig. 47. Winged object (harpoon shaft weight), Old Bering Sea culture (length ca. 21 cm). (After Willey 1966.)

151

The Birnirk culture, which was situated on the northwest Alaskan coast from Cape Nome to Point Barrow, dates from about A.D. 500 to 1000. It was contemporaneous with Punuk, and ancestral to the Thule culture that expanded rapidly eastward and southward around A.D. 1000. Birnirk people took over the area that had previously been inhabited by the Ipiutak folk. Their harpoon heads and other artifacts show derivation from the Okvik–Old Bering Sea tradition, and also indicate Birnirk influence on the Punuk culture. The small chipped flint tools of Birnirk suggest that the deeper roots of this culture lie in the Arctic Small Tool tradition. Birnirk assemblages also comprise numerous kinds of artifacts that are paralleled in the ingenious tool kit of the modern Eskimos. These include various weapons and gadgets used in hunting seals, whales, caribou, and birds, fishing, travelling over snow or water (sleds, kayaks, umiaks), preparing food, making clothing from skins, and building houses.

The Thule culture developed from Birnirk in northwestern Alaska shortly before A.D. 1000, and soon spread rapidly eastward as far as Greenland, replacing the Dorset culture everywhere by A.D. 1400. Thule pottery, bearing paddle-stamped curvilinear impressions identical to those which decorate Birnirk pots, has recently been discovered at sites on Ellesmere Island, just west of Greenland. After persisting for a while in making pottery of poorer quality, the eastern Thule gave up the ceramic craft altogether and made their cooking vessels of soapstone instead. The Thule people also made less use of chipped stone tools for working bone and ivory, using tools made of meteoric iron instead.

The Thule expansion may have occurred in response to the onset of a warmer climate, which may have caused a reduction of the seal population or changes in the distribution and migration routes of whales. The growth of the Alaskan Eskimo population, augmented by immigration from Siberia, may also have provoked the Thule migration. The introduction of slat armor and daggers from Siberia (Maxwell 1980), not long before the migration began, suggests that warfare was becoming more frequent, perhaps reflecting an imbalance of human population and food resources on the Alaskan coast. Thule immigrants and Dorset folk seem to have coexisted for a while in some areas, such as northern Labrador, before the Dorset culture disappeared; however, the Thule culture picked up very little from Dorset. Since cultural fusion did not occur, we may suspect that Thule–Dorset relations were generally less than cordial; but no clear evidence of Thule-inflicted violence has been reported from late Dorset sites. Perhaps the Dorset people avoided open conflict by moving to less favored areas, where they succumbed to starvation – an ever-present threat in the Arctic. The process of cultural replacement remains to be clarified by further research.

Thule houses on Ellesmere Island have yielded pieces of chain mail, woolen cloth, even iron rivets from boats, which prove that the Eskimos had some contact with the Vikings who settled in Greenland in A.D. 986 (McGhee 1984). Apparently, Norse explorers traveled up the western shore of Greenland to reach Ellesmere Island by A.D. 1200 or 1300. As is well known, other Vikings sailed westward from Greenland, encountering the coast of Labrador. Around A.D. 1000, one party, perhaps Leif Ericson's, spent the winter at L'Anse aux Meadows, on the northern tip of Newfoundland. The foundations of their turf long houses, and traces of their iron-working, have been excavated there. Newfoundland was probably the "Vinland" of the Norse sagas, even though wild grapes did not grow there. The native "Skraelings" of the region, with whom the Norse had several hostile encounters, were probably Algonquian-speaking Indians, rather than Eskimos. This conclusion, based on archaeological evidence, is difficult to reconcile with Norse references to the Skraelings' skin boats; only Eskimos used kayaks. However, the sagas also recount an incident when the Vikings surprised and killed several Skraelings who had been sleeping under their boats. This would not have been possible with a kayak, but could have been done if the boat was an Algonquian birch-bark canoe. Perhaps the Vikings mistook the birch-bark, seen from a distance, for skin. Farther north, in Greenland, Eskimo–Norse contact certainly occurred. The Norse colonists evidently could not adjust to the colder conditions brought on by the Little Ice Age that began in the thirteenth century: some died of starvation, others were killed in Eskimo raids, and perhaps the rest sailed back to Iceland or Scandinavia, leaving the Greenland villages deserted by 1500.

The cold climate that set in during the thirteenth century may also have been responsible for the migration of some eastern Thule back into more western areas. The late Thule people in the eastern Arctic no longer wintered in large semi-subterranean houses: instead, they built snow houses on the fast ice, where they hunted seals, as modern Eskimos do, by waiting patiently beside their breathing holes. Over the course of several centuries prior to the historic era, Thule-descended groups adapted somewhat differently to the regions they had occupied. Some emphasized coastal sealing, like the Copper Eskimos; others relied heavily on caribou-hunting, as the historic Nunamiut and Kobukmiut did; and whaling was an important activity for the Point Barrow Eskimos.

KODIAK ISLAND AND THE ALEUTIANS

The early Aleutian culture represented at Anangula, ca. 6000 B.C., differed from the contemporary Arctic Small Tool cultures of the Alaskan mainland in its use of large blades. The next cultural phase found in the

Aleutians dates to about 4000–3000 B.C.: called the Ocean Bay tradition, it is better known from sites on Kodiak Island and the Alaska Peninsula. This tradition is characterized by large leaf-shaped chipped stone points or knives, as well as scrapers and a few adzes. Ocean Bay harpoons featured barbed heads, instead of the toggling heads used by most Eskimos. Later Aleuts persisted in the use of such harpoons for sea mammal hunting. They also continued to use chipped stone points and knives, only adding ulus and other polished slate tools to their kit after A.D. 1000 or 1500. This change was probably related to the southward expansion of the Thule culture that occurred around that time. In contrast, Ocean Bay descendants on Kodiak Island began making points of polished slate as early as 2500 B.C. An increased use of polished slate tools, including the ulu, is evident in Kodiak assemblages dating between 1500 B.C. and A.D. 1000. Barbed harpoons like the Aleuts', and other implements, were made of bone. After A.D. 1000, Thule influence is reflected in the introduction of pottery and in the convergence of some local artifact types with Thule types. The end result of this convergence was the culture of the historic Koniag (Dumond 1983).

PROTO-ATHAPASKAN CULTURES OF THE INTERIOR

As noted earlier, the bearers of the Northern Archaic tradition retreated southward after 2000 B.C., probably in response to the onset of a colder climate. After a long period for which there is little evidence, their presumed descendants are represented in interior Alaska by assemblages from Klo-kut, Kavik and Chimi (Campbell and Cordell 1975). Klo-kut was situated at a caribou crossing on the Porcupine River in the northern Yukon. An unbroken stratified sequence runs from about A.D. 500 to the recent past, when the site was occupied by the Kutchin Athapaskans. Klo-kut yielded stemmed, serrated stone points, stone scrapers, bone and antler arrowheads, bone and antler leister (fish-spear) prongs, and antler wedges. The Kavik site lies 480 km (300 miles) west of Klo-kut, at a caribou crossing on the Anaktuvuk River. The assemblage here, which may be about 500 years old, includes crude lozenge-shaped and stemmed points, knives, scrapers, and artifacts made of antler: leister prongs, a wedge, and a decorated comb. At Chimi, in the boreal forest of the southern Yukon, 700 year-old leister prongs were found, similar to those from Kavik and Klo-kut. Proto-Athapaskan cultures were regionally diversified, both in their artifact assemblages and their differing emphases in the use of local forest resources. Where copper was available, hammered points, knives, and awls were added to the tool-kit. At Proto-Athapaskan sites along the lower Yukon River, typically Eskimo artifacts, such as toggling harpoons and ulus, have been found. Trading contacts in

154

this area between Eskimos and Indians, resulting in the latter's adoption of Eskimo artifacts and customs, were also reported by ethnographers.

ARCHAIC ADAPTATIONS IN CENTRAL AND SOUTH AMERICA

In South America, as in North America, the Paleo-Indians' descendants adapted to the changing post-Pleistocene environments. As mastodon, horse, and ground sloth died out, early Archaic hunters shifted their attention to deer and guanaco. They also hunted and trapped small mammals, such as rabbits and guinea pigs. They began to do more fishing and shellfish-collecting, and gathered more plant foods. Such broad spectrum foraging ultimately led, in Mesoamerica and Peru, to the development of agriculture; we will examine that process in detail in the next chapter. Here, we will look briefly at other South American foraging adaptations that paralleled those of North American Archaic cultures.

South American Paleo-Indians had already hunted deer and camelids, along with the soon-to-be extinct megafauna, so the transition to hunting of surviving species was not a drastic one. Trapping of smaller animals and birds, and gathering of nuts, berries, and roots had also begun by 9000 B.C., but these activities probably became more important after the extinction of the megafauna. In the Andes, broad spectrum Archaic adaptations are attested at several sites in the 9000–7000 B.C. range, including Guitarrero Cave, Chobshi Cave, Inca Cueva 4 (Argentina) and several sites near Ayacucho. Willow leaf-shaped Ayampitín points and sitemmed Paiján points replaced fishtail points in the tool-kits of the hunters of the Peruvian highlands and coast. Elsewhere, well-made points were rare or absent. In Colombia, only simple flake tools were used by the inhabitants of La Sueva rockshelter (ca. 8900 B.C.) and the El Abra rock-shelters (7100–5300 B.C.). These tools were associated with remains of deer, guinea pigs, and other small animals. A diversified subsistence base, including mammals, birds, mussels, fish, eggs, snails and palm nuts, is also represented by several early Archaic sites in the highlands of eastern Brazil which date from between 9000 and 4000 B.C. The stone tools at these Brazilian sites were generally simple; points were seemingly not made (Lynch 1983).

A few sites located near the Pacific coast have yielded evidence of very early use of marine resources. At a campsite of the Paijanense culture of Peru, fish and shellfish, as well as snails and lizards, were eaten. This site, PV 22–13, where a human skeleton was also found, has been C14 dated to about 8250 B.C. At the Chilean site of Quereo, remains of whale and sea-lions and marine shellfish were excavated from a deposit that dates from before 7400 B.C. Associated bones of mastodon, horse and camelid show

1 Guitarrero Cave
2 Chobshi Cave
3 Ayacucho
4 El Abra
5 Quereo
6 Quebrada Las Conchas
7 Cerro Mangote
8 Quiani
9 Englefield Island
10 Brazilian sambaquis (shell middens)
11 Banwari Trace
12 Fell's Cave

Fig. 48. Archaic sites in South America.

156

that the site's inhabitants also relied on land hunting. Another site in Chile, Quebrada Las Conchas, which might be as early as 7700 or 7500 B.C., yielded mollusk shells and fish bones, sea mammal bones, and also remains of camelids (Llagostera 1979). Far to the north of the Chilean sites, on the coast of Ecuador, the lowest level of the Las Vegas shell midden has been dated to about 8200 B.C. (Stothert 1985). These early Archaic sites seem to represent seasonal stops at the shore by cyclically wandering bands of foragers, rather than permanent settlements, which began to be established several thousand years later on the Peruvian coast.

The rate of sea level rise slackened around 5000–4000 B.C., resulting in stabilization of the coastline. Submergence of the former coast created lagoons, estuaries, and swamps that were colonized by mollusks and fish. Although it is clear that earlier foragers made some use of coastal resources, it seems that many more groups were attracted by the abundant resources of this new environmental zone after 5000 B.C. Coastal sites of the period from 5000 to 3000 B.C. include: Cerro Mangote, in western Panama (4850 B.C.); the Quiani midden of northernmost Chile (4220 B.C.); the Englefield Island shell midden at Tierra del Fuego (prob-

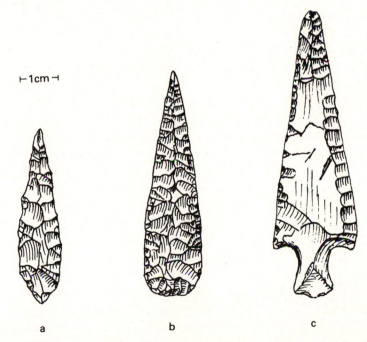

Fig. 49. Archaic points from western South America: (A) willow-leaf; (B) Ayampitín; (C) Paiján (length 10 cm). (A and B after Lynch 1980; C after Willey 1971.)

able date ca. 4000 B.C.); the shell middens or *sambaquis* on the coast of Brazil, some of which date from 4000 B.C.; and Banwari Trace, on the island of Trinidad (5000 B.C.). This early campsite on Trinidad suggests that marine-adapted people were using boats off the coast of Venezuela by 5000 B.C.; by 3000 B.C. they had probably occupied the islands of Cuba and Hispaniola.

In most regions of South America, hunter–gatherers either adopted agriculture or were displaced by farming groups at some time after 2000 B.C.; however, a few areas were still inhabited by foragers at the time of contact with Europeans. The Ciboneys of far western Cuba were coastal foragers who had adopted neither farming nor pottery; their tools were made of conch shells and ground-stone. Some tribes in Venezuela and Guyana were living by hunting and fishing at the time of contact, but these people may have been one-time farmers who had reverted to a foraging way of life. Similarly, Amazonian tribes such as the Siriono, who lived by hunting, gathering, and a little farming, are suspected to have abandoned farming after they were pushed away from the riverbanks by stronger groups. Some of the Macro-Ge-speaking tribes who lived on the crest of the plateau in eastern Brazil were hunter–gatherers; others practiced some farming, growing mainly sweet potatoes or maize. To the west, the inhabitants of the dry plains of the Gran Chaco had probably lived exclusively or primarily by foraging until the time of contact. The tribes of the Argentine pampas practiced some farming, but to the south, the Puelche and Tehuelche of Patagonia and the Ona of northeastern Tierra del Fuego were plains hunters. They used bolas and the bow and arrow, armed with stone or bone points, to hunt guanaco, deer and the ostrich-like rhea. Small, rigidly territoria bands lived in semi-sedentary villages, composed of skin wind-breaks or pole and mat tents (Willey 1971).

The direct prehistoric antecedents of the Ona are represented by the Magellan V culture of Patagonia, which is characterized by small, stemmed, corner-notched stone points. Similar but slightly larger points were typical of the preceding Magellan IV phase, in which they were accompanied by end- and sidescrapers and bolas. Magellan IV may have begun around 3000 B.C. The archaeological sequence in southern Patagonia begins with Magellan I, the Paleo-Indian, fishtail point-making culture present at Fell's Cave at 9000 B.C. Magellan II, typified by bone points and long stone points that resemble the leaf-shaped points of the early Andean Archaic cultures, has no C14 dates, but probably dates to about 8000 B.C. Magellan III assemblages contain willow leaf-shaped points, similar to the Ayampitín points of Peru; this phase probably dates to 4000 B.C. or earlier. A few stemmed points also appear in Magellan III, suggesting that a gradual local transition occurred to the plains-adapted hunting culture represented by Magellan IV. The archaeological record therefore implies that the Ona of the historic period inherited a cultural tradition which, except for minor changes in artifact styles and in hunting methods (e.g. adoption of the bow and arrow), had remained basically unaltered for at least 5,000 years; indeed, some features of the Paleo-Indian Magellan I culture may have persisted among the Ona.

Southwest of the Ona, the Alacaluf, Chona, and Yahgan lived by collecting shellfish and hunting sea mammals along the cold, wet, forested coast of Tierra del Fuego, and on the offshore islands. Small extended family bands shifted camp frequently, often travelling by canoe. This marine adaptation had begun to develop by about 4000 B.C. The shell midden of this age on Englefield Island seems to represent the transitional period when land-oriented hunters, using Andean-style willow leaf points, as well as bolas, were adapting to the coastal environment (Willey 1971).

It is interesting to note that linguistic evidence corroborates the implication of the similarities between the stone point styles of the Andean and Patagonian–Fuegian Paleo-Indian and Archaic cultures. The Fuegian languages shared a common ancestry with the main Andean languages, Quechua and Aymara; however, while the more southern peoples remained hunters and coastal foragers, their northern cousins developed agriculture and pastoralism and created a complex civilization. The sharp contrast between these cultural trajectories must be attributed primarily to the differing capacity of the respective environments to support large human populations.

Fig. 50. Point types of the Magellan sequence, Patagonia: bottom Magellan III, ca. 5000 B.C. (ca. 3.5 cm, 7.5 cm); middle, Magellan IV, ca. 3000 B.C. (ca. 3.5 cm); top, Magellan V, ca. A.D. 500 to contact (ca. 2 cm, 1.2 cm).

5

The origins of agriculture and village life

More than 100 species of plants, including several upon which much of the world's population is dependent today, were originally cultivated and domesticated by native Americans. The most familiar and widespread of these crops are maize, which came from Mexico, and potatoes, which were first grown in the highlands of Peru. The roster of American cultigens also includes sweet potatoes, manioc, several kinds of beans, squash and pumpkins, tomatoes, chili peppers, avocados, sunflowers and amaranths. In addition to their use as food, cultivated plants provided native Americans with stimulants (tobacco, coca), fiber (cotton) and containers (gourds).

Archaeologists have traditionally viewed agriculture, or "food production", as a radical and momentous break with earlier hunting and gathering lifeways. The Australian prehistorian, V. Gordon Childe, referred to a "Neolithic Revolution" which agriculture had triggered in the societies of the Near East and Europe. Agriculture yielded much more food than foraging; with an assured food supply, Neolithic populations increased rapidly. Permanent villages were established, as farmers settled down beside their fields. Freed from the daily search for undependable wild resources, farming people had more leisure time to develop crafts such as pottery-making and weaving. If they harvested more food than was immediately needed, it could be stored, and the surplus could be used to trade with other groups for luxury items. The surplus could also be used to free some members of the community from subsistence tasks: specialist craftsmen, merchants, priests, and a ruling élite. Thus, agriculture paved the way for social and economic stratification.

The concepts and techniques involved in the relationship of man to nature in agriculture as opposed to hunting and gathering seemed so radically different to many scholars that they thought it unlikely that food production could have been invented more than once. In the 1950s, geographer Carl Sauer suggested that agriculture, initially utilizing root crops that could be easily grown from cuttings, was begun by fishing peoples in southeast Asia, and spread from this "hearth" to the Near East, and across the Pacific to tropical America (Sauer 1952). The theory that agriculture diffused world-wide from a single point of origin is no longer very popular, but it still has a few adherents (e.g. Carter 1977, Lathrap 1977, Jett 1983, Isaac 1970). If confronted with the obvious question: Why aren't the same staple crops found throughout the world?, diffusionists can offer two responses. One is that it was only the idea of agriculture that spread, not the plants themselves. Once an agricultural mindset was established, through cultural contact or migration, people in a given region would experiment with cultivation of the most promising wild plants in that environment. The second answer is that, if one closely examines the archaeological record, one will in fact find traces, at an early stage of agricultural development, of exotic, imported cultigens. In discussions of agricultural origins in the Americas, attention has focussed on two possible imports from the old World: cotton and gourds. Cotton was domesticated in Mexico before 3000 B.C., and it was being woven into textiles on the coast of Peru by 2500 B.C. The Mexican and Peruvian cottons are of different species and were probably domesticated independently from local wild varieties. What complicates the issue is that the genetic structure of both species can only be explained as the result of hybridization with African cotton. While diffusionists would say that this is evidence of trans-Atlantic canoe voyages, an alternative explanation is that African wild cotton rafted across the ocean and hybridized with New World species without human assistance; this probably occurred many thousands of years before man had even reached South America. The case of the gourd is similar. Bottle gourds are generally thought by botanists to be native to Africa; but gathered or cultivated specimens have turned up in very early contexts in Mexico and Peru. To explain these occurrences as the result of cultural diffusion, one must postulate an implausibly early trans-Atlantic voyage by African fishermen–farmers, followed by transmission by cultivators across the Amazon basin, to get gourds to Mexico by 7000 B.C. and to coastal Peru by 6000 B.C. (Lathrap 1977). The stumbling-block for this scenario is the complete absence of evidence of farming groups in either West Africa or lowland South America at such an early date. Gourds can remain viable after weeks of immersion in salt water, so they could have reached American shores by floating across from Africa. Given the stream-side locations where African gourds habitually grow, they must have been carried off into the ocean with some frequency. But once on the American side, the gourds had another problem, since they could not establish themselves on sandy beaches. Somehow, they had to get inland. We must either speculate that some early South American cultivator happened by and took the stranded gourd's seeds inland to plant them, or accept that the seeds might have been eaten by some animal that conveniently excreted the undigested seeds in a sunlit, stream-side spot where they could grow. The only other way to account for the early American gourds is to suggest that wild forms may once have existed throughout the tropics, but that the wild American variety became extinct, leaving only its domesticated descendant (Pickersgill and Heiser 1977). It is ironic that this last theory is favored by scholars who now reject an analogous explanation of the origin of maize as a descendant of a vanished wild form. The origin of the New World gourd remains a disturbing problem.

The consensus among archaeologists today is that the dichotomy between hunting and gathering and agriculture was too sharply drawn by past theorists. Ethnographically observed hunter–gatherers of the recent past knew how plants and animals reproduced. In some cases, they intentionally fostered the growth of preferred species. Australian aborigines planted root cuttings and scattered grass seeds. Shoshoni Indians dug irrigation ditches to bring water to stands of seed-bearing grasses. A common ecological management practice of many hunter–gatherers was periodic burning of vegetation, which cleared the way for grasses that provided food for both humans and game animals. One can also point to hunter–gatherers who actually practiced gardening in a minor way, but never became dependent on cultivation for their subsistence. A good example of this is the growing of tobacco by the hunter–gatherers of California and the fishing tribes of the Northwest Coast. Agriculture, it becomes clear, was not the unique discovery of a lone prehistoric genius; it was a logical development of subsistence practices that were already common among hunters and gatherers. Furthermore, the supposed advantages of an agricultural lifeway were probably not immediately obvious to hunter–gatherers. Ethnographic studies have shown that hunting and gathering is not a desperate daily struggle for survival, as it was formerly portrayed. Even in the marginal, arid environments where extant hunter–gatherers such as the !Kung San and Australian Aborigines live today, they enjoy nutritionally adequate diets for which they do not have to work very hard. Each adult !Kung San puts in an average of two or three hours per day at subsistence chores. The rest of the day is spent chatting, visiting or sleeping. So much for the notion that hunter–gatherers do not have enough leisure time to elaborate their culture!

Ethnographic and archaeological evidence can disabuse us of other time-honored misconceptions about hunting and gathering and agriculture. As the large villages of California and the Northwest Coast illustrate, sedentism can develop in the absence of agriculture. We have examined archaeological evidence of substantial dwellings at Archaic sites, such as Koster, where there is no indication of cultivation. With regard to the development of crafts by non-agricultural societies, it seems that pottery was first manufactured in the New World by foraging groups in northern South America. Basketry was developed into an art form in non-agricultural California. The stone-carving of the Hopewell culture, which on present evidence was based mainly on efficient foraging, was quite sophisticated, as was the wood-carving of the Northwest Coast. The indications of stratification in Hopewell societies, and the hints of status distinctions in earlier Eastern Archaic societies, imply that social stratification does not presuppose an agricultural subsistence base. Long-distance trade was evidently not dependent on the availability of agricultural surpluses; the Hopewellian trade network stretched from the Ohio Valley to Wyoming, and earlier Late Archaic trade routes ran from the Gulf Coast to the Great Lakes. Clearly, foragers in rich environments could also amass socially useful surpluses.

Did agriculture bring about any improvements in the quality of life? Probably not. Reliance on a few cultivated crops, instead of the wide variety of resources exploited by hunter–gatherers, left farmers vulnerable to starvation if the crops succumbed to drought or insects. The bones of early farmers' skeletons often contain growth arrest lines, resulting from episodes of malnutrition during childhood. The average stature of early farming populations was smaller than that of hunter–gatherers, probably because of a worsening of nutrition, particularly a loss of protein from the diet. The farmers' teeth were worn down by particles of grit from their grinding stones, and riddled with cavities which resulted from their high carbohydrate intake. The denser populations and unsanitary conditions in agricultural villages encouraged the spread of infectious diseases, which were rare among hunter–gatherers.

If agriculture had so many drawbacks, why would anyone have chosen it over the easier, healthier hunting and gathering lifeway? For want of a good answer to this question, archaeologists began to suggest in the late 1960s that the transition to agriculture had not been a matter of choice. Instead, hunter–gatherers had been forced to take up farming, because the alternative was starvation. The problem they had had to contend with was one of too many people and not enough naturally-occurring food (Cohen 1977a). This is the essential idea that underlies the various population pressure theories of agricultural origins that have been proposed by archaeologists during the last decade. There is another basic premise that these theories share: the events that must be explained were world-wide in scale. Agricultural development began in the Near East around 9000 B.C.; within several thousand years, it had also started in southeast Asia, China, Mesoamerica, and Peru. Assuming that diffusion was not responsible, how then can we account for the appearance of agriculture in these regions at about the same time?

It can hardly be irrelevant that the origins of agriculture coincided with the end of the last Pleistocene glaciation. Among the environmental changes that this entailed, the extinction of the megafauna and the rise of

163

the oceans have been most often cited as possible causes of agricultural development. In our review of the Archaic, we have already examined the responses of the Paleo-Indians to the disappearance of the Pleistocene megafauna. They turned for food to smaller game, birds, fish, shellfish and plants. Increased dependence on and knowledge of plants could have led to their cultivation and domestication in some areas. Agriculture would thus have been a response to an imbalance or disequilibrium in the relationship of people to resources, caused by a sudden reduction in available food. While it is an explanation that may be applicable to the New World, faunal extinction cannot account for the origins of agriculture in the Near East, China, or southeast Asia. In the Near East, the earliest cultivators continued to hunt gazelle, deer, and wild cattle, as their ancestors had done for thousands of years before.

Rising ocean waters could have caused disequilibrium either directly or indirectly. By swallowing up large coastal regions, such as the continental shelf of the northeastern U.S., the sea may have pushed thousands of hunter–gatherers inland. This influx would have upset the delicate ecological balance maintained by the groups that were already living in the interior. New food sources would have to be found to support the denser population; this situation could have led to experimental cultivation, begun as a way of increasing the yields of wild plants. A theory of indirect effect, proposed by Lewis Binford in an influential article (1968), stresses the creation of rich new coastal environments in ocean-flooded estuaries and marshes. Those groups that took advantage of the abundant coastal resources could meet their subsistence needs without moving about much, so they established permanent villages. Sedentism allowed mothers to raise more children, which led to rapid population growth in these coastal villages. When population threatened to exceed the environment's carrying capacity, some people would leave the village and head off into the interior. This migration would have caused a population disequilibrium in the interior, thus having the same effect as the direct displacement postulated in the previous theory.

Binford's theory does not stand up very well in light of our current knowledge of post-Pleistocene coastal changes. As we have seen, sea level did not stabilize, allowing formation of tidal and estuarine ecosystems, until about 4000 B.C. Recent fieldwork in Belize suggests that the earliest coastal adaptation there dates to ca. 4200 B.C. A few other coastal sites in Central America seem to be of comparable antiquity, but most are later than 3000 B.C. By that time, plants had already been cultivated in the Mexican highlands for at least 2,000 years. While Binford's theory thus seems invalid for Mesoamerica, it might be applicable to Peru, where there is evidence of coastal villages before 5000 B.C. However, recently reported finds of cultivated beans from 7000 B.C. or earlier at Guitarrero Cave, in the Andes, suggest that, as in Mesoamerica, experiments in food production by inland-dwelling groups preceded the establishment of coastal villages.

These disequilibrium theories assume that, like modern hunter–gatherers, prehistoric groups maintained stable populations, well below environmental carrying capacities, by employing practices such as birth spacing, abortion and infanticide. Only in extraordinary situations would this equilibrium be upset. But according to another recent view, human populations have grown continuously since the early Pleistocene, despite such attempts to suppress their growth artificially (Cohen 1977a). The easiest way to relieve the resulting pressure on resources was for some people to migrate into new territories; however, by the end of the Pleistocene, all habitable areas had been occupied by hunter–gatherers. With migration no longer feasible, subsequent population growth could only be dealt with by finding new food sources.

This is a reasonable theory, and it does account rather well for the archaeological evidence of the development of "broad spectrum" subsistence strategies by the Epipaleolithic inhabitants of the Nile Valley and the Near East, the Mesolithic population of Europe, and, of course, the Archaic peoples of the Americas. From this perspective, agriculture appears to have been merely a special local variant of widespread Archaic adaptations. But the obvious question then arises: Why didn't agriculture develop everywhere as a logical extension of Archaic gathering practices? To take a specific example, why did agriculture develop in Mexico, but not in the Great Basin? Around 7000 B.C., the lifeways of the inhabitants of both regions were quite similar: they collected cactus leaves, roots, seeds, and other vegetal foods, and occasionally they hunted antelope or deer, and trapped rabbits and other small animals and birds. However, by about 2500 B.C. the Basin lifeway was virtually unchanged, but the Mexicans were living in villages and harvesting domesticated crops, some of which, such as maize, had been radically altered from their wild forms.

To explain these differing outcomes, the possibilities that come to mind are: 1) there may have been some distinctive features of the Mexican environment that were conducive to agriculture; 2) the plants collected by the Mexicans may have been more readily cultivated and domesticated than their Basin counterparts; 3) Mexican harvesting practices may have differed from those of Basin gatherers in some way which fostered desirable changes in plants. Whatever the distinctive features that we may discover in Mexico, we should find analogous features in the environment, native plants, or subsistence techniques of the Andean region, where agriculture also developed.

THE BEGINNINGS OF FARMING IN MEXICO

Our knowledge of agricultural beginnings in Mexico is largely derived from the fieldwork of Richard "Scotty" MacNeish. In 1949, MacNeish discovered some tiny corncobs in a cave in the Sierra de Tamaulipas, in northeastern Mexico. These turned out to date to about 2500 B.C., approximately the same age as maize found in Bat Cave, in New Mexico. It was clear that corn had been domesticated at an earlier date, somewhere farther south. Based on the modern distribution of corn varieties, botanists had guessed that it was first domesticated somewhere between Mexico and Peru. MacNeish set out to find dry cave sites in this region, hoping to excavate preserved specimens of early maize. He could not find dry caves in Honduras or Guatemala, but in the state of Chiapas in southeastern Mexico, he excavated a large cave called Santa Marta. Although he uncovered pre-ceramic remains dating back to 7000 B.C., maize pollen was not present in any of the strata that pre-dated 3500 B.C. This was not much earlier than the Tamaulipas corncobs, which implied that the first domestication had occurred somewhere between Tamaulipas and Chiapas. The reported discovery of maize pollen, dating from about 4000 B.C., in a core taken near Mexico City, pointed to an origin south of that city, but north of Chiapas. The search narrowed when Paul Mangelsdorf, the botanist who had analyzed the Tamaulipas finds and who had attempted to recreate ancient maize by back-crossing modern varieties, told MacNeish that his research indicated that the wild ancestral maize had flourished in an arid highland valley. There were three such valleys between Mexico City and Chiapas: southern Oaxaca, the Tehuacan Valley in Puebla, and the valley of the Rio Balsas in Guerrero. MacNeish's survey of Oaxaca did not yield any promising rock shelters (some years later, however, early botanical remains were recovered from shallow but stratified caves that he had not investigated). MacNeish moved on to the Tehuacan Valley, where, after initially discouraging results, he discovered remains of early maize in Ajuereado Cave. MacNeish subsequently undertook a major archaeological project in the Tehuacan Valley, intensively excavating nine sites and testing 18 others. The results allowed him to trace a cultural sequence from about 9500 B.C. to A.D. 1531, when the Spaniards arrived. Excellent preservation of plant and animal remains and even human feces in the dry caves of the valley enabled MacNeish to reconstruct, in remarkable detail, the subsistence strategies of the ancient Tehuacanos. To aid him in this effort, he enlisted the services of botanists, zoologists and geologists, who studied the modern environment as well as the prehistoric remains (MacNeish 1964, 1972, 1978; Byers and MacNeish 1967–76).

MacNeish has divided the Tehuacan cultural sequence into phases, which are named after the excavated sites in the valley. During the first phase, Ajuereado, ca. 9500–7000 B.C., Paleo-Indians used leaf-shaped spear-heads to hunt horse, antelope and deer. This activity may have provided some 50 to 60% of the diet before 8000 B.C. Additional meat was obtained by catching jackrabbits; this may have involved cooperative hunts by men, women and children from normally dispersed family bands, similar to the rabbit drives of the Shoshoni. The Ajuereado stone tool kit is dominated by butchering and hide-working tools, and few plant remains were found in occupation levels of this phase. Small bands, consisting of one or a few families, seem to have roamed widely and randomly throughout the valley. Their subsistence activities did not vary much from one season to the next. Around 8000 B.C., horse, antelope, jackrabbits, giant turtles, and several rodent species became extinct, perhaps because of the onset of warmer, drier conditions and shrinkage of grassland in the valley. The inhabitants' response to the faunal extinction was probably increased dependence on deer-stalking and plant-collecting.

Based on the number of occupations found, the Tehuacan population may have tripled during the next phase, El Riego (7000–5000 B.C.). Deer-hunting continued as an important subsistence activity, relied on almost exclusively during the dry winter. Trapping of small animals and cutting of cactus leaves also provided a small percentage of the diet during the winter and other seasons. In the spring, seed-collecting contributed more to the diet than hunting. Net bags and coiled baskets may have been useful for collecting seeds, which were processed with ground-stone manos and metates or mortars and pestles. Seed-collecting continued during the relatively wet summer months. In the fall, fruit-picking, a minor activity at other seasons, provided about as many calories as hunting.

The El Riego settlement pattern reflected these seasonally scheduled activities, as microbands (families) camped, for one or two seasons, in or near whichever of the valley's five micro-environments (oasis, humid river bottoms and steppe, alluvial slopes, travertine slopes, canyons) was most productive at that time of year. There seem to have been three clusters of microband campsites in the valley, which may represent three bands that had established mutually recognized territories. Each microband site cluster is linked to a macroband campsite. These larger camps, where the usually dispersed families congregated in groups of 25 to 30, were most often located in the humid, lush river bottoms; they were occupied in the relatively wet summer season, when cactus leaves and grass seeds could be harvested and there were animals in the area to be hunted.

Toward the end of the El Riego phase, there is rather dubious evidence of the first steps toward agriculture; squash, amaranth, chili pepper, and avocado may have been planted. Only three or four squash seeds, not definitely of cultivated type, were found in El Riego levels; and the remains of the other plants were indistinguishable from those of wild forms. This is a problem that is frequently encountered when dealing with the earliest stages of agriculture. When humans first take plants or animals from their natural habitats and begin to tend them, those organisms will remain genetically and physically indistinguishable from their wild relatives. In the case of plants, such cultivated but genetically unchanged forms are called "cultivars". After generations, perhaps centuries, of human control and selection for desirable characteristics, such as large seeds, soft seed-cases and less brittle stalks, the plant may undergo genetic and morpho-

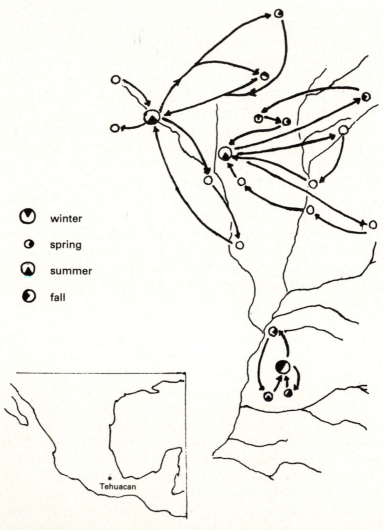

winter

spring

summer

fall

Tehuacan

Fig. 51. El Riego phase settlement pattern in the Tehuacan Valley (5.5 cm = 50 km). (After MacNeish 1978.)

logical changes which distinguish it from the wild form. At that point, it has become a domesticated "cultigen". Some plants may have been cultivated for centuries without developing such distinctive mutations. A possible example is *setaria*, which was more intensively collected than maize during the El Riego and Coxcatlan phases in the Tehuacan Valley; it might have been artificially planted and tended, but its seeds retained their wild appearance. In the cases of chili and avocado, the argument for their cultivation rests on the fact that they are not native to the Tehuacan Valley, and would have required irrigation to grow there. However, the possibility that they were brought back to campsites by long distance foragers cannot be excluded. In any case, even if planting and simple stream irrigation were practiced, they did not require expenditure of much time or labor, nor did they result in significant additions to the diet. Incipient agricultural activities did not yet affect seasonal movements or settlement patterns.

It is in the next, Coxcatlan phase (5000–3400 B.C.), that maize first appears in the archaeological record of Tehuacan. It was cultivated along with beans, mixta and moschata squash, gourds, amaranths, chili peppers, and trees that bore chupandilla plums, zapotes, and avocados. Of these plants, only mixta squash, amaranths, and chupandilla were native to the valley; the rest must have been imported from other parts of Mesoamerica where they were already under cultivation.

But what about maize? The tiny corncobs recovered from Coxcatlan levels had all the characteristics that Mangelsdorf had predicted would be present in the wild ancestral plant: a light husk, a single seed spike to which were attached a few pod-enclosed kernels, and a pollen-bearing tassel growing from the end of the spike. These traits would have allowed the plant to pollinate and disperse its seeds without human assistance. MacNeish therefore had good reason to think that his search had paid off, that he had discovered the very spot where maize was transformed from a wild to a domesticated plant. However, the absence of wild maize remains in the earlier El Riego levels should have aroused suspicion. If the wild ancestral maize was a native plant of the Tehuacan Valley, why had El Riego phase seed-collectors ignored it, while they gathered large quantities of setaria? And if wild maize was not native to Tehuacan, the Coxcatlan specimens, primitive-looking though they were, must have been first cultivated elsewhere and intentionally brought to the Valley. The issue of maize's origin was further clouded when other botanists began to question Mangelsdorf's assumption that maize was descended from a now-extinct wild ancestor. Apart from MacNeish's finds, the only evidence of this hypothesized plant was the presence of 80,000 year-old grains of maize pollen, found in lake bed cores from the Valley of Mexico. Since this was long before agriculture could have been practiced in the area, indeed long before the arrival of human beings, these pollen grains must have come from a wild form of maize. However, it is very doubtful whether maize pollen can be distinguished on the basis of size, surface configuration, or any other criteria, from pollen of a closely-related Meso-american grass, teosinte. Unlike the hypothetical wild ancestral maize, teosinte still grows wild in Mexico, Guatemala, and Honduras (but, interestingly, not in the Tehuacan Valley). It can be hybridized with maize, and in fact some of the Mesoamerican races of maize were evidently created by such crossing. Not surprisingly, genetic and morphological studies have shown that maize and teosinte are very closely related. Mangelsdorf and MacNeish have recently acknowledged this evidence of a close teosinte–maize relationship by suggesting that both may be descended from a common ancestor, "proto-maize–teosinte" (MacNeish 1978). But to accept this idea, we must believe that, while maize mutated so as to become more useful to human cultivators, teosinte regressed over time, developing smaller, more firmly encased seeds. It is

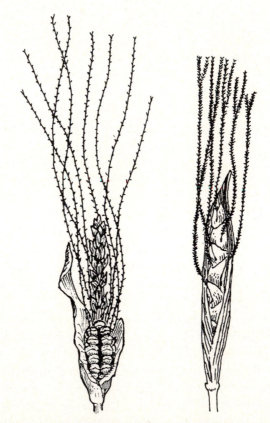

Fig. 52. Coxcatlan maize (reconstructed) (A) and (B) teosinte (¾ actual size). (After MacNeish 1964.)

more credible, as George Beadle (1977) and Mangelsdorf's former ally, Walton Galinat, have concluded, that today's wild teosinte is the surviving form of the ancestral plant from which maize was developed through human selection. If teosinte is indeed the ancestor of maize, the tiny corncobs from Tehuacan must be early domesticated specimens, differing from the wild form in having a tough spike with a cob and soft fruit-cases. These traits, which would have made maize more suitable for human use, could have appeared through mutations of a single gene, the tunicate allele (Flannery 1973).

MacNeish has estimated, on the basis of food remains preserved on living floors and in human feces, that the various cultivated plants constituted about 14% of the Coxcatlan phase diet. Seasonal subsistence activities differed little from those of El Riego times, except that while seeds were collected in the spring, crops were also planted, to be harvested during the summer.

The results of a recent analysis of human bones from Tehuacan suggest that the transition from El Riego to Coxcatlan may have entailed a much more abrupt dietary shift than MacNeish had originally hypothesized (Farnsworth et al. 1985). This conclusion is based on the ratios of isotopes of carbon and nitrogen found in bone collagen. Maize and other grasses differ from other plants in their intake of carbon 13, and the resulting distinctive isotope ratio is also found in the bones of humans or animals that consume these grasses. Unfortunately, bone collagen had not been preserved in many of the skeletons from Tehuacan; Farnsworth et al. had only one usable sample from the El Riego phase and one from the Coxcatlan phase, and these could only be compared to bones from a much later period, when agriculture was fully established in the area. However, other studies indicate that individual isotope ratios do not deviate significantly from population averages, so the small sample size may not be all that problematic. Another problem is the reliance, for several calculations, on assumptions of dubious validity. In any case, the observed ratios in the El Riego and Coxcatlan bones are quite different, and the latter resemble the ratios in the bones of later agricultural people. Farnsworth et al. estimate that 90% of the Coxcatlan diet consisted of maize or other grass seeds (e.g. *setaria*), or maguey and cacti, or meat from animals that fed on these plants. This tentative evidence of an abrupt dietary transition fits well with indications that maize and other cultigens were introduced to Tehuacan from elsewhere.

There are actually fewer occupations from the Coxcatlan phase than from the preceding phase; however, the macroband campsites were two or three times bigger, and both they and the microband camps were occupied longer, usually for two consecutive seasons. Because of the availability of spring-planted crops, spring through summer camps were most common. The territorial divisions of the preceding period apparently continued.

In the Abejas phase, 3400–2300 B.C., agriculture may have provided 25% of the diet. MacNeish excavated one site which, he reports, consisted of pit-houses arranged in a line along a stream terrace. This hamlet, he suggests, had been occupied year-round. However, multi-season macro-band camps were still in use, as were microband camps that were most frequently occupied during the winter. The stored agricultural produce was seemingly insufficient to allow bands to stay together through the lean winter months: they still had to disperse into family units to make it through this season by hunting.

Actually, the evidence for waterway hamlets is very slim (Flannery 1972). At one site, Ts 381, MacNeish and his team excavated an oval pit-house, about 4 m wide and 5.25 m long. Its sides had been reinforced with stone slabs, and post-molds showed that it had been roofed by laying brush and twigs on two upright posts and several slanting ones. Although this house lay in the midst of an extensive scatter of occupational debris, no other similar dwellings were discovered at this site. Plant remains were not found at Ts 381, so any statements about the seasonality or duration of the occupation are questionable. At another Abejas phase site, Ts 388, three groups of stone slabs, like those placed against the walls of the Ts 381 house, protruded above the surface, seemingly in alignment. Unfortunately, this site could not be excavated, because it lay in a field that was then under cultivation.

Abejas phase population seems to have been perhaps twice as large as that of the preceding phase; there may have been 300 to 600 people in the valley. Based on site clustering, they appear to have been divided into four territorial bands.

The next phase, Purron, 2300–1500 B.C., is very poorly represented in the Tehuacan Valley. We can say nothing about subsistence, population, or settlement pattern. What is known is that pottery-making was introduced during this phase, probably as a result of diffusion rather than independent invention. In the following Ajalpan phase, 1500–850 B.C., there may have been three or four hamlets, composed of wattle and daub houses in the valley. Agriculture is thought to have provided about 40% of the diet; the remainder was divided equally between hunting and gathering of wild plants. The hamlets were occupied year-round, task groups camping more briefly at other localities while they engaged in seasonal collecting and hunting. The Tehuacan sequence continues up to historic times, but already in the Ajalpan phase the valley was becoming marginal, as complex societies began to emerge in other parts of Mesoamerica.

The fact, alluded to before, that some of the earliest cultivated plants in the Tehuacan Valley, possibly including maize, were seemingly imported from elsewhere, implies that there should be evidence of comparably early or even earlier agricultural experimentation in other Mesoamerican regions. MacNeish himself found such evidence in the northeastern state of Tamaulipas, where gourds, chili peppers and pumpkins may have been cultivated before 5000 B.C. Pumpkins were definitely cultivated between 5000 and 3000 B.C., as were yellow and red common (kidney) beans. By 2500 B.C., maize of a domesticated variety, Nal-Tel, had been brought to Tamaulipas from the south.

Closer to Tehuacan, there is evidence of early agriculture in the Valley of Oaxaca, which MacNeish had bypassed because of its unpromising-looking shallow caves. The evidence comes from two such shallow caves, Guila Naquitz and Cueva Blanca. The three levels with Archaic remains at Guila Naquitz have been C14 dated to between 8700 and 6900 B.C., contemporaneous with the Ajuereado phase of Tehuacan. The preserved plant remains included: acorns, pinyon nuts, mesquite beans, prickly pear and organ cactus fruits, wild onions, hackberries, maguey, and representatives of more than a dozen other species. About 7000 B.C., small black beans, bottle gourd rinds and some squash or pumpkin seeds were deposited in the cave. These remains probably attest to the beginnings of cultivation in Oaxaca. Pollen samples from the cave deposits contain a few grains of another squash species (*C. moschata*) and pollen from either maize or teosinte. If these pollens were indeed brought in inadvertently by humans, as appears most likely, they constitute further evidence of incipient cultivation. Teosinte–maize probably could not have survived without human assistance in the cool, arid savanna thought to have existed in Oaxaca around 7000 B.C. (Schoenwetter 1974).

The occupation of nearby Cueva Blanca is C14 dated to about 3300 B.C. The material is very similar to that of the Coxcatlan phase of Tehuacan, showing a mixed economy based on collecting, hunting, and some cultivation of maize, beans, and squash. The dietary staples and the seasonal scheduling of their utilization were essentially the same at Cueva Blanca and Coxcatlan Cave, despite the difference in the environmental settings of these sites. Coxcatlan lies in an arid tropical thorn forest dominated by stands of cacti; Cueva Blanca is situated in a temperate woodland zone, which includes oaks and pinyon pines among its flora. Nevertheless, at both sites, the most important food plants were maguey (best known to modern North Americans as the plant from which tequila is distilled), organ cactus, prickly pear, and the tree legumes, mesquite and guaje. Maguey, which had to be roasted for from one to five days to render it edible, was one of the few plants available during the dry season. Cactus fruits were collected at the end of the dry season, before the summer rains turned them to mush. Mesquite and guaje pods could be collected during the wet summer season. The most important meat sources in Tehuacan and Oaxaca were white-tailed deer and cottontail rabbits; both species were available year-round. However, toward the end of the dry season and early in the rainy season, when families coalesced into macrobands, priority was given to rapid collection of maturing plants. No one could be spared for hunting, so only cottontails and other small animals that blundered into traps were eaten at these times. In late fall and winter, most plants no longer bore fruit, but deer-hunting was at its best. But as the dry season continued, the deer grew wary of the hunters and moved off into the mountains. With hunting becoming less productive, people now had to turn to collecting "starvation" plants such as maguey and pochote (Ceiba) root.

As long as the human populations in the Mexican highlands remained small, as was dictated by dry season scarcity, they posed no threat to the plants and animals on which they relied for food. Although variations in abundance would occur from year to year, the hunter–gatherers could have continued to get by indefinitely by exploiting these resources in their usual cyclical fashion. However, as Kent Flannery (1968a) has suggested, this equilibrium system was destabilized by the small, accidental genetic changes that occurred in teosinte–maize. The harvesting of teosinte and other annual grasses, such as *setaria*, had been only a minor subsistence activity; but the tough spike and cob and the soft fruit-case of the mutant maize made it more profitable to plant and harvest. Thus was set off a positive feedback system. The more maize was cultivated, the greater the chance that hybridization would occur, resulting in varieties offering higher yield. Higher yields permitted the growth of human population, which led to the adoption of more intensive forms of cultivation. Maize had to be planted in the spring and harvested in the early fall; these activities cut into the time that could be devoted to collecting wild plants or hunting during those seasons.

Maize alone could not have provided the ancient Mexicans with adequate nutrients: it lacks lysine, an amino acid that human beings require. However, if beans are eaten with maize, they supply the missing lysine, thus making maize a good source of protein. It is astonishing, at first glance, that since 5000 B.C. Mexicans have been eating maize and beans together. Obviously, they were not aware of the biochemical processes that make this practice beneficial, so how did the complementary use of maize and beans develop? Perhaps farmers simply took advantage of the plants' habits; bean vines are often found in fields of maize, clinging to the stalks (Flannery 1973). However, beans were evidently cultivated in some parts of Mesoamerica (e.g. Tamaulipas) and in Peru many centuries prior to the cultivation of maize in those areas; so it would be a mistake to conclude that beans were domesticated and eaten just because they happened to grow in the vicinity of maize. Perhaps the custom spread

174

because those groups that did combine maize and beans in their diet enjoyed better health and a lower mortality rate than those that did not, and so held a competitive advantage over them.

Even when complemented by beans, maize does not provide enough protein for lactating women or young children (Kaplan 1971). The early Mexican farmers obtained most of their high-quality protein from deer, rabbits, and other hunted game; but as the population grew and more land was put under cultivation, game must have become scarce. Unlike the farming peoples of the Old World, the farmers of Mesoamerica did not domesticate any large herbivores. There were few species native to the region that were potentially domesticable. Horse and camel had become extinct by 7000 B.C., and the ranges of bison, antelope, and mountain sheep did not extend south into Mexico. Deer, which were present, appear to have been unsuitable for domestication, since they were not domesticated in the Old World. Perhaps the pig-like Mesoamerican peccary was also too difficult to tame. However the Mexicans did domesticate dogs, turkeys, and ducks. The famous ceramic Colima dogs seem to portray animals that were intentionally fattened prior to slaughter and consumption, and large numbers of burnt and split dog bones have been found at late prehistoric sites in Mexico. Michael Harner (1977) and Marvin Harris (1977) have suggested that hunted game and these few small domesti-

Fig. 53. Colima ceramic dog (42 × 25 cm).

cates did not supply enough protein for the millions of people who lived in late prehistoric Mesoamerica. They speculate that cannibalism, associated with human sacrifice, may have arisen as a cultural response to protein scarcity. Human sacrifice was a feature of Mesoamerican civilizations going back to the Olmec (ca. 1000 B.C.); there are even hints of sacrificial rites in the decapitation and charred bones in a collective burial in the El Riego phase of Tehuacan (MacNeish 1964). However, human sacrifice reached its bloody climax among the Aztec, who annually sacrificed tens of thousands of war captives. According to Spanish accounts, the privilege of partaking of the victims' flesh was reserved for priests, nobles and outstanding warriors. Clearly, sacrificial cannibalism was not a solution to the problem of protein scarcity, since the great majority of the Aztec population was excluded from consumption of human flesh.

In the Old World, the larger domesticated animals, such as cattle, water buffalo, and horse, were used to haul plows and wheeled vehicles. In the New World, the simple digging stick was never abandoned, nor were wheeled vehicles used. However, ancient native Americans were not ignorant of the principle of the wheel. Toy ceramic dogs, mounted on four wheels, have been found in Mexico, near Veracruz. Presumably, in the absence of beasts of burden to pull them, full-sized wheeled vehicles would not have been much more efficient than human porters or litter-bearers. Ultimately, the failure of the New World civilizations fully to exploit the wheel's potential precluded the development of a complex technology such as that which emerged in medieval Europe. The technological advantage enjoyed by the Europeans facilitated their conquest of the New World.

Fig. 54. Dog figurine on wheels, Veracruz, Mexico, Classic period.

Flannery's hypothesis of a positive feedback loop set into motion by accidental mutation of teosinte–maize offers one plausible answer to the question posed earlier (p. 165): Why did agriculture develop in Mexico but not in the Great Basin? The simple reason could be that teosinte grew in Mexico but not in the Basin. However, this explanation is not entirely satisfying, because cultivation of other plants – amaranths, squash, chili and avocado – seems to have preceded the domestication of maize, at least in the Tehuacan Valley if not everywhere in Mesoamerica. There is no comparable evidence of cultivation of native plants by the Desert Archaic inhabitants of the Great Basin. Why didn't pickleweed or Indian rice grass, on which the Basin gatherers depended so heavily, develop large seeds or other traits favored by man?

Perhaps the answer lies in differing techniques of gathering. In the Great Basin, grass seeds were beaten into baskets. This meant that the gatherers were selecting for the same characteristic – an easily shattered rachis – that was necessary for naturally-occurring seed dispersal. In contrast, one of the early human-selected traits of maize was its less brittle spike. If seeds are picked by hand, as is the traditional practice in Mesoamerica, seed-cases that don't shatter when touched will be selected for, and then replanted to create a population of plants with this desirable trait. Basin-style seed-beating would not have discriminated between small and large seeds, so it would not have encouraged the segregation of large-seeded races, unlike Mesoamerican hand-picking. However, it now appears that seed-beating may have been an innovation of the Shoshoni; pre-Shoshoni gatherers seem to have used horn sickles. Since the effects of this technique should have been similar to those produced by hand-picking, differences in harvesting techniques do not fully explain why agriculture should have developed only in Mesoamerica. A recent reassessment (Bettinger and Baumhoff 1982) of the evidence from the Great Basin suggests that the pre-Shoshoni inhabitants were more dependent on hunting than on seed-gathering. Their reliance on this male-dominated activity may have entailed population control by means of female infanticide. In contrast, the population of the Tehuacan Valley seems to have grown continuously after 7000 B.C., while the percentage of meat in the diet steadily decreased. Perhaps differences in the availability of game, in the diversity of edible plants, and in the rates of population growth, may account for the emergence of agriculture in Mesoamerica but not in the Great Basin. It should be noted that while agriculture did not develop indigenously in the Basin, at a relatively late date (ca. 900–1300 A.D.) maize-growing was adopted by the Fremont culture of the northeastern Basin.

One interesting fact that emerges from a review of the earliest evidence of cultivation in Mesoamerica is that most of the first probable cultivars

– gourds, squash, chilis, avocados and amaranths – were not staple foods. This suggests the possibility that cultivation originated among hunter–gatherer bands that already had adequate supplies of essential wild plant foods. The location of stands of these staple wild plants probably determined the seasonal movements of these bands through their territories. The contribution of such plants as avocado or chili peppers to the diet was probably too slight to warrant long side-trips to the distant spots where they grew naturally; but these plants were nevertheless desirable. If their seeds could be taken and planted in the vicinity of the band's usual seasonal encampments, the need to go on repeated long trips to retrieve small quantities would be obviated. Once the habit of cultivation was established, it could later be extended to other plants. Theoretically, it is probably easiest to explain agriculture as emerging from an already sedentary context. People who were permanently encamped in an area of abundant wild resources would have been unwilling to go very far away to harvest other wild resources. They would have had a stronger incentive than other, more nomadic groups to transplant stands of desirable plants from their native environments to locations closer to the village.

However, the cultural sequence from the Mexican highlands actually shows that a gap of 2,000 or more years intervened between the beginning of agriculture and the establishment of permanent villages. This evidence is in marked contrast to that from the Near East, where the first villages, such as the lake-side settlement at Eynan, in northern Israel, seem to have been occupied at the same time (ca. 9000 B.C.) as the first cultivation of cereals and legumes and the first herding of sheep and goats. As we have seen, there is evidence in the New World of pre-agricultural villages at Koster and other Archaic sites.

Recent controversial finds at Zohapilco, in the Valley of Mexico, hint at the existence of a sedentary lake-side occupation there as early as 6000 B.C. (Niederberger 1979). No remains of actual structures have been found, but pollen grains, plant remains and animal bones attest to the variety of resources that were available at this site through the year. At all seasons, fish and water-fowl could be taken from the lake, and deer and rabbits could be hunted or trapped in the forests on the nearby mountain slopes. During the wet summer, supplements to the diet included snakes, turtles, axlotls (a kind of amphibian) and several plants: teosinte, squash, amaranth and ground cherry (*Physalis*). Grinding stones show that seeds were processed at Zohapilco, but there is no conclusive proof that cultivation was practiced.

At other sites in Mesoamerica, there is much later evidence of sedentism. It is possible that pit-house hamlets were occupied year-round during the Abejas phase (3400–2300 B.C.) in the Tehuacan Valley, but we have already seen how slim the evidence is. There is similarly meager evidence of village life in one of the Chantuto shell middens on the Pacific coast of Chiapas, where an apparent house floor of clay dates to about 2700 B.C. (Stark and Voorhies 1978). MacNeish has recently reported his discovery of large villages, subsisting on fish and shellfish, on the coast of Belize; these villages are said to date from the "Melinda" phase, 4200–3300 B.C. (details have not yet been published). During the next phase, "Progreso", 3300–2500 B.C., there seems to have been a population movement from the coast to the flood-plains of rivers, where agriculture may have been practiced (Zeitlin 1984). This shift in settlement and subsistence may account for the initial occupation of the Cuello site at around 2000 B.C. (2400 B.C., calibrated date). Flotation of soil samples from Cuello has recently yielded evidence of the cultivation of both maize and root crops. From the beginning, the inhabitants of the site produced well-made pottery; some 25 varieties of "Swasey" ware have been recognized. Most of the pottery is red-slipped, and some vessels bear incised decoration. A lime-plastered platform, upon which a thatch-roofed hut had presumably once stood, was built at Cuello at about 1800 B.C. (2200 B.C., calibrated date). Layer upon layer of platforms and courtyards, many seemingly of a ceremonial character, were laid down above this structure over time, culminating around 200 A.D. in the construction of a pyramid. This structure and its associated artifacts are clearly Mayan, and the continuity of occupation of the same spot strongly suggests that the earliest inhabitants were also Maya (Hammond 1977, 1982b; Hammond et al. 1979).

The first really solid evidence of permanent agricultural villages in the Tehuacan Valley comes from the Ajalpan phase, 1500–850 B.C. In Oaxaca, villages were first established around 1700 B.C. It appears likely that the widespread shift to sedentary agriculture in Mesoamerica after 2000 B.C. resulted from the improvement of maize, which only now began to exceed wild mesquite in its yield (200 kilograms of shelled kernels per hectare). This was three times the yield of the earliest cultivated maize. It now became worthwhile to settle down beside cornfields, rather than wander between naturally occurring stands of other plants (Flannery 1973).

EARLY FARMING, VILLAGES AND CERAMICS IN ECUADOR

Maize was apparently adopted rapidly by people living in Central America and northern South America, even before the Mexican farmers had developed its most productive varieties. By 3200 B.C., maize had reached the Peruvian highlands. Radiocarbon dates from recently excavated sites in northern Argentina and Chile indicate that maize was introduced to those areas as early as 3000 to 2700 B.C. (Lynch 1983).

Maize had probably been brought to the coast of Ecuador by 2500 B.C., and perhaps much earlier. Recently, maize phytoliths are reported to have been found in the Las Vegas shell midden, in levels dated to 6000 or even 7000 B.C. (Stothert 1985). Corroboration of this startling discovery is necessary; if valid, it could call into question the presumed Mexican origin of maize.

Fairly convincing evidence of maize cultivation in Ecuador around 3000–2500 B.C. comes from Real Alto and other sites of the Valdivia culture. Designs on Valdivia pottery have been plausibly interpreted as portraying large and small varieties of maize, and a single probable kernel impression has been found on a vessel's surface (Zevallos et al. 1977). Phytoliths recovered from the soil of Real Alto have been identified as derived from maize. The numerous manos and metates found at Valdivia sites, and the presence of sites at inland locations suitable for agriculture, also seem to imply cultivation and consumption of maize. Various traces of other cultigens have recently been reported from Valdivia sites: phytoliths of achira (a root crop), Canavalia beans, and imprints of cotton textiles. Numerous clay and stone spindle whorls (used to make cotton into yarn) offer further proof of cotton-weaving (Damp 1984).

Not everyone is convinced that the Valdivia people grew maize. A study of an admittedly rather small sample of human teeth from a Valdivia cemetery revealed no caries (cavities) among them – a most unusual state of dental health in a population that was supposedly eating a lot of carbohydrate-rich, plaque-forming maize (Turner 1978). Caries *do* occur in teeth that belonged to members of the culture that followed Valdivia in coastal Ecuador, the Machalilla culture (ca. 1400–900 B.C.). Recently, maize kernels were recovered by flotation of soil at a Machalilla site called La Ponga, which lies 15 km east of Valdivia (Lippi, Bird, and Stemper 1984). Thus, maize was definitely present in coastal Ecuador after 1400 B.C., but its earlier presence is still debatable. Nevertheless, the accumulating evidence that maize was present much farther south in the Andes by 3000–2500 B.C. tends to support the inference of its cultivation in Ecuador at that time.

The Valdivia culture has been the focus of a heated argument between proponents of diffusion and independent invention. Valdivia sites contain some of the earliest pottery in the New World, dated by several C14 assays to about 2700 B.C. (there is also an inconsistently early date of 3200 B.C., uncalibrated). Only the site of Puerto Hormiga, on the coast of Colombia, has yielded pottery that may be earlier (ca. 3100–2500 B.C., uncalibrated). Valdivia pottery was thick-walled and not perfectly symmetrical. The vessels were built up from clay coils. Their surfaces were usually smoothed and highly polished, and were occasionally covered with a red slip. Various techniques of surface decoration were employed:

incision, grooving, scraping, rocker-stamping, punctation, excision and appliqué. These techniques, the decorative motifs used and the shapes of the vessels have close parallels in Early to Middle Jomon pottery, found at sites on the Japanese island of Kyushu. This Jomon pottery dates from the same period as the Valdivia material, but it has antecedents in Japan as early as 10,000 B.C., whereas the fairly sophisticated Valdivia pottery seems to appear quite suddenly, without such a long developmental sequence behind it. Betty Meggers and the late Clifford Evans, who

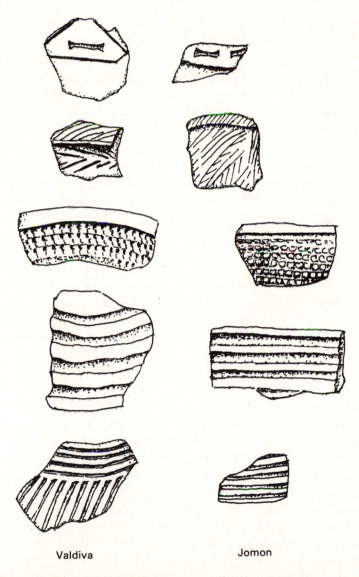

Valdiva   Jomon

Fig. 55. Valdivia potsherds (left) compared with Jomon potsherds (right).

excavated at the Valdivia sites, have argued (1969) that the Jomon–Valdivia stylistic similarities show that pottery-making was introduced to the natives of coastal Ecuador by Japanese fishermen, who had been blown from their home waters by a storm and carried across the Pacific by ocean currents. This diffusionary explanation of Jomon–Valdivia similarities would probably be accepted without qualms by other archaeologists, were it not for the great distance of 15,000 km (8,000 nautical miles) separating the proposed donor and recipient cultures, and if the sensitive issue of Old World–New World contact were not involved. Critics of the Meggers–Evans theory have argued that small dug-out canoes, which the Jomon culture is known to have possessed, would not have been capable of a drift voyage across the Pacific (McEwen and Dickson 1978). The crew of such a vessel would have had to survive more than a year and a half in the cold North Pacific, and in order to reach Ecuador they would have had to steer their boat across several countervailing currents that would have carried them off to the west. Taking another tack, critics of the diffusion theory have suggested that the similarities between Valdivia and Jomon surface decorations merely reflect the limited potential range of variation in designs that can be created by incising clay. The resemblance of these wares, according to this view, is the result of accidental convergence, not culture contact. The case for convergence has been strengthened by recently discovered evidence of an earlier, somewhat less sophisticated pottery style, called San Pedro, which was stratified below Valdivia pottery at the site of Valdivia itself (Bischof and Gamboa 1972). The lowest strata, which lay below the San Pedro level, did not contain any pottery. The San Pedro pottery, while more primitive than the Valdivia material, is still too well-made to mark the first tentative steps in ceramic manufacture; and the absence of earlier, cruder proto-types in the underlying levels suggests that pottery-making was introduced to coastal Ecuador from elsewhere. However, the incised linear decorations on San Pedro sherds do not bear much resemblance to Jomon motifs, so the case for a Japanese stimulus to Valdivia pottery-making is weakened. Nevertheless, some other external source for Valdivia pottery must still be sought. The most likely source is Colombia, where comparably early and stylistically similar pottery is known from Puerto Hormiga. The presence of maize at Valdivia sites also points to influence from a more northern group, situated closer to the Mesoamerican center of maize domestication.

The Valdivia site of Real Alto, excavated in 1974–5, provides evidence of a culture as advanced as any known contemporary culture, either in Mexico or Peru, in the latter half of the third millennium B.C. (Lathrap, Marcos and Zeidler 1977). The site was originally occupied by shellfish-collectors, but people using pottery of Valdivia II style settled there around 2600 B.C. (3400 B.C., calibrated date). Most of the excavated material comes from the following Valdivia III period, about 2200 B.C. (2900 B.C., calibrated date). The Valdivia III settlement took the form of a roughly rectangular plaza, flanked by two low mounds. The so-called "Fiesta" mound measured 50 by 37 meters at its base, and 13 by 9 meters at its summit. It had been re-surfaced with yellow clay at least four times, and eight successive structures had been built on top of it. Pits dug into the floors of these buildings contained seafood delicacies such as lobster, scallops, and turtles, as well as deer bones and broken drinking bowls; these were presumably the remains of ceremonial feasts. The doorway of the Fiesta house faced the "Charnel House" mound across the plaza. The ovoid charnel house situated on top of this mound contained a number of burials, mostly secondary bundles. At the threshold, a woman had been buried in a grave lined with manos and metates. The remains of a dismembered male had been placed in a grave beside the woman's, and another nearby secondary grave held the re-deposited bones of seven men. It has been suggested that the eight males may have been sacrificed to accompany the deceased woman. If so, we may infer that at least some women enjoyed high status in Valdivia society. There are other grounds for this inference. The average dwelling at Real Alto was an elliptical pit-house, with walls of upright logs coated with mud, measuring 12 by 8 meters. A house of this size could have held an extended family of 10 or more people. Such large households are most common in societies where matrilocal residence is the norm, i.e. where women remain in their mothers' households after marriage. In matrilocal societies, women's status tends to be higher than in those where other residence modes prevail; women may own the fields or houses, and may even enjoy political power, as, for example, among the Iroquois of western New York. Another possible indication of the importance of women in Valdivia society is the predominance of female representations among the stone and ceramic

Fig. 56. Female figurine from Valdivia.

figurines found at Valdivia sites. Until more evidence becomes available, these speculations about high female status must remain tentative. In any case, if Real Alto's population was really about 1,500, as its excavators estimate, at least a rudimentary differentiation of the inhabitants according to ranked statuses was probably necessary to maintain order.

THE DEVELOPMENT OF SEDENTISM AND AGRICULTURE IN PERU

By 3200 B.C., maize had been brought to the highlands of Peru. Its impact there was not revolutionary, since the people of that region had already been cultivating plants for many centuries. In fact, agriculture may have begun in the Andes before it did in Mexico.

Peru, like Mesoamerica, is a region of great ecological diversity. It is divided into three radically different environmental zones. The Pacific coastal strip is an extremely arid desert, which receives less than 10 cm (4 ins) of rain a year. However, the moisture of mid-winter fogs supports isolated patches of green meadow, called *lomas*, on the upper slopes of hills, facing the sea. There is good evidence that the lomas were more widespread in early prehistoric times than they are at present. Their shrinkage may have been caused by climatic change, but more probably human over-exploitation was responsible. Among the lomas plants were some that bore tubers, bulbs, or rhizomes, on which human gatherers could have subsisted. The lomas vegetation also provided food for deer and other smaller mammals that could have been hunted or trapped. The coastal strip is cut across by some 40 river valleys, in which trees and seed and pod-bearing plants flourished in prehistoric times. Apart from the resources that were available in the lomas and river valleys, the abundance of marine resources – fish, shellfish, birds and sea mammals – that could be obtained at, or close to, the Pacific shore, also drew settlers to the coastal region.

The narrow coastal strip reaches a maximum width of about 100 km (60 miles) in northern Peru, but it is much narrower to the south. It is everywhere abruptly terminated to the east by the Andes mountains. The rugged peaks and plateaus of the Andes, rising higher than 4,800 m (16,000 ft) above sea level, constitute the second major environmental zone of Peru, the *sierra*. The sierra actually comprises several diverse micro-environmental zones, which are found at different altitudes. The *puna*, a cold, damp grassland, is located between 3,600 and 4,100 m (12,000 and 13,500 ft) above sea level. Early inhabitants of the puna could have hunted native *vicuña* (a deer-sized wild camelid), white-tailed deer, *huemal* deer, and perhaps the *guanaco* (another wild camelid). Below the puna, at 2,900 to 3,600 m (9,500 to 12,000 ft), lie humid woodlands, which include some fairly large trees. The fauna of this zone, which could have been hunted by the ancient inhabitants, include deer, guanaco, wild guinea pig, and rodents. Today, root crops are grown in the woodland zone, and in the lower reaches of the puna. A zone of thorn forest scrub lies below the woodlands, at an altitude of 2,300 to 2,900 m (7,500 to 9,600 ft). This zone bears a resemblance to the ecological setting of Coxcatlan Cave in the Tehuacan Valley; however, maguey and mesquite, which are common in the Andean scrub zone today, were probably imported from Mexico after the Spanish conquest. The dry and wet seasons are well defined in this zone, and deer, guanaco and rodents are seasonally available. Where permanent streams run through the thorn forest, gallery forests line their banks. Today, in this riverine microenvironment, maize, beans, lucuma and other crops are grown. Below 2,300 m (7,500 ft) lies a very hot, dry zone, with desert vegetation.

On the eastern slopes of the Andes, there is a rapid descent from the puns to the lowland jungles, or *selva*, of the Amazon basin. Stratified between these extremes are a vertical series of micro-environments, containing a wide variety of plants and animals. Some parts of the eastern slopes are unforested; other areas, with heavy vegetation, are called the *montaña*. Very little archaeological evidence is available from either the *montaña* or the selva, but finds made in the sierra and on the coast suggest that the tropical forest zone may have been the original source of Andean agriculture.

As we have seen (Chapter 4), big game hunters, using fluted fishtail points, had occupied the sierra by about 9000 B.C. They hunted horse and giant sloth for a while, but when these animals became extinct, they came to rely more heavily on hunting deer and camelids and trapping smaller mammals. The shift to smaller game may be reflected in the replacement of fluted points, after 9000 B.C., by stemmed, triangular, and ovoid types. Such points have been found at Pachamachay Cave in the puna zone, and at Guitarrero Cave and several caves near Ayacucho, which lie in the thorn forest and humid woodland zones.

The hunting bands that camped at Pachamachay from 7000 to 1500 B.C. preyed almost exclusively on *vicuña*. Deer, rodents and birds also provided them with a small amount of meat. This meat diet was supplemented by a little vegetal food, including *Opuntia* (cactus) fruit, *Chenopodium* and amaranth seeds, wild legumes, and totora roots. Various grasses were collected to be used for fiber or fuel, and other plants recovered from the cave deposits may have been used medicinally. These resources may have enabled the inhabitants of Pachamachay to camp there year-round (Rick 1980).

In the Lauricocha caves, which are also situated in the puna, there were more deer than camelid bones in the layers dated from 7500 to 6000 B.C.

However, after 6000 B.C., camelid hunting became predominant.

Guitarrero Cave (Lynch 1980) lies in a high mountain valley, the Callejón de Huaylas, at an elevation of 2,580 m (8,500 ft) above sea level; the dominant vegetation in the area is thorn forest scrub. There are some inconsistencies in the C14 dates and artifact types from the lowest strata of the cave, but it seems most likely that they date to about 8500 B.C. These levels, referred to as complexes I and II, yielded remains of a wide variety of hunted and trapped animals. Deer provided most of the meat during this early period; other minor sources of meat were rabbits, rodents, skunks and birds (tinamou and pigeon). A few bones of camelids were present in Complex II, ca. 8000–5600 B.C. Complexes III and IV were, unfortunately, badly disturbed, and therefore cannot be dated with any confidence. However, there is evidence of increasing dependence upon camelids, and less hunting of deer, such that camelids surpassed deer in dietary importance in Complex IV. This change in relative frequency may reflect the introduction of camelid herding.

The inhabitants of Guitarrero Cave also collected a variety of plants which they used for food, fiber and fuel. Grasses were used as bedding. Fiber, made from the leaves of plants of the pineapple family, was used for cordage, and to make twined baskets and bags. Among the food items found in Complex II, rhizomes and tubers provided carbohydrates, fruits (lucuma, pacay, *Solanum hispidum*) and squash provided vitamins and minerals, and beans added protein to the diet. Chili peppers (*ají*) were used to flavor meals, but they also had nutritional value. Remarkably, the common beans and lima beans from Complex II were apparently domesticates. A few beans were recovered from level IIa, as was a single seemingly domesticated pepper. This may mean that beans and peppers had been domesticated prior to about 8600–8000 B.C., somewhere in the Andean region; however, in view of the small number of beans found in the whole of Complex II – only 5 – and the evidence of widespread disturbance of the cave deposits, there is good reason to be skeptical of this conclusion. Dates for domesticated common beans in a reportedly very secure context in Complex IIe (5730 B.C.) and lima beans in IId (ca. 6500 B.C.) are more credible. Wild beans, it should be noted, do not grow in the Andean sierra, near Guitarrero Cave; but they are native to the *montaña*, the forested eastern slopes. Lima beans and peppers were also probably brought to the highlands from the eastern slopes or the Amazonian lowlands. The conclusion is inescapable: agricultural experimentation must have begun in the tropical forest, perhaps before 8500 B.C., certainly before 6500 B.C. Trade and other forms of social interaction presumably resulted in the spread of cultigens westward and upward into the highlands.

Maize cobs were present in Complex III of Guitarrero Cave, and their uniformity suggests that they were deposited not long after the initial introduction of corn from the north. The Complex III maize may date from some time between 5000 and 3000 B.C.; this date agrees with evidence from the Ayacucho region, where maize first appeared around 4000 to 3000 B.C.

The Ayacucho project was organized by Richard S. MacNeish, whose central role in the investigation of early Mesoamerican agriculture has already been discussed. Like his earlier Tehuacan project, MacNeish's Ayacucho project was an attempt to trace the development of agriculture from a gathering–hunting base, in a highland valley. He and his colleagues succeeded in finding and excavating sites in a variety of micro-environmental settings; but unfortunately the preservation of plants at these sites was poor, so the transition to agriculture could not be documented in the kind of detail that was possible in Tehuacan (MacNeish 1971, 1977, 1978).

The earliest phases recognized by MacNeish are of dubious significance. The "tools" of the Pacaicasa complex, 20,000–13,500 B.C., appear to be nothing more than jagged chunks of rock, fallen from the roof of Pikimachay Cave (Lynch 1983). The next complex, Ayacucho, 13,500–11,500 B.C., includes some undoubted artifacts, but is inadequately dated by a single C14 determination, which is probably too early. The Huanta phase, represented by a small number of artifacts, corresponds to the Paleo-Indian big game-hunting stage, preceding 9000 B.C. The following Puente phase is dated at 9000 to 7100 B.C. Six microband camps of this period have been excavated. The families that occupied these sites probably moved seasonally between micro-environments. During the wet season (October to March), they camped in the riverine thorn forests, where they trapped wild guinea pigs and other small mammals, and also did some hunting of larger game. The microbands moved up to the humid woodlands during the dry season (April to September). There they hunted deer and a smaller number of camelids.

There seems to have been a population increase during the next phase, called Jaywa (7100–5800 B.C.); twelve excavated components and one surface site date to this phase, twice as many sites as are known from the preceding phase. The seasonal scheduling of resource use and camp location remained the same. A few bits of plant material recovered from human feces, some charred seeds, and a grinding stone, suggest that in addition to the trapping of small animals, plant-collecting provided some food during the wet season.

Population growth evidently continued through the Piki phase, 5800–4550 B.C., which is represented at 18 surface sites and 24 excavated components at seven caves. The wet-season microband camps of this period became larger, as people began to exploit new food sources. Piki phase living floors at Pikimachay Cave yielded few animal bones, but did contain wild seeds, gourd rinds, and seeds of domesticated quinoa (Chenopodium) and squash; these remains attest to greater reliance on plant-gathering, and the beginnings of agriculture. It is noteworthy that farming seems to have begun somewhat later in Ayacucho than at Guitarrero Cave. On the other hand, the people of Ayacucho apparently took the first steps toward the domestication of the guinea pig. At Puente Cave, the bones of these creatures occur in such large numbers, relative to other small mammals that were trapped in the vicinity of the cave during the wet season, that it seems probable that the guinea pig had been tamed.

Cultivation of maize, potatoes, squash, gourds, common beans, lucuma, quinoa, and possibly coca, is attested at sites of the Chihua phase, 4550–3100 B.C. These crops, supplemented by some wild plants and meat from guinea pigs and hunted game, supported large, multi-family wet-season camps in the riverine and dry thorn scrub forest zones. Higher up, in the puna, microband hunting from dry season camps continued, but stone hoes found at these campsites suggest that potatoes may have been cultivated as well. An increase in the number of surface sites (from 18 of the Piki phase to 27 Chihua sites) indicates some population growth, although the rate of growth may have been slower than in earlier periods.

The valley's population continued to increase in the next phase, Cachi,

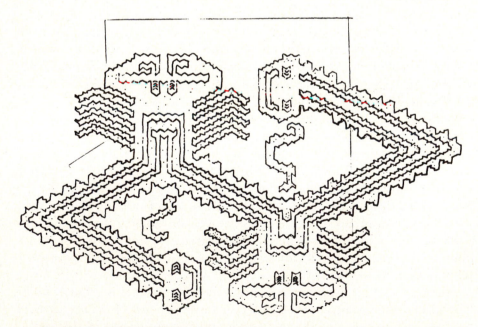

Fig. 57. Textile from Huaca Prieta, with design showing stylized crabs and snakes (original length ca. 40 cm; drawing by J. Reilly). (After Bird 1963.)

188

3100–1750 B.C., which is represented at 50 sites. Two separate subsistence and settlement systems developed at higher and lower elevations. Some groups herded tame camelids and hunted wild ones in the high puna during the dry season, and moved down to the low puna or woodlands to cultivate potatoes during the wet season. At lower altitudes, agricultural hamlets were occupied year-round. Seasonally, task groups from these permanent sites camped at caves, while they planted or harvested crops, collected wild plants, or hunted. Camelid herding may have begun somewhat earlier in the Ayacucho region than at the puna site of Pachamachay to the northwest, where the transition from hunting to herding occurred between 2200 and 1500 B.C.

It is obviously premature to jump to general conclusions on the basis of the Ayacucho data, which have as yet been only sketchily reported. The evidence that has been published appears to support the population pressure theory of agricultural origins. The population of the Ayacucho region seems to have grown steadily after 9000 B.C. Pressed to find more food, the inhabitants first developed an efficient seasonal schedule (Puente phase); next, they began to eat more seeds and roots (Jaywa phase); then they experimented with plant cultivation and animal domestication (Piki phase). Increasing reliance on agriculture followed (Chihua phase); this led to sedentism, but did not result in any marked acceleration of the population growth rate, which had been faster in the preceding phases.

Archaeological data from the Peruvian coast also suggest that the adoption of agriculture, which occurred much later than in the highlands, was the result rather than the cause of rapid population growth (Cohen 1977b, Patterson 1971). The coastal sequence is best known from surveys and excavations conducted in or near the Chillón, Lurín, and Chilca river valleys on the central coast. Little can be said about the earliest inhabitants of this region; a possible kill site suggests that they may have hunted mastodon and giant ground sloth. After the extinction of the megafauna, the coastal bands probably shifted to hunting deer and collecting plants and marine shellfish. The archaeological record becomes clearer after 6000 B.C. Small temporary campsites of the Arenal and Luz complexes (6000–5000 B.C.) have been found in areas that, in ancient times, supported lomas vegetation. The refuse from these sites consists of marine mollusk shells and bones of fish, birds, and land mammals. Judging from the relative amounts of shell and bone, hunting was a more important activity than shellfish-collecting. The styles of the spear-points used by the Arenal hunters indicate their close relationship to the Jaywa phase inhabitants of Ayacucho. In addition to the animal remains, rinds of bottle gourds have been recovered from the lomas sites. It is not certain whether these were wild or cultivated plants (see p. 161), but in any case, they could not have grown in the arid coastal environment where the sites are located, so they must have been brought to the lomas from the Chillón river valley. A few grinding stones suggest that seeds of wild plants were a minor dietary supplement.

Seeds evidently became a more important food source in the following phase, Canario (5000–4200 B.C.). More seeds of wild plants, and more grinding stones, have been found at Canario sites than at sites of the preceding period. Marine shellfish also increase in number, while remains of land mammals decrease. Canario artifact styles correspond to those of the related Piki phase of Ayacucho. But unlike Ayacucho, where quinoa and squash were cultivated by this time, there is no evidence of agriculture at the Ancón-Chillón sites.

About 100 km south of the Ancón-Chillón area, near the valley of the Chilca River, a permanent village of oval pit-houses was established at the site of Paloma before 5000 B.C. The year-round occupation was apparently based not on agriculture but on efficient harvesting of wild resources of the coast, lomas, and river valley, from a convenient central location. A similar situation permitted year-round occupation of base camps near the Lurin valley. The inhabitants of these camps subsisted primarily on fish and shellfish.

Only three sites of the Corbina phase, 4200 to 3600 B.C., are known in the Ancón-Chillón area. The next phase, Encanto, is better represented by 15 temporary campsites. The excavated refuse at these sites was dominated by shellfish and fish; a small number of deer bones were also present, as well as gourds and wild legumes and fruits. Large piles of grass seeds, and the grinding stones used to process them, point to a significant amount of seeds in the diet. The first evidence of cultivation of edible plants in the Ancón-Chillón region – 26 large squash seeds – also comes from Encanto phase sites.

Population growth over time is not obvious from the number of sites of each phase in the Ancón-Chillón sequence. An estimated growth rate of less than .01% per year can only be inferred indirectly, from the steady decrease in bones of hunted deer, the increasing reliance on shellfish and seeds, and the movement of campsites ever farther away from the river valley (Cohen 1977b). By Encanto times, hunting and gathering seem to have been degrading the lomas vegetation, which may also have been adversely affected by climatic change. The evidence of continuous contact with highland groups that were practicing agriculture before 6000 B.C. suggests that the Ancón-Chillón people knew about agriculture, but only turned to it after 3600 B.C., when they were forced to do so by population growth and the depletion of local wild resources.

The first permanent village in the Ancón-Chillón region was the Pampa site (2500–2300 B.C., 3300 B.C., calibrated date). Sedentary life was probably related to increasing reliance on cultivation. Great quantities of squash remains occurred in the Pampa refuse; three species were represented – two domestic, one wild. Other plants newly included, in small amounts, in the villagers' diet were pacae, achira (a starchy root), guava and jack beans. Cotton was used for nets and textiles. These plants must have been grown at river valley sites that have since been obliterated. In addition to cultigens, wild tubers and rhizomes were also collected. There was hardly a trace of land mammals at the Pampa site; meat was provided instead by shellfish, birds and sea-lions.

The settlement and subsistence patterns remained essentially the same during the following phases, Playa Hermosa (2300–2100 B.C.) and Conchas (2100–1900 B.C.). Peppers first appear in Playa Hermosa refuse deposits; lima beans, lucumas and sapindus seeds were added to the diet of Conchas villagers, while squash seems to have become less important. Fishing and shellfish-collecting remained the most important subsistence activities.

On the north coast of Peru, in the Chicama valley, the mound of Huaca Prieta was occupied at about the same time as the Conchas phase sites on the central coast. The primary food sources at Huaca Prieta, as at the central coast sites, were fish and shellfish, and the cultivated plants were about the same. Although thousands of gourd fragments were found, only two gourds, discovered in a grave, bore incised decorations. These depicted, in one case, stylized faces, and in the other, stylized human figures and birds, perhaps condors. The late Junius Bird's painstaking analysis of the twined cotton fabrics from Huaca Prieta revealed traces of angular stylized designs, representing human figures, birds, crabs and snakes (Bird 1963).

At least 100 villages like Huaca Prieta dotted the Peruvian coast by 2000 B.C. These were small communities, each occupied by no more than a few hundred people. In the Ancón region, villages had been established near almost every shellfish bed on the coast by the Gaviota phase, 1900–1750 B.C. Several inland sites were also occupied at this time, including a large town or ceremonial center at Chuquitanta. The population of this site has been estimated as somewhere in the range of 1,000 to 4,000. Nine stone buildings, including what seems to be a temple on top of an artificial mound, covered an area of 900 by 650 meters. The construction of this huge complex must have involved a large, well-organized work force, which implies the existence of a central authority and, possibly, a ranked society. The excavations at Chuquitanta have yielded remains of cultivated plants, including cotton, gourds, lima beans, guavas, achira, lucumas, pacae, and pijama. Peanuts and sweet potatoes have been identified at other Gaviota phase sites. The absence of maize is surprising, since it had already been grown for centuries in the highlands. Perhaps the native Peruvian tubers were an adequate source of carbohydrates.

It has been estimated that, between 2500 and 1750 B.C., the population of the Ancón-Chillón region increased from 200 or 300 to 3,000–6,000 persons. The implied yearly growth rate of 0.4 to 0.7% is 40 times greater than the growth rate that has been tentatively proposed for the earlier phases (Cohen 1977b). Clearly, the shift to a more sedentary way of life, the development of an efficient marine adaptation, and the adoption of agriculture were conducive to population growth, although the relative contribution of each factor is arguable. Michael Moseley (1975a) has argued that the emergence of large central places such as Chuquitanta was based primarily on efficient harvesting of the abundant marine resources of the coast. Opponents of this theory (Wilson 1981, Raymond 1981) argue that the heaps of shell at coastal sites are deceptive – the nutritive value of mollusks is actually slight, so they could not have been a satisfactory dietary staple. Furthermore, shellfish, fish and shore bird populations are occasionally decimated when the upwelling cold waters of the Peru Coastal (Humboldt) Current are replaced by warm currents from the north. Human groups that depended solely on marine resources would have been hard-pressed to survive under these *Niño* conditions. Moseley's critics stress the presence at coastal sites of cultivated plants that must have been taken from the river valleys. Nevertheless, it is clear that fish, shellfish, and sea mammals furnished necessary protein for the central coast people for centuries (Quilter and Stocker 1983). Not until 200 B.C. to A.D. 600 do alternative sources of protein – domesticated llamas and guinea pigs – appear on the central coast, although they were present much earlier elsewhere along the coast.

We will consider the argument over the subsistence base of the civilizations of coastal Peru again, when we examine the origins of complex societies. But for now, having traced the origins of Peruvian agriculture up to the point when it became established on the coast, we leave Peru to examine the spread of farming into other regions.

EARLY AGRICULTURE IN AMAZONIA

The early occurrence at sites in highland and coastal Peru of cultivated plants that were probably native to the eastern slopes of the Andes or to the tropical forest (selva) of the Amazon Basin, has given rise to the suspicion that agriculture may have begun independently, at a very early date, in the tropical forest. Unfortunately, it has been very difficult to obtain the data necessary to confirm or disprove this surmise. Fieldwork is not easily conducted in Amazonia, and the chances of discovering preserved plant remains in such a humid environment are slim. Nevertheless, Anna Roosevelt's (1980) recent success in recovering carbonized maize from a site near the Orinoco River, in Venezuela, shows that in certain favorable situations, remains of early cultigens may survive. However, the plant that is most likely to have been grown in the tropical forests at an early date is manioc, which does not produce seeds. Lacking carbonized seeds, archaeologists have not been able to demonstrate the presence of manioc at sites. Perhaps the new technique of phytolith analysis will yield direct evidence of prehistoric manioc cultivation. Meanwhile, archaeologists must make do with indirect clues.

Manioc, a starchy tuber, was the staple crop of most Amazonian and Caribbean tribes at the time of European contact. Although rich in carbohydrates, it is a poor source of protein; therefore a manioc-based diet must include supplemental protein, derived from meat or fish. Despite the seeming profusion of life forms in the tropical forest, it actually supports few large animals, so hunting is not very productive. On the other hand, the Amazon and Orinoco and smaller tributary rivers teem with fish. Furthermore, the rivers constantly deposit fresh silt along their banks, so that the best soils for farming occur in the riverbank zone, or *várzea*. The combination of fish and good soil makes the *várzea* the most desirable area for human occupation (Meggers 1971, Roosevelt 1980). Unfortunately, in the course of time, many settlement sites in this zone must either have been washed away or buried deeply under silt. Houses and many artifacts were made of organic materials which have disintegrated, but pottery has survived. Although there may have been people living in Amazonia before pottery was introduced, only after its adoption (ca. 2000 B.C.) can occupied sites be recognized, and cultural traditions distinguished. Ceramic artifacts can also provide strong, albeit indirect, evidence of manioc cultivation.

There are two varieties of manioc, sweet and bitter. Both contain poisonous prussic acid. In the sweet form, it is concentrated in the outer skin, and can be easily removed by peeling before consumption. However, the poison is pervasive in bitter manioc, so that the tuber must be peeled, grated, washed and squeezed before it is eaten. After this preparation, the manioc flour is toasted on large ceramic griddles, called *budares*. Where such griddles have been found in archaeological contexts, it is likely (but not really certain) that bitter manioc was cultivated and processed. Small flint flakes that have been found at some archaeological sites may have been set into boards and used like recent manioc-graters; however, on closer inspection, the prehistoric flakes are not identical to the modern grating tools, and may have had other uses (De Boer 1974). Curiously, the bitter variety of manioc seems to be the further developed one; it was favored by farmers because of its greater yield of starch. Modern Indians

1 Valdivia and Real Alto
2 Ayacucho
3 Chillón, Lurín, and Chilca valleys
4 Huaca Prieta
5 Malambo
6 Tutishcainyo
7 Puerto Hormiga
8 Marajó Island
9 Orinoco delta (Barrancos)
10 Middle Orinoco (Parmana)
11 Manacupurú
12 Caiambé
13 Paredão
14 Santarém
15 Mojos
16 La Tolita
17 Manta
18 San Agustín
19 Milagro
20 Calima
21 Quimbaya
22 Tairona
23 Chibcha (Muisca)
24 Sitio Conte
25 Capá

Fig. 58. Central and South American sites representative of prehistoric farming tribes and chiefdoms.

make a kind of beer out of sweet manioc; archaeological finds of large urns and small bowls, comparable to those used today to serve the beer, may be indicators of the cultivation of sweet manioc.

At sites in the Middle Orinoco, ceramic griddles have been found that are tentatively dated to about 2100 B.C. (the C14 dates may be too early, due to contamination by lignite and recent charcoal). Apart from this occurrence, the earliest known budares come from sites of the Malambo culture, on the north coast of Colombia; these date to around 1100 B.C. Malambo pottery is similar to the Barrancoid pottery that was made by the inhabitants of the mouth of the Orinoco from about 1000 B.C. onward. Manioc griddles are also present at Barrancoid sites. Far to the west, on the upper Rio Ucayali, budares and other Barrancoid-like ceramics appear in the Hupa-Iya phase, dating from roughly 200 B.C. to A.D. 1. Pottery of an earlier phase, Tutishcainyo, found at the same site, probably dates to about 2000–1600 B.C., judging from its similarity to early pottery of this age from Kotosh, in the Andes. Tutishcainyo vessels include urns and bowls which may have been used to drink manioc beer. Thus, indirect evidence suggests that bitter manioc was cultivated by 1000 B.C., and sweet manioc perhaps by 2000 B.C. (Lathrap 1968, 1970); however, the excavator of Tutishcainyo, Donald Lathrap, has speculated that manioc cultivation may have begun by at least 5000 B.C. Citing the early occurrence of gourds at sites in Mexico and Peru, Lathrap (1977) has suggested, rather implausibly, that agriculture was introduced to the eastern lowlands of South America by fishermen from West Africa, 14,000 years ago. More plausible is his contention that manioc cultivation began in the lowland tropical forests of Colombia, Venezuela, and Ecuador. As the population of this area grew, farming groups seeking new land would have expanded into Amazonia, western Ecuador, and eastern Peru. The Valdivia culture of coastal Ecuador might have been founded by one such migrant group. However, the evidence from Valdivia sites – a possible carbonized maize kernel, supposed ceramic depictions of maize, probable maize phytoliths, and manos and metates – attests to the cultivation by the Valdivians of maize, not manioc. It should be noted that the ceramic vessels found at Valdivia sites do not include budares. Pottery as early as or earlier than the Valdivia pottery was made at Puerto Hormiga, near the Caribbean coast of Colombia, around 3000 B.C. There is no clear evidence of agriculture at Puerto Hormiga. Some grinding stones were found, but they may have been used to process seeds of wild plants, while hammer and anvil stones were probably used to crack palm nuts. In addition to these presumed plant foods, the inhabitants of Puerto Hormiga ate shellfish, fish and small animals. Apart from the manufacture of pottery, their mode of subsistence and their crude stone tools were basically the same as those of the earlier Archaic inhabitants of the coast.

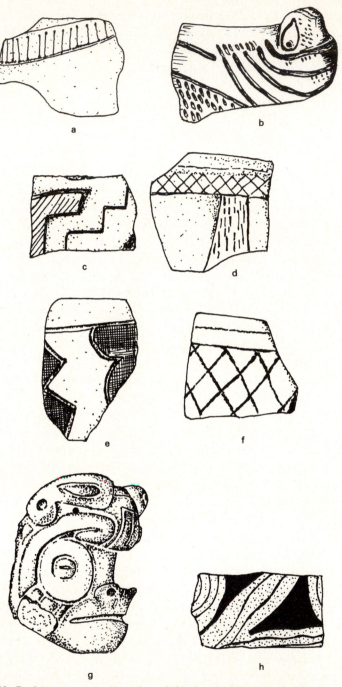

Fig. 59. Prehistoric ceramic styles of the South American lowlands: (A, B) Puerto Hormiga; (C–F) Zoned Hachure style (C and D, early Tutishcainyo, E and F, Ananatuba style from Marajó Island); (G) a Barrancoid adorno (height ca. 5 cm); (H) Saladoid sherd (red paint on natural-color background). (A, B, C, D, G, H after Willey 1971; E and F after Meggers and Evans 1983.)

196

If, as the evidence suggests, the Puerto Hormiga folk were foragers, not farmers, we have another illustration of the fact that there is no necessary connection between pottery and agriculture, as the making of pottery by prehistoric Eskimos also clearly demonstrates.

CERAMIC TRADITIONS OF THE ORINOCO AND AMAZON BASINS

Archaeologists working with material from the tropical lowlands are still engaged in the basic task of establishing a chronological framework into which the bewildering array of ceramic assemblages from this vast region can be fitted. Comparisons of pottery from widely separated areas have often revealed obvious stylistic similarities that are most simply explained as the results of rapid long distance migrations. Such migrations could be undertaken by people canoing down the major rivers and their tributaries. The migratory expansion of Tupian speakers from Amazonia into Brazil, and of the Caribs from northern Amazonia into the Caribbean islands, was still in progress when Europeans arrived in the sixteenth century. Arawakan-speakers had probably engaged in similar migrations some centuries earlier, and these historically and linguistically attested movements provide a model for widespread diffusion of prehistoric ceramic complexes (Lanning 1974b). Although archaeologists have generally agreed that migrations occurred, they have disagreed sharply over the origins of Amazonian cultures and their direction of movement. Meggers and Evans (1983) have sought the origins of Amazonian ceramics, cultivated plants and other cultural traits in the Andes; in recent years, they have emphasized the role of the coast and highlands of Colombia as a donor area. In contrast, Lathrap (1970, 1977) has argued that cultural innovations and waves of migration issued from central Amazonia.

The earliest Tutishcainyo pottery (ca. 2000–1600 B.C.) was often decorated by incising fine parallel or cross-hatched lines within zones defined by deeply incised outlines. Far to the east, at the mouth of the Amazon, similar "zoned hachure" decoration occurs on pottery from Marajó Island. This pottery is assigned to the Ananatuba phase, which dates to around 1400 B.C. The typical Ananatuba vessel forms were rounded bowls and jars; manioc griddles were absent, and there is no other evidence of agriculture. The small refuse heaps imply that the settlements were small, perhaps consisting of multi-family communal residences. Farther up the Amazon, the zoned hachure style occurs at the site of Jauarí, and it is also found in the Pastaza phase of southeastern Ecuador, which has a C14 date of about 1900 B.C. The point of origin of this widespread ceramic style is not known, but Meggers and Evans (1983) suggest that it may have been derived from the coast of Colombia.

About 1000 B.C., Barrancoid pottery began to be made by the inhabitants of the Orinoco delta. This style featured curvilinear incised decoration, and applied, modelled animal and human faces, called *adornos*. Griddles imply the cultivation of bitter manioc by Barrancoid groups. At Tutishcainyo, incised decoration reminiscent of Barrancoid pottery appears in the Hupa-iya phase, dated at around 200 B.C. On Marajó Island, there was a brief occupation, ca. 1000–800 B.C., by people who made plates with flat-topped, incised rims. The homeland of these intruders is not known; incised-rim pottery has been found elsewhere along the lower Amazon and upper Orinoco, but is not securely dated in those areas. The source of the Barrancoid tradition is also uncertain – its ultimate source is probably the Puerto Hormiga tradition, but a presumed intermediate phase, somewhere in Venezuela, has yet to be identified.

Pottery of the Saladoid style was being made on the middle Orinoco after 600 B.C., and perhaps considerably earlier, if Roosevelt's dates from Parmana are accurate. Saladoid pottery featured white-on-red painted decoration, but incised patterns and adornos were also employed, showing the effect of interaction with the Barrancoid tradition. The origin of Saladoid pottery is disputed; Meggers favors a source in Mesoamerica or the Andes, while Lathrap looks to central Amazonia. The Saladoid culture moved rapidly along the Orinoco to the coast of Venezuela, and beyond to the Caribbean islands, around A.D. 50. On the middle Orinoco, Saladoid pottery was replaced by that of the Corozal culture, which may have come from western Venezuela. Roosevelt (1980) dates this change at 800 B.C., but Meggers suggests that it occurred during the early centuries A.D. Carbonized maize kernels, absent from the Saladoid levels, begin to occur in the Corozal phase. The adoption of maize seems to have sparked a rapid growth of the local population, which increased to four times its former size in less than four centuries. The presence of budares at Corozal sites shows that manioc was still being grown along with the new crop.

Around A.D. 1, vessels painted in red and/or black, on a white-slipped surface, began to be made on the middle Amazon. This polychrome style was carried southwest, up the Rio Madeira, by A.D. 200, and had reached Marajó Island, to the east, by A.D. 400. There, polychrome pottery occurred, along with many plain vessels, in the Marajoara phase. Marajoara dwellings were built on top of artificial mounds, probably to avoid flooding during the rainy season. A few mounds were used for burials; the largest was 10 meters high, measuring 255 by 30 meters at its base. Secondary and cremation burials found within the mounds had been placed inside anthropomorphic urns, accompanied by pots, ceramic pubic covers (*tangas*), and animal bones. Similar anthropomorphic urns have been found at Polychrome sites on the middle Amazon. The association in some cases of a number of burials in plain jars, with a single one placed in a painted urn, suggests that Marajoara society may have been ranked, with painted urns being reserved for élite funerals. Meggers believes that the Marajoara culture originated in western Venezuela or Colombia, and that it never became fully adapted to Amazonian conditions. Consequently, she sees evidence of gradual decline, in the increasing simplicity of pottery and uniformity of burial treatment, until a simpler village farming culture, Aruã, from Guyana, replaced the Marajoara culture around A.D. 1300. In contrast, Roosevelt (1980) suggests that Marajoara originated in central Amazonia, that the decline in quality of its ceramics need not be an indication of general cultural deterioration, and that the Aruã culture took over Marajó Island only in the sixteenth century, after the complex Marajoara culture had been weakened by contact with Europeans.

The incised-rim tradition seems to have persisted in the middle Amazon region until A.D. 900. Incised-rim bowls have been found at Manacupurú (C14 date, A.D. 425), Caiambé (A.D. 630–640), and Paredão (A.D. 870–880). Manacupurú is a huge midden, which stretches for more than two kilometers along the river's northern bank and inland for 400 meters. Paredão is also a large midden, its black soil (*terra preta*) covering several hectares. Budares found here attest to the cultivation of bitter manioc, and ceramic spindle whorls imply the weaving of cotton. These sites must be the remains of large villages or towns, with hundreds of inhabitants (Willey 1971).

After A.D. 400, Arauquinoid pottery replaced Corozal ceramics on the middle Orinoco. Typical decoration of the new ware consisted of parallel straight incised lines, sometimes associated with dots made by excision or punctuation; modelled adornos, with coffee-bean eyes, also appear. Budares were no longer made, and numerous carbonized kernels of maize show that it had replaced manioc as the staple crop. The Barrancoid pottery made by the inhabitants of the lower Orinoco after A.D. 750 shows Arauquinoid influence in its increased emphasis on incised and punctate decoration. In Amazonia, an "incised and punctate" tradition, related to the Arauquinoid, began to affect polychrome pottery, whether by diffusion, migration, or exchange. Polychrome painted pottery was still being made in far western Amazonia after 1300, in the Napo phase of the Rio Napo and the Caimito phase of the Rio Ucayalí. This decorative tradition continued into the historic period among the Shipibo and Cashibo. However, to the east, the incised and punctate style became dominant along the Amazon and its southern tributaries after A.D. 1000. The most flamboyant examples of this style come from Santarém, at the mouth of the Rio Tapajós, where they date to around

A.D. 1300. Vessels were festooned with adornos in the form of humans, crocodiles, jaguars, monkeys, birds and frogs. These profuse ornaments would have prevented everyday use of the pottery; the vessels may instead have been used for funerary rites, such as Europeans observed among the Tapajós Indians of this region at the time of contact. The Tapajós ground up the bones of the dead, then mixed the powder into beer which they drank during the funeral ceremonies. Perhaps the Santarém vessels were used for this purpose (Willey 1971).

When the Europeans encountered the Tapajós and their western neighbors, the Omagua, in the 1500s, they observed an almost continuous strip of villages along the river. Some settlements were inhabited by 300 to 700 people, and one town is reported to have contained 500 families. The houses were made of cedar planks and roofed with thatch. The Tapajós and Omagua were organized as chiefdoms, comparable in complexity to those of the Intermediate Area; village chiefs were subservient to paramount chiefs. War captives were kept as slaves. The Omagua are reported to have grown both manioc and maize; the Tapajós also grew manioc, but maize was their principal crop. Turtles and fish taken from the river provided additional protein (Meggers 1971).

The Europeans also found chiefdoms in the far southwestern corner of the Amazon Basin, in the lowlands of Bolivia. Archaeological surveys of the Mojos region have revealed the presence of an extensive system of ridged fields, causeways, and mounds used for villages and burials. These earthworks kept crops and houses above the flood-waters that covered the grasslands for six months each year. The ridged fields are reported to cover some 50,000 acres (Parsons and Denevan 1967). General similarities in pottery decoration suggest that the poorly-known cultures of the Mojos region, which date from about A.D. 500 and afterward, were related to the polychrome tradition cultures found elsewhere in Amazonia (Willey 1971).

Fig. 60. Santarém vessel (height 18.5 cm).

AGRICULTURE AND VILLAGE LIFE IN THE SOUTHWEST

We have already traced the southward spread of maize, which was adopted in the Peruvian highlands around 4000 to 3000 B.C. Maize was also carried northward from its Mexican hearth, reaching southwestern New Mexico perhaps as early as 3500 B.C. That is the probable date of the small, primitive maize cobs that were found in 1948 in Bat Cave. The same layer of the cave also yielded squash seeds, which were also of Mexican origin. The plant remains were associated with artifacts of the Chiricahua phase of the Cochise culture. Unfortunately, the cave deposits had been disturbed, so the date of these finds is uncertain; the true age might be as late as 1500 B.C. Nevertheless, the resemblance of the Bat Cave maize to early specimens from the Tehuacan Valley tends to support the earlier date. Additional evidence that maize was present in the Southwest no later than 2000 B.C. comes from another Cochise site, Cienega Creek, which is 160 km (100 miles) west of Bat Cave. At Cienega Creek, 4,000 year-old maize pollen was recovered. It is remarkable that no maize remains of comparable age have been found at any site lying between Bat Cave and Tehuacan, which are almost 3,200 km (2,000 miles) apart. Despite this fact, it is likely that maize and squash were transmitted northward, from one band of foragers to the next, along the eastern flanks of the Sierra Madre Occidental. The inhabitants of this area belonged to the same cultural tradition as the Cochise people of the Southwest, and they probably spoke closely related Uto-Aztecan languages.

As we have seen, the subsistence pattern of the Cochise culture was "pre-adapted" for agriculture, in that wild grass seeds, roasted and then ground using the mano and metate, were an important food source. In later Southwestern farming cultures, maize kernels were prepared in the same way, by roasting or drying prior to grinding. These methods differed from the traditional Mexican practice, in which the kernels were softened by soaking them in a lime solution before grinding them. Initially, maize cultivation provided the Cochise foragers with a minor dietary supplement, but it did not provoke an immediate, drastic change in their accustomed pattern of seasonal band movements between patches of wild resources.

By about 1000 to 400 B.C., a third Mexican crop, common beans, had been added to the San Pedro Cochise diet. Around 500 to 300 B.C., an important genetic change occurred in Cochise maize, as evidenced by remains from the middle levels of Bat Cave and from Tularosa Cave, which lies 40 km (25 miles) west of Bat Cave, in the Mogollon Mountains. Whether this change resulted from selection by local cultivators or importation of a new Mexican strain is not certain. In any case, the new, drought-resistant Chapalote race could be grown not only in the high-

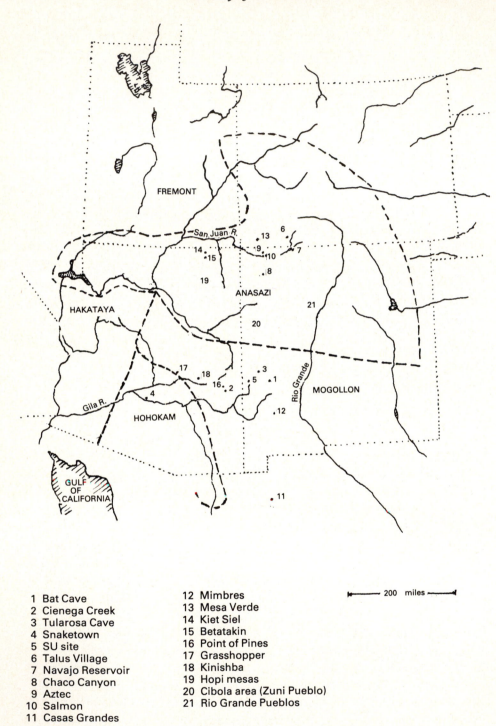

1 Bat Cave
2 Cienega Creek
3 Tularosa Cave
4 Snaketown
5 SU site
6 Talus Village
7 Navajo Reservoir
8 Chaco Canyon
9 Aztec
10 Salmon
11 Casas Grandes

12 Mimbres
13 Mesa Verde
14 Kiet Siel
15 Betatakin
16 Point of Pines
17 Grasshopper
18 Kinishba
19 Hopi mesas
20 Cibola area (Zuni Pueblo)
21 Rio Grande Pueblos

200 miles

Fig. 61. Southwestern sites and culture areas.

lands but in hotter, drier lowland areas. By about A.D. 300–400, Chapalote maize had been adopted by groups in southern Utah and southwestern Colorado (Woodbury and Zubrow 1979).

THE HOHOKAM

While these foragers were slowly adding maize and other cultigens to their diet of wild foods, a completely new economic and settlement pattern appeared quite suddenly in southern Arizona. Village life based on intensive irrigation agriculture was apparently brought into the Gila River valley around 300 B.C. by immigrants from Mexico, who established a settlement at Snaketown. They began to grow maize, beans and squash, watering these crops by means of a long, wide canal running from the river. Irrigation probably allowed the villagers to plant two crops a year, in March and August, and to harvest them in July and November. A significant part of their diet was provided by gathered foods, such as cactus fruit and mesquite pods, and by hunted game, primarily deer and rabbits. The earliest evidence of irrigation systems in Mesoamerican highland valleys dates to about 900 B.C. (Nichols 1982), and they became more widespread after 600 B.C. Perhaps irrigation agriculture triggered a rapid growth of population, which forced some marginal groups to emigrate to less densely populated regions, as the Snaketown colonists seem to have done. Apart from their irrigation system, other traits of the early (Pioneer period) Hohokam of Snaketown that link them to Mexico are pottery, clay figurines, stone vessels on which animals were carved in bas-relief, turquoise mosaics, and carved shell ornaments (Haury 1976).

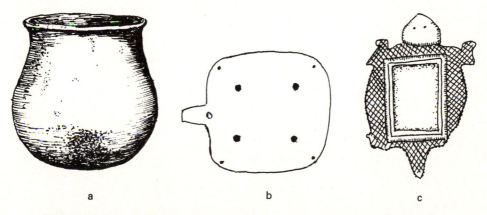

a   b   c

Fig. 62. Early Hohokam artifacts: (A) Pioneer period jar (Vahki Plain style), diameter 25 cm; (B) Vahki phase pit-house (length ca. 8 m); (C) zoomorphic stone palette.

The earliest Hohokam houses were almost square, measuring 10 to 15 m (30 to 50 ft) per side. The floor was formed by removing enough soil to expose a hard underlying layer of calcium carbonate (*caliche*). The flat roof and sloping side walls were made of poles covered with brush or grass. The size of these houses suggests that they were occupied by extended families. They were loosely grouped together, in no particular order, into small villages; the population of Snaketown is thought to have been about 100.

Pioneer period pots were generally thin-walled and plain, grey or brown in color. Some vessels of the first phase (Vahki) were red-slipped. During the second Pioneer phase, Estrella(A.D. 1–200), some pots bore simple geometric designs – chevrons or parallel lines – painted in red on a grey background. By A.D. 350, the pottery was better made, designs were more complicated, and vessel shapes were more varied.

By the end of the Pioneer period, ca. A.D. 550, the area of Hohokam settlement had begun to expand from the central region of the Gila and Snake river valleys into smaller river valleys and into desert areas where there was no surface water. During the next period of cultural development, known as Colonial (A.D. 550–900), Mexican civilization seems to have exerted its influence again over the Hohokam. This influence is most evident in two kinds of public structures that now appeared in Colonial villages – platform mounds and ball-courts. Mound-building actually began late in the Pioneer period, when rubbish was piled together with clean soil into large mounds which were shaped, levelled, and coated with lime plaster. Later Colonial and Sedentary (A.D. 900–1100) mounds were made of the same materials, but were more carefully built. Like Mexican pyramids, they were frequently remodelled, but unlike the Mexican prototypes, they were not approached by ramps or stairs. Colonial period ball-courts were long, oval depressions, 52 to 65 m (ca. 170 to 215 ft) long, bordered by ridges. Stone markers were often placed at the center and ends of the courts. It is not certain that the semi-sacred Mesoamerican ball game was played in these features; an alternative suggestion is that they were used primarily as communal dance floors. However, their similarity to Mexican ball courts is apparent, and rubber balls have been found at Hohokam sites (although unfortunately not in direct association with the supposed courts). Other items of Mesoamerican origin that have been found in Colonial and Sedentary sites include cast copper bells, macaws (valued for their colorful feathers), and mirrors composed of bits of iron pyrite.

The public ceremonies and games that took place on top of the mounds and within the ball courts presumably brought together large numbers of people from several villages, thus fostering the integration of Hohokam communities into larger social, political, and religious organizations.

Such integration was made necessary by the continuing growth of the Hohokam population and its dispersion over a widening area, estimated at 26,000 square km (10,000 square miles) by A.D. 1000. Greater crop yields, needed to feed more people, were achieved by digging much longer and deeper canals, which brought water to many more cultivated areas than had been possible before. In the Gila Valley, between the modern towns of Florence and Coolidge, a canal system has been identified, which served a number of small villages and a single larger site (Doyel 1979). The smaller Colonial villages usually lacked the public structures found in the larger villages; the latter also contained most of the elaborate artifacts made by the Hohokam, such as acid-etched and carved shell, delicately chipped, thin barbed points, and finely carved stone palettes. The Hohokam dead who were cremated in the larger villages were accompanied by richer grave offerings than those who were cremated in the smaller settlements. These lines of evidence point to increasing social differentiation in the later stages of Hohokam development. Perhaps, the larger sites were occupied by members of higher-ranking lineages, who enjoyed greater wealth than their distant kinsmen in the smaller villages.

The Hohokam have long troubled archaeological theorists, who have often cited large-scale irrigation systems as a major cause of the emergence of centralized political authority and social stratification. Yet the Pima, the presumed descendants of the Hohokam, are known to have maintained an extensive canal system without recourse to centralization. When ditches had to be cleaned or dug, or dams built, men from several villages worked together. Their effort was organized and directed by a "ditch boss", but he retained no authority after the work was done. This ethnographic case, and the archaeological case of the Pima's canal-digging Hohokam ancestors, seem to contradict the supposed general rule that water control systems lead to political centralization and ultimately result in the development of states. However, it is probably a mistake simply to retroject the social institutions of the historic Pima into prehistory. Pima canals were not constructed on the same scale as the Hohokam works, and their population was dramatically reduced by disease soon after contact with whites; so post-contact accounts may not apply to the Hohokam. The observed differences in size, architectural elaboration and artifactual wealth of Hohokam sites suggest that water control did indeed stimulate the development of a more complex social and political organization.

THE MOGOLLON

The arrival of the Hohokam colonists seems to have had a major impact on the neighboring hunter–gatherers of Arizona and New Mexico. They had been cultivating Mexican-derived crops for 2,000 years, but only as supplements to the foods they gathered. The addition of maize to their diet had permitted larger groups to camp together, for somewhat longer periods, but the traditional pattern of seasonal movement from one resource zone to the next continued. It was only around A.D. 250 that this pattern changed. Perhaps the new strains of maize that were developed locally or introduced from Mexico around this time offered a greater caloric reward for the labor and time invested in their cultivation. The Hohokam intrusion might have caused some displacement of hunter–gatherers, leading to an imbalance of population and resources in neighboring areas. An improvement in storage techniques might have permitted more efficient use of agricultural surpluses. Whatever the causes may have been, the Cochise hunter–gatherers of southeastern Arizona and southwestern New Mexico became more sedentary around A.D. 250. The primary indicator of this transition is the appearance of villages, which typically consisted of some 15 pit-houses. The pit-houses varied in shape from round to quadrangular, and were dug to a depth of less than 1.5 m (4 ft); the walls and roof were made of logs, with mud and branches filling the chinks. The house was entered through a narrow passageway. Another marker of the new sedentary lifeway was the first appearance of pottery, which partially replaced baskets for some cooking and storage functions. Round bowls and jars, red to brown in color, were made; this undecorated ware is called Alma Plain. Pottery-making was probably learned from the Hohokam. The establishment of pit-house villages and the adoption of pottery mark the transition from the late Archaic San Pedro Cochise to the initial phase of the Mogollon tradition. Archaeologists recognize five chronological phases of this tradition, from about A.D. 250 to 1150. These phases are distinguished mainly on the basis of changes in pit-house shapes and pottery types. In Mogollon 2, the interiors of brown bowls were sometimes decorated with red paint, and the designs became more varied in Mogollon 3 (A.D. 650–850). The bow and arrow replaced the dart, and cotton was cultivated. Around A.D. 700, Mogollon pottery and dwellings began to reflect the influence of their northern neighbors, the Anasazi. This influence, probably accompanied by immigration, grew increasingly dominant during Mogollon phases 4 and 5, so that by A.D. 1100 there was no longer a separate Mogollon tradition.

The early Mogollon villages were usually perched at the ends of high mesa tops, 90 to 180 m (300 to 600 ft) above the valley floors where the inhabitants grew their crops. The purpose of this siting was apparently defensive; the village was protected on three sides by steep cliffs, and a wall built from cliff to cliff deterred attack from the mesa top. After

A.D. 600 the threat of attack seems to have abated, for villages were built in the river valleys (Martin and Plog 1973).

Some Mogollon villages, like the 28-house SU site in New Mexico, were relatively large; others were small. There is some evidence of a tendency for one large site to be surrounded by a cluster of smaller villages. The large villages usually contained an oversized pit-house, which was probably used, like the kivas of recent Pueblo Indians, for ceremonies. One or two of the pit-house dwellings in the larger villages were bigger than the others, and had more associated storage pits; these houses were often located close to the ceremonial structures. It has been suggested that these patterns of settlement location and community layout may be indicative of a simple ranked society (Lightfoot and Feinman 1982). The bigger houses might have belonged to headmen, who were responsible for the redistribution of food and exotic trade items, such as shells and turquoise, at communal feasts that were held in the kiva-like structures and attended by both the residents of the large village and their kinfolk from the smaller satellite communities. Analogous multi-village tribelets existed in aboriginal California.

THE ANASAZI

The hunter–gatherers who lived to the north of the Cochise-Mogollon, on the Colorado Plateau, took up sedentary life at about the same time, or a little later. Since about 1890, archaeologists have referred to these incipient farmers, who did not yet produce pottery, as "Basketmakers". At the 1927 Pecos Conference, where Alfred Kidder and his colleagues established a tentative chronological framework for the Southwest, the Basketmaker period was divided into three phases. At the time, no Basketmaker I sites pre-dating A.D. 1 were known; Basketmaker I has since been recognized as equivalent to Archaic, and the latter term is now applied to the earliest material. The artifacts of Basketmaker II (A.D. 1–450) were essentially identical to those of the earlier Desert Archaic. Many normally perishable artifacts were extraordinarily well-preserved in dry caves and rock shelters. They included baskets, bags, woven fiber sandals, wooden scoops and clubs, atlatls and darts, snares and nets, rabbit-fur blankets, gaming pieces and crude figurines. The cultivation of maize and squash probably contributed more to the Basketmaker II diet than it had previously, but hunting and gathering were still very important. While occupation of natural shelters continued, some groups constructed substantial houses. At the Talus Village site, near Durango in southwestern Colorado, round houses, 4 to 6 m (12 to 18 ft) in diameter, were built on terraces cut into the rubble slope alongside a cliff. The house walls, which sloped inward toward a domed roof, were made of logs laid horizontally and covered with mud mortar. At any one time, nine houses were occupied. No other sites of this period have yielded evidence of quite the same building technique, but traces of horizontal logs on the edges of oval house floors were found at Navajo Reservoir, in northwestern New Mexico. The sites in that area also produced a small amount of polished brown pottery, similar to early Mogollon ware. Like early Mogollon villages, the Basketmaker II communities were situated at high points, on mesa tops or old river terraces, presumably for defense.

Basketmaker II represents the beginning of a long-lived cultural tradition, centered in the "Four Corners" region of the Colorado Plateau, where New Mexico, Colorado, Arizona, and Utah meet. Archaeologists refer to this tradition as Anasazi, from the Navajo word for "ancient alien ones". This ancient tradition is still extant today, carried on by the Hopi and Zuni of Arizona, and the various Pueblo groups who live along the Rio Grande in New Mexico. The lifeways of these native peoples have provided archaeologists with invaluable models that they have used in reconstruction and interpretation of the prehistoric remains in the Southwest.

During the Basketmaker II phase (A.D. 450–750), beans were added to the diet, and the Anasazi became more committed to agriculture as their primary means of subsistence. This orientation is reflected in the location of sites near deep, well-watered soils. Grinding slabs were replaced by troughed metates and two-handed manos, which were more efficient tools for processing maize. Domesticated turkeys were introduced, as a supplement to the deer and rabbit meat obtained by hunting and trapping. Around A.D. 700, the bow and arrow replaced the atlatl and dart. During the previous phase, what little pottery the Basketmakers had made was imitative of Mogollon ware. In Basketmaker III, pottery, now distinctive in style from that of the Mogollon, became more common. The clay was formed by coiling and scraping, then fired in a reducing atmosphere. The resulting bowls and jars were grey or grey-white in color; their interiors were often decorated with geometric patterns, painted in black. More Basketmakers settled down in permanent villages, which consisted of pit-houses. These varied in shape from round to rectangular, and in size, from 2.7 to 7.5 m (9 to 25 ft) across. The house floors were dog to a depth of 30 cm to 1.8 m (1 to 6 ft) below the surface. The domed roofs, made of logs and mud, were supported in each case by four central posts, and the walls were either plastered or lined with upright stone slabs. The central firepit was protected from the drafts that came through the entrance by a deflector slab. Other typical pit-house features were a ventilator shaft in the roof, sub-floor storage cists, and a *sipapu*. This small hole in the floor, near the firepit, is thought by modern Pueblo peoples to be the mythical place where ancestors emerged from the underworld. So it would seem that at this time, each family's dwelling was invested with a sacred character.

Shabik'eshchee, in Chaco Canyon, was a typical village. It was composed of 18 pit-houses, of which half had been occupied at one time. A larger slab-lined pit-house, with wall benches and a roof entry, probably served as a kiva (ceremonial room). The houses were arranged in a rough crescent. Some other villages were larger, consisting of more than 50 pit-houses. At least one village, the Gilliland site in southwestern Colorado, is known to have been surrounded by a stockade; other sites may have had stockades too, but the excavators did not look for them. The stockade shows that relations between neighboring groups were occasionally hostile.

Usually, a row of small storage rooms was built on the surface, to the north of the pit-house dwellings, using wattle and daub (called *jacal* in the southwest). In the succeeding Pueblo I period (A.D. 700 or 750–900), the Anasazi began building larger jacal surface structures, forming two contiguous rows; the smaller back rooms were still used for storage, while the larger front rooms, now equipped with firepits, became dwellings. The kiva was meanwhile becoming a more specialized version of the earlier pit-houses; pilasters set along the walls replaced central floor-posts as the supports for roof-beams, wall niches were emplaced for storage of ritual paraphernalia, and sometimes a ventilation tunnel was installed. Pueblo I pottery included a greater variety of vessel forms, and decorated vessels were now frequently covered with a white slip prior to painting. Large collecting baskets and winnowing trays seem to have gone out of use, perhaps reflecting the decreasing importance of wild seeds in the diet. The Anasazi began to cultivate cotton, which was woven into clothing on the loom. Physical anthropologists once interpreted the broad skulls of Pueblo I Anasazi as evidence of the intrusion of a new population that replaced the long-headed Basketmakers; however, the broad skulls are now recognized as resulting from the intentional flattening of infants' heads against cradleboards, a practice that began during this period. Both cranial deformation and weaving were probably borrowed by the Anasazi from the Mogollon.

The Anasazi population reached its peak during the next period, Pueblo II (A.D. 900–1150). Small pueblos, occupied by extended families or small lineages, wre scattered across the Colorado Plateau, often in upland areas where today there is not enough water to drink, let alone to farm with. This wide distribution of sites suggests that the region may have received more rainfall during Pueblo II times than it gets now. Indeed, tree-rings and pollen studies indicate that this was a relatively warm and wet period; few severe droughts occurred, and summer rainfall was abundant. Besides relying on rain for dry farming, the Anasazi watered their fields by controlling run-off, sometimes building small check-dams in gulleys, and terraces and stone grids on hillsides. Despite the relatively favorable climate of this period, agriculture was still a risky enterprise on the Plateau, and there is evidence that crop failure sometimes drove the Anasazi to desperate acts. At several village sites in northern New Mexico, dating to around A.D. 900–950, burned, cut, and split human bones showed that the inhabitants had been killed and cannibalized (Flinn et al. 1976).

The best-watered soils were occupied before the marginal upland areas, and villages in these preferred areas grew to a larger size, sometimes comprising more than 100 rooms. These larger pueblos seem to have been formed by the aggregation of several extended families or minimal lineages; the same social units, living independently, occupied the smaller pueblos. These small pueblos were typically composed of a block of contiguous surface dwellings and storage rooms, with a kiva and dump to the south or southeast. The pueblo buildings were often constructed of stone, instead of the jacal of earlier times.

THE CHACO "PHENOMENON"

The biggest Pueblo II communities flourished in Chaco Canyon, a 15 km-(12 mile-) long, silt-filled, barren valley in the San Juan Basin of northwestern New Mexico. Eight towns were built within the canyon, four others on nearby mesas. Each town contained several hundred contiguous rooms, arranged in tiers around a central plaza, and rising to four storeys at the rear. The largest of them was Pueblo Bonito, which covered 1.2 hectares (three acres) and contained 650 to 800 rooms. It was a planned community, laid out in the form of a giant D. The pueblo was situated at the northern edge of the canyon floor, with its back, the arc of the D, toward the mesa cliff. The walls of the outermost rooms formed a continuous four- or five-storey-high shell that would have offered some protection against attack. A single row of rooms blocked entry into the plaza at the front. Another row of rooms split the central plaza in half. This plaza was dominated by a great kiva, 20 m (65 ft) in diameter. Four other large kivas were situated along the northern edge of the plaza, and 33 smaller ones lay along the arc of the room block, toward its interior face. The great kiva was flanked by a number of rectangular rooms, which may have been used for storage of food or of ritual paraphernalia. The walls of Pueblo Bonito consisted of rubble cores faced with well fitted courses of thin, tabular stones. Thousands of large wooden beams were used for the roofing of Bonito and other pueblos; these logs were carried to the canyon from highland areas 75 km (47 miles) away. Ring-dated beams indicate that construction of Bonito began in A.D. 919, and was completed by A.D. 1085 (Canby 1982).

On the southern side of the canyon there were 200 to 350 small villages, each containing 10 to 20 rooms, which seem to have been inhabited at the same time that the great pueblos were flourishing. Not counting Bonito, there were another 2,000 rooms in the great pueblos. Based on the total number of rooms, and allowing for the abandonment of some rooms and the use of others for storage or for rituals, one can reasonably estimate the population of the canyon as about 15,000, of whom some 1,200 people lived at Bonito.

Emigrants from Chaco Canyon seem to have set up colonies elsewhere in the San Juan Basin, as far as 160 km (100 miles) from the canyon. Chaco "outlier" sites can be recognized by their planned, D-shaped layout, neat masonry, and kivas, which duplicate those of the pueblos within the canyon. Some 70 outliers have been identified to date; among them are two sites located near Farmington, New Mexico, Aztec Ruins and Salmon Ruins. The recently excavated Salmon pueblo contained 300 rooms. It was begun in A.D. 1088, and completed six years later. Outlier sites were often situated on high points, surrounded by clusters of smaller villages.

In recent years, sophisticated analysis of aerial photographs has revealed the existence of a system of roads, many of them 9 m (30 ft) wide, that linked the towns within Chaco Canyon and ran in straight lines from the canyon to outliers as far as 75 to 100 km (65 miles) away. The Chacoans appear to have been determined to lay their roads out straight; where they encountered cliffs, they carved stairs or footholds into the

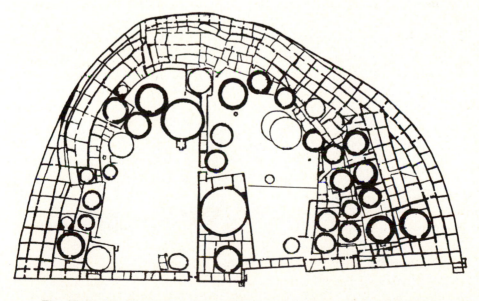

Fig. 63. Pueblo Bonito (ca. 160 × 100 m). (After Willey 1966 and Jennings 1974.)

rock, instead of skirting them. The great amount of labor expended on construction of the road system makes no sense in terms of practical cost–benefit analysis. The Chacoans had no wheeled vehicles, and roads could not have made travel on foot much easier. We can only surmise that the road network had symbolic significance, perhaps as a concrete manifestation of the unity of the Chacoan socio-political system. The far-flung road network is a strong indication that the large Chaco pueblos were not independent, socio-political units, but rather were integrated components of a larger, complex system. How was this system organized, and why did it emerge in this inhospitable near-desert environment?

One theory attributes the origin of the Chaco "phenomenon" to the arrival in the southwest of Mexican *pochteca* (merchants), who were looking for turquoise and other exotic materials. Copper bells and skeletons of macaws have been found at Chaco sites, showing that there was indeed some trade with Mexico. However, such finds are too few to support the idea that a Mexican élite had actually taken up residence in the canyon. Some archaeologists have claimed to detect Mexican elements, such as colonnades and the rubble core walls, in Chacoan architecture; but such basic features as the room block and the subterranean kiva have local antecedents, while distinctively Mexican structures, such as ball-courts and temple mounds, are absent. The characteristic Chacoan pottery – black-on-white painted ware with hachured geometric designs, and corrugated cooking vessels whose coils were not smoothed away – is, like the architecture, clearly derived from the indigenous Anasazi tradition.

On the other hand, thousands of turquoise beads, and the waste flakes

Fig. 64. Anasazi pottery: (A) Chacoan style; (B) Mesa Verdean style. (After Canby 1982.)

212

resulting from their manufacture, were found in the great Chaco pueblos, and some of those beads might have been destined for export to Mexico. If trade with Mexico was largely responsible for the Chacoans' sudden florescence, the equally rapid abandonment of the great pueblos might perhaps be attributable to a re-alignment of trade routes. Around A.D. 1150, as the Chacoan system collapsed, a Mexican group took over the Mogollon-related village of Casas Grandes, in northern Chihuahua, 620 km (390 miles) south of Pueblo Bonito. Under the Mexicans' control, the village expanded into a small city, covering 36.5 hectares. Its 1,600 apartment-like rooms housed more than 2,200 people. Public facilities of a distinctly Mexican cast included a market-place, platform mounds, ball-courts, plazas, and a water supply and drainage system. Food for the city's inhabitants was produced in the surrounding area, where a sophisticated system of water control and soil retention works was installed. Casas Grandes seems to have been the economic and administrative center of a region of 77,000 square km (48,125 square miles). Its control over the out-lying territories was secured by means of a network of forts, roads, way-stations, and signal towers. Casas Grandes was also a major trade and craft production center. Ornaments were fashioned there, using marine shells imported from the Gulf of California, 480 km (300 miles) to the west, turquoise from New Mexico, and the feathers of macaws from south-ern Mexico. These birds were kept and bred at Casas Grandes in aviaries.

We can entertain the possibility that Mexican pochteca, using Casas Grandes as their base, achieved direct access to turquoise sources in New Mexico which had formerly been monopolized by the Chacoans. The resulting disruption of Chacoan trade might also account for the sudden collapse of the Classic Mimbres culture around A.D. 1130. The Mimbres people, descendants of Mogollon pit-house dwellers, occupied a river valley in southwestern New Mexico, more than 320 km (200 miles) south of Chaco Canyon. About A.D. 1000, the Mimbres population grew rapidly. Many pueblos were built, some small, others housing several hundred people. At the same time, the Mimbres culture achieved an artistic peak, most evident in its ceramics. Classic Mimbres black-on-white pottery included both vessels with geometric designs and bowls with paintings of humans and animals. These bowls were "killed"; that is, a hole was punched through, and the vessel was then buried in a grave, covering the face of the corpse. Today, collectors will pay as much as $60,000 for a Mimbres bowl. Looters, searching for these valuable pieces, have destroyed almost every site in the area. Fortunately, archaeologists have managed to salvage some information from sites where a few rooms were left undisturbed by the pot-hunters. The Mimbres pueblos may have served as waystations for Chacoan porters en route to Mexico, in exchange for a share of the profits. If the Mimbres economy was tied to the

Chacoan system, the simultaneous collapse of both cultures, around A.D. 1130–1150, may have been caused by the Mexican take-over at Casas Grandes. Around A.D. 1150, adobe pueblos and Casas Grandes-style pottery appeared in the Mimbres Valley, showing that it had been incorporated into the Casas Grandes zone of control. This situation ended around A.D. 1300, when Casas Grandes was destroyed, perhaps by an uprising of the native population.

Despite the plausibility of the foregoing model, which attributes the florescence and decline of both Chaco Canyon and Mimbres to external influences, it is questionable whether the turquoise trade was so crucial to the Chacoan economy that disruption of the trade would have caused a total cultural collapse. It seems more likely that unforeseen environmental changes triggered the Chacoan decline. However, no clear evidence has been found of a major climatic deterioration in the early twelfth century.

Fig. 65. Classic Mimbres bowl. The sitting figure's head-dress is reminiscent of the costume of Mesoamerican warriors. Such violent scenes are rare in Mimbres art. (After Canby 1982.)

Diffusion and trade are relegated to minor roles by those archaeologists who attribute the rise and fall of Chaco Canyon to local factors. Gwynn Vivian (1970) has suggested that the great pueblos housed an emerging élite, whose privileged position, relative to the inhabitants of the smaller villages, was based on their control of the water distribution system. Pueblo Bonito and several other great pueblos in the canyon were built near the mouths of side canyons, which channeled run-off during summer storms. The run-off was controlled and distributed by means of a system of diversion dams, canals, ditches and stone-bordered garden plots. Irrigation has frequently been cited as the prime mover in the development of other complex societies, such as Teotihuacán. In theory, it leads to population growth, concentration of settlement in the restricted area served by the water-works, and the centralization of power and authority in the hands of an élite who oversee construction and maintenance of the irrigation system and enjoy privileged access to the best-watered, most productive land.

The discovery of the impressive Chacoan road system has shifted attention from water control to redistribution as the possible primary cause of centralization. James Judge, director of the National Park Service's Chaco Research Center, has suggested that the great pueblos functioned as the administrative centers of a vast redistributive network. If any outlying area suffered crop failure due to a local drought, the administrators in Chaco Canyon could be informed by means of messengers or signal fires. They would dispatch bearers carrying surplus food, which had been collected from the entire region and stored in the great pueblos against such emergencies.

Anthropologist Elman Service (1975) has emphasized that redistribution is the crucial function performed by the chief in those societies that he has termed "chiefdoms". Typically, redistribution is accomplished by means of ceremonial feasts, supervised by the chief and his assistants, and held at the large central community where they reside. It has been suggested that a need for redistribution of hunted and gathered foods might account for the emergence of chiefly élites among the Hopewellians of the eastern woodlands. It is conceivable that the Chacoan system was also a chiefdom, and that redistributive ceremonies were held in the great kivas. However, several aspects of the archaeological record are difficult to reconcile with the chiefdom model. One problem is that there are so many great pueblos; instead of a single large center in the canyon, there were a dozen. Assuming for the sake of argument that the biggest of these sites, Pueblo Bonito, was the chiefdom's capital, where at Bonito did the chief and his family live? There are no particularly large, elaborately decorated or equipped, or spatially segregated living rooms at Pueblo Bonito where a hypothetical ruling élite might have resided. If we had a

215

good sample of burials, differences in status and wealth might perhaps be evident in the variable treatment of the dead, but unfortunately the cemetery of Pueblo Bonito has never been discovered. In view of the fact that some 10,000 people must have lived and presumably died at the site during the two centuries when it was inhabited, the absence of burials is puzzling. A possible explanation is that the Bonitians actually spent most of their time in the smaller pueblos, only gathering at the great pueblo on special occasions. An analogous practice by modern Pueblo Indians is the periodic occupation of Acoma Pueblo by normally dispersed families, who gather there for important ceremonies.

The presumed political and economic integration of the Chacoan system has no parallel among recent Pueblo groups. Most historic pueblos were independent social and political units, although in the case of the Hopi, members of one tribe occupied several pueblos. Pueblo societies were basically egalitarian, without major differences in wealth or status of individuals. The population was usually divided into exogamous clans, each named for a totemic animal or plant, and each possessing its own fetishes and secret rituals. Many of the Rio Grande Pueblos were divided into halves, or moieties; each moiety had its own kiva, and had the responsibility to perform certain rituals. Most Pueblo societies were matrilineal and matrilocal; that is, women owned the houses, fields, and stored crops, and clan membership was passed on in the female line of descent. A married man left his own family to live with his wife and her mother and sisters. However, men dominated the political and religious spheres. The governing body in secular matters was a council of elders; a council of priests tended to religious matters. Many pueblos recognized the authority of a priest–chief; there was also a war-priest, of equal authority, and a warrior society, which functioned both externally, as a military force, and internally, as a police force. At Zuni, prior to contact, there may have been a supreme council of war-priests, who represented the six separate Zuni villages (they later coalesced into a single community). In all pueblos, a number of specialized religious cult groups were responsible for the worship of particular supernatural beings, and for periodically staging ceremonial dances. Each of these cults had its own priests, fetishes and kiva (Ortiz 1979).

Presumably, the smaller kivas at Pueblo Bonito were used by cults, similar to those that met in the kivas of recent pueblos. The great kivas of Chaco Canyon, however, have no modern counterparts. The apparent partition of the plaza of Pueblo Bonito into two halves suggests that the population may have been split into two moieties, practicing marriage exchange and performing complementary roles in ceremonies. Evidence from a thirteenth-century Arizona pueblo, Grasshopper, which was almost as big as Pueblo Bonito, suggests that a moiety organization also existed there. The lack of indications of a high-ranking wealthy élite in Chacoan society seems to render a chiefdom model inapplicable – we might instead envision a sort of tribal confederacy, like that of the Iroquois. The governing body of such a league might have been a council of priests and elders from each great pueblo: the closest analogue among the recent Pueblos might be the supreme council at Zuni. The great kivas may have been used for council meetings; they may also have been the settings for major pan-tribal ceremonies. Such ceremonies must have played a crucial role in the integration of the Chacoan system. We can readily imagine the dancers decked out in elaborate costumes, incorporating jingling copper bells and colorful macaw feathers, imported from Mexico. The elaboration of ceremonial outfits and paraphernalia might well have been a socially sanctioned way of displaying wealth and competing for prestige; it certainly had this aspect in recent pueblos.

Much more research must be done if we are ever to move beyond such speculative reconstructions of Chacoan society. Some clues concerning inter-site relationships might be generated by analysis of the distribution of micro-stylistic elements in painted pottery. The results of recent excavations at Salmon Ruins and at Pueblo Alto, where the roads from the northern outliers merged as they entered Chaco Canyon, may shed some light on the relations between the Canyon sites and the outliers. However, the operations of social and political systems are hard to extract from archaeological data under the best of circumstances, and many Chacoan sites were excavated decades ago, using collecting and recording strategies that were designed to answer different questions. Another problem that has confronted archaeologists who have sought evidence relevant to Chacoan socio-political organization is the re-use of sites. For example, after the outlier pueblo of Salmon Ruins was abandoned by the Chacoans, it was re-occupied by Anasazi from the Mesa Verde area. The newcomers cleaned out many rooms and filled them with their own debris. Unfortunately, questions about the distribution of wealth, localization of craft production, linkages between domestic groups and the like cannot be answered when the contents of rooms have been so thoroughly disturbed.

MESA VERDE

The intrusive Mesa Verdean occupation at Salmon can be recognized on the basis of several distinctive features that also appear in the core area of this culture, in southwestern Colorado. Compared to Chacoan pottery, the geometric designs that were painted in bands on the highly polished Mesa Verdean black-on-white ware included more solid elements, combined with hatched lines. Characteristic Mesa Verdean vessel forms

Fig. 66. Cliff Palace, Mesa Verde.

included long-handled ladles, and mugs which look like small beer steins. Mesa Verde kivas resembled those of Chaco Canyon, except that they were often built with a deeply recessed chamber at the southern end, for air intake; this makes them look, in plan, like key-holes. There were very few great kivas in the Mesa Verde pueblos. The pueblo walls were made of large hewn stones, instead of the thin sandstone slabs of Chacoan masonry.

Mesa Verde, as its Spanish name implies, is more green than Chaco Canyon; because it receives more rainfall, the mesa is covered with trees – cedar, pinyon, spruce and oak. Water is also provided by nuamerous springs. Many small villages, with an average of eight surface-built rooms each, were situated on top of the mesa as early as A.D. 700. After A.D. 900, villages became even smaller, with an average of six rooms each, and the population may have declined. However, this fall-off was soon followed by renewed growth. Villages grew larger, and they were built using improved masonry techniques. By A.D. 1050, about half the villages were being constructed within the large caves that pock the upper walls of the deep canyons that cut through the mesa. By 1150, most of the area's inhabitants were living in large cliff houses, in the shelter of the caves. Presumably their motive for choosing these inaccessible sites was defense against attack. This concern for security is also evident in the construction, beginning around A.D. 950, of round or rectangular towers. These towers, often two or three stories high, were frequently situated next to kivas, perhaps to allow lookouts to warn the men assembled for rituals underground of the approach of raiders. The towers might also have had ceremonial or astronomical functions.

The peak of building activity at Mesa Verde occurred between A.D. 1230 and 1260. It is estimated that there are some 500 to 1,000 cliff houses of this period in Mesa Verde National Park. Some small cliff houses are located outside the park, and there are hundreds of medium-sized pueblos on top of the mesa. The population of the whole mesa may have been in the order of 7,000. Cliff Palace was the largest pueblo in the area, with 200 living rooms and 23 kivas. Spruce Tree House contained 120 rooms and eight kivas, and there were 150 rooms at Long House. To the north and west of Mesa Verde there are many extensive mounds, the ruins of pueblos that may each have held hundreds of people in the thirteenth century (Martin and Plog 1973, Canby 1982, Lipe 1983).

KAYENTA

At the same time (A.D. 1230–1300) that Mesa Verdean population was peaking, multi-storied cliff dwellings such as Kiet Siel and Betatakin rose in the canyons of the Kayenta region of northeastern Arizona. The masonry of these pueblos was not as well-finished as that of Mesa Verde. Lots of mortar was applied, and some walls were made of wattle and daub. The circular Kayenta kivas were simpler than those at Mesa Verde; they lacked pilasters, and had flat instead of cribbed roofs. Late Kayenta pueblos had rectangular kivas. Kayenta pottery included both corrugated and painted wares. The painted vessels were profusely decorated with geometric designs, using four color schemes: black-on-white, black-on-red, polychrome (red on an orange-red ground, the designs outlined in black), and red-on-orange.

ANASAZI INFLUENCE ON THE MOGOLLON; WESTERN PUEBLO

Anasazi influence began to be exerted on the Mogollon culture during Mogollon 4 (A.D. 850–1000), as evidenced by the replacement of red-on-white by black-on-white pottery. The Mogollon culture became thoroughly submerged within the Anasazi tradition during Mogollon 5 (A.D. 1000–1100). Surface pueblos replaced pit-houses and population grew, probably due, to some extent, to Anasazi immigration. Planned pueblos were built in Arizona in the late 1200s; they contained both great kivas and square-shaped small kivas. The Anasazi-like pottery found at these sites includes black-on-white, polychrome and corrugated wares. The population of the northern Mogollon area clustered in a few large pueblos, such as Kinishba, Point of Pines, and Grasshopper. Grasshopper comprised two separate room blocks, with a total of more than 500 rooms, arranged in two storeys; ceremonial events took place in a rectangular great kiva. Under its floor, high-status individuals were buried, accompanied by rich grave goods. Skeletons of four birds, one of them a macaw, were found in the graves; they may have been clan totems. Both the location and certain attributes of the burials, and the separation of the room blocks, suggest that the community was divided into moieties. The population seems to have included both Anasazi immigrants from the Kayenta region and Mogollon-Anasazi people from the Upper Little Colorado.

Abandonment of the western pueblos began in the late 1300s, but some sites were still occupied in the early 1400s. Many emigrants from this area probably went to the Hopi, Zuni, and Acoma pueblos, where they contributed to the formation of the Pueblo cultural tradition that has survived at those communities down to the present day.

ABANDONMENT OF THE COLORADO PLATEAU

Most of the large pueblos of the Four Corners area were abandoned in the late 1200s. Various explanations of this abandonment have been proposed: invasion by hostile Athapaskan or Numic-speaking nomads; warfare between pueblos; and climate change, particularly drought. The movement of settlements to inaccessible cliffs, and the construction of lookout towers, suggest that the Anasazi were troubled by the threat of attack in the twelfth and thirteenth centuries. However, the Athapaskan-speaking ancestors of the Navajo and Apache, who originally lived in western Canada, did not arrive in the Southwest until about A.D. 1500, and the Numic-speaking Paiute and Ute spread eastward only after many of the Colorado Plateau sites had already been deserted. It is therefore more likely that the apparent concern for defense was prompted by increasingly frequent attacks by one pueblo upon another. This was not a new phenomenon: as noted before, there is evidence of violence, even cannibalism, at tenth-century sites on the Plateau. However, there may have been a marked escalation of the levels of conflict, caused by the increasing pressure of population on arable land. That pressure was exacerbated by climatic deterioration (Martin and Plog 1973, Lipe 1983). After about A.D. 1150, the climate of the Plateau became cooler and drier, and droughts of longer duration became more frequent. Narrow tree-rings attest to a particularly severe drought that lasted from A.D. 1276 to 1299. The changing climate, over-use of valley bottomlands for farming, and felling of trees on the hillsides, may have caused accelerated erosion, resulting in the loss of topsoil and lowering of water tables. There is evidence that arroyo-cutting erosion had begun by A.D. 1100, and became worse in the 1200s. Both flood-water and irrigation farming would have been rendered more difficult by this erosion. The shortened growing season and reduced rainfall may have forced Anasazi farmers, who had occupied the marginal uplands when the climate was more favorable, to abandon their villages and move into the alluvial valleys in search of better-watered land. However, even under the best of circumstances, the valleys could not have supported this excess population; as it was, arroyo-cutting was already making farming more difficult for the valleys' inhabitants. Faced with mounting violence over access to farmland, and an environment in which farming was becoming ever more precarious, the Anasazi abandoned the Plateau pueblos and moved to the south and southeast, where summer rains were more reliable. They re-settled on the Hopi mesas of northeastern Arizona, in the Cibola region, where the Zuni and Acoma pueblos are situated today, in some parts of the Mogollon highlands, and in the Rio Grande valley. By 1450, the Mogollon highlands were also deserted, and by 1600, Pueblo groups were living at approximately the locations that they still occupy today.

The small villages of earlier periods were no longer built; instead, the late prehistoric Puebloans lived in towns with populations of 200 to 2,000. A more elaborate ceremonial system was adopted, which helped to integrate the kin groups that coalesced into these large pueblos. The new religious cult centered on the kachinas, benevolent anthropomorphic spirits who were associated with clouds and rain, and who were impersonated by masked dancers. Rock art depictions of kachina masks suggest that the cult originated in the Jornada Mogollon region of southern New Mexico (Schaafsma and Schaafsma 1974). It was adopted by the Rio Grande and western Anasazi after 1300, as shown by the appearance of masks, dancers, and symbols of the cult in paintings on kiva walls and on pottery. One of the symbols associated with the kachina cult was the horned or plumed serpent, presumably a representation of the Mexican god, Quetzalcoatl. Mexican influence is also evident in the stylized macaw design that was employed on some Pueblo IV painted pottery.

6

Chiefdoms and states: the emergence of complex societies

INTRODUCTION

As we saw in Chapter 3, the evidence for Paleo-Indian social organization, meager though it is, is consistent with the assumption that they formed egalitarian bands, comparable to those of recent hunter–gatherers. In these societies, there are no significant differences in individuals' wealth or power, and leadership roles are transitory. An individual may be temporarily vested with authority in order to coordinate the group's activities; for example, a "rabbit boss" directed the rabbit drives of the Shoshoni. However, such authority does not extend beyond the particular task. Certain individuals, particularly eloquent older men, may be more influential than other band members in the discussions that result in consensual decisions; but they do not exercise coercive power.

However, we have also seen that positions of authority were more rigidly defined among the contact period foragers of the Northwest Coast and California. Chiefs were responsible for organizing both subsistence activities and ceremonial events, and for managing relations with neighboring groups. Their positions were inherited, and they enjoyed special privileges, including greater wealth in shell beads and other valued items. The traditional hunter–gatherer ethic of sharing was maintained, so that chiefs were expected to be conspicuously generous, providing their followers with gifts of food and other goods. This aspect of the chiefly role is exemplified by the potlatches of the Northwest Coast. Clearly, the emergence of "redistributor" chiefs in these foraging societies was related to the presence of permanent villages, occupied by groups numbering in the hundreds (as opposed to the 25–50 people reported for most bands), and to the economic emphasis on abundant and storable foods (dried fish and fish oil on the Northwest Coast, acorns in California). It is quite possible that prehistoric Archaic groups which occupied rich environments, where permanent villages could be established, were organized like the tribelets of contact period California.

Apart from their temporary secular leaders, most hunter–gatherer societies recognize certain individuals as particularly adept at dealing with supernatural powers, for purposes of curing disease or divining the future. These shamans represent a significant exception to the general principles of band societies. Their knowledge of the spirit world is esoteric, shared only with selected disciples. In aboriginal California, shamans did not freely dispense their healing skills, but expected to be paid for their services (see Kroeber 1925: 35). Shamans also have a capability for coercion, as they can cast disease-causing spells on others. Shamans are often believed to communicate with spirits that take the form of animals, such as bears, rattlesnakes or jaguars; sometimes the shaman is thought to be transformed into an animal. The frequent motif of composite human-felines, found in the art of Mesoamerica, Peru, and the Intermediate area, suggests the persistence of the shamanic belief complex in those civilizations.

The esoteric aspect of shamanic activities could be extended to larger groups, open only to initiated men. For example, in California, the Wintun and other tribes had a secret society, called Kuksu, whose members held dances in which they impersonated spirits (Kroeber 1925). The leader of this cult was always a shaman. There were several basic similarities between the Kuksu cult and the various secret men's societies of the Southwestern Pueblos: all-male membership, a separate subterranean lodge for cult meetings, a foot-drum set into the lodge floor, and impersonation of spirits by dancers. Whether these similarities arose by convergent development, or reflect a common Archaic cultural substrate shared by the peoples of California and the Southwest, is uncertain. In any case, secret societies also existed among village-dwelling tribes in other regions, for example, the "False Face" curing society of the Iroquois. A common feature of such societies (or "sodalities") is the wearing of masks, which serve both to impersonate supernatural beings and to conceal the identity of the wearer. Depictions of masks on figurines from early Mesoamerican villages lend credence to Flannery's (1972) suggestion that sodalities, drawing their members from separate coresident kin groups, helped to integrate the early villages.

By means of such socio-religious organizations, and simple political institutions such as councils of village elders, societies with populations numbering in the hundreds, even several thousands, could be effectively integrated, whether for ceremonies, agricultural labor or warfare. In terms of Elman Service's (1962) scheme of socio-political evolution, these societies are "tribes". As populations grew, however, more centralized systems of distribution and control became necessary. Anthropologists refer to these larger scale socio-political systems as chiefdoms and states.

The generalized conception of the chiefdom as a stage of political evolution is based largely on ethnohistoric observations of Polynesian and African societies. Anthropologists have also drawn upon contact period accounts of chiefdoms in Central and South America and southeastern North America. The populations of chiefdoms generally numbered in the tens of thousands. There was usually a central community, larger than the rest, where the chief, his relatives and retainers lived. This central place also contained a ceremonial precinct, where priests conducted worship of the gods (a mediating role that had developed from that of the shaman). In theory, the people of the chiefdom varied in status according to their respective genealogical distance from the central chiefly line of descent. As relatives of the chief, they could expect him to treat them generously in return for their allegiance and payments of tribute. Most of the population resided in smaller villages or hamlets, only visiting the central place for ceremonial feasts by which the chief displayed his generosity. Each of the smaller communities might be ruled by a lesser chief, subordinate to the central ruler. The most complex chiefdoms might have three administrative levels: village chiefs, district chiefs, and the paramount. Chiefdoms usually had a theocratic cast, much of the chief's authority deriving from his supposed relationship to ancestral spirits and other supernatural beings. Often the chief also served as high priest. The stages of his life – birth, initiation, marriage and death – were marked by public rituals. In economic terms, the chief functioned as the central node of a redistributive network, collecting tribute from communities situated in diverse micro-environmental zones, and accomplishing the transference of food and goods among these communities by means of periodic ceremonial feasts.

Several archaeological manifestations are usually interpreted as denoting prehistoric chiefdoms. Large-scale constructions, typically earthen mounds, imply the mobilization and direction of numerous workers by a central authority, presumably a chief (or high priest, or an individual combining these roles). Such mounds often contain the remains of a limited segment of the ancient population; if many burials are incorporated, those that are most centrally located may have the most elaborate tombs and richest accompanying grave goods. According to ethnohistoric accounts, upon the death of a Natchez chief his wives were strangled so as to accompany him. Archaeological evidence of wife and/or retainer sacrifice is known from sites such as Kolomoki (Georgia), Cahokia (Illinois), Coclé (Panama) and Kaminaljuyú (Guatemala). Concentrations of artifacts made from exotic imported materials in a small number of burials suggest that a chiefly élite had privileged access to display items that underlined their special status. Settlement patterns characterized by a single large center, surrounded by smaller sites, may also imply a chiefdom organization; a two- or three-tiered hierarchy of settlement sizes can be plausibly interpreted as reflecting a two- or three-level administrative structure. Based on ethnohistoric accounts and on these archaeological criteria, chiefdoms are thought to have developed in the southeastern United States, Central America, the Caribbean, Ecuador and Colombia, and in parts of the Orinoco and Amazon basins. Also, the prehistoric societies of Mesoamerica and Peru seem to have passed through an early chiefdom phase as they developed into states.

Although states bear much resemblance to chiefdoms, they differ in certain respects. There is a difference of scale: states can incorporate hundreds of thousands, even millions of people. The Inca state, for example, controlled some six to eight million subjects. The society is no longer conceptualized as a kin-based unit; instead, it is divided into classes: royalty, nobles, commoners, and slaves. Bureaucrats appointed by the ruler replace heads of local lineages and clans as administrators (although the kin-based *ayllu* and *calpulli* retained important functions in the Inca and Aztec states, respectively). Although an organized religion continues to provide the regime with ideological support, increasing reliance is placed on threatened or actual use of military force to compel subjects' obedience and payment of taxes or tribute. The central community expands from a chiefly residence and ceremonial site to a full-fledged city, occupied not only by nobles and priests but by bureaucrats, specialist craftsmen, and farmers as well (this urban pattern was characteristic of Mesoamerican states, but was absent in some Peruvian states, notably that of the Inca). The capital is surrounded by satellite communities of three or more sizes. The state takes over the chief's role as central collector and redistributor of food and goods. In Mesoamerica, a parallel redistributive market system developed, with some degree of independence from state control, but in the Andes, the Inca state maintained strict control of production and distribution of commodities.

Archaeologically, it can be difficult to distinguish states from complex chiefdoms. Everyone agrees that Teotihuacán, with an estimated population of more than 125,000, was a city-state. But was the Maya site of Tikal, with some 30,000 residents, the center of a small state or a big chiefdom? If Tikal was a state, does that mean that we must also designate Cahokia, with a nearly equivalent population, as a state? Must a state have cities? If so, the Inca empire would not qualify, for its capital, Cuzco, was essentially a royal ceremonial center.

Why did complex socio-political systems develop? Anthropologists have proposed a number of theories that emphasize, to varying degrees, the causative roles of irrigation agriculture, warfare, population pressure, redistributive exchange and long distance trade. Karl Wittfogel (1957) suggested that, in river valleys, coordination of work crews to build and maintain levees and canals, and adjudication of disputes over access to water, required the establishment of a strong, centralized bureaucratic state. Sanders and Price (1968) contend that, in the specific case of

Teotihuacán, intensification of agriculture by means of terracing and irrigation permitted rapid population growth, which caused competition between rival communities for scarce land, leading to warfare and state formation. Robert Carneiro (1970) has pointed out that inter-tribal warfare, sparked by competition for land, is common among village farmers; but he suggests that it will only lead to the emergence of chiefdoms and states where "environmental circumscription", lack of productive land in the surrounding region, compels defeated groups to remain in place as tribute-paying subjects of the victors. Morton Fried (1967) suggests that ranking originally develops as a consequence of population growth and the emergence of a redistributive economy. Ultimately, increasing population pressure on agricultural land causes land-owning lineages to become increasingly exclusive of outsiders. When such privileged groups seek to restrict the access of other members of the society to land, water or other key resources, they must create repressive state institutions. Elman Service (1975), in contrast to Fried, has stressed the beneficial aspects of the chiefdom, which he sees as an embryonic form of the state. The chief as redistributor facilitates the exchange of diverse resources among groups that occupy differing ecological niches. As several archaeologists have also suggested, such an extensive symbiotic system provides security against local shortfalls, because it is unlikely that all resources and all areas within a broad region will be equally hard-hit by natural disasters. This "security in diversity" theory has been employed to explain the towns and roads of Chaco Canyon, the Hopewell mounds, as well as the expansion of the Inca empire.

These theoretical perspectives should be kept in mind as we examine the archaeological evidence pertaining to the chiefdoms and states of prehistoric America.

RANKING AND CHIEFDOMS IN THE EASTERN WOODLANDS: ADENA, HOPEWELL AND MISSISSIPPIAN

As we saw in the first chapter, fascination with the impressive and enigmatic mounds of the Ohio and Mississippi valleys was a major stimulus to the growth of American archaeology. By the end of the nineteenth century, the long-popular idea that the mounds were the work of a vanished pre-indian race had been convincingly refuted. Cyrus Thomas' research had proven that the mounds had been raised by native Americans, and that mound-building had even continued, in some areas, down to the time of European contact.

Archaeologists remained reluctant, however, to postulate a strictly indigenous origin for mound-building. Instead, diffusion of the practice from some area where it was already well-established seemed to be the best way to explain its apparently sudden and relatively late appearance in the eastern woodlands. A few archaeologists suggested that mound-building had diffused, along with cord-marked Woodland pottery, across the Bering Strait from Asia; but they had to admit that the absence of both traits in the intervening regions was problematic. According to another theory, the idea of raising mounds for the dead, and techniques of pottery manufacture, had been brought across the Atlantic from Bronze Age Scandinavia. But the most widely accepted diffusionist theory attributed the mounds to Mexican influence, exerted either by transmission of ideas or by an actual immigration of colonists. The apparent physical distinctiveness of the round-headed occupants of the Ohio mound graves from their long-headed Archaic predecessors seemed to support the theory of Mexican colonization. The great size of some mounds and earthwork complexes implied the existence of a large labor force, with enough leisure time to devote to construction projects. The work of specialist craftsmen, freed from subsistence tasks, seemed to be manifest in the fine quality of the artifacts buried in the mounds. Leisure time and craft specialization were inconceivable except as by-products of agriculture, and so archaeologists assumed that the mound-builders were farmers, who grew maize, beans, and squash. These staple crops were, of course, of Mexican origin. One could construct a neat diffusionary model, based on this evidence: Mexican emigrés brought their staple crops, pottery-making, and mound-building into the woodlands, and imposed themselves upon the local inhabitants as a privileged élite.

The credibility of the Mexican hypothesis was weakened as archaeologists realized that the Ohio mounds were older than those of the Mississippi Valley; one would have expected the age of sites to decrease as one moved northward, away from the supposed Mexican homeland. Archaeological expeditions to the northeastern corner of Mexico failed to produce evidence of any ancestral mound-building culture. Furthermore, as village sites in Ohio and Illinois were excavated, it became clear that the early mound-builders of the Adena and Hopewell cultures had grown little, if any, maize.

The faltering case for a Mexican connection received a much needed boost when radiocarbon dates placed the Poverty Point culture of Louisiana as early as 1200 B.C. The huge complex of concentric earth ridges and mounds at Poverty Point was earlier than the Adena mounds of the Ohio Valley, which were built around 500 B.C. The southerly location of Poverty Point, near the mouth of the Mississippi and not far from the Gulf coast, made it a plausible first stop for hypothetical Mexican culture-bearers. Its date suggested a relationship with the Olmec, who constructed a massive earth platform at San Lorenzo at about the same time. Some archaeologists, eager to demonstrate the Olmec link, thought they saw Olmec-like characteristics, such as the slit forehead, in the ceramic figurines of the Poverty Point culture. However, the pottery that was found, in small quantity, at Poverty Point was derived not from Mexico, but from the fiber-tempered ware of the Southeastern Archaic. In most other cultural traits, e.g. soapstone bowls, atlatl weights, and broad spear-points, Poverty Point was clearly related to other Late Archaic cultures of the Southeast. As in the case of the later Adena culture, maize was conspicuously absent, although squash may have been grown. However, squash had evidently diffused throughout the Southeastern woodlands by 2000 B.C., so its presence at Poverty Point would not indicate a particularly close relationship to Mexico. Today, the majority opinion is that Poverty Point represents a localized, indigenous florescence of a Southeastern Archaic culture in a rich environment where efficient harvesting of wild foods yielded a socially useful surplus (Gibson 1974a, Muller 1983).

There are no specific traits that connect Adena to Poverty Point; the earthworks are different, and the diagnostic Poverty Point artifacts, clay balls that were probably used in place of stones for boiling, are not found in Ohio. It therefore seems most likely that Adena mound-building was an independent development.

A special concern for the dead had already become evident in several Late Archaic societies of the Northeast. In the Orient culture of Long Island (ca. 1000 B.C.), numerous spear-points and steatite bowls that had been punctured to symbolize death were deposited in cremation burials. Both single and collective graves were situated on the summits of high sand hills. Tools and ornaments were placed with the dead at Port au Choix, Newfoundland, and at other Maritime Archaic sites; in the same region, the earliest known mound burial had been made around 5500 B.C. Another Late Archaic culture that displayed fairly elaborate mortuary behavior was the Glacial Kame culture. This culture, which occupied Michigan, Ohio, Indiana and southern Ontario around 1500 to 1000 B.C., gets its name from the custom of interring the dead on top of hills of glacial gravel. The dead were sometimes provided with ornaments of copper and marine shell. These exotic items attest to the maintenance of long-distance exchange networks. The presence of formal cemeteries in Late Archaic contexts suggests that populations were becoming more sedentary. Seen against this backdrop of Late Archaic mortuary ceremonialism, Adena mound-building appears to be simply an elaboration of widespread, pre-existent cultural tendencies. It was, after all, only a minor innovation to entomb the dead within artificial hills instead of burying them on top of natural ones.

1 Grave Creek Mound
2 Scioto Valley Hopewell sites
   (Seip, Harness, Mound City)
3 Rice Lake sites
4 Trempealeau
5 Marksville
6 Copena
7 Santa Rosa – Swift Creek
8 Crystal River
9 St Johns
10 Serpent Mound
11 Cahokia
12 Spiro
13 Poverty Point
14 Moundville
15 Etowah
16 Aztalan
17 Havana (Illinois Hopewell)
18 Crab Orchard (Illinois Hopewell)
19 Kansas City Hopewell
20 Weeden Island
21 Kolomoki
22 Delmarva Adena
23 Meadowood, Owasco, Iroquois
24 Porter Hopewellian
25 Miller
26 Glacial Kame
27 Powers Phase
28 Goodall
29 Cooper
30 Fort Center
31 Plaquemine-Natchez
32 Middle Missouri
33 Central Plains
34 Northeastern Plains

Fig. 67. Adena, Hopewell, and Mississippian sites and regions.

230

ADENA

Some of the Adena burial mounds may pre-date 500 B.C., but most were raised after that time. The greatest concentration of Adena sites occurs in the central Ohio Valley, within a 480-km (300-mile) circle around the town of Chillicothe (Dragoo 1964, Griffin 1983). Most of the estimated 300 to 500 Adena sites that have been recorded since the beginning of the nineteenth century are mounds, and most, but not all, of the Adena earthworks contained burials. One notable non-funerary construction is the famous Serpent Mound (although there was a burial mound nearby). Unlike so many other Ohio mounds, which have been bulldozed away to make room for streets, shopping centers, and parking lots, this site has been preserved as a state park. The great snake's undulating body measures 382 m (1,254 ft) from head to tightly coiled tail, and rises 1.2 to 1.5 m (4 to 5 ft) above ground level. The snake is about to devour an oval object, which may represent an egg, or perhaps a frog. We can only speculate about the meaning of this symbolism. The Adena people also built enclosures, usually circular but sometimes in the form of squares or pentagons. These "sacred circles" average 90 m (300 ft) in diameter. Burial mounds were often built either inside or outside them. Although there is little hard evidence to go on, it is easy enough to imagine periodic rituals being conducted within these enclosures.

One of the largest Adena mounds was the Grave Creek Mound in West Virginia. It was about 73 m (240 ft) in diameter, and 21 m (70 ft) high; some 54,500 metric tons (72,000 tons) of earth were piled up, basketful by basketful, to construct it. Some Adena mounds were built in one episode; others, such as the Cresap Mound in West Virginia, seem to have risen gradually through several burial and construction phases.

Post-hole patterns found at the bases of some excavated mounds show that they were built on top of circular houses that were intentionally burned down before construction began. It is possible that corpses may have been placed temporarily in these houses, until the flesh had decayed enough so that the exposed bones could be coated with red ochre. Usually, the dead were buried in the center of the mound, lying on their backs in an extended position; but flexed burials, bundles of disjointed bones, mutilated and decapitated skeletons, and separate skulls and bones, were also placed within the mounds. In late Adena burials, large rectangular log tombs were built to hold one to three bodies, which were smeared with red ochre or black graphite; earth was then heaped on top. Cremation was actually a more common means of disposal than interment. In Adena villages, the dead were burned in round clay basins. Sometimes, cremated remains were deposited in the mounds.

Adult males seem to have been placed preferentially in central locations within Adena mounds, and to have been buried with objects denoting their high status; but grave goods were more often associated with children. Most grave goods were utilitarian items, such as chipped stone blades, drills, and scrapers. Also included in graves were the typical Adena and Robbins spear-points, which were related to types found elsewhere in the eastern woodlands. More exotic grave goods included crescents and sheets of mica, imported from North Carolina, and various objects – bracelets, beads, crescents, celts, adzes and gorgets – made of copper from Lake Superior. Gorgets are perforated objects of polished stone or, rarely, copper, which are believed to have been tied to strings worn around the neck. The distinctive Adena gorget type was shaped like a simple fishing line reel. A small amount of marine shell, imported from the Gulf coast, was deposited in the mounds. The Adena dead were often buried with tubular stone pipes. Some late examples were carved in effigy form; the most famous of these, from the Adena Mound, seems to depict a goiterous dwarf. The pipes were presumably used to smoke tobacco. If one recalls that the contact period hunter–gatherers of California and the Northwest Coast, who grew no food plants, cultivated tobacco, it should not be surprising that the basically non-agricultural Adena people also grew it.

Late Adena grave goods sometimes included stone tablets, engraved with highly stylized representations of buzzards or other birds of prey. These tablets may have been used to prepare red ochre for ceremonial use, or to sharpen bone awls, perhaps for tattooing. Trophy skulls, sometimes polished, were occasionally buried with late Adena individuals. Head-dresses, usually fashioned from the skullcaps and antlers of deer or elk, but sometimes imitations made of thin hammered sheets of copper, were also placed in late Adena tombs. In the Ayers Mound in Kentucky, a man who may have been a shaman was buried with the artificially thinned upper jaw of a wolf stuck in his mouth. While he was alive, his upper incisor teeth had been knocked out to make room for the wolf palate, which must have been part of an elaborate dance costume. Similarly modified wolf jaws have been found in two other Adena mounds.

The Adena mound-builders apparently gathered periodically for funeral ceremonies and construction, but for most of the year the population was widely dispersed in small, temporary villages. The round Adena houses varied in diameter from 6 to 24 m (20 to 80 ft). Some must have been occupied by single families, but others were big enough to have held 40 people. Some villages consisted or 10 or more houses; others had only two to four. Even allowing for the possible disappearance of sites due to river action and modern development, the estimated population density for the Ohio Valley in Adena times is very low – less than 0.39 persons per square kilometer (Griffin 1983).

232

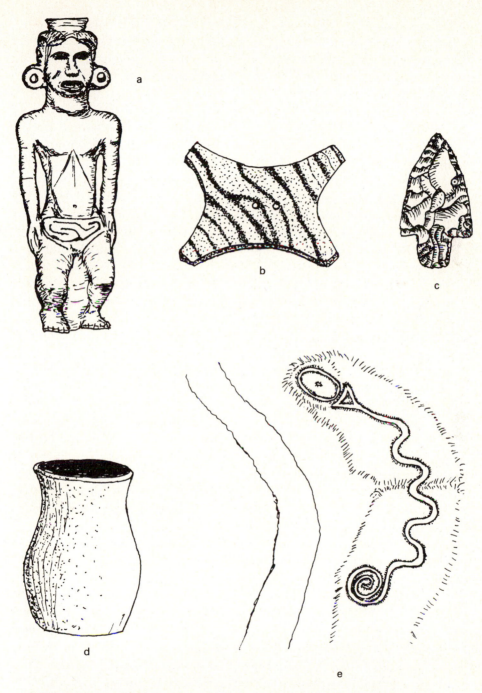

Fig. 68. Adena artifacts: (A) stone pipe, in form of goiterous dwarf (?), from the Adena Mound (height ca. 20 cm); (B) reel-shaped gorget, made of banded slate (ca. 10 cm); (C) lobate-stemmed Adena point (about ½ actual size); (D) ceramic vessel; (E) Serpent Mound (the serpent is 382 m long, from the tip of the upper jaw to the end of the tail). (B–D after Dragoo 1964.)

The diversity of Adena mortuary treatments, and particularly the labor expended on log tombs for a few individuals, suggest that there were different statuses in Adena society. The fact that the occupants of the log tombs were generally adult males may imply that high status was achieved rather than inherited.

A major difficulty we face in trying to reconstruct Adena social and political organization is the lack of appropriate recent analogs. Recent hunter–gatherer societies which occupied the rich environments of California and the Northwest Coast developed ranking. Unfortunately, they did not undertake construction projects comparable to the Adena mounds. Their funerary rituals tended to be overshadowed by major ceremonies connected with initiation, or held to ensure the regeneration of nature. The degree of craft specialization represented by Adena effigy pipes, polished stone artifacts, and copperwork is more easily matched, by the intricate basketwork of California and the sophisticated wood-carvings of the Northwest Coast. The sheer size of Adena sites like the Great Serpent Mound and the Grave Creek Mound implies the collaboration of people from numerous villages; perhaps they were participants in a pan-tribal cult, analogous to the Kuksu cult which linked the tribelets of California.

The spread of a funerary cult may explain how Adena-style artifacts reached far-off sites in the Northeast. The Augustine Mound in New Brunswick, and a group of mounds on Long Sault Island in the St Lawrence River, seem to have been built in imitation of Adena practices. A surprising concentration of Adena-style artifacts, such as stone tubes, Adena points, birdstones, gorgets, and shell and copper beads, has been found in multi-stage graves at sites on the Delmarva Peninsula, on the eastern side of Chesapeake Bay (Dragoo 1976a, Ford 1976). At first, archaeologists interpreted these finds as evidence of short-lived colonies, established by Adena refugees from the Ohio Valley. However, it is now generally believed that Adena-style artifacts reached groups to the east through an exchange network, and that the custom of lavishing these valued items on the dead was spread by the same mechanism.

Despite the continuities noted earlier with Late Archaic cultures, the Adena culture is classified as Early Woodland, primarily because of the presence of the aforementioned pipes and, more importantly, of pottery. Early Adena pots, like those that were made elsewhere in the eastern woodlands after 1000 B.C., had rounded or cone-shaped bottoms. Their surfaces were plain, or bore the impressions of a cord-wrapped paddle. Some of the pottery was check-stamped, using a carved wooden paddle. A later Adena style of pottery, Montgomery Incised, was decorated with incised lozenges.

HOPEWELL

Around 100 B.C., the Adena culture in the Ohio Valley was transformed into the Hopewell culture. At about the same time that Hopewell pottery and other traits began to appear in Ohio, they also appeared in southern Illinois. Illinois Hopewell may in fact be a little earlier, which raises the possibility that the Adena-to-Hopewell transition in Ohio may have somehow been sparked by diffusion or immigration from Illinois. Immigration might account for the replacement of the round-headed Adena population by the long-headed Hopewell people; like earlier Archaic populations of the Midwest, the Illinois Hopewellians were long-headed. However, this change in head shape may simply have been the result of abandonment of the Adena custom of intentionally deforming infants' skulls. The Ohio Valley situation is complicated by radiocarbon dates that suggest that Adena and Hopewell groups may have coexisted there for several centuries. In any case, even if Hopewell ceramic styles originated in Illinois, the florescence of the Hopewell tradition, as evidenced by lavish grave goods and enormous mounds and earthworks, clearly occurred in the Scioto Valley of Ohio. It is also obvious that in many respects Hopewell is simply an elaboration of Adena traditions.

As in the case of Adena, available evidence points to intensive harvesting of wild plants and hunting as the predominant subsistence activities of the Hopewell culture. Small amounts of maize have been recovered from a few sites, such as the McGraw village in Ohio (Prufer 1964). However the inference, based on the paucity of its remains, that maize was not a significant part of the Hopewell diet has been strengthened by the results of the application of a new analytical technique to human skeletal material (Bender, Baerreis and Steventon 1981). The basis of this technique is the recent discovery that maize and some other plants that grow in arid or semi-arid regions absorb more of the C13 isotope of carbon than most plants do. Humans who consume maize as a staple food will consequently absorb into their flesh and bones a greater than usual amount of C13, relative to other isotopes. As expected, tests of skeletal samples showed that Archaic inhabitants of New York, Illinois and Wisconsin did not eat maize, while Late Woodland and Mississippian peoples did. Bones of Hopewell people from Wisconsin, Illinois, and Ohio were also tested, and they showed about the same ratio of C13 as the Archaic skeletons – a strong indication that they had not consumed much maize. Apart from maize, other cultigens of Mesoamerican origin – squash and gourds – were known to, but evidently not much used by, the Hopewellians. Beans, an essential complement to maize in the Mexican diet, have not been found in any Hopewell sites. Apparently agriculture based on Mesoamerican cultigens was not the economic foundation of the Hopewell florescence. Some archaeologists have nevertheless suggested that gardening (horticulture) was an important subsistence activity, but that it involved native plants, such as marsh elder, amaranth, chenopodium and sunflower (Yarnell 1965, 1977). The sunflower and marsh elder had been domesticated during the Early Woodland period; the status of the other seed-bearing plants is more ambiguous, but their occurrence at sites lying outside their native habitats is suggestive of some sort of cultivation. However, available evidence indicates that cultivated seeds were insignificant in the Hopewell diet in comparison to nuts, especially hickory (Ford 1979). Other important food sources were deer, small mammals, turkeys, fish and shellfish. Garden-grown seeds only supplemented these foods procured by hunting and gathering. Hopewell settlements were concentrated on or near river bottomlands, not for floodplain agriculture, but because wild resources were most abundant in those micro-environments.

Early archaeologists understandably concentrated their attention on the mysterious and artifact-rich Hopewell burial mounds; thus, habitation sites were largely ignored. Although the situation has improved somewhat in recent years, we still do not know very much about Hopewell community organization and settlement patterns. In the Illinois Valley, villages ranged in extent from 0.1 to 6 hectares; the largest villages could not have held more than a few hundred people. They were generally located at the foot of a bluff, near the river and about 20 km (12½ miles) away from the next large village. Faunal remains from the Scovill site, a late (A.D. 450) Hopewell village on the Spoon River in the lower Illinois Valley, show that it was abandoned in the early spring and late autumn (Munson, Parmalee and Yarnell 1971). The houses that comprised the villages were rectangular or oval-shaped; they were built of wooden posts and were probably covered with mats or with sheets of bark, like the wigwams of contact period Indians.

We must turn to the mortuary evidence for more clues to Hopewell economic, social and political organization. The grandest mounds and richest graves were found in the Ohio Valley. The Hopewell culture got its name from a Captain M. C. Hopewell, the owner of the farm near Chillicothe where an extensive mound complex, excavated in the early 1890s, was located. At the Hopewell site, 38 mounds were contained within a rectangular enclosure, 45 hectares (110 acres) in extent. The central mound, no. 25, is the largest burial mound in North America. At Mound City, there were 24 mounds inside a 5.25-hectare (13-acre) enclosure. The other four major excavated sites – Seip, Turner, Harness and Tremper, range in size between these extremes. The Seip Mound, 9 m (30 ft) high, 76 m (250 ft) long and 46 m (150 ft) wide, is the second largest Hopewell mound. The Ohio mounds average about 30 m (100 ft) in basal diameter and 9 m (30 ft) in height. Their average volume is almost 14,000 cubic m (half a million cubic feet), representing more than 200,000 man-hours of labor.

The Hopewellians continued the Adena custom of building mounds within sacred circles, but their earthworks were on a much grander scale. The complex of circles, square and octagon, linked by earthen avenues, at Newark, Ohio, covered 6.4 square km (4 square miles). Earthworks of this sort generally appear to have had ceremonial rather than defensive functions, but some hilltop enclosures, seemingly equipped with bastions, may have been fortifications.

The remains of more than 1,150 individuals were recovered from the six major Ohio sites. Modes of disposal included cremation, extended and flexed primary burial, and bundle and partial secondary burial. It has been estimated that three-quarters of the Hopewell dead were cremated, burial in the flesh having been reserved for the élite. Both cremated remains and extended corpses were placed in charnel houses made of wooden posts; these houses were then burned, and mounds built over their ruins.

The Hopewell élite were often buried, like their Adena predecessors, in log tombs within the charnel houses; but they were accompanied by more and richer grave goods than had been provided for the Adena dead. In the

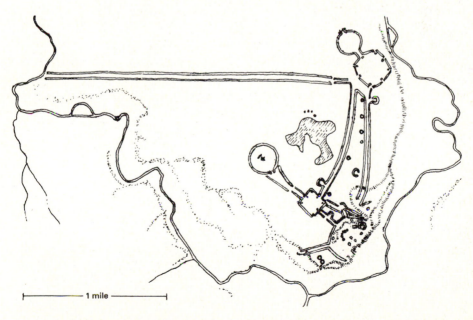

Fig. 69. Hopewell earthworks at Newark, Ohio (diameter of central circle is 358 m). (After Prufer 1964.)

237

log tomb within the Seip Mound, four adults and two children were buried with thousands of freshwater pearls, and tools and ornaments made of copper, mica, tortoise shell, and silver. In the central mound at Hopewell, a tall young man lay beside a young woman. She was bedecked with, and surrounded by, thousands of pearl beads and buttons made of copper-covered wood and stone; she also wore copper bracelets. Both individuals wore copper ear-spools, copper breast-plates, and necklaces of grizzly bear canines. Also, a row of copper ear-spools had been laid out along one side of the grave. A rather strange touch was the presence of artificial copper noses; another example was found on the face of a skeleton in the Seip Mound. A cremated male, buried in Mound 11 at Hopewell, may have been a master obsidian worker; apart from two sheets of mica, a few pearl beads, and a polished piece of green chlorite, he was accompanied by several hundred pounds of obsidian fragments. This man may have made the several hundred obsidian spears found in an altar deposit in Mound 25. Three thousand sheets of mica and 90 kilograms of galena were buried with one man in Mound 17. Among the other items found

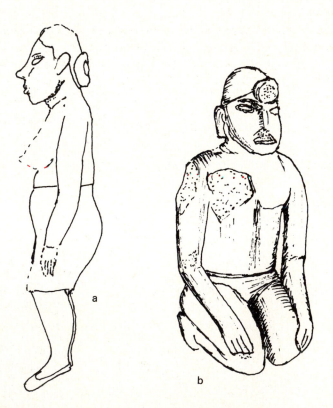

Fig. 70. Ohio Hopewell clay figurines: (A) woman (height 18 cm); (B) man with hair-knot on forehead, from Turner mound (height 11 cm)

either in association with burials or in large caches within the Ohio mounds were: copper axes; copper and mica cutout effigies of fish, birds, snake heads, claws, human heads and hands, as well as swastikas and other geometric cutouts; imitation deer antler head-dresses; flint and chlorite discs; polished stone atlatl weights, ear-spools, and effigy pipes; copper pan-pipes; copper and stone reel-shaped gorgets; painted fabrics, woven from plant fibers; perforated human jaws and engraved human bones. A few human figurines of fired clay provide evidence of the Hopewellians' appearance. Women went bare-breasted; they wore calf-length skirts, belted at the waist. Men wore loincloths. Their hair was sometimes worn in a scalp-lock ("Mohican"), but other, longer hairstyles were also known. One figure from the Turner mound group wears his hair bunched in a knot on his forehead; this was the mark of a shaman among contact period Plains Indians.

The raw materials for Hopewell grave goods were brought in from distant sources. Trace element analysis has shown that most of the obsidian came from what is today Yellowstone Park, in Wyoming. Conch and turtle shells, shark and alligator teeth and barracuda jaws were acquired from the coast of Florida. Mica and chlorite came from North Carolina and Tennessee. Most Hopewell copper was mined near Lake Superior, but some came from the southeast. Chunks of galena were obtained from the upper Mississippi Valley and the Ozarks. Large amounts of bluish flint were imported from Indiana, and chalcedony from North Dakota also reached Ohio. While "down the line" inter-village exchange mechanisms may have accounted for some of the imports, long-range trading or mining expeditions also seem to have been involved, for example in the acquisition of the western obsidian.

ILLINOIS VALLEY HOPEWELL

The Illinois Valley may have been the birth-place of the Hopewell tradition, but it never matched the Ohio Valley in the grandiosity of its mortuary cult. In Illinois, there was very little cremation, no elaborate charnel houses, no big mounds (the largest, at the Ogden-Fettie site, was 4 m (12 ft) high and 61 by 53 m (183 by 159 ft) at its base), and no extensive geometric earthworks.

The Illinois Hopewellians built conical mounds on the crests of bluffs, and loaf-shaped mounds on the flood-plains. In each case, the honored dead were laid out in extended position in a central rectangular log vault, as in Ohio. Other bodies were buried in the doughnut-shaped earthen ring surrounding the central tomb. Bones of still other individuals were collected into secondary bundle burials and placed either in small auxiliary mounds or in pits dug alongside the main mound. There were twice as many males as females in bundle burials. In the flood-plain mounds, very few burials were placed around the central chamber.

Some of the log tombs were occupied by only a single adult male. In other cases, women, adolescents and children, presumably relatives of the deceased males, were also present. This hints at the possible operation of a rudimentary system of ranking according to heritable ascribed status.

The men of highest rank, and some select members of their families, were buried in the log chambers of the flood-plain mounds. They were accompanied by such grave goods as quartz crystal pendants, wolf jaws, copper necklaces, ear-spools, platform pipes (probably imported from Ohio), mica sheets, and carved marine shell vessels.

Skeletal analyses by physical anthropologist Jane Buikstra have yielded intriguing clues to Illinois Hopewell social organization (Struever and Holton 1979). The males buried in the central log tombs often suffered from arthritis of the elbow, while those buried in the surrounding earth rings had arthritis of the wrists instead. This suggests that the central, presumably high-ranking males may have been hunters who frequently used spearthrowers, which caused stress on the elbow joint, while the peripheral males may have been craftsmen. Another ailment that often afflicted high-status males was the growth of bony tumors in their ear cartilage, which probably impaired their hearing. Today, such tumors occur most frequently in individuals who do a lot of swimming and diving. It has therefore been speculated that the high-status males may have enjoyed the exclusive privilege of diving to the river bottom to collect pearl-bearing mussels. Apart from their peculiar maladies, the high-status males also differ from the rest of the population in that they were

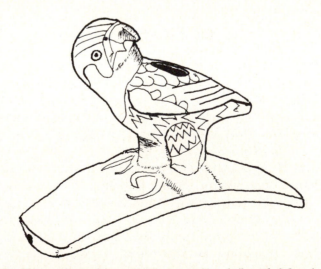

Fig. 71. Hopewell platform pipe, in form of hawk (length 8.3 cm).

always taller, though there is no skeletal indication that their diet was better than others'. It is possible that the short stature of commoners was caused by frequent marriage within their local, inbred community. The "big men", by virtue of their role as mediators in inter-tribal exchange and other external affairs, may have had more opportunity to take wives from distant communities, thereby imparting a "hybrid vigor" to their children.

THE EXPANSION OF HOPEWELL

From southern Illinois, Hopewell culture traits appear to have spread, by diffusion and/or migration, northward into Wisconsin (Trempealeau culture) and Michigan (Goodall culture); westward into Missouri (Kansas City and Cooper cultures), and southward, through western Tennessee (Copena culture), to Louisiana (Marksville), Mississippi (Miller), Alabama (Porter) and Florida (Santa Rosa and Swift Creek cultures). The Ohio Valley Hopewell may also have had a direct impact on the southeastern Hopewellian cultures, and its influence was certainly felt by mound-building groups in western New York (Squawkie Hill phase), southern Ontario (Rice Lake sites), and Pennsylvania. Hopewell influence is most clearly expressed in a widely adopted style of pottery, which features zoned, rocker-stamped decoration, sometimes depicting abstract birds of prey or ducks. Copper artifacts, such as ear-spools, breast-plates and pan-pipes, are also markers of Hopewell influence, as is the practice of mound construction.

The strength of Hopewell influence on these peripheral cultures evidently depended on factors other than simple distance from the heartland areas. Thus there are only pale reflections of classic Hopewell in the Copena (Copper + Galena; culture of western Tennessee and northern Alabama. A total of only 154 imported copper objects other than beads, some 50 low, small mounds containing burials with few grave goods, and rare finds of Hopewell-style ceramics, are all that there is to show the impact of Hopewell on the local inhabitants (Walthall 1980). In contrast, the burial mounds, earthworks, and decorated pottery of the Marksville culture of Louisiana so strikingly resemble those of the classic Hopewell centers as to suggest the possibility of actual colonization from the north. Hopewell-like Marksville pottery was used not only as a funerary accompaniment, but for domestic purposes as well. In most other societies within the Hopewell sphere of influence, the Hopewell-style ceramics, ornaments, and mortuary rites seem to have been grafted on to the ongoing local cultural tradition.

The spread of Hopewell artifacts may denote acceptance of an ideology that stressed elaborate funerary rites. This mortuary cult would have been most eagerly espoused by local "big men", who saw in it a way to enhance their own status. Secondary centers or nodes within the far-flung Hopewell exchange network, exemplified by Marksville, may have arisen wherever the local economy generated enough wealth to attract a disproportionate flow of raw materials, finished goods and craftsmen. Even before such societies were drawn into the Hopewellian network, they might well have developed redistributive economic systems, in which big men organized ceremonial feasts, where food from diverse local microenvironments was brought, to be doled out to the assembled villagers. Recent anthropological analyses of ceremonial exchange and feasting systems in tribal and chiefdom-level societies – e.g. the kula ring by which shell ornaments passed from one man to another in the Trobriand Islands, or the Northwest Coast potlatch – suggest that ritualized exchanges often mask the exchange and redistribution of material necessities. The compulsion to perform the ritualized exchanges may

Fig. 72. Hopewellian pottery with stylized bird motifs: (A) Marksville, Louisiana (height 11 cm, diameter 8.2 cm); (B) Illinois (Havana culture), height 13.4 cm, diameter 16.4 cm; (C) Ohio (height 24 cm).

ensure that the more mundane, but nevertheless essential, goods will also be redistributed. It may thus be hypothesized, but has not yet been proven, that the periodic aggregation of Hopewellian villagers for mortuary rites facilitated the redistribution, by big men, of the food-stuffs collected in diverse micro-environments, and thereby counteracted the potentially disastrous effects of local resource fluctuations.

THE DECLINE OF HOPEWELL

The poorly understood collapse of the Hopewell "interaction sphere" around A.D. 400 might have been caused by the disruption of such redistribution networks. One interesting suggestion relates this decline to increasing dependence on agriculture (Hall 1980). Villagers with an assured supply of stored maize would have had less motivation to participate in the collective mortuary and redistributive ceremonies. However, on present evidence, maize agriculture was not widely adopted in the northeastern woodlands until about A.D. 800, several centuries *after* the decline of Hopewell.

It has been speculated, on the basis of the observed increase in the number of sites in the Illinois Valley from Middle (Hopewell) to Late Woodland, that unchecked population growth might somehow have strained the integrative capabilities of the Hopewell socio-political system (Muller 1983). It has also been noted that the Hopewell decline coincides with the disappearance of finely-made atlatl weights (birdstones and boatstones) from the archaeological record. This must reflect the replacement of the spearthrower by a new weapon system – the bow and arrow (Ford 1974). In fact, small points, probably from arrows, occur at Illinois sites dated around A.D. 400 to 600. The greater range and accuracy thus achieved may have affected hunting practices, and, perhaps, warfare. An increased incidence of warfare in the Ohio Valley in late Hopewell times has been inferred from the seemingly defensive location and layout of some hilltop enclosures, which occasionally also show signs of having been burnt (Prufer 1964).

Climate change has also been cited as the primary cause of the Hopewell collapse. It became colder, world-wide, around A.D. 400. As long as archaeologists assumed that Hopewell subsistence was agricultural, it was reasonable to theorize that the colder weather might have caused crop failures, thus weakening the economic foundations of Hopewell. However, now that agriculture is generally thought to have played an insignificant role in Hopewell subsistence, this theory is no longer tenable in its original form. Nevertheless, the possibility remains that the Hopewell decline was caused by climatic deterioration, which might have led to decreasing yields of wild resources. This climatic explanation has the advantage of accounting for the fact that some of the south-eastern societies that had been integrated into the Hopewellian exchange network continued to flourish after the more northerly centers in Ohio and Illinois declined.

POST-HOPEWELLIAN CULTURES OF THE SOUTHEAST

In the lower Mississippi Valley, the ceramics of the Marksville culture underwent some slight changes as it was transformed into the Troyville and Issaquena cultures (Greengo 1964); sites of these cultures date to about A.D. 450 to 800. The Issaquena folk lived in small villages in the flood-plain. They seem to have built both conical mounds and flat-topped "platform" mounds, which were possibly substructures for élite residences. Contrary to earlier Hopewellian norms, many of the Issaquena mounds were evidently not used for burials. This is an important difference, because in the later Mississippian cultures, mounds functioned primarily as substructures for temples or chief's houses.

Typical Hopewellian artifacts had been carried through the exchange network as far as the Fort Center site in south-central Florida. The Santa Rosa and Swift Creek cultures of northwestern Florida and adjacent Georgia were part of that network, as shown by the Hopewellian pottery, copper ornaments, etc., that have been found in Florida, and by the objects of Gulf Coast origin that reached Ohio (Brose and Greber 1979). While the Hopewellian network farther north was breaking apart, the societies of Florida's Gulf Coast were thriving. Changes in ceramic styles around A.D. 400 mark their transition into the Weeden Island phase, a period of population growth. The largest Weeden Island site is Kolomoki, in southern Georgia (Muller 1983), which covered an area of 120 hectares (297 acres). There were numerous burial mounds and a rectangular mound, 17 m (55 ft) high, with a flat top, on which a structure may have stood. The size of the resident population of Kolomoki is uncertain, but it may have been about 1,000.

Pottery vessels, sometimes in the shape of humans, birds, or animals, were often deposited in caches on the eastern side of Weeden Island mounds. They were usually "killed" by punching a hole through the bottom. Some vessels were apparently made exclusively for the funerary ritual, as they were neatly punctured even before they were fired. Among other grave goods were spear-points, blades, shell cups and beads, copper ornaments, mica sheets and clay elbow pipes.

The Kolomoki burial mounds seem to have been built in a single stage, beginning with the burial of a single individual, who was laid on the ground or in a pit. Other burials, in bundles, flexed, or comprising only the skull, were occasionally added as the mound rose. It has been suggested that these might have been retainers or slaves, sacrificed at the death of a chief. If this interpretation is correct, Kolomoki would have been the center of a ranked, chiefdom-level society. In any case, Kolomoki is a uniquely large site; other Weeden Island mounds seem to have been built by kin groups, either from a single village or from several villages that formed a tribe.

THE MISSISSIPPIAN TRADITION A.D. 700–1500

The early appearance of what seem to be platform mounds in Hopewell-influenced Southeastern cultures is important, because it suggests an indigenous origin for a major diagnostic trait of the Mississippian tradition. The standard plan of Mississippian communities – platform mounds capped by temples and élite residences, arranged around an open plaza, and often surrounded by numerous dwellings – is one of the features that have given rise to theories of a strong diffusionary influence, perhaps even migration, from Mesoamerica. Additional traits that hint at a Mexican connection are maize cultivation and certain religious symbols and artistic motifs, particularly those that appear in the paraphernalia of the so-called "Southern Cult". However, there is also clear evidence of continuity from Hopewell into Mississippian, *via* the Hopewellian cultures of the Gulf Coast. As in the case of Adena and Hopewell, proponents of diffusion must contend with the absence of any complex society in

Fig. 73. Weeden Island vessel, "killed" before firing (height ca. 22 cm).

northeastern Mexico that might have been the source of the supposedly diffused Mississippian traits. Furthermore, not one Mexican-made artifact has been found in the Southeast. On the other hand, such features of Mississippian art as the comic balloon-like glyph that signifies speech in some engravings, or the jaguar or ocelot effigy pipe from Moundville, are too similar to Mexican prototypes for the resemblance to be a matter of chance. Perhaps a few Mexican objects reached the Southeast after a long series of "down the line" exchanges; or, perhaps some enterprising Mexican merchant-warriors (like the Aztec pochteca) made their way overland, or along the coast by canoe, to trade directly with the Mississippians. In any case, the absence of linguistic traces of Mesoamerican intrusion in the Southeast, and the archaeological evidence of continuous development from the Gulf Coast cultures into the Mississippian, rule out migration as an explanation.

Although there is little doubt that the platform mound-builders of northwestern Florida and Louisiana played an important part in the development of the Mississippian tradition, the exact point of origin of that tradition is, in fact, unknown. Cultures with Mississippian characteristics began to flourish in the valleys of the Mississippi, Tennessee, Cumberland and lower Ohio rivers around A.D. 700 or 800. The peak period of Mississippian development was about A.D. 1200 to 1500. The distinctive Mississippian traits shared by these cultures included: the aforementioned mound–plaza community layout; sophisticated shell-tempered pottery, including painted and effigy vessels; the bow, and arrows tipped with small triangular points; flood-plain cultivation of maize, squash and, after A.D. 1200, beans; a religious system largely

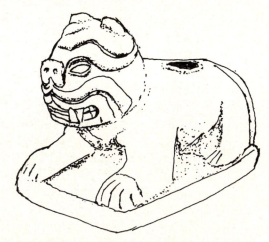

Fig. 74. Pipe in form of ocelot or jaguar, from Moundville, Alabama (length 15 cm).

246

devoted to ensuring agricultural fertility, and centered on a god with solar attributes and associated with fire (Muller 1983).

The spread of Mississippian cultural traits was facilitated by the operation of a widespread exchange network, comparable to the earlier Hopewellian system. Long distance trade is attested, not only by the distribution of raw materials such as shell and copper, but by the occurrence of virtually identical Southern Cult objects at sites in Georgia, Alabama and Oklahoma. In some cases, Mississippian lifeways were adopted by local Woodland groups that had become acculturated through their participation in the exchange network; however, there is evidence that in some areas, Mississippian expansion was the result, not of trade or acculturation, but of outright colonization. A particularly clear example is the Powers Phase Mississippian settlement of southern Missouri (Price 1978). Mississippian colonists set up hamlets, fortified villages, and a fortified temple-town, around A.D. 1275. By about A.D. 1325 to 1350, the colony had proven to be a failure; the Powers Phase people packed up their belongings, set fire to their communities, and abandoned the area. The stockaded village at Aztalan in southern Wisconsin may have been another Mississippian colony.

The major Mississippian settlements were situated in the flood-plains of large rivers, although there were also some shifting farmsteads in the upland stream valleys. Not only did the flood-plains offer rich, well-drained, easily tilled alluvial soils, conducive to the cultivation of maize, squash and beans, but the large numbers of fish and water-fowl available in backwater oxbow lakes were an important source of protein (Smith 1978). Harvesting of wild foods, especially nuts, still provided a significant percentage of necessary protein and fat. Despite these varied food sources, analyses of skeletal remains of Mississippians show them to have been less well-nourished, and shorter-lived, than their hunting and gathering ancestors. Their teeth were also much worse, because of their increased dependence on carbohydrates. The adoption of agriculture by Mississippian and contemporaneous Late Woodland groups may have been a response to the growth of population beyond the carrying capacity of wild resources. On the other hand, by about A.D. 900, selective breeding had created a race of maize, "northern flint", which could thrive in the shorter growing season and shorter summer nights of the northern United States. Widespread adoption of this hardy variety might have provided a new source of food, encouraged sedentism, and thereby provoked population growth. Hunting with bow and arrow is another innovation which, by destabilizing the traditional balance of humans and game animals, might have pushed Late Woodland hunter–gatherers into adopting new subsistence strategies.

It was probably increasing competition of growing populations for scarce agricultural land that caused the marked increase in warfare between Mississippian societies. This trend is manifested archaeologically in several ways. Many Mississippian sites were fortified with palisades; skeletons with imbedded arrowheads are not uncommon; beheading (or perhaps scalping) is depicted by a stone effigy pipe from Spiro Mound, in Oklahoma; and there are numerous portrayals in Mississippian art of severed trophy heads (Larson 1972, Gibson 1974b, Dickson 1981).

The major river flood-plains actually constituted a circumscribed environment (Hall 1980); the prairies lying just to the west could not be farmed using aboriginal digging sticks or stone hoes, and the nearby upland forests did not approach the carrying capacity of the flood-plains. According to the influential theory of anthropologist Robert Carneiro (1970), this sort of situation has repeatedly led to the emergence of primitive states. The losers in the continual struggles for scarce farmland cannot leave the area, because the surrounding region is so inhospitable; therefore, they remain on their former territory as a subservient lower-status group, paying tribute to the victorious élite. In the Mississippian case, there is evidence of environmental circumscription, warfare, and long distance trade – all factors that have been cited as critical in the development of states. This raises the very interesting question: Why didn't states appear in the prehistoric Southeast?

Fig. 75. Stone effigy pipe from Spiro Mound, Oklahoma. A warrior, wearing armor, prepares to behead (or scalp) a crouching captive (height 25 cm).

CAHOKIA

Some archaeologists (O'Brien 1972) contend that, in fact, at least one state *did* emerge in the Mississippi Valley, and that its capital was Cahokia. This site, which lies just east of East St Louis, Illinois, has been partially destroyed in recent times to make way for highways, stores and housing developments, but fortunately the central area has been preserved as a state park. Cahokia's central and dominant feature is Monks Mound, the largest of all North American mounds. It rises, in four terraces, to a height of 33 m (100 ft); it measures 316 by 241 m (1,037 by 790 ft) at its base, and covers 6.5 hectares (16 acres). Some 613,800 cubic m (21,690,000 cubic ft) of earth are contained within it. About 45 other, smaller mounds still stand at Cahokia; originally there were probably about 120. The mounds were situated on top of a natural ridge that runs from east to west. They seem to have been clustered around several plazas; the largest of these secondary mounds formed a group, surrounding Monks Mound. This central mound complex was encircled by a defensive palisade of large upright wooden posts. There are traces of another, much longer palisade that protected the whole northern side of the town.

At its peak, around A.D. 1050 to 1250, Cahokia extended over 13 square km (5 square miles). Eight hundred hectares (two thousand acres) were covered by houses, several to a hectare. Calculating on the assumption that there were five or six people per household, one arrives at a population estimate of 30,000 – about as many people as are thought to have lived in and around the major Mayan center at Tikal. On the basis of population size alone, we may therefore suspect that Cahokia may have been the seat of a society as complex as the Mayan city-states.

Additional evidence of Cahokia's organizational complexity has been provided by archaeological surveys of the surrounding flood-plain, known as the American Bottom. The sites around Cahokia, which appear to have been occupied at the same time, fall into three size categories. There are four sites that cover more than 50 hectares (124 acres) and contain several mounds; five sites with a single mound, surrounded by habitation debris; and more than 40 hamlets and farmsteads, only a few hectares in extent (Fowler 1975, 1978, 1980; Fowler and Hall 1978).

This settlement size hierarchy presumably reflects the structure of a political hierarchy. In the large, complex chiefdoms for which we have ethnographic data, the political hierarchy generally comprises two or three tiers. A higher-ranking or "paramount" chief controls a number of lower-ranking chiefs, each of whom collects tribute from the territorial district or social unit which he controls. In the chiefdoms of the Society Islands of Polynesia, the most complex chiefdoms for which there are historical accounts, a third level of administrators, called *ra'atira* or "stewards", were subordinate to the lower-ranking chiefs. The chiefs, sub-chiefs, and stewards lived at centers composed of ceremonial court-yards (*marae*) and associated chiefly residences and assembly houses. The size and elaborateness of marae varied according to the resident administrator's place in the hierarchy; those of the stewards were smallest, that of the paramount chief, the grandest. The commoners who comprised the bulk of the population lived in scattered farmsteads (Steponaitis 1978).

Seeking analogues for Cahokia's organization, we can turn to another historically known chiefdom, the Natchez, whose institutions may well have been directly derived from those of Mississippian societies. Archaeological evidence suggests that the Natchez were the final phase of a cultural tradition, called Plaquemine, that resulted from the infusion, around A.D. 1150, of Cahokia-derived traits into the local Coles Creek culture. The Natchez were still building mounds in the lower Mississippi Valley when the French arrived there in the seventeenth century.

There were two administrative levels in the Natchez hierarchy. At the upper level, the whole tribe was ruled by a supreme chief, known as the Great Sun, and a war chief, called "Tattooed Serpent", who was a younger brother of the Great Sun. Below this level, lower-ranking chiefs each controlled one of the nine districts into which the chiefdom was subdivided (as the Natchez population declined in the early eighteenth century, the number of districts decreased). The Great Sun and Tattooed Serpent lived in the "Grand Village", which actually consisted of only nine or fewer cabins, in addition to a temple built on top of an earthen mound. There were at least four secondary centers which functioned as district capitals. Most of the people lived in isolated hamlets or farmsteads. They paid tribute to the Great Sun at the monthly ceremonial feasts that he organized. He received food both from the people of his own district and from the sub-chiefs, who sent him what remained from their own feasts (Steponaitis 1978, Farb 1968).

The Natchez were a small-scale society compared to Cahokia; at the end of the seventeenth century, already decimated by European-introduced diseases, they numbered only 3,500 people. The populations of the complex Polynesian chiefdoms ranged from 940 to more than 4,000. The population of the society whose center was Cahokia must have been well over 40,000. If Cahokia was so much larger than these complex chiefdoms, might it then have been a state? A recently established rule of thumb in the interpretation of settlement patterns is that three or more levels of administration above the level of the individual household, as represented archaeologically by a hierarchy of site sizes with three or more levels, usually indicate the existence of a state. By this criterion, Cahokia seems to have been a state, because, apart from the small, dispersed farmsteads that were probably occupied by single families, there are indeed three site size categories. However, the Society Islands chiefdoms would also qualify as states by this criterion. Perhaps this simply goes to show that the chiefdom/state distinction is, to some extent, only a semantic quibble. Apart from its sheer size, the state is usually considered to differ from the chiefdom in the more effective monopoly of coercive force by the ruling élite; in the increased social stratification based on unequal access to valued resources; and in the decline of kinship-based organization and its replacement by a class structure, in which the ruler and his subjects are no longer considered relatives with mutual kin obligations.

Social stratification was quite rigid among the historic Natchez. The immediate relatives of the Great Sun, called Suns, constituted the aristocracy; all important officials came from their ranks. The next lower rung of the social ladder was occupied by the Nobles; beneath them were the Honored Men, and at the bottom were large numbers of despised commoners, referred to (behind their backs) as Stinkards. An odd feature of this social system was its built-in downward mobility. Members of the upper classes had to marry Stinkards. The children of high-status females retained their mother's rank, but children of high-status males dropped to the rank below that of their father. It is noteworthy that a Stinkard male could move up to Honored rank through his prowess in warfare. It has been suggested that such upward mobility might also have been possible in Mississippian societies, and that status-striving might have been the immediate cause of endemic Mississippian warfare, while the *ultimate* cause was population pressure on scarce land (Gibson 1978b, Dickson 1981).

The Great Sun exercised despotic power over his subjects; according to a French observer, "If he demands the life of any one of them, he comes himself to present his head." The ruler's feet never touched the bare ground; he was usually carried about in a litter, and if he had to walk for some reason, mats were spread before him. Only the Great Sun and a few priests whom he appointed were permitted to enter the temple on the mound, in which a sacred fire was kept burning continuously and the bones of former Great Suns were preserved. At the death of a Great Sun, his wives, guards and retainers were killed, to accompany him into the afterlife (Farb 1968).

There is archaeological evidence of a similar custom at Cahokia (Fowler 1975). The skeletons of more than 50 young women, between the ages of 18 and 23, had been neatly placed in a pit in Mound 72. There was no evidence of violence, but it is nevertheless likely that the women had been strangled. Nearby lay the bodies of four men, whose heads and hands had been cut off. The individual whose death may have occasioned this mass sacrifice was an adult male, whose body had been laid out on a platform composed of 20,000 shell beads. Next to him were placed the bundled or partially disarticulated remains of several individuals. Evidently as part of the same funeral rite, the bodies of six high-status individuals – three men and three women – had been buried nearby. They were accompanied by 800 arrowheads, sheets of mica and copper, and 15 double-concave discs of polished stone, which had probably been intended for use in the spear-throwing game that historic Southeastern Indians called "chunky". Perhaps the people accompanied by these luxury items had been close relatives of the dead chief.

Cahokia was by far the largest Mississippian community. There were several other large towns, however, that seem to have reached their peaks around A.D. 1250 or thereafter – a development that was probably related to the evident decline of Cahokia's power around that time. At Moundville, which lies beside the Black Warrior River in Alabama, 20 platform mounds were raised between A.D. 1200 and 1500. The total area of the site was over 121.5 hectares (300 acres), and the resident population may have numbered about 3,000. Moundville was the major ceremonial center of a three-tiered settlement system, which also included ten minor ceremonial centers, each comprising a single mound and associated village, and numerous villages and hamlets (Peebles 1978). This is the sort of settlement pattern that we would expect in a chiefdom. Other major Mississippian sites of the same period were Etowah, in Georgia, and Spiro, in eastern Oklahoma.

THE SOUTHERN CULT

At these major sites, around A.D. 1250, highly distinctive artifacts were deposited in mortuary mounds. These artifacts were the symbolic paraphernalia of a religious cult in which the chiefly élite were apparently the foremost participants (as an analogy, bear in mind that among the Natchez, the Great Sun also functioned as chief priest; he worshipped the stone and clay images in the temple every morning and evening). Among these "Southern Cult" objects were: axes with the head and shaft carved from a single piece of stone; polished or chipped stone batons or maces; copper pendants decorated with circles or weeping eyes; shell gorgets depicting woodpeckers, fighting cocks, rattlesnakes or spiders; pottery vessels decorated with circles, crosses, hands, skulls, rattlesnakes, flying horned serpents, and feathered serpents; copper plates and engraved shell cups portraying male figures (perhaps warriors, or shamans, or deities), wearing eagle or falson costumes and sometimes carrying a baton in one hand and a trophy head in the other.

Some of the items shown in the engravings have full-size counterparts,

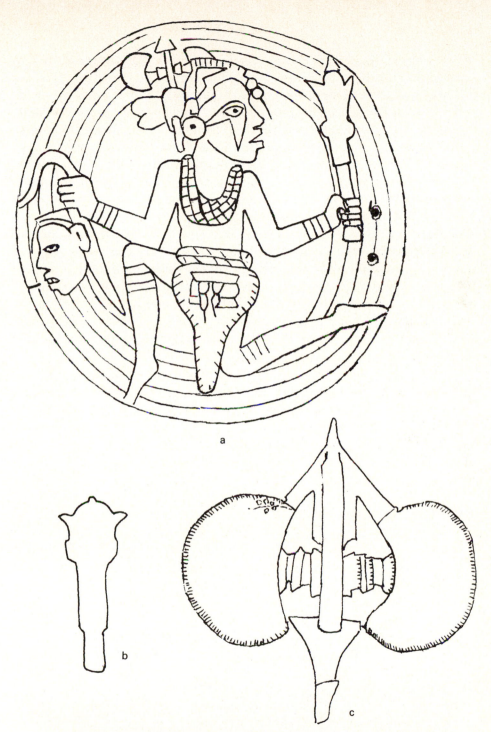

Fig. 76. (A) Mississippian engraved shell gorget, from Tennessee (diameter 10 cm); (B) polished stone mace (length 35 cm), from Spiro Mound, Oklahoma. Note similarity to object carried by the figure on the gorget; (C) copper ornament in form of "bilobed arrow", probably worn in the hair; from Etowah, Georgia.

253

which were excavated either at the same site or at far-distant sites. For example, a so-called "bi-lobed arrow" of hammered copper from Etowah is duplicated by the hair ornament of a feathered "warrior" depicted on a copper sheet from the same site, but also shown on an engraved shell ornament from Tennessee. Each of these figures carries a mace; an almost identical full-size specimen, of polished stone, was found at Spiro. A few of the highest-status individuals buried in the Moundville mounds were accompanied by artifacts of the sort carried or worn by the eagle warriors: these included axes, flints, and hair plumes made from sheet copper. These individuals were also associated with skulls and infant skeletons (Peebles 1971). The skulls may have been trophy heads, and the infants may have been sacrificed, like the infants whose bodies paved the way for the litter in which was borne the corpse of the Great Sun of the Natchez. It is noteworthy that at the second-order centers around Moundville, people of high status were buried with items that bore representations of eagle warriors, but not with the actual objects. These seem to have been reserved for burials of the highest rank, in the primary center of the chiefdom.

A plausible explanation of this limited distribution of cult symbols is that the shell and copper depictions represent a deity, and that members of the chiefly lineage were regarded, as was the Great Sun of the Natchez,

Fig. 77. Mississippian pottery: (A) and (B) from Moundville, Alabama; (C) frog effigy vessel, from Arkansas (height of A 11.5 cm; length of C, 29.2 cm; A and B after Walthall 1980).

as descendants and confidants of the deity. Thus, they alone were entitled to wear the same divine regalia that he did.

THE MISSISSIPPIAN DECLINE

When the Spanish conquistadors arrived in the Southeast in the sixteenth century, the lower Mississippi Valley was inhabited by the Natchez and the Tunica, among whom the Mississippian temple–town pattern persisted. It was formerly believed that the abandonment of Cahokia and the other great Mississippian centers had been the result of a catastrophic loss of population due to the introduction of European diseases; however, as radiocarbon dates have since made clear, the decline occurred more than a century before Europeans set foot in the region. Construction at Cahokia ceased in the fourteenth century, and the site was abandoned by 1500. At about the same time, Moundville, Etowah and Spiro were also vacated. Like the Hopewellian collapse that occurred 1,000 years earlier, the Mississippian decline has not yet been satisfactorily explained. There is no evidence of a decrease in population – in fact it probably grew – but people were now dispersed across the landscape in many small settlements instead of concentrated in a few large sites. The end of the Mississippian climax coincides with the onset of the "Little Ice Age", during which annual temperatures were about 1°C colder than today. Perhaps this climatic change had an adverse effect on Mississippian agriculture. However, some tribal level farming groups, such as the Iroquois of western New York, who lived near the northern limits of maize cultivation, flourished during this cold spell. Another intriguing possibility is that the introduction of beans into the Mississippian region after A.D. 1200 provided a good alternative protein source, so that people no longer needed to rely on the fish they caught in the flood-plain's oxbow lakes. Thus settlements could now be established in the uplands, away from the flood-plains. With the loss of the circumscription factor, despotic chiefs were deprived of the tribute that had constituted their economic base, and so the complex chiefdoms, and the extensive trade networks that linked them, fell apart (Hall 1980). In any case, when the French entered the middle Mississippi Valley in the seventeenth century, they encountered tribal groups that practiced agriculture, supplemented by hunting and gathering.

TRIBAL FARMER–HUNTERS
ON THE MISSISSIPPIAN PERIPHERY

The influence of the Mississippian tradition was carried, by diffusion and migration, far beyond its heartland area in the central Mississippi Valley.

To the east and northeast, a generalized Mississippian influence can be seen in the Late Woodland cultures that developed after about A.D. 900. This influence is evident in the adoption of maize–bean–squash agriculture, the bow and arrow (signalled by the appearance of triangular points), and the construction of fortified villages. However, ceramic types show continuity from the local Middle Woodland traditions; for example, in New York, cord-marked Owasco pottery developed from Point Peninsula pottery. The Owasco culture, in turn, developed into that of the Iroquois of the historic period. The distinctive Iroquois long houses, which were occupied by matrilineal clans, appeared around A.D. 1300. The Iroquois' matrilocal–matrilineal social system may have been an outcome of women's assumption of a key economic role when agriculture was adopted. Iroquois men were often involved in raids on neighboring tribes; already in the preceding Owasco phase, skeletons with embedded points attest to the occurrence of warfare, and scattered finds of human bones in rubbish deposits suggest that cannibalism may have been practiced. The Iroquois tribal confederacy, which impressed European observers and remained a potent military and political force until the late eighteenth century, was probably established before the time of contact (Tuck 1978b, Ritchie 1965, Funk 1983).

Why was it not until A.D. 1000 that farming and village life were adopted in the Northeastern woodlands? Climatic amelioration may have played a role; it seems to have become warmer about this time. Perhaps maize could now thrive in northern areas. Possibly, too, it had taken a long time to breed a race of maize that was adapted to northern latitudes, but such a variety was now finally available. Population pressure is another possibility. This may have been caused, to some extent, by local population growth, but there may also have been a sort of ripple effect, emanating from the densely inhabited Mississippian zone. Resultant pressure on resources would account both for the shift to cultivated crops and for the well-attested intensification of warfare. Interestingly, population densities remained quite low among the Iroquois and the related Hurons of southern Ontario, compared with other village farmers. It has been suggested that cultural mechanisms may somehow have adjusted the population, keeping it below the level where deer might be over-hunted (Gramly 1977). Deer were essential not only for their meat but for their hides, from which clothing was manufactured.

West of the Mississippi Valley, some groups living in the river valleys of the Plains had begun to make pottery, perhaps as early as 250 B.C. The shapes of their vessels were derived from the pottery of the eastern Woodland tradition, which accounts for the designation of these western cultures as "Plains Woodland" (Wedel 1961, 1983). The zoned decoration and rocker-stamping of some vessels show the influence of the Hopewell culture, which is further attested by the presence of platform pipes. The Hopewellian custom of mound burial was adopted by the inhabitants of the Kansas City area; around A.D. 300–400, they placed secondary burials and cremations in stone chambers, covered by mounds of earth. Hunting of deer and small mammals, and gathering of wild plants, remained the most important subsistence activities for the Plains Woodland folk, although very small amounts of maize and squash show that some gardening was practiced, particularly at later sites. This mixed economy was apparently reliable enough to form the basis for a fairly sedentary way of life; the Kansas City Hopewellians lived in semi-permanent villages that sometimes covered 3 or 4 hectares (7½ to 10 acres). The inhabitants of the northeastern Plains also raised mounds, under which the dead were buried in log-covered pits. These mounds, in the eastern Dakotas and southern Manitoba, were either linear or conical in shape. The biggest ones were about 3 to 4 m (9 to 13 ft) high, and 25 to 30 m (80 to 100 ft) in diameter. Frequently, the skeletons or skulls of bison were deposited in the mounds, suggesting the animals' economic and religious importance. Gorgets made of marine shell, engraved with Southern Cult designs, were found in some of the Manitoba mounds (Wedel 1961); they indicate that some of the mounds were contemporaneous with the Mississippian cultures. While Woodland people were settling in the valleys of the eastern Plains, the Archaic pattern of hunting, gathering and bison drives continued as before in the northwestern Plains.

Beginning about A.D. 900, a second wave of village-dwelling farmers migrated from the eastern woodlands into the Plains, occupying the stream valleys from the Dakotas to Texas. They built their villages on ridges or blufftops; they grew cold-resistant varieties of maize and beans in the valley bottoms, and also hunted and gathered in the wooded bottomlands and grassy uplands. The shared features of these Plains Village cultures included: multi-family lodges; permanent settlements, sometimes fortified with dry moats and stockades, and equipped with storage pits; pottery, some of which resembled Mississippian wares; and various artifacts made of stone, bone, horn and shell (Jennings 1974, Wedel 1983). A particularly characteristic tool was the bone hoe, which was usually made from the shoulder blade (scapula) of a bison. The widespread occurrence of small chipped stone points shows that Plains Village hunters used the bow and arrow. It has been suggested that the villagers' entry into the Plains occurred in response to the improved climatic conditions of the neo-Atlantic period, and that the newly available cold-resistant crops made their expansion possible (Wedel 1983). Another factor leading to migration may have been competition for land against the more highly organized Mississippian societies.

Emigrants from southwestern Minnesota and northwestern Iowa

settled in the middle reaches of the Missouri River in South Dakota. The Middle Missouri tradition that they began was characterized by square or rectangular houses, 9 to 20 m (30 to 65 ft) long, and by grit-tempered pottery, often in the form of globular, wide-mouthed jars. Villages consisted of six to 20 houses, with populations of 50 to 300. A second wave of immigrants, from the same area as the original settlers, settled mainly in North Dakota. Violent conflicts with the earlier settlers must have erupted frequently, because sites were fortified, and there is skeletal evidence of massacres and scalping. The Huff site, occupied about A.D. 1400 to 1600, is a well known example of a late Middle Missouri village. It was situated on the western bank of the river. More than 100 houses lay within a palisade and earth embankment, which had 10 projecting bastions. The 9 m- (30 ft-) long houses had walls of wattle and daub, and were probably roofed with sod (Jennings 1974).

The farming groups who occupied the central Plains (Nebraska and Kansas) from A.D. 1000 to 1400 constructed their houses and made their pottery somewhat differently from the Missouri River people. The square or rectangular houses, with rounded corners, covered from 36 to 67.5 square m (388 to 727 square ft), and were made of timbers covered with earth. The roof was supported by four central posts. Central Plains villages were smaller and less compact than those of the Middle Missouri, and they were not fortified. In Nebraska, the globular, handled pots were shell-tempered, like Mississippian pottery. In the fifteenth century,

a   b

Fig. 78. (A) Plains Village pot, Nebraska phase; (B) Mississippian pot, Langston phase (northeastern Alabama).

drought seems to have forced many groups to leave the central Plains; they moved into the Middle Missouri region, where their arrival was marked by the introduction of a new form of house. It featured four posts supporting the roof, as in the earlier central Plains houses; however, these later earth lodges were no longer rectangular, but circular. Such dwellings were typical of the "Coalescent" culture, which spread northward, up the Missouri, between 1450 and 1680. The Arikara were the post-contact bearers of this cultural tradition. Farther north, the contact period Mandan and Hidatsa represented a late stage of the Middle Missouri tradition. The historic Pawnee were descended from villagers who had remained in the central Plains (Wedel 1983).

For many people, the historic Plains Indians are *the* Indians. Their superb horsemanship, bison hunting, tepees, war bonnets, peace pipes (calumets) and sign language are familiar from countless books and movies. However, it is not often realized to what extent the historic Plains cultures had developed in response to contacts with Europeans. Certainly, as archaeology has demonstrated, bison herds had been hunted successfully by foot-nomads. However, when the Indians learned how to ride horses, which the Spanish had re-introduced to the Americas, it became much easier to follow the migrating herds. Rifles, which the Indians began to acquire by the eighteenth century, also aided bison hunting. The acquisition of horses must have encouraged some tribes, who had formerly supplemented their farming with seasonal bison-hunting, to rely increasingly on hunting, so that ultimately they stopped farming altogether and abandoned their villages. This is what happened in the case of the Dakota Sioux and the Cheyenne. On the other hand, the Blackfoot, Arapaho, and Assiniboin were descended from bison-hunters. Farming had been largely a female occupation, so as it was de-emphasized, women's economic role was devaluated and their social status diminished accordingly. For example, the Arikara are thought to have shifted from matrilocal to patrilocal residence during the eighteenth century. James Deetz (1965) has interpreted the increasingly random association of attributes in Arikara pottery during the years 1700–80 as a reflection of the break-up of extended matrilocal households. Deetz suggests that in the earlier villages, the women of each large matrilocal family possessed their own distinctive micro-traditions of pottery making. These ideas and techniques would be passed on from grandmothers to granddaughters. However, when the matrilocal families broke up in the mid-eighteenth century, and the dispersed women came into contact with many unrelated women, a more random mixing of ideas occurred. This process, Deetz argues, is reflected by the more random associations of attributes in later Arikara ceramics.

MESOAMERICAN CIVILIZATIONS

The Olmec

As we have seen, the formation of permanent villages in Mesoamerica was delayed for several thousand years after the beginnings there of agriculture. It may have taken that long for maize cobs to become large enough for a cultivated field to produce more food than a comparable area of wild plants; this would have made it profitable for people to set up permanent dwellings alongside their fields. The development of effective storage techniques was undoubtedly another factor that facilitated this shift to a sedentary way of life. The first villages seem to have been established around 2500 B.C., but the rapid spread of village farming throughout Mesoamerica apparently occurred after 1500 B.C. The lifeways of the "Formative" villagers have been most intensively studied in the Valley of Oaxaca, by Kent Flannery (1976) and his students. Formative villages in Oaxaca generally consisted of eight to 12 houses, occupied by some 50 to 60 people. The houses were built of wattle and daub; they were rectangular, with a floor area of about 25 square m (270 square ft). In the center of the village there was a plaza, which may have served as a dancing ground for public rituals.

Around 1200 B.C., a new level of cultural complexity was achieved by the inhabitants of the hot, humid, forested lowlands of the Gulf Coast, near modern Vera Cruz. Archaeologists refer to the founders of this earliest Mesoamerican civilization as the Olmec. This name, which means "rubber people", was used by the Aztec to designate the much later inhabitants of this region, where rubber trees flourished. We don't know how the so-called Olmec referred to themselves, nor are we even sure what language they spoke. Some scholars believe that their language belonged to the Mayan family, but others have suggested that they spoke a language of the Mixe-Zoquean family. These languages, which are related to Mayan, are still spoken in areas close to the Olmec heartland.

Several features of Olmec society set it apart from earlier and contemporary Mesoamerican societies. The major Olmec sites – San Lorenzo, La Venta and Tres Zapotes – contained large ceremonial structures. Evidently, the labor of at least hundreds of individuals must have been mobilized for the construction of these monuments. A considerable expenditure of time and labor was also required to transport, from their source 95 or 130 km (60 or 80 miles) away, the huge pieces of basalt that Olmec craftsmen sculpted into 2.8 m- (9 ft-) tall heads. These menacing-looking heads, which are probably portraits of chiefs, tend to support the inference, from the scale of the monumental architecture, that centralized political authority was wielded by an élite. Apart from the giant heads and

other monumental pieces such as stelae and altars, the skill of Olmec
stone-workers is also evident in smaller pieces, such as jade axes and
figurines. The motifs that appear repeatedly in Olmec art offer glimpses
of a complex ideology, elements of which seem to have been adopted by
later Mesoamerican civilizations.

Much work remains to be done before we can fully understand why
civilization should have arisen so precociously in a seemingly inhospitable environment. Very little is known of the local village farming phase
that is assumed to have preceded the florescence of Olmec civilization. In
fact, some scholars have suggested that the ancestral Olmec arrived on
the Gulf Coast with their culture already fully developed, after a
migration from Guerrero or Oaxaca. However, most archaeologists are
inclined to look for indigenous factors which might have caused the transformation of tribal farmers into a civilization. The most obvious factor is

1 San Lorenzo	18 Dzibilchaltún
2 La Venta	19 Uaxactún
3 Tres Zapotes	20 Cerros
4 Chalcatzingo	21 El Mirador
5 San José Mogoté	22 Lamanai
6 Monte Albán	23 Becan
7 Tlatilco and Tenochtitlán	24 Calakmul
8 Cuicuilco	25 Copan
9 Teotihuacán	26 Palenque
10 Kaminaljuyú	27 Bonampak
11 Tikal	28 Yaxchilán
12 Cholula	29 Piedras Negras
13 Cuello	30 Coba
14 Colha	31 Uxmal
15 Chalchuapa	32 Tula
16 Izapa	33 Chichén Itzá
17 Altar de Sacrificios	34 Mayapán

Fig. 79. Mesoamerican civilizations (3 cm = 400 km).

high agricultural productivity. The Olmec settled near sluggish rivers; when these overflowed, they dumped fertile silt along their banks. Using simple slash and burn methods, Olmec farmers could have harvested 1,450 kg (3,200 lb) of maize from each acre of these alluvial soils – almost twice the yield that could be achieved by farming on the hillsides. Even in areas away from the riverbanks, the lime-rich soil of the Olmec region retained its fertility better than most easily leached tropical soils. Thus, even with a simple, non-intensive agricultural system, the Olmec could provide enough food to sustain a growing population and an élite of rulers, priests, and craftsmen (Coe 1968a).

San Lorenzo, occupied from about 1200 to 900 B.C., seems to have been the predominant center of Olmec civilization in its earliest phase (Coe 1968b, 1981). There were two other sites nearby – Tenochtitlán (not to be cofused with the Aztec capital) and Potrero Nuevo. San Lorenzo was situated on top of a plateau which rose 45 m (150 ft) above the surrounding savanna; the plateau was about 1.2 km (three-quarters of a mile) long, from north to south. The uppermost 7.5 m (25 ft) seems to have been an artificially constructed platform of clay, sand, and rock. On the plateau stood some 60 stone ornaments, including carved heads. Its surface was pocked by more than 20 artificial ponds, from which water was drained by a system of buried basalt-lined troughs. The purpose of this elaborate

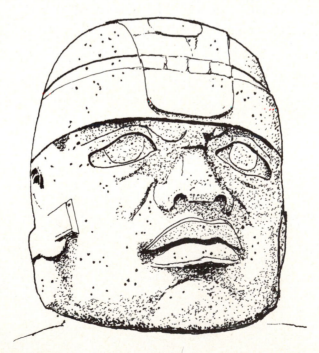

Fig. 80. A giant stone head from San Lorenzo (height 2.8 m).

drainage system is unknown; it has variously been explained as a water storage facility, an irrigation network, or a sort of aquatic farm for the breeding of sacred crocodiles. The great majority of the several hundred mounds situated on top of the plateau had once served as the bases of dwellings. The resident population of San Lorenzo is estimated at about 1,000; another 1,000 people may have lived at Tenochtitlán, and 250 at Potrero Nuevo. What little is known of the subsistence economy suggests that maize was the staple crop, while domesticated dogs, fish, turtles, and deer and other hunted game supplied protein.

The earliest pottery found at San Lorenzo pre-dated 1300 B.C. It is not very similar to the wares associated with the Olmec constructions. In addition to this discontinuity in ceramics, the absence at the site of antecedents to the fully-formed Olmec art style which appeared around 1200 B.C. suggests that the Olmec civilization did not evolve *in situ* at San Lorenzo.

A possible clue to Olmec origins is provided by the oddly shaped clay mound at Le Venta, which lies 85 km (50 miles) northeast of San Lorenzo. This mound, the largest structure at the site, was about 33.5 m (110 ft) high, and measured 128 m (420 ft) across at its base. It was built in the form of a fluted cone. It has been speculated that this mound may have been intended as an imitation of the similarly shaped natural volcanic cones that occur in the Tuxtla mountains, 100 km (60 miles) west of La Venta (Heizer 1968). If so, this might imply that this mountainous region was the original homeland of the Olmec, to which they remained sym-

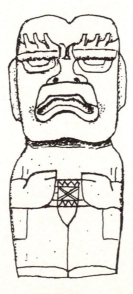

Fig. 81. Olmec jade celt (height 31 cm).

bolically tied by recreating its landscape in their new lowland home. However, one should generally regard such suggestions, that mounds are artificial replicas of mountains, with skepticism.

The fluted mound was the dominant structure in a whole complex of mounds, platforms, pyramids and plazas which extended over an area greater than five square km. This ceremonial center was built on an island in a swamp, near the Tonala River. All the major structures were aligned on an axis 8° west of north, probably in line with some star or constellation.

La Venta seems to have become the major center of the Olmec region around 900 B.C., usurping the dominant role that had previously been played by San Lorenzo, which was abandoned at about the same date. Most of the stone monuments at San Lorenzo had been intentionally mutilated, which suggests a violent overthrow of the local élite, either by a rebellious peasantry or by invading warriors of a rival chiefdom. Some of the toppled monuments had been carefully buried, as though their destroyers feared that they might still retain some of their former sacred power. In fact, such careful treatment of the monuments raises doubts about the conquest or rebellion hypothesis. Perhaps we are dealing instead with a ritual of destruction, carried out when a ruler died, or a calendrical cycle was completed, or a sacred site was abandoned. The importance of burial in Olmec rituals is illustrated by several finds at La Venta. In one instance, 425 cubic m (15,000 cubic ft) of clay were dug out, serpentine blocks were put on the bottom of the pit, and it was then refilled. Also, three mosaic pavements were found at La Venta; in each case, some 485 serpentine blocks had been arranged in a 4.5 by 6 m (15 by 20 ft) rectangle, seemingly representing a stylized jaguar mask. Soon after their construction, the pavements were intentionally covered with layers of clay and adobe. Perhaps, the burial of the stone monuments had a similar religious significance.

Whatever the cause of the abandonment of San Lorenzo, La Venta replaced it as the primary Olmec center after 900 B.C. La Venta was

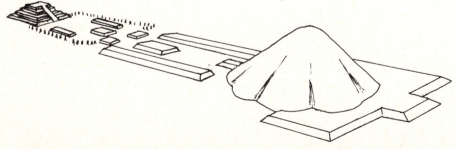

Fig. 82. La Venta: fluted mound and associated structures. (After Coe 1968a).

abandoned around 600–500 B.C.; again, as at San Lorenzo, the center's downfall was marked by the mutilation of its stone monuments. Tres Zapotes then rose to prominence; by the time it was abandoned, around A.D. 1, the Olmec had been eclipsed by emergent civilizations in the high-lands, whose development had been spurred by Olmec influence.

Olmec ideology must be reconstructed primarily on the basis of their art. It has long been thought that the jaguar was the inspiration for the fanged, snarling, trapezoid-mouthed infantile beings who are so fre-quently depicted in figurines and ceremonial jade axes. A few statues, which seemed to depict jaguar–human copulation, inspired the idea that the fanged infants were "were-jaguars", the offspring of such mythical unions (Davis 1978). Another interpretation of the jaguar traits held that the figurines portrayed stages in the transformation of shamans into jaguars (Furst 1968). However, the fangs and other characteristics of the were-jaguars have recently been re-interpreted as stylized represen-tations of the features of caymans and crocodiles (Stocker et al. 1980). Michael Coe (1968a), one of the foremost authorities on the Olmec, has tentatively identified, on an Olmec statue that was discovered in 1965, representations of five gods who were worshipped by later Meso-americans. They include Xipe, the Lord of Spring; the Fire "Serpent" (with crocodilian attributes) who carried the sun across the sky; Quetzal-coatl, the Feathered Serpent, god of wisdom and life; Tlaloc, the rain god (represented by the were-jaguar); and the death god.

Other elements of later Mesoamerican religions seem to be pre-figured in Olmec iconography. The great stone heads appear to wear helmets; this may indicate that Olmec chiefs took part in the sacred ball-game. Even if this interpretation of the helmet-like head-gear is incorrect, clay figurines of ball-players from San Lorenzo show that the Olmec did know, and probably originated, the Mesoamerican ball-game, which was still being played when the Spanish arrived. A number of Olmec sculptures show men, presumably priests, who bear infants or dwarves in their arms. These scenes can be plausibly interpreted as depictions of ceremonies preceding human sacrifices. The sacrifice of an adult war captive may be depicted in a stone relief found far to the west of the Olmec heartland, at Chalcatzingo, in the central Mexican state of Morelos (Grove 1968). Three masked men, possibly priests, carrying long clubs, stand before a bearded, sitting figure whose bared genitals and bound wrists mark him as a humiliated war captive (Coe 1968a). The occurrence of charred and split human bones in refuse deposits at San Lorenzo can be credibly interpreted as evidence of cannibalism, which might have been the after-math of human sacrifices, as it was among the much later Aztec.

Among the most remarkable finds at La Venta were a number of con-cave mirrors, made of highly polished iron ores. It has been shown that these mirrors could have been used to cast images on blank surfaces, or to start fires by reflecting sunlight (Coe 1968a). Obviously, ownership of such devices must have conferred mystical power and prestige; in fact, Olmec rulers are shown in sculptures, wearing such mirrors on their chests. A small concave mirror was also found, in pyramid fill, at the earlier site of San Lorenzo. However, most of the mirrors found at San Lorenzo were not curved but flat. They were made of magnetite, and seem to have been imported from Oaxaca, where evidence of their manufacture has been found (Flannery 1976). In contrast, the La Venta mirrors were evidently made at the site, using material from local sources. In later Mesoamerican civilizations, down to the Aztec, mirrors remained highly prized objects with sacred connotations.

The Chalcatzingo petroglyphs are not the only example of Olmec presence or influence outside the core area on the Gulf Coast. Paintings executed in Olmec style have been found at Juxtlahuaca Cave in Guerrero, more than 320 km (200 miles) southwest of San Lorenzo. Ceramic figurines whose mouths and eyes had been depicted in typically Olmec fashion have been found at Las Bocas, Morelos, and at Tlatilco, in the Valley of Mexico. It is noteworthy that at the latter site, many figurines in a clearly local, non-Olmec style were also excavated. Other examples of Olmec-like artwork are scattered along the Pacific coast of Chiapas and Central America, as far as western El Salvador. These traces of Olmec influence raise an obvious but important question: What is typically Olmec art doing in places so far away from the Olmec heartland?

The answer clearly involves trade. We have already noted that the basalt used for Olmec monuments was hauled and rafted to the Gulf

Fig. 83. Stone relief in Olmec style, Chalcatzingo, Morelos. (After Grove 1968.)

Coast from remote mountain areas. The jade and serpentine that Olmec craftsmen fashioned into axes and statuettes were also imported; bluish jade may have come from Morelos, greenish jade from Guatemala, and serpentine from Puebla. Some Olmec jade may even have originated in Costa Rica. Michael Coe (1968a), the excavator of San Lorenzo, envisions Olmec merchant-warriors, analogous and ancestral to the Aztec pochteca, plying trade routes between the Gulf Coast and the jade sources, and establishing combined military outposts and trading depots along the way. Coe interprets the Tlatilco evidence as indicating conquest of the local villagers by Olmec aristocrats.

An alternative interpretation of the diffusion of Olmecoid art objects and style also involves trade, but this model is more complicated (Flannery 1968b). As the Olmec culture was taking shape in the Gulf Coast region, agricultural villages were springing up elsewhere in Mesoamerica. As populations grew and prime agricultural land became scarce, ranked societies emerged, in which the kin groups residing in the larger, better-situated villages claimed higher status than was accorded the inhabitants of satellite villages. To bolster their new position, the village big men adopted the theocratic ideology of the Olmec chiefs, and exchanged local materials and craft products (e.g. the mirrors from Oaxaca) for prestigious Olmec art and ritual objects. In Oaxaca Formative villages, imports from the Gulf Coast are occasionally found, such as sting ray spines, which were probably used for ritual blood-letting, turtle shells, which may have been used as drums, and even a crocodile jaw, which may have been part of a dance costume (Flannery 1976). The small percentages of Olmec-style figurines and decorated pottery relative to local styles at sites in Oaxaca and the Valley of Mexico tend to support this exchange network model instead of the colonial expansion model. Even at Chalcatzingo, where the stone reliefs clearly demonstrate ties with La Venta, the pottery found at the nearby ceremonial center is predominantly local, not Olmec, in style (Grove 1981). During the period when the reliefs seem to have been carved, ca. 900 to 600 B.C., the number of villages in the vicinity of Chalcatzingo increased dramatically, terracing and irrigation projects were undertaken, and Chalcatzingo became the focus of local craft production and redistribution (Grove et al. 1976). The site probably also functioned as the export center for local goods that were destined for the Gulf Coast. Perhaps the local élite, who seem to have occupied a larger than average house which also contained wealthy burials, may have been tied by marriage to the Olmec rulers, who sought thereby to ensure their access to trade goods for which other newly emergent highland chiefdoms were beginning to compete. Olmec sculptors might have arrived in Chalcatzingo as members of the entourage of the in-marrying nobles.

267

Chiefdoms and early states in the highlands

The local élite of the Mexican highland villages, whose prestige had been bolstered by their participation in the Olmec trade network, seem to have consolidated their own power after La Venta's influence waned. Chiefdoms and nascent states emerged in the Valley of Oaxaca and the Basin of Mexico around 600 B.C.

In Oaxaca, by 550 B.C., the town of San José Mogoté had grown to be 15 times the size of the next largest site in the region. By about 400 B.C. even this large town was overshadowed by the new center of Monte Albán, constructed on top of a high, steep bluff in the middle of the valley. Monte Albán's population at this time is estimated to have been about 5,000. Set into the face of a stone platform were 140 stone slabs, bearing carved representations, in Olmec-like style, of contorted human figures. Their odd positions have led to their being called "*danzantes*" (dancers); but the contortion, nudity, and closed eyes of the figures suggest that they represent enemies, humiliated, killed, and sometimes mutilated by the ruler of Monte Albán. It is noteworthy that each "danzante" is identified by a distinctive carved glyph, indicating that the Zapotecs of Oaxaca had

Fig. 84. A "danzante" from Monte Albán (height 1.4 m). (After Willey 1966.)

already devised (or perhaps borrowed from the Olmec, who had occasionally carved glyphs on jade objects) a rudimentary writing system. Other slabs, bearing carved glyphs and bar and dot numerals, show that the 52-year "calendar round" system, known from later Mesoamerican civilizations, was in use at Monte Albán. This calendar involved the meshing of the 260 days of the Almanac Year with the 365 days of the solar year. The Almanac Year was composed of 20 named days, with names such as dog, reed, serpent, crocodile, which inter-meshed with the numbers 1 to 13. A day in the Almanac Year would meet its counterpart in the solar year every 52 years. The added refinement of the Long Count, which may have been devised by the Olmec, was employed only by the Maya. In this system, the length of time elapsed since the arbitrary starting date of 3113 B.C. was calculated in terms of periods of varying length: 144,000 days, 7,200 days, 360 days, 20 days, and one day. Thus, a bar-and-dot Long Count date, inscribed on Stela C at the late Olmec site of Tres Zapotes, is 7.16.6.16.18, which corresponds to 31 B.C. in our own calendrical system (Coe 1962).

The slopes of Monte Albán were levelled off to form more than 2,000 terraces, which were used as both farm plots and house supports. Over the course of several centuries, the site grew to be an enormous ceremonial center and élite residence. At its peak, between A.D. 200 and 700, Monte Albán may have had 30,000 inhabitants. It was the nucleus of a complex of public buildings, terraces, and residences that covered some 40 square km (15 square miles) (Blanton 1978, Blanton and Kowalewski 1981).

Monte Albán was established in a section of the Valley of Oaxaca that had previously been only sparsely inhabited, because of its limited agricultural potential. This fact has led Richard Blanton (1978, 1980) to propose that Monte Albán was founded at a neutral site, as the capital of a league of semi-autonomous polities. The capital's location at the junction of the three "arms" of the valley made it a most convenient place from which to coordinate political administration and economic exchange throughout the league's territory. Blanton notes the existence of similar leagues in late prehistoric Mexico, and draws an analogy with the founding of Washington, D.C. at a neutral site between the northern and southern states. A contrary explanation of Monte Albán's emergence has been offered by Robert Santley (1980), who claims that, if irrigated, the land that lay within walking distance of the site could have been highly productive. He suggests that as the Formative population of the Valley of Oaxaca increased, pressure on farmlands would have led to more frequent conflicts. People would have clustered into larger communities for protection, and Monte Albán's hilltop location made it a particularly good choice for defensive purposes. Ultimately, its centrality and its rich resource base enabled Monte Albán to conquer the rest of the valley. The "danzantes" and other evidence point to a significant level of military conflict in Oaxaca during the Monte Albán I period. Blanton also takes note of this evidence, but he suggests that the conflicts were not between rival centers within the valley, but instead involved defensive campaigns by the valley-based league against marauders from the surrounding mountains. Santley's argument that population pressure led to stratification and internal conflict is somewhat weakened by Stephen Kowalewski's (1980) calculation, based on the estimated maize-producing potential of Oaxaca farmland, that during Monte Albán I the valley's population was only 8% of that which could have been supported.

The Basin of Mexico

The Basin of Mexico, 2.4 km (one-and-a-half miles) high and 7,800 square km (3,000 square miles) in extent, is ringed by hills; in pre-Conquest times, its center was largely filled by a great shallow lake. Irregular rainfall and winter frosts deterred early farmers from occupying the basin, although recent finds at Zohapilco suggest that Archaic villages may have been established by the lake-shore. The earliest agricultural settlements were founded about 1500–1300 B.C., in the southern part of the basin, where rainfall agriculture could be most easily practiced. One of the first villages, Coapexco, lay close to a pass that led southward through the mountains to Morelos, and the similarity of the villagers' pottery to the Formative ceramics of Morelos suggests that they may have been colonists from that region. Archaeological surveys have located nine sites of the initial phase; four of these were villages with several hundred inhabitants, the rest, hamlets occupied by fewer than 100 people. By 1150 B.C. the population numbered about 5,000, occupying 14 sites. The largest of these villages was Tlatilco, which may have had as many as 1,500 inhabitants. Unfortunately, this site was largely destroyed by looting and by the operations of a brick factory; nevertheless, a famous collection of artifacts was recovered from the village cemetery. The dead had been provided with pottery, shell ornaments, obsidian and bone tools, jade and serpentine objects, and clay figurines. Some of the dead, including infants, were more richly provisioned than others, possibly indicating some form of ranking. Particularly intriguing are several collective graves, in which women appear to have been the central figures, accompanied by men and children who may have been sacrificed when the women died. This might be evidence of the high status of women, a possibility that is also raised by the great predominance of female representations among the numerous clay figurines of this period. It is noteworthy that, besides pottery and figurines of the local Morelos-like types, incised vessels and baby-faced figurines in the Olmec style were also found in the Tlatilco graves. These pieces have been variously explained as indicators of Olmec colonization or political domination, or as souvenirs of religious pilgrimages to the Olmec heartland (Tolstoy 1979, Grenne-Ravits and Coleman 1976).

The population of the southern Basin increased rapidly between 1150 and 650 B.C., reaching an estimated 25,000 at the end of this period. Population density increased also, as the previously settled area filled up with more tightly clustered sites. Of the 75 known sites of this phase, eight were large villages, a few of which had more than 1,000 inhabitants. The marked disparity in the size of communities, and the variations of wealth in burials, suggest that high-ranking lineages may have occupied the large villages, and low-ranking lineages the smaller satellite villages and hamlets. Recently, traces of a simple canal system that re-directed run-off from a rain-swollen ephemeral stream in a gulley (*barranca*) have been discovered on the western side of the Basin, and dated to 900 to 750 B.C. (Nichols 1982) – this is the earliest evidence of irrigation in the Basin. In view of the low density of population that then existed in the area served by the canals, it does not seem that this was an attempt to ease pressure on land by opening up more cropland; more probably, the system was a way of ensuring that crops would not be lost due to either late spring rains or early fall frosts.

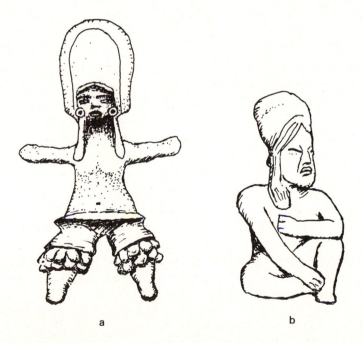

a   b

Fig. 85. Tlatilco figurines: (A) local style (height 16 cm); (B) Olmec style (height 10 cm).

271

The Basin's population continued its rapid growth during the next phase, First Intermediate 2 (650–300 B.C.), reaching 75,000. The communities of this period comprise three, perhaps four, hierarchical levels, according to size; the largest site was Cuicuilco. Although excavation has been severely impeded by a layer of lava, which blanketed Cuicuilco during a volcanic eruption around A.D. 300, it has been possible at least to determine the approximate extent of the site at successive stages of its existence. An estimated 5,000–10,000 people lived at Cuicuilco during First Intermediate 2. Five other sites in the Basin had between 1,000 and 3,500 inhabitants each; these sites have yielded traces of the region's earliest civic architecture – temple platforms, more than 5 m (15 ft) high. Faunal remains indicate that, throughout prehistory, more than 90% of the meat in the diet of the Basin's residents came from hunted deer. It is therefore startling to realize that, according to calculations of the available deer population, deer meat probably accounted for less than 1% of the diet, even as early as this period (Sanders, Parsons and Santley 1979). The size of Cuicuilco, and the hierarchy of site sizes, suggest that a fairly large and complex chiefdom had emerged in the southern Basin during the First Intermediate 2 phase. Excavations at the large village of Loma Torremote have yielded some evidence of residential patterns and social organization during this period. This community is estimated to have held some 400 to 475 compounds, each consisting of wattle and daub houses along with their associated patios and gardens. Three to six such compounds, sharing common walls, tended to be clustered together. The groups of 15 to 40 people who lived in these compound clusters may have constituted a lineage or lineage segment, and the lineages may have been ranked, according to their relative distance from the chief's line of descent. In a typical excavated cluster, only one compound incorporated a shrine containing figurines and ceramic censers, numerous storage pits, and a concentration of exotic items, including obsidian cores. This special compound may have been the residence of the lineage head (Sanders, Parsons and Santley 1979). However, there is not enough difference in burial wealth or house size or elaboration to suggest that really major status distinctions existed at this local level. One can only conjecture about the power and prestige that may have been enjoyed by the élite residents of Cuicuilco.

During First Intermediate 3, 300–100 B.C., the Basin's population doubled, reaching 145,000. There was now a four-level site hierarchy, including two very large regional centers – Cuicuilco in the southwest and Teotihuacán in the northeast. Cuicuilco now covered more than 400 hectares (1,000 acres) with at least 20,000 inhabitants. The site was dominated by a massive circular temple platform, 118 m (387 feet) in diameter and 23 m (75 feet) high. Teotihuacán appeared in the northeastern Basin, in a sparsely inhabited area where no large communities had existed before. This new center soon covered 6 to 8 square km (one-and-a-half square miles), with a population of about 20–40,000. Teotihuacán was situated next to a group of about 80 to 100 springs, on the gently sloping lower piedmont, at the head of an alluvial plain. Although direct evidence is lacking, it is presumed that the rapid growth of Teotihuacán was made possible by capturing the springs' water in canals for irrigation of the alluvial soils, and by draining some 1,000 hectares (2,500 acres) of swampy land near the springs to create fertile *chinampas*. Even with such methods, it was probably impossible to meet the subsistence needs of a large population by farming only in the immediate vicinity of the site, so tribute demands may have been imposed on surrounding communities. Cuicuilco, the only center that might have competed with Teotihuacán for hegemony over the Basin, was crippled around 150 B.C. by a natural catastrophe – a massive lava flow that covered much of the town and its farmland. Cuicuilco was still inhabited by a few thousand people until it was completely engulfed by a second lava flow around A.D. 300.

After more than 1,000 years of continuous growth, the population of the Basin seems to have decreased, to about 80,000–110,000, during First Intermediate phase 4, 100 B.C. to A.D. 100. In contrast to this region-wide downturn, Teotihuacán grew to three times its former size, with a population of well over 60,000, occupying 20 square km (8 square miles). More than 90% of the inhabitants may have been farmers, who left their city residences periodically to tend their fields (Sanders, Parsons and Santley 1979). These people must have been drawn into Teotihuacán from rural villages and hamlets, whether voluntarily or forcibly. This "implosion" at Teotihuacán left the remainder of the Basin thinly settled by only some 15,000 farmers. Those who were re-located in the city were put to work on massive construction projects. A great central avenue, now known as the "Street of the Dead", was laid out, running slightly east of north. On the eastern side of the avenue, a massive flat-topped pyramid, traditionally said to have been devoted to the sun god, was constructed. When completed, around A.D. 200, it was 64 m (210 ft) high, 210 m (650 ft) square at its base, and it contained about 1 million cubic meters of earth, adobe, and rubble fill, which was faced with stone. Tourists who visit the site today see five terraces, but this is the result of an erroneous modern reconstruction; actually there were only four. As tourists do today, the ancient priests would have climbed up a staircase on the western side to reach the top of the pyramid. A temple built of wood and thatch, which has long since disappeared, probably stood on the summit. At the northern end of the avenue, another major pyramid, said to have been that of the moon goddess, was built; it was about half as big as the Pyramid of the Sun. More than 20 other temple complexes were constructed along the central avenue during this period. The construction and maintenance of the temple complexes may imply that the city was ruled by a priestly élite, whose authority grew out of their religious functions. If, as seems likely, the de-population of the countryside involved coercion, we may infer the existence of secular authorities who controlled a military force. There is very little evidence to substantiate these reasonable inferences about Teotihuacán's political organization. Apart from the great mass of farmers and the presumed small élite class, the population also included a small number of full-time craft specialists. About 2% of the population

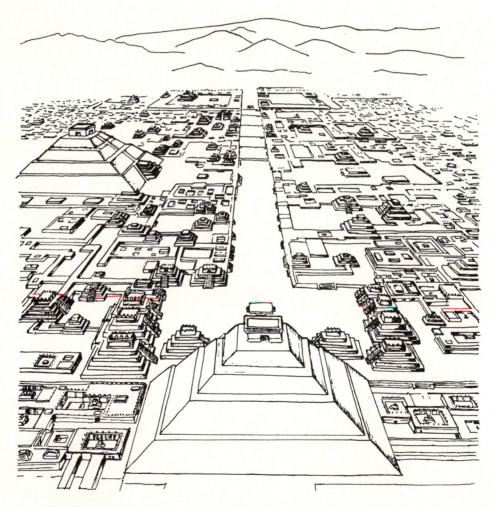

Fig. 86. Teotihuacán, ca. A.D. 400: perspective view down the central avenue (Street of the Dead). Pyramid of the Moon is in foreground, Pyramid of the Sun is to the left. The Ciudadela lies far down the avenue, to the south. Opposite it, on the right, is a large open plaza that may have served as a market-place. (After Swanson et al. 1975.)

is estimated to have been engaged in manufacture of obsidian tools, and other craftsmen may have accounted for the remaining 4%.

Around A.D. 150–200, a huge compound, known as the Ciudadela, was built, about 1.2 km (three-quarters of a mile) south of the Pyramid of the Sun. At its center stood a temple, its stone facade decorated by sculpted heads of feathered serpents, alternating with heads whose goggle eyes may be symbolic of the rain god, Tlaloc. The feathered serpents are the basis for this building's name, the "Temple of Quetzalcoatl". It has been suggested that the great compound in which it stood was the residence of the rulers of Teotihuacán.

About A.D. 200–450, there was a marked change in the residential areas of the city, as the earlier insubstantial houses were replaced by permanent, stone-walled compounds. These residential compounds formed blocks in the city's grid pattern, and the largest of them may have housed 100 people. The variations in layout, artifactual contents, and mural decoration of the compounds suggest that in some, the resident families were equal members of a kin group, while in others, more privileged families were surrounded by less well-to-do clients. Varying amounts of floor space also suggest that, from compound to compound, there were differences in wealth and power: the most affluent groups seem to have lived closest to the main avenue. The compounds formed distinct clusters, apparently neighborhoods (or, in Spanish, *barrios*), whose residents tended to practice the same occupation, such as obsidian-working or pottery-making. One such barrio, in the western part of the city, seems to have been occupied from A.D. 400 onward by natives of Oaxaca, whose domestic pottery and burial customs show their continuing ties to their homeland, 320 km (200 miles) to the southeast. Stylistic similarities in the art of Teotihuacán and Monte Albán suggest that an especially close relationship, perhaps a political alliance, linked these centers after A.D. 400 (Millon 1967, 1973, 1981).

At its height, A.D. 450–650, Teotihuacán held a resident population of about 125,000, perhaps even as many as 200,000 people. It is estimated that two-thirds of them were farmers, while craftsmen, merchants and bureaucrats comprised the remainder. About the same number of people now lived in provincial centers, villages and hamlets elsewhere in the Basin. This re-population of the region seems to have been the result of a deliberate policy which began to be implemented around A.D. 100. The peasants were re-settled in planned villages where they could till nearby lands, to produce surplus crops that they brought to Teotihuacán, to offer as tribute or to trade in the markets. The standardized planning and architecture of the satellite communities indicate that they were tightly controlled by Teotihuacán administrators (Sanders, Parsons and Santley 1979).

275

Teotihuacán's buildings had distinctive *talud-tablero* facades, consisting of rectangular panels with insets, set above sloping batters. The interiors of élite residences and temples were decorated with painted murals, depicting humans, gods and animals such as jaguars and coyotes. Only a few pieces of monumental stone sculpture are known, but life-sized masks were carved from greenstone, basalt, jade, and other materials. The most distinctive ceramic type made by Teotihuacán's potters was the cylindrical vase, with three slab-shaped feet and a knobbed lid. The vase's surface was carved or else stuccoed over and painted after firing. Such vessels were acquired by trade or imitated by neighboring peoples, even by the Maya of far-off Guatemala. Obsidian, mainly in the form of blades, was probably the most economically important of Teotihuacán's exports. More than 400 obsidian-knapping workshops have been identified within the city; 100 other workshops produced items of ceramic, shell, and ground-stone. Numerous clay figurines were made, using molds; these appear to represent 10 male and female deities, whose attributes permit their identification with gods worshipped in sixteenth-century Mexico, including the rain god (Tlaloc), the "Feathered Serpent" (Quetzalcoatl), the sun god, moon goddess, water goddess, and Xipe Totec, who symbolized the renewal of vegetation. A few glyphs found on pottery and murals show that a form of writing was probably known, but if there were any written documents on perishable materials, none have survived (Coe 1962). There is no way of ascertaining the language or ethnic identity of the Teotihuacános, but it seems most likely that they were Nahua-speakers, like the later Toltecs and Aztecs, whose cultural debt to Teotihuacán is obvious.

In its heyday, A.D. 450–600, Teotihuacán was the most important economic, political and religious center in Mesoamerica. Its close relationship to Monte Albán has already been noted. Its influence was also strongly felt at Cholula, in the valley of Puebla. Far to the southeast,

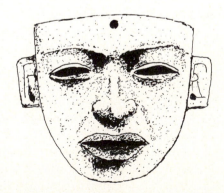

Fig. 87. Stone mask from Teotihuacán (original is life-size).

Fig. 88. Tripod vessel from Teotihuacán (height ca. 20 cm; drawing by J. Reilly).

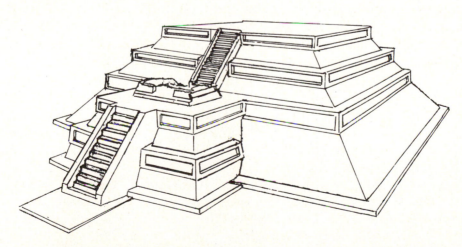

Fig. 89. Kaminaljuyú, Guatemala: pyramid with talud-tablero facade (length 27 m). (After Henderson 1981 and Willey 1968.)

at Kaminaljuyú in the Guatemalan highlands, pyramids with talud–tablero facades and tombs full of Teotihuacán pottery suggest that something more than intermittent trade contacts was involved. At Tikal, one of the most important centers of the lowland Maya, a monument marking the inauguration of a ruler known as Curl Snout shows him in Teotihuacán-style costume and pose. This stela was erected in A.D. 376; 46 years later, Curl Snout was buried in a tomb stocked with Teotihuacán imports. His successor, Stormy Sky, marked the twentieth year of his reign by raising a stela, on which he is shown wearing typical Maya regalia, but two accompanying warriors are equipped with Teotihuacán-style shields, spearthrowers and head-dresses (Henderson 1981). Whether these indications of Teotihuacán's influence reflect imperial domination of the Maya, or resulted from other forms of economic and cultural interaction, is not clear. Long-distance trading expeditions, organized by armed merchants like the later Aztec pochteca, might account for the widespread distribution of such portable items as ceramic vessels and obsidian blades; however, the talud–tablero-style buildings at Kaminaljuyú must reflect some other mechanism of cultural diffusion. Architects and craftsmen must have been brought to the site from Teotihuacán, perhaps to serve a colonial Mexican élite who dominated the local population. The continuation of the Pre-Classic Kaminaljuyú custom of burying the élite dead in rich graves within platforms, and the presence of Maya-style ceramics, imply some acculturation of the intrusive Teotihuacános to local ways, perhaps through marriage to members of the local aristocracy. There is no evidence that Teotihuacán built forts, depots, or roads, to facilitate administration of an empire; but these features were also lacking in the later Aztec empire. The Aztecs ran their empire by intimidation: recalcitrant tribute-payers were liable to be attacked by punitive military expeditions, dispatched from the Aztec capital. Teotihuacán might have maintained control of an empire in the same way. There are depictions of warriors, not only at Tikal, but also in the artworks of Teotihuacán itself, so it would seem that warfare was at least occasionally employed as a foreign policy option. An apparent increase in the number of warrior representations, as well as the construction of defensive walls at the city's center, suggest that Teotihuacán may have become more militaristic toward the end of its heyday (Millon 1967, 1973).

Around A.D. 600, the Maya of the Peten stopped importing pottery from Teotihuacán, an apparent indication that the city's influence beyond the Central Plateau of Mexico was waning. Nevertheless, large quantities of foreign pottery were still reaching Teotihuacán during the Metepec phase (A.D. 650–750), showing that long-distance trade had not ceased. There seems, however, to have been a major decline in the urban population during this period, to around 30,000–40,000. The weakened city was destroyed and burned about A.D. 750. Why did Teotihuacán collapse? It has been suggested that a possible decrease in rainfall, or erosion caused by forest-cutting, might have caused disastrous crop failures (Coe 1962); however, it appears most likely that Teotihuacán's decline was caused by the rapid growth of a rival city-state, Cholula, in the Valley of Puebla, to the southeast. Cholula had at first been only a regional center, culturally influenced and probably politically dominated by Teotihuacán; but it was in a better strategic position for control of the trade routes to

Fig. 90. Stela marking twentieth year of the reign of Stormy Sky, Tikal, ca. A.D. 445. The ruler is flanked by warriors in Teotihuacán-style dress; the figure on the right carries a shield with depiction of Tlaloc, the central Mexican rain god. (After Henderson 1981.)

Oaxaca, the Gulf Coast and the Peten. A huge complex of plazas and public buildings was built at Cholula at about the same time that Teotihuacán was burned to the ground; indeed, Cholula may have been responsible for that destruction. The style of the ceramic ware used by the Basin's inhabitants during the ensuing period, Second Intermediate 1, probably originated in Cholula (Sanders, Parsons and Santley 1979). This suggests that the Cholulans may have moved quickly to fill and political vacuum left in the wake of their rival's collapse.

THE EMERGENCE OF CIVILIZATION
IN THE MAYAN LOWLANDS

The Maya created the most sophisticated civilization of ancient America. Their achievements in art, architecture, writing, astronomy and calendrical notation were unsurpassed. Yet the jungle environment of the Peten, where Classic Maya civilization flourished, seems to be a most unlikely place for a complex society to have developed. The climate is uncomfortably hot and humid, the forest is dense and tangled, the insects are annoying and the poisonous snakes terrifying. The soil is thin and leached of its nutrients by heavy seasonal rains. To enrich the nutrient-poor soil, the modern-day descendants of the Maya practice a form of slash and burn agriculture, known as *milpa* cultivation. Trees are cut down in December; brush and secondary growth are cut during the ensuing rainless months, and the dried vegetation is burned in April. This process leaves behind a layer of nutrient-rich ash, into which the farmer pokes holes with his digging stick and drops in seeds of maize, beans, squash and peppers. If the rains come on time, soon after the May planting, the seeds will be well-watered and produce a good crop. The more vegetation that is burned, the more ash will be deposited, and thus the higher the yield will be. Therefore, the farmer must leave his plot unworked for a long time, to allow the forest to grow back. In the lowlands, some plots can be worked for only two seasons, and must then be left fallow for as long as 20 years.

Not long ago, most archaeologists assumed that the ancient Maya, like their modern descendants, practiced milpa agriculture (Dumond 1961, Cowgill 1962), however, it was difficult to explain how such shifting cultivation could have produced enough food for large urban populations. Archaeologists could evade this problem by denying that the Maya had ever been truly urban. The Maya "cities", it was suggested, were really ceremonial centers, periodically visited by peasants from surrounding hamlets, but vacant during most of the year, save for the few resident priests who looked after the shrines.

In recent years, this reconstruction of Maya settlement patterns and subsistence has been greatly altered, in light of new discoveries. Surveys of the important site of Tikal have revealed that house-mounds, which once supported Maya dwellings, are rather densely concentrated around the temple–palace complexes of the city's core. Estimates of Tikal's population at its height, around A.D. 700, range from 20,000 to 80,000, and the recently explored site of El Mirador may have held as many as 80,000 inhabitants. During the Classic period, A.D. 300–900, the Maya lowlands may have supported as many as five million people. Recent fieldwork has also provided evidence that all these people were not fed by slash and burn agriculture alone. Archaeologists have found traces, dating to as early as 100 B.C., of fields that were artificially raised above surrounding wetlands by piling up soil. Aerial surveys using radar imagery have disclosed extensive networks of canals, which the Maya dug to drain swampy areas, thus converting them into highly productive arable land. This would explain why so many of the largest Maya centers were situated on the edges of swamps (Harrison and Turner 1978).

The region inhabited by the ancient Maya, which includes modern Guatemala, Belize, southeastern Mexico, and the western parts of Honduras and El Salvador, actually comprises three different ecological zones. In the south, near the Pacific coast, the highlands rise above 300 m (1,000 ft), with volcanic peaks as high as 3,900 m (13,000 ft). The dissected landscape consists mostly of ridges and ravines, but there are a few broad valleys that have been important foci of human settlement since prehistoric times. Pine trees and grasses cover the slopes and ridges, while oaks grow in the ravines. Particularly in the lower-lying areas, the soil is thicker and more fertile than that of the lowlands, so milpa cultivation does not require very long fallow periods. A massive limestone peninsula juts northward from the highlands. Its southern half is the Peten, its northern half, Yucatan. One hundred and eighty to 230 cm (70 to 90 ins) of rain fall in the Peten during the wet season, from May to October, but much of the water percolates into the porous limestone – thus there are few lakes, and rivers occur only in the west and southeast. The most important river system is that of the Usumacinta, which flows northwest from the highlands through the Peten to the Gulf of Campeche. The scarcity of surface water in the lowlands during the long dry season was a major consideration for early Maya farmers, who were compelled to settle either close to the rivers or beside clay-clogged sinkholes, known as *cenotes*, which offered permanent supplies of drinking water. Annual rainfall decreases as one moves northward into the Yucatan, which causes differences in the vegetation cover of the southern and northern lowlands. The Peten is covered by a high monsoon forest, dominated by tall mahogany trees, sapodillas, logwood and breadnut (*ramon*) trees. Interspersed among the forests are patches of grassy savanna. In Yucatan, the tall trees give way to a low,

281

thorny forest, which in turn is replaced by dry scrub vegetation on the northern coast.

Recent fieldwork conducted in Belize by Richard MacNeish has yielded evidence that Paleo-Indian hunters inhabited the lowlands as early as 9000 B.C. This initial occupation was followed, after 7500 B.C., by several Archaic phases (Zeitlin 1984). Population grew over time, and settlements became larger and more permanent. A pattern of seasonal resource exploitation developed, as greater reliance was placed on coastal marine resources and plant foods. It is not yet clear how this coastal Archaic sequence was related to the appearance of the first agricultural villages. The earliest such site, also in Belize, is Cuello, where well-made pottery was found, associated with the remnants of house platforms. Radiocarbon dates put the initial occupation of Cuello as early as 2000 B.C. (calibrated date 2400 B.C.; see Hammond et al. 1979). Since this site was excavated in 1975, similar "Swasey" pottery has been found at several other sites in the lowlands. A C14 date from the site of Colha, not far from Cuello, indicates that Swasey ware was still being made there as late as 750 B.C. Either this style had an exceptionally long-lived popularity, or perhaps the earliest dates from Cuello must be re-assessed (Marcus 1983). In any case, it is by now apparent that the village–farming way of life was adopted at least as early in the Maya lowlands as in the Mexican highlands.

There is little archaeological evidence from the Formative period (2500 B.C.–A.D. 250) that pertains to the subsequent development of ranked societies among the Maya, but the lack of data has not discouraged scholars from advancing theories to account for this process. The proposed causative factors include population pressure, warfare, agricultural intensification, trade and diffusion. William Rathje (1971) suggested that the Maya of the Peten had to resort to long-distance trade in order to obtain vitally necessary materials that were not locally available, particularly salt, obsidian, and hard stones suitable for grinding corn. The Peten Maya had little of any material value to exchange for these commodities, so instead they offered their neighbors a chance to participate in their complex religious system. The leaders who oversaw the transportation and distribution of the trade goods, and purveyed the cult, emerged as a powerful hereditary élite. Rathje has been criticized, however, for underestimating the utility of locally available chert, limestone, and salt. A somewhat different trade model has been proposed by David Freidel (1979), who suggests that élites, arising at about the same time all over the lowlands, enhanced each other's prestige by long-distance exchange of valued items such as jade. William Sanders (1977), David Webster (1977) and Joseph Ball (1977) have advanced warfare models, which are essentially variants of Robert Carneiro's (1970) theory on the origin of chiefdoms and early states in "circumscribed" environments. According to this model, certain lowland areas, particularly the Usumacinta and Belize river systems, had greater agricultural potential than others. The population of these favored areas grew more rapidly, to the point where land became scarce and conflicts broke out between communities. The need for military leaders, and for authoritative individuals to allocate land, led to the emergence of an élite. Population density was already high everywhere in the lowlands, so the losers in inter-village warfare could not emigrate. They had to remain in their homes and pay tribute to the conquering chief, whose power was thereby enhanced.

Of course, the Maya were not the first people to create a civilization in the tropical lowlands of Mesoamerica. The Olmec had raised their monuments hundreds of years earlier on the Gulf Coast, some 500 km (300 miles) to the west of the Peten. One would expect to find some connection between these cultures; and indeed there is clear evidence of a strong Olmec influence upon early Maya civilization, but most of this influence was indirect and delayed. Initially, contact with the Olmec seems to have had little effect on the Formative villagers of the Peten. In most areas, local traditions of pottery manufacture continued, with the inclusion of a few Olmec-inspired designs. No large centers were built in the lowlands. However, there was a much stronger Olmec presence in the eastern highlands, manifested by a civic center with monumental architecture, stone reliefs, and Olmec-style pottery, at Chalchuapa in El Salvador. Perhaps the Olmec set up a colony in this area in order to get a steady supply of cacao (chocolate), which was still grown on the Pacific slopes at the time of the Spanish conquest. Cacao was considered extremely valuable in Mesoamerica, both as a medium of exchange and as a drink for aristocrats.

After 800 B.C., the lowland Maya villages seem to have become more closely connected with one another in an exchange network; this is inferred from the widespread distribution of the Mamon pottery style. It may be that the coalescence of this new interaction sphere disrupted the long-distance trade routes by which exotic goods had formerly reached the Olmec heartland, and thus contributed to the Olmec decline.

By around 400 B.C., fairly large structures had been built at several sites in the lowlands. A group of platforms, one of which was 5 m (16 ft) high, was constructed at Altar de Sacrificios in the Peten, and large platforms and a communal sweathouse were built at Dzibilchaltún in the northern Yucatan. In the highlands, the people of Kaminaljuyú, on the outskirts of modern Guatemala City, began to erect large clay platforms, flanking open plazas. More than 200 such platforms, some of which were surmounted by temples, others by élite dwellings, were constructed at Kaminaljuyú during the Late Formative (also called Pre-Classic), between 400 B.C. and A.D. 250. Mound E–III–3 was a flat-topped, stepped clay pyramid, which rose to a height of 18 m (60 ft). The mound had taken shape in stages, as new platforms were added following the burials of chiefs within the structure. The honored dead had been placed in wooden chambers, accompanied by several human sacrifices, numerous pots and rich offerings, such as jade beads, obsidian blades, and pyrite-encrusted plaques (Coe 1966, Henderson 1981, Culbert 1983). Also found at Kaminaljuyú were stelae, which bore long hieroglyphic inscriptions and representations of gods and rulers, carved in the Izapan style. Other monuments carved in this style have been found at the type site of Izapa and at many other sites, from Tres Zapotes, to the Pacific plain of Chiapas and Guatemala, to the Guatemala City area of the highlands. A number of Izapan stelae can be dated precisely, because they bear dates calculated by the Long Count system that was later used by the lowland Maya. The earliest Long Count date, which was carved on a stela at Chiapa de Corzo, corresponds to 36 B.C. The first dated stela in the lowlands is Stela 29 from Tikal, dating from A.D. 292; it is similar in style to the Izapan monuments. The Izapan style is clearly transitional between

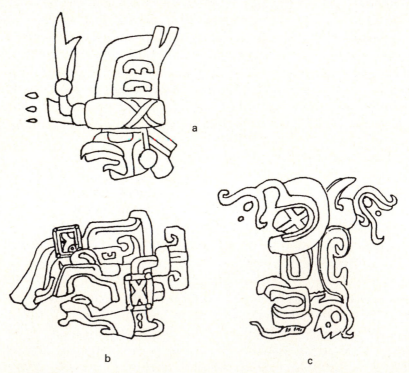

Fig. 91. Olmec, Izapan, and Maya treatments of the same theme (a mask with toothless jaw): (A) Chalcatzingo, (B) Kaminaljuyú, (C) Bonampak. (After Henderson, 1981.)

Olmec and Maya art. The scenes of rulers and gods, and the use of Long Count dates and hieroglyphics, demonstrate that the stela cult, a central focus of the art and ideology of the lowland Classic Maya, was derived from the Izapan culture of the highlands. Olmec influence thus seems to have reached the Maya mostly indirectly, through the Izapan culture (Coe 1966, 1977; Quirarte 1977).

In the lowlands, rapid population growth seems to have occurred during the Late Formative (300 B.C.–A.D. 250). A two-tiered settlement hierarchy developed; chiefdom centers, distinguished by their monumental structures, were surrounded by subordinate satellite villages. At Tikal, around A.D. 1, three large temple platforms and two smaller ones were built on the North Acropolis. The larger platforms, whose earth and rubble cores were faced with stucco, were about 4 to 4.5 m (14 ft) high. Their stairways had been decorated with modeled and painted stucco masks, probably representing supernatural jaguars. Similar stucco masks decorated the facades of platforms at Uaxactún and Cerros. Monumental buildings were also constructed during the Late Formative at El Mirador, Lamanai, Cuello, and Altar de Sacrificios in the Peten, and at Dzibilchaltún in the northern Yucatan. The deities who were represented by the stucco masks, and were worshipped in the temples on the platforms, may have been claimed as ancestors by chiefly lineages. The rich burials found within Tikal's North Acropolis hint at this sort of special relationship between deities and rulers. The style of the stucco masks is clearly derived from Izapan art, and highland influence is also evident in the spread of a decorative form of pottery, known as Floral Park ware. Vessels of this highland-derived type, with black and red geometric designs painted on an orange background, were used for tomb offerings and in other ritual

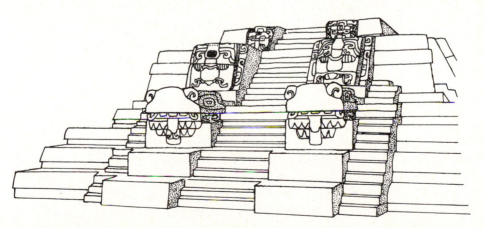

Fig. 92. Uaxactún: platform facade with stucco masks (height ca. 8 m). (After Henderson 1981.)

285

activities, by the élite of the Peten centers. Commoners continued to use Chicanel pottery, a plain ware that had developed locally from Mamom pottery (Henderson 1981).

At Becan in central Yucatan, around A.D. 200, a ditch and embankment, 2 km in circumference, were constructed, presumably as a fortification, which lends support to the idea that population pressure may have been causing more frequent conflicts between Late Formative communities. A comparably large ditch, 1,200 m (4,000 ft) long, was excavated at Cerros, a Late Formative center on the coast of northern Belize, around 100 B.C. (Scarborough 1983). This ditch describes an arc around the southern edge of the 37 hectare (92.5 acre) site, which is bounded on its north side by the waters of a bay. The ditch may have been useful for defense, but it seems to have functioned primarily as a canal, in which wet-season run-off was drained from fields and collected, to be used for pot irrigation of gardens during the dry season. The coastal location of Cerros has been interpreted as evidence that long-distance trade, involving the use of sea-going canoes, was a major factor in the rise of Late Formative Maya chiefdoms. It is interesting that the construction of monumental temple platforms at Cerros seems to have begun about a century *after* the water control system was installed. This suggests that planning and maintenance of such hydraulic systems may have been a vital function performed by the emergent élite at Cerros; their authority may thus have had an economic basis at first, instead of developing from a religious function.

The recently surveyed site of El Mirador, in Guatemala, may have been the pre-eminent lowland center of the Late Formative (or Pre-Classic) period (Dahlin 1984). This huge site consisted of two groups of monumental buildings, connected by a 1 km-long causeway, which seem to have been aligned to astronomical positions. Buildings with civic and religious functions, and élite residences, occupied the western acropolis, which was enclosed by a stone wall and ditch on the southern and eastern sides, and by steep slopes to the north and west. This fortified acropolis was much bigger than the north acropolis at contemporary Tikal, and its two pyramids dwarfed Tikal's temples. Six causeways radiated out from El Mirador, extending as far as 23 km (14½ miles) to the southeast. Pilgrims from the hinterland must have walked along these causeways, bearing offerings, tribute, or trade goods; several large open areas at El Mirador may have functioned as market-places.

The erection of the first Long Count-dated monuments in the lowlands marks the beginning of the Classic period, around A.D. 250. Curiously, in the highland centers, where the custom of erecting stelae had begun in the first century B.C., they were no longer set up after A.D. 250. This might reflect a major disruption of highland communities, caused by a volcanic eruption that occurred about that time. The earliest dated stela in the lowlands is Stela 29 from Tikal; carved in the Izapan style, it bears a date corresponding to A.D. 292. Until A.D. 434, dated stelae were put up only at Tikal, Uaxactun, and other nearby sites. After this date, the beginning of Long Count cycle 9, the stela cult spread eastward to Copan and north-ward to sites in Yucatan. The stelae evidently commemorated the ances-tors of the chiefly lineages.

The transition from chiefdom to state organization appears to have occurred in the Peten around A.D. 534 (Marcus 1983). The stela cult reached its maximum extent, a state artistic style took shape, and the symbolic system used for monuments became more standardized. Where formerly there had been a two-level hierarchy of sites, there were now four levels, presumably indicative of a more complex administrative structure. Large and small centers tended to be regularly spaced, with 13 to 26 km (8 to 16 miles) between them. At the pinnacle of the hierarchy, four huge primary regional centers were emerging, each with its own emblem glyph and ruling dynasty. These centers were Tikal, Calakmul, Copan and Palenque. The political influence of these city-states is reflected in the occurrence of their emblem glyphs on monuments at smaller, subordinate centers. For several centuries, the rulers of the Maya centers jockeyed for power; but in accordance with their scheme of cosmological order, the Maya recognized only four centers as paramount at any one time. Each of these four was assigned to one of the cardinal directions.

A typical Classic center was composed of a series of stepped platforms surrounded by masonry superstructures, arranged around plazas or courtyards. At Tikal and other large centers, several such complexes were linked by causeways. The grandest structures were the tall, steep-sided temple pyramids, built of limestone blocks facing a rubble core. At Tikal there were six pyramids; the tallest of these rose to a height of 70 m (229 ft). The pyramid's height was accentuated by the addition of an extension to the temple's roof; this "roof comb", and the temple facade, were decorated with painted stucco reliefs. Besides pyramids, a typical complex included a number of lower platforms, which supported single-storey buildings with as many as several dozen rooms. Although they do not seem very comfortable, these structures are generally assumed to have been élite residences. In these "palaces", doorways and ceilings fre-quently took the form of corbelled vaults, in which each of the higher courses of stone projected a little farther inward, up to the top of the vault, which was capped by flat stones. The corbelled vault was a distinctive feature of Maya architecture; it was not used by other Mesoamerican civilizations. Other structures commonly found in central complexes were ball-courts and reservoirs.

For many years, scholars believed that Maya hieroglyphic inscriptions signified only ideas, not sounds, and dealt only with astronomical and calendrical records. However, in the 1950s, the Soviet scholar Yuri Knorosov showed that besides the numerous glyphs that were pictographs or ideographs (signifying whole words or concepts) there were other phonetic glyphs that stood for syllables. In 1958, Heinrich Berlin identified the emblem glyphs associated with particular centers. Soon after this breakthrough, Tatiana Proskouriakoff (1960, 1961) demonstrated that groups of stelae recorded significant events in the lives of particular rulers – their births, accessions, marriages, births of offspring, alliances, military victories and deaths. The decipherment of Maya texts is far from complete, but we have already gained valuable insights into Maya politics and history. We can trace the careers of individual rulers, such as Stormy Sky of Tikal, Bird Jaguar of Yaxchilán, and Pacal of Palenque.

Fig. 93. A typical Maya pyramid: Temple I at Tikal (total height 47 m). (After Andrews 1975.)

Pacal reigned at Palenque from A.D. 615 to 683; under his rule this center became predominant in the western lowlands. When Pacal died, he was buried in a subterranean crypt, over which was raised a stepped pyramid, now known as the Temple of the Inscriptions. A valuted staircase descended from the floor of the temple on top of the pyramid, through its core, to Pacal's tomb. The entrance to the staircase was discovered by Mexican archaeologist Alberto Ruz Lhuillier in 1949. It took him four years to clear out the rubble with which the 25 m- (80 ft-) long staircase had been intentionally filled. He finally reached an antechamber that held the skeletons of five or six young adults, apparently sacrificial victims. A huge stone slab blocked the far end of the antechamber. Upon removing the slab, Ruz entered Pacal's tomb. Pacal's skeleton lay in a monolithic sarcophagus, covered by a 3.8 m- (12 ft-) long rectangular limestone slab. A jade mosaic mask, ear-spools, necklaces, rings, and numerous other ornaments of jade and mother of pearl had been placed in the sarcophagus. Two jade figurines lay beside Pacal; one represented the sun god. The body and grave goods had been sprinkled with red cinnabar. Pottery vessels and two portrait heads made of stucco lay on the floor of the burial chamber (Ruz-Lhuillier 1953). The scene carved in relief on the sarcophagus lid has been interpreted as depicting Pacal being swallowed by an underworld monster, like the sun sinking below the western horizon – the implication of this symbolic equation seems to be that, like the sun, the deified ruler will ascend again to the heavens. Monuments commemorating the accession of Pacal's son and successor, Chan-Bahlum, show Pacal associated with symbols of the sun god. Pacal's symbolic identity with the sun god was further emphasized by Palenque's architects. As the sun sets on the day of the winter solstice, its last rays illuminate the relief scenes of Chan-Bahlum's accession in the Temple of the Cross, and as seen from the Palace, the setting sun's oblique descent appears to follow the line of the stairway down to Pacal's tomb (Henderson 1981).

Women appear to have been prominent members of Palenque's royal lineage. A woman named Kan Ik ruled the center from A.D. 583 to 604, and Zac Kuk, who was probably Pacal's mother, ruled from 612 to 615. Palenque was not unique in this respect; inscriptions at other centers, such as Piedras Negras and Coba, refer to women who acted either as regents or as permanent rulers. Pacal seems to have married his sister, Ahpo Hel. Marriage to noble ladies was one of the ways by which the leaders of secondary centers were allied to the rulers of primary centers. For instance, in 682 a royal woman from Tikal was sent off to marry the lord of Naranjo, a secondary center. Monumental inscriptions recording the birth of their son in 687 repeatedly mention his link, by the maternal line, to Tikal, while his lower-ranking father is virtually ignored (Marcus

Fig. 94. The lid of Pacal's sarcophagus (length 3.8 m).

1983). The Classic Maya nobility seem to have reckoned their lines of descent bilaterally, stressing whichever line, male or female, enhanced their status more. Commoners, on the other hand, probably reckoned descent in the male line.

The accomplishments of Maya architects have already been mentioned; and the great skill displayed by Late Classic artists should also be acknowledged. They excelled in carving bas-reliefs, that often feature portraits of elaborately dressed nobles and highly stylized and complex representations of gods. A few surviving examples in wood show that this material was carved as exquisitely as stone was. The walls of palaces and temples must once have been covered by colorful frescoes, but the only examples that have survived intact in the tropical climate of the Peten are the murals of Bonampak. Dated around A.D. 760, these paintings depict a victory won by the ruler of this minor center. In one of three scenes, he stands with his warriors and noble spectators on top of a

Fig. 95. A section of the Bonampak murals.

291

stepped platform. Stripped and bleeding captives sit on the steps below him, begging for mercy. Some indication of what the vanished murals must have been like is provided by the beautifully painted exteriors of bowls, dishes and cylindrical vases, which often depict scenes from the lives of Maya aristocrats. An outstanding example is a 25 cm- (10 in-) high painted vase that was found in the grave of a young woman at Altar de Sacrificios (Stuart 1975). Dated by glyphs to 21 April 754, it shows the ritual self-sacrifice of a young woman, presumably the occupant of the

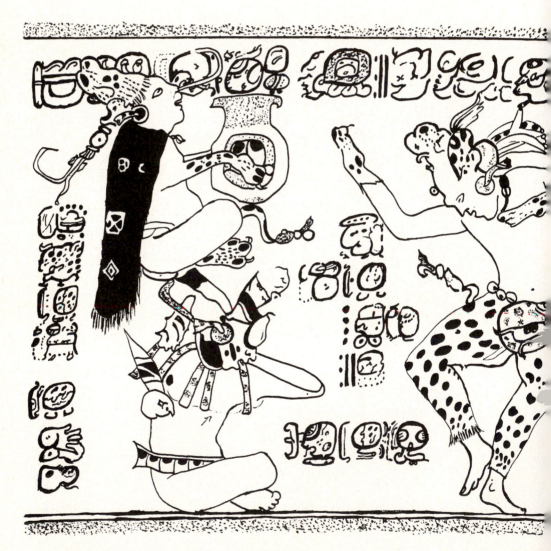

Fig. 96. Scene on vase from Altar de Sacrificios (height 25 cm; drawn by J. Reilly). (After Stuart 1975 and Henderson 1981.)

grave. She was probably obligated to accompany in death an older noble-woman who was buried in the grave below hers. In the painting, she has slit her throat with a leaf-shaped flint blade, in the company of dancing celebrants dressed in costumes representing the god of the underworld. Glyphs identify these figures as visiting aristocrats. One of them is Bird Jaguar, the ruler of Yaxchilán, or perhaps his envoy, while another has come from Tikal. Distinctive pottery vessels from these two centers, and also a third site, were found as offerings in the older woman's grave.

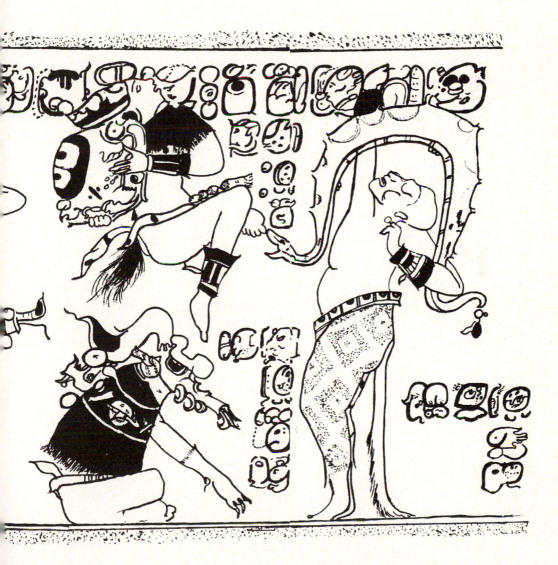

THE CLASSIC MAYA COLLAPSE

The rulers of Palenque and other centers in the western lowlands stopped erecting stelae around A.D. 800. At about the same time, or shortly thereafter, at center after center monumental construction ceased and population declined. There seems to have been a sort of domino effect, as the wave of decline moved rapidly eastward. At Tikal, no major buildings rose after A.D. 830, and the latest Long Count date at the site was 10.3.0.0.0 (A.D. 889). The city's population dropped to 10% of its eighth-century size. The very last Long Count date, carved on a jade piece from eastern Yucatan, is 10.4.0.0.0 (A.D. 909). By this time, the state organizations of all the southern lowland centers had collapsed, and by A.D. 950, all of the central ceremonial precincts lay in ruins, occupied only by small groups of squatters. The disaster hit not only the urban élite, but the rural peasants as well; most of the Peten was depopulated, and has remained so to this day.

Why did this dramatic decline of Classic civilization occur? Among the causes that have been speculatively advanced are an epidemic disease, such as malaria or yellow fever; earthquakes; drought; agricultural collapse; severing of trade routes; peasant revolution; and an invasion by Mexicans (Culbert 1973). The mosquito-borne diseases can be discounted, because they were almost certainly introduced after 1492, and there is no evidence of unusually violent earthquakes. It is possible that the growing population of Late Classic times may have finally overtaxed the limited agricultural potential of the Peten. Some Late Classic skeletons, mostly commoners but some aristocrats too, show the effects of malnutrition – stunted growth, scurvy, anaemia and peridontal disease. An obvious short-term solution to the problem of food shortages would have been to shorten the fallow intervals between cultivation of milpas and in the long run this practice would have resulted in soils depleted of nutrients. Burning off too much vegetation cover would have caused erosion of soil from hillsides, and the slopewash might have clogged canals. It is even possible that removal of too much forest cover might have affected the region's rainfall pattern, causing more frequent droughts. Such theories of agricultural exhaustion and ecological catastrophe must now be re-assessed, in light of the recently discovered evidence that the Maya supplemented slash and burn with more intensive forms of agriculture. As population increased, why didn't they simply dig more canals and drain more swampland? Intensive agriculture, involving raised and ridged fields, terraces, and canals, has not been practiced in the lowlands in modern times, so there is no good basis for estimation of the maximum crop yields that might have been produced by such methods. Proponents of the peasant revolution theory (Hamblin and Pitcher 1980) cite the Bonampak murals and other Late Classic depictions of wel-dressed rulers subduing enemies who wear only simple loincloths. An obvious reason for hesitation in identifying the conquered figures as peasant rebels is that in Mesoamerica, nakedness was regarded as a sign of humiliation, which would probably have been inflicted as readily on captured nobles as on commoners. Mutilation and destruction of monuments, which has been ascribed to triumphant and vengeful peasants, could as easily have been the work of a rival ruler's army. Elimination of the aristocracy alone, who must have constituted only a small minority of Maya society, would not account for the near-total depopulation that accompanied the centers' collapse. It should be noted, however, that in a few places, such as the Belize valley, villages evidently continued to flourish for at least a century after the demise of the élite centers.

Toward the end of the eighth century, increasing amounts of "fine paste" pottery appeared at western Maya centers, suggesting intensified contact with Mexican groups. This ware also appeared at Tikal, but only after the city's decline had already begun. Fine paste pottery is very rare at eastern lowland sites. This distribution may indicate changing trade patterns, but by itself does not prove that an invasion occurred. Depictions of Mexicans at western sites during this period do, however, show that there was some population movement into the lowlands (Henderson 1981).

Obviously the Classic Maya collapse was a complex process, doubtless entailing the interplay of several causative factors, which probably operated somewhat differently in each locality. The following is a plausible scenario. The decline, then fall of Teotihuacán (A.D. 600–750) created a power vacuum in Mesoamerica. The rival Maya city-states tried to win control of the trade routes to the west, which were now "up for grabs". Their jockeying for power involved more frequent outbreaks of warfare and an intensified construction of monuments, designed as conspicuous displays of the rulers' prestige. Population growth was encouraged, because the élite needed soldiers for their armies and workers for their construction crews. The rulers organized large scale water control and land reclamation projects, in an effort to meet the food demands of the growing population. Their network of external alliances and their systematic tribute collection and redistribution at second and third-order administrative centers ensured that, despite any local crop failures that might occur, the commoners could be provided with food as well as more exotic items. Ultimately, the political unrest engendered by Teotihuacán's fall spilled over the eastern edge of the Mexican highlands into the Maya world. Mexican merchants and immigrants, who may have arrived peacefully sometimes, aggressively at other times, began to dominate the western Maya centers culturally, then politically. The decline of the élite in the western centers set off a crisis of confidence among their allies and in-laws to the east. As the élite lost their grip, they could no longer control disgruntled peasants, who may no longer have been so impressed by the rulers' claims of divine support. The overthrow or collapse of the ruling dynasties led to the disintegration of the intricate system of exchange and redistribution that they had managed, and deterioration of the agricultural works they had maintained. This break-down of the economic system caused famines. Many peasants died; those who survived returned to slash and burn farming, or emigrated northward to Yucatan, where the Classic societies did not suffer a decline in the ninth century.

The most influential of the Yucatan centers, toward the end of the Late Classic, were Uxmal in the Puuc hills to the west, Dzibilchaltún to the north, and Coba in the east. The distinctive Puuc architectural style, typified by Uxmal's magnificent pyramids and palaces, featured intricate stone mosaic upper facades and engaged columns. These Yucatan centers flourished from about 800 to 1000. Traces of Mexican influence were already visible at Uxmal during this period, and the Toltec invasion that followed led to the site's decline and abandonment.

POST-CLASSIC CIVILIZATIONS

As Teotihuacán declined in the eighth century, the population of the Basin of Mexico fell by one third. The distribution of settlements during the period from A.D. 750 to 950 suggests that the Basin was divided among a series of small, hostile states. The people of each state tended to settle close to their regional center, probably for security against attack.

New centers of political and economic power and cultural influence emerged in areas to the south and north of the Basin. At Cholula, in the Valley of Puebla, a huge acropolis of plazas and public buildings was con-structed. After A.D. 950 much of this area was incorporated into the base of Cholula's Great Pyramid, which exceeded Teotihuacán's Pyramid of the Sun in volume. The adoption of Cholulan-style pottery at sites in the southern Basin suggests that Cholula may have controlled the area. A largely unoccupied buffer zone separated the sites of the southern Basin from those of the northern section, which was probably controlled by the Toltecs.

The Toltecs' capital city was Tula, situated in an arid plain 60 km (37½ miles) north of the Basin of Mexico. Later Aztec legends lavish praise on the Toltecs for their great wealth and superior craftsmanship, and describe Tula as a sort of paradise. In reality, however, Tula was a city of moderate size, and its public buildings were neither particularly impressive nor well-constructed (Diehl 1981). It covered about 9 square km (3½ square miles) and estimates of its population range from 30,000 to 60,000. Another 60,000 farmers occupied the villages and hamlets of the surrounding region. The seeming aesthetic poverty of Tula can be at least partially blamed on the Aztecs, who carried off much of the site's artwork to their own capital city. The largest structure, Pyramid C, was completely vandalized, but some of the artwork of Pyramid B was left in place, perhaps because the pieces were too big to be easily moved. Pyramid B was a terraced temple platform. The roof of the temple that once stood on the summit was supported by stone columns. Some of them were carved in the form of warriors, others bore carved representations of feathered serpents, with their tails raised, and some square columns were decorated with reliefs depicting soldiers. The facade of the pyramid was decorated with bas-reliefs, showing jaguars, coyotes, feathered serpents, and eagles tearing at hearts. These creatures probably symbolized warrior orders, similar to those of the Aztec knights. In the temple and the ceremonial precinct around it were found a number of *chacmool* sculptures, showing reclining men holding round dishes on their bellies. The real function of these figures is unknown, but it has been speculated that the hearts ripped from the chests of sacrificial victims were placed in the dishes. Whether or not this was the case, there is other evidence confirming that the Toltecs did practice human sacrifice. Stone carvings at

Fig. 97. Stone column in form of a warrior, Pyramid B, Tula (height ca. 4.6 m).

Tula depict *tzompantlis,* the wooden racks on which the Toltecs, like the Aztecs, displayed the skulls of those who had been sacrificed. The style of Toltec art owes something to the contemporary styles developed by the Cholulans of Puebla and the Mixtecs in Oaxaca, but was largely derived from the Teotihuacán tradition. However, as can be inferred from the brief foregoing description of Tula's monumental art, Post-Classic art has a distinctive sanguinary aspect. Teotihuacán art includes some depictions of warriors, and one mural from the city, showing a priest who carries a knife and bleeding heart, does suggest that human sacrifices were occasionally performed there. However, the much greater emphasis placed by Post-Classic artists on symbols and scenes of death, warfare, and human sacrifice, distinguishes their work from that of their Classic predecessors.

Tula grew rapidly between A.D. 750 and 950. Archaeological and legendary evidence indicates that the city absorbed immigrants both from the north and the south. From the arid northwestern frontier of Meso-america came the Chichimecs, simple village farmers who were regarded as barbarians by the more sophisticated peoples of central Mexico. The other major group that migrated to Tula was the Nonoalca, who were probably craftsmen, priests, and other civilized refugees from the warring statelets to the south. The legends that recount the struggle between the peaceful ruler, Topiltzin-Quetzalcoatl, and the fierce god, Tezcatlipoca, may reflect the uneasy relationship of these factions.

It is difficult to separate the kernel of historical truth in the story of Topiltzin-Quetzalcoatl from later mythical accretions. Topiltzin does seem to have been a real person, born in A.D. 935 or 947, who was later identified with the divine "Feathered Serpent", Quetzalcoatl (Coe 1962). He is said to have moved the Toltec capital from a place called Colhuacan to Tula. Topiltzin is characterized in the legends as something of an intellectual pacifist, who abhorred human sacrifice. This attitude enraged the god, Tezcatlipoca, who, by means of several cunning stratagems, drove Topiltzin-Quetzalcoatl from Tula. The deposed ruler and his retinue made their way to the Gulf coast, where, according to one version of the tale, he set himself on fire and was transformed into the Morning Star. Another version has him sail off to the east on a raft made of serpents, promising to return some day. The legends describe Quetzalcoatl as fair-skinned and bearded. When the Aztec ruler, Moctezuma, heard of Cortes' landing in 1519, he feared that the conquistador might be Quetzalcoatl, returning to reclaim his kingdom.

It is intriguing to note that, according to Maya historical legends, a man named Kukulcan conquered Yucatan in A.D. 987 and established his capital at Chichén Itzá. "Kukulcan" is the Maya translation of the Nahua title Quetzalcoatl, or "Feathered Serpent". Might Kukulcán, conqueror of the Yucatan Maya, have been the very same Topiltzin-Quetzalcoatl who had fled from Tula? Many scholars, noting the frequent conflation and confusion of events and individuals in Maya legendary history, have hesitated to accept this identification of Kukulcán. Nevertheless, archaeological evidence confirms that, around A.D. 1000, the Maya center at Chichén Itzá was occupied by Toltec invaders. The new rulers initiated an ambitious construction program, laying out a plaza flanked by a pyramid, temple platforms, colonnaded halls, an I-shaped ball-court (the largest in all Mesoamerica), and a tzompantli (skull rack). The Temple of the Warriors is virtually the twin, but on a larger scale, of Pyramid B at Tula, and the other buildings at Chichén Itzá so closely resemble their counterparts at Tula as to suggest that whoever designed

Fig. 98. Gold plate depicting human sacrifice, from the sacred cenote at Chichén Itzá (diameter 23 cm; drawn by J. Reilly). (After Emmerich 1977.)

them was intimately familiar with Tula's central precinct and sought to replicate it in Yucatan. If the legendary Topiltzin was involved in the Toltec conquest of Yucatan, his supposedly pacific nature is belied by depictions, at Chichén Itzá, of Toltec warriors attacking the Maya. Such conquest scenes occur in murals painted in the Temple of the Warriors and the Temple of the Tigers, and on gold discs that had been thrown as offerings into Chichén Itzá's famous sacred cenote (sink-hole). The Toltecs' relations with the native population evidently improved during the two centuries of their rule, for Maya nobles and deities appear in the murals and reliefs of Chichén Itzá, and the buildings of this period incorporate certain features of the Puuc architectural style.

The Toltec empire collapsed in the mid-twelfth century, and Tula was destroyed and burned around A.D. 1168. The cause of the collapse remains to be clarified, but one contributing factor was the arrival of large numbers of desperate Chichimec immigrants, village farmers and nomadic hunter–gatherers driven from the northwestern frontier by prolonged drought. Tula may also have been weakened by competition with Cholula and with other rival states on its western and eastern borders.

The ambitious rulers of small states, who had formerly been tribute-paying vassals of Tula, moved to fill the political vacuum left by its downfall. The Mixtecs had been gradually extending their control over Oaxaca, by means of conquest and strategic royal marriages. By 1350, they were infiltrating Zapotec territory in the Valley of Oaxaca. Monte Albán, the one-time Zapotec capital in the valley, had been deserted since about A.D. 900, and the intrusive Mixtecs buried their own dead in the city's old tombs. A Mixtec lord was laid to rest in Tomb 7, accompanied by his sacrificed servants and a spectacular treasure, which included thousands of pearls, turquoise mosaics, engraved jaguar bones, silver bowls, necklaces composed of rock crystal, amber, jet, and coral beads, and 3.6 kg (8 lb) of gold objects – pectorals, rings, necklaces, nose and ear ornaments, lip-plugs, tweezers, false fingernails, diadems, and miniature masks (Caso 1932). The Mixtec goldsmiths had used the lost wax process, which, along with other metal working techniques, had been brought to Mexico by traders from the Andes or Central America around A.D. 900. Mixtec artists excelled not only in metal and stone working, but also in sculpture and in painting of pottery, plastered walls, and folding books made of bark-paper or deerskin. These codices recounted the exploits of Mixtec rulers, from the seventh century onward, using a mixture of pictographs and rebus-like phonetic symbols. A number of them miraculously survived the Spanish conquest.

In Yucatan the power of the Mayanized Toltecs waned, and they abandoned Chichén Itzá by A.D. 1224. A new Maya-dominated state was established by the Cocom dynasty; its capital was Mayapán, in northern

Yucatan. Mayapán's temples and palaces were shoddy imitations of those at Chichén Itzá – this has usually been interpreted as an indication of cultural decline, although it has recently been suggested that it reflects the rise of a merchant class that had no reason to invest its capital in impressive public architecture (Sabloff and Rathje 1975). Some 11,000 to 12,000 people were crammed together in 4 square km (2½ square miles), protected by a low stone wall. The Cocom rulers kept the titular lords of their provinces as virtual hostages at Mayapán, thus ensuring their continued payment of tribute. Such tactics did not endear the Cocom to the subordinate nobles, who rebelled and destroyed Mayapán around A.D. 1450. The former Cocom domain was broken up into 16 small rival states. Merchants based in these states managed the coastal trade routes, along which salt, cotton cloth, cacao, honey, jade, feathers, obsidian and copper were transported in ocean-going canoes. This was the political and economic situation that the Spanish encountered as they began their conquest of northern Yucatan in 1528. The Maya were not as easily subjugated as the more centralized Aztec and Inca empires; the Spanish had to contend with guerrilla tactics and frequent rebellions. It was not until 1697 that the last independent Maya kingdom fell to the Spanish; this was Tayasal, which had been founded in a wilderness region of the Peten around 1450, by refugees from northern Yucatan.

THE RISE OF THE AZTECS

In the century of chaos that followed Tula's collapse, Toltec refugees and Chichimec immigrants streamed southward into the Basin of Mexico, where they inter-married with the local inhabitants. In the process, the rustic Chichimecs learned the more civilized ways of central Mexico. The newly merged populations formed more than 50 tiny statelets, whose ruling dynasties claimed descent from the Toltecs and adopted the Toltec ideology of divinely authorized kingship. The statelet centers were generally built in areas that had been virtually uninhabited in earlier times.

The last of the Chichimec immigrants to arrive in the Basin were the Tenochca or Mexica, whom we know as the Aztecs. They seem to have begun as a semi-civilized agricultural tribe, forced by drought or overpopulation to leave their home town of Aztlan, which was probably located in western Mexico. By the time the Aztecs arrived in the Basin, there was not much vacant land left to be colonized, and they settled as squatters at one spot after another, only to be driven off by the landowners, who were repelled by their savage ways. The people of Colhuacan allowed them to remain in their territory as serfs; but when the Aztecs sacrificed a Colhuacan princess who had been offered as a wife for their chief, and her father, arriving for the marriage ceremony, beheld a priest dressed in his daughter's flayed skin, the Aztecs were expelled from Colhuacan too. They resumed their wandering until they came to some uninhabited swampy islands near the western shore of Lake Texcoco. It was here, according to Aztec legend, that they saw an eagle, with a snake in its beak, sitting on a cactus – the prophesied marker of the site where they should establish their capital. The twin Aztec towns of Tenochtitlán and Tlatelolco were founded on the islands in 1325 or 1345. In 1367, the Aztecs started serving as mercenary soldiers for Tezozomoc, the ruler of the Tepanec city-state of Azcapotzalco, who was competing against the rulers of Texcoco for recognition as paramount lord of the new Chichimec states. Also in 1367, Acamapichtli was appointed as *tlatoani* ("speaker", or ruler) of Tenochtitlán. He and his successors collaborated with the traditional tribal council, composed of lineage elders and priests. About 1400, Tezozomoc rewarded the Aztecs of Tlatelolco for their support by giving them his son as their first king, and he gave one of his daughters in marriage to Acamapichtli's son. The Aztec cities grew larger and more wealthy. The Aztecs were delegated more responsibility for the administration of conquered states, and they were awarded a share of the land and tribute won by Tezozomoc when he finally defeated the Texcocans in 1418.

Following Tezozomoc's death in 1426, his eldest son, Maxtla, seized the throne of Azcapotzalco from his half-brother, who had been chosen by their father to succeed him. Maxtla then murdered the Aztec rulers, who had supported his rival. This provoked a rebellion by the Aztecs, who, with the aid of the Texcocans, destroyed Azcapotzalco in 1428. The victorious tlatoani, Itzcoatl, carried off an internal power play at Tenochtitlán, depriving the lineage heads of any significant role in decision-making or the administration of conquered lands. In 1434, the rulers of Tenochtitlán, Texcoco, and the less powerful city of Tlacopan formed the Triple Alliance. The rulers of the other small states in the Basin were induced to become tribute-paying vassals of the Alliance through a combination of inter-dynastic marriages, offers to share in the tribute from newly conquered areas, and occasional threats or applications of force. Most of the agricultural tribute collected from the vassal lords was kept by the tlatoani, but the rest was distributed to high-ranking nobles who had distinguished themselves in battle. After securing control of the Basin, the rulers of the Triple Alliance began large scale water control and construction projects, and embarked on the conquest of outlying areas. Toward the end of his reign, Itzcoatl ordered construction of a causeway that linked Tenochtitlán to the towns on the shore of Lake Xochimilco, and he conquered towns in Morelos and northern Guerrero, 100 km (62.5 miles) to the south. His successor, Moctezuma I (1400–69), undertook renovation of the temple of the Aztecs' patron god,

Huitzilopochtli; he also ordered construction of a great palace, a 16 km- (10 mile-) long dike across Lake Texcoco, a canal leading to Tlatelolco's market area, and an aqueduct that brought fresh water to Tenochtitlán from the springs at Chapultepec. His armies achieved numerous conquests in areas to the south and east of the Basin. By 1500, the Triple Alliance controlled a territory of about 200,000 square km (125,000 square miles) and a population of as many as 10 million. Aztec domination of the Alliance was strongly asserted for the first time when Moctezuma II (1502–20) seized conquered iand from Texcoco and then, in 1506, forced the Texcocans to appoint his nephew as their ruler (Davies 1973, Coe 1962, Calnek 1982, Rounds 1982, Brumfiel 1983).

Tenochtitlán by this time covered 12–15 square km (5 square miles), with a resident population of 150,000 to 200,000. The city proper was linked by canals and causeways to nearby provincial centers and suburbs, forming a "Greater Tenochtitlán" with 400,000 inhabitants. An additional 600,000 people lived in centers, villages and hamlets in the rest of the Basin of Mexico. It is not surprising that the Spaniards who arrived in 1519 were awestruck by their first glimpse of Tenochtitlán, for it was bigger than most European cities of the time – five times the size of contemporary London, for example. The Spaniards compared the Aztec capital to Venice, for Tenochtitlán's "streets" were canals. The canals, laid out in a north–south grid pattern, were filled with a steady traffic of canoes laden with passengers or cargo. Much of Tenochtitlán itself, and the surrounding farm plots that produced food for its inhabitants, had been created by an enormous drainage and land reclamation project. The canals functioned not only as thoroughfares but as drainage ditches, which reduced the water content of the swampland around the original islands to the point where it could be farmed. Mud from the lake-bed and rotting vegetation were piled on top of the drained plots, raising them higher and thereby lessening the danger of flooding. Defense against rainy-season floods was also provided by the dike that had been built across a narrow neck of Lake Texcoco; the dike also prevented the salty waters of the eastern lake from polluting its western third, which the Aztecs had filled with fresh water, piped in by their aqueduct. Chinampa agriculture was highly productive: 0.4 hectares (1 acre) could provide enough food for six to eight people (Palerm 1955, Sanders, Parsons and Santley 1979).

At the center of Tenochtitlán was a sacred precinct, dominated by a 60 m- (200 ft-) tall pyramid, on which stood the twin temples of Tlaloc, the rain god, and Huitzilopochtli, the sun god. Smaller temples were devoted to Tezcatlipoca, Xipe Totec and other gods. The precinct also included the priests' quarters, a large ball-court, and a tzompantli on which the skulls of tens of thousands of sacrificial victims were displayed. The buildings of the central precinct were torn down by the Spaniards, and the buildings of colonial Mexico City rose upon their ruins. Only in 1978 did Mexican archaeologists begin to excavate the giant twin temple pyramid. The archaeologists moved in after workers laying in an electric cable stumbled upon a huge circular stone, which bore a carved relief depicting the dismembered goddess, Coyolxauhqui. This stone lay in the plaza where the corpses of sacrifices landed after rolling down the steps of the Great Temple. Excavation has revealed 11 construction stages, and more than 50 rich offering caches that had been buried within them. Among the 200 objects found in a typical cache were human skulls, flint and obsidian blades, and stone sculptures; in addition, many hundreds of stone beads were generally included (Matos Moctezuma 1980. Molina Montes 1980).

Surrounding the sacred precinct were the palaces of Tenochtitlán's rulers. Moctezuma II's palace contained his luxurious private residence and pleasure gardens, which included an aviary, a zoo, and apartments for human freaks. It was also an administrative center, with a council room, law courts, a treasury, store rooms for tribute, a jail, an arsenal, guest

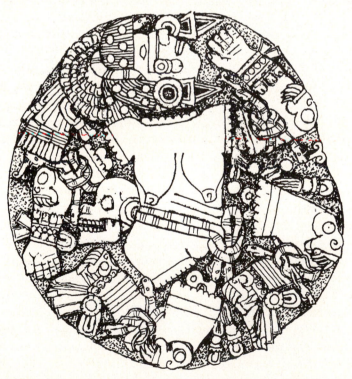

Fig. 99. Stone with relief of the goddess Coyolxauhqui, found in Mexico City in 1978 (diameter 3.25 m).

rooms, a hall for music and dance performances, and quarters for 3,000 servants and workmen.

There were two major market-places, one located near the temple precinct, the other in Tlatelolco (the twin city that was finally absorbed around 1500). Spanish observers reported that the Tlatelolco market was bigger than those of Rome and Constantinople. All manner of exotic imports, food, even slaves were offered for sale in the markets. The Aztecs used cacao beans, cotton cloaks, and quills filled with gold dust as standard units of value in their commercial dealings.

Aztec society was stratified into classes, yet it seems to have retained a few traces of an earlier kinship-based organization (Adams 1966). The highest class, the nobles or *pilli*, were all relatives of the king; they may have comprised 5% of the population. The nobles had their own inherited estates, as well as tribute-paying lands that were granted to them by the tlatoani as rewards for the services they rendered him as administrators or warriors. Most of the population were commoners, or *macehuales*. Each of them belonged by birth to one of 20 clans, or *calpultin*. Members of a *calpulli* occupied their own ward in the city, jointly owned and farmed chinampa plots in the suburbs, maintained their own temple, set up schools for the military education of their young men, and went to war as a combat unit. The calpulli members were often not just kinsmen, but also practiced the same specialized craft. Each calpulli was internally ranked, on the basis of closeness to the founding ancestor of the lineage. Calpultin of different rank together comprised each of the four quarters into which Tenochtitlán was divided. The lowest class were the *mayeques*, displaced and conquered farmers who, having no rights to calpulli land, worked as tenants on the estates of the nobles. Also occupying the lowest rungs of the social ladder were porters and slaves, who were usually recruited from among the ranks of captives and debtors. There were two groups who were able to achieve some upward mobility in the Aztec hierarchy: long-distance traders in exotic goods, the *pochteca*, could amass great wealth, but they avoided public displays which might provoke the nobles' enmity; and warriors who distinguished themselves in battle might be granted estates of their own and waivers of tribute payments.

The Aztecs were almost incessantly at war. One aim of this warfare was to conquer other peoples and force them to pay tribute. About one-third of Tenochtitlán's food needs were satisfied by the 6,300 metric tons (7,000 tons) of maize and 3,600 metric tons (4,000 tons) each of beans, sage seed and amaranth, that were received yearly as tribute from the provinces. More exotic items, such as cloth, metal, jade, quetzal feathers, cacao and the like were also required as tribute. When subject peoples rebelled against the heavy payments imposed upon them, the Aztec army, more than 100,000 strong, would take the field against them. Some groups, notably the Mixtecs, Tarascans, and Tlaxcalans, successfully resisted the Aztecs. When Cortes arrived in Mexico, the Tlaxcalans became his allies in battles against the Aztecs.

The Aztecs also had a less obviously pragmatic reason for waging war, which was to obtain captives who would be sacrificed to their gods. So important was this motivation that during the reign of Moctezuma I (1440–68), a series of pre-arranged battles were fought by the armies of the Triple Alliance against those of Tlaxcala and Huexotzingo; the sole purpose of these "Flowery Wars" was for each side to capture sacrificial victims from the other (flowers and blood were poetic equivalents for the Aztecs).

Human sacrifice was not an Aztec innovation in Mesoamerican religion: the Toltecs and Maya had certainly practiced this custom, and it may have originated in the time of the Olmecs or even earlier. However, the scale of Aztec sacrifice seems to have surpassed anything that came before. Basing his estimate on the figures given in several post-Conquest sources, S. F. Cook (1946) calculated that each year about 2,000 people were sacrificed at Tenochtitlán, and another 8,000 to 18,000 in the other cities and towns of the Basin of Mexico. To celebrate the dedication of the renovated Great Temple in 1487, sacrifices went on for 4 days straight. A steady stream of prisoners, probably numbering about 14,000, was led up to the pyramid's summit. There, four priests grabbed each victim's arms and legs, bent his body backwards over a stone, and a fifth priest slit the victim's chest open with a flint knife and pulled out the heart, which was burnt as an offering to the gods. War captives were the most common sacrifices, but slaves and children were also killed. The highlight of some ceremonies was the sacrifice of a privileged young man or woman who had been pampered for a year as the impersonator of a god or goddess. These sacrificial victims were flayed, and their putrid skins were worn for 20 days by priests or penitents, in imitation of the god of spring, Xipe Totec.

The Aztecs believed that to prevent the destruction of the universe, which had already occurred four times in the past, the gods must be supplied with a steady diet of human hearts and blood. Several anthropologists have wondered whether this religious explanation for human sacrifice might have served to rationalize or obscure some more mundane function. Sherburne Cook (1946) suggested that human sacrifice was an unconscious means of population control. By ceremonially killing 15,000 people a year, the Aztecs raised the death rate of the Basin's population by 15%; an additional 5% increase could be attributed to the wars that were waged to acquire captives. Cook argued that the 20% increase in annual mortality was a significant factor in damping the growth of a population that was on the verge of exceeding the carrying capacity of its environment. However, as Marvin Harris (1977) has observed, the great majority of battlefield casualties and sacrificed captives were male adults, and the deaths of these men could have been easily offset by an increased birth rate. Thus, only by sacrificing more women could the Aztecs have effectively controlled population growth by this method. Harris himself embraces a theory proposed by Michael Harner (1977), who has suggested that human sacrifice was a pretext for, and prelude to, cannibalism. The lack of high-quality protein and fat in the Aztec diet might have produced a craving for meat that, in the absence of large domesticated animals, only human flesh could satisfy. Harner cites post-Conquest accounts by eye-witnesses, who described how, after the body of a sacrificial victim was rolled down the pyramid's steps, old men called *Quaquacuiltin* carried it to the house of the military officer who had presented that prisoner to the temple. At the house, the body was cut up and the limbs were prepared to be cooked, often in a stew flavored with peppers and tomatoes. Victims' trunks are said to have been fed to the animals in the royal zoo.

Archaeological evidence does tend to verify Harner's assumption that protein scarcity was a problem in the Basin of Mexico in Late Horizon times (1350–1519). Hunted deer probably accounted for less than 0.1% of the diet. Other meat sources – dogs, turkeys, ducks, rabbits and fish – existed, but were probably available only to the nobility. Aztec commoners had to derive their protein from such sources as water fly eggs and spirolina algae, skimmed from Lake Texcoco's surface. Harner's ecological explanation of Aztec sacrifice and cannibalism seems quite plausible in the light of this evidence of protein scarcity, but unfortunately his theory doesn't show how cannibalism might have alleviated this problem. The flesh of 15,000 sacrificed humans, divided among the one or two million inhabitants of the Basin of Mexico, would not have been a significant dietary supplement. In fact, the historical sources indicate that most of the human flesh was consumed by high-status warriors, nobles, and priests – the same group who enjoyed privileged access to the other scarce meats. It is not at all clear why these well-fed members of the élite should have regarded a few morsels of human meat as a more desirable reward than the enhanced prestige they gained by offering their captives to the gods. Ironic as it may seem to us, human sacrifice in Mesoamerica was a civilized trait; in practicing it, the Aztecs were emulating their more sophisticated neo-Toltec tutors. Earlier Toltec depictions of skulls impaled on tzompantli suggest that they too sacrificed large numbers of victims; the Aztecs' intensification of the custom may simply have been a proportional increase, commensurate with the larger numbers of people involved in Late Horizon warfare. Human sacrifice was probably an ecologically neutral practice, which neither reduced the Basin's population effectively nor added significantly to the average Aztec's protein intake; on the other hand, once this custom and the ideological system to which it was integral had become established in Mesoamerican civilizations, its continuation posed no threat to the ecosystem. We in Western societies should be familiar enough with the phenomenon of men going to deaths for the sake of abstract causes; and what cause could have been more worth killing and dying for than the preservation of the universe?

CHIEFDOMS OF THE INTERMEDIATE AREA

The so-called "Intermediate Area", comprising most of Ecuador, the highlands and coastal plain of western Colombia, western Venezuela, and Central America east of Honduras, lies between Mesoamerica and Peru. This is a region of great environmental diversity, including hot, wet tropical forests on the Pacific coast and high temperate basins in the northern Andes, and the series of gradually differentiated environmental zones that lie between them. If interaction between populations occupying diverse, altitude-defined micro-environments is the *sine qua non* for the development of civilization, we should expect to find traces of full-fledged civilizations in the Intermediate Area, comparable to those of Mexico and Peru. In fact, however, there was no architecture in this area on the scale of Tikal's pyramids or Moche's Huaca del Sol, no cities approaching the size of Teotihuacán or Chan Chan, no states to rival those of the Aztecs or Incas. However, while they did not attain the level of socio-political organization of their neighbors to the north and south, the peoples of the Intermediate Area did achieve quite a high level of artistry in certain crafts, particularly ceramics and metallurgy.

Small chiefdoms may have developed in coastal Ecuador as early as 2200 B.C., as suggested by the construction of mounds at Real Alto. The pottery-using Valdivia culture, represented at Real Alto, was followed by the Machalilla culture around 1400 B.C. Machalilla developed into the Chorrera culture, which flourished from about 1000 to 500 B.C. Chorrera pottery displays several distinctive shapes and decorative techniques. Some vessels had pinkish, iridescent painted surfaces, and spouted jars were made with handles that whistled. Pottery bearing pink iridescent paint appeared at about the same time (1500–1000 B.C.) in the Ocos culture, on the Pacific coast of Guatemala. This trait is so unusual that most archaeologists agree that its presence in these cultures must indicate that they were in contact. Similar pottery has not been found at any sites lying between them, so it seems most likely that sea-borne traders travelled between Ecuador and the west coast of Mesoamerica. Ecuadorian traders may already have been sailing along the coast in balsa rafts like those seen by the Spaniards in the sixteenth century, and copied by Thor Heyerdahl to make his famous "Kon-Tiki" raft.

A "Regional Development" period is recognized as having begun in Ecuador around 500 B.C. and lasted until A.D. 500. Nine localized traditions of pottery manufacture can be distinguished during this period. Widespread ceramic forms include vessels with three or more feet, pedestals, or ring-bases; spouted and bridge-handled vessels, and jars, bottles, and bowls with everted lips. White-on-red and negative painting were common decorative techniques. Ceramic artifacts other than vessels included figurines, masks, whistles, stamps, ear-spools and spindle whorls (Willey 1971, Feldman and Moseley 1983).

In most areas, the people of this period lived in small villages, probably at a tribal level of organization. However, more complex societies occupied the north coast of Ecuador and the southern highlands of Colombia. At La Tolita, in Ecuador's Esmeraldas province, 40 earth mounds were built between 400 B.C. and A.D. 200. The tallest of these was 9 m (30 ft) high, and measured 45 by 20 m (150 by 65 ft) at its base. Some of the other mounds were circular or ovoid. Several mounds were built at the edges of a wide plaza. La Tolita is famous for its mold-made ceramic figurines, which depict, in a naturalistic style, human beings, animals and gods. The metal-workers of La Tolita made various ornaments, pins, needles and fishhooks out of gold, copper and *tumbaga* (a gold–copper alloy).

Some 320 km (200 miles) south of La Tolita, the contemporary site of Manta, in Manabí province, seems to have been a chiefdom center during the Bahía phase. Terraced pyramid platforms, destroyed during expansion of the modern city, are said to have been as large as 175 by 50 m (575 by 165 ft). Most Bahía figurines are stylized, often grotesque. Another type is more naturalistic, and includes portrayals of men, possibly high-status individuals, wearing pointed helmets and other strange head-gear. Among the other ceramic objects of the Bahía phase are models of houses with gabled, curving roofs, and concave head or neck-rests. These artifacts, along with gold tee-shaped ear-plugs, pan-pipes, and dragon or serpent motifs, have been cited as evidence of possible trans-Pacific contacts with East Asian cultures; but this proposed relationship requires more conclusive proof.

Another important chiefdom of the Regional Development period was situated less than 320 km (200 miles) east of La Tolita, in the highlands of southern Colombia. Remains of this culture, including mounds, terraces, canals, drainage ditches and roads, have been found at more than 30 sites, in a 500 square km (312 square miles) area around the modern town of San Agustín. Shaft-tombs and beaten gold jewelry seem to date from the earlier phase of the San Agustín culture; around A.D. 1, earth mounds began to be constructed, and a distinctive style of stone sculpture developed. Mound-building and sculpture then continued for more than 700 years. The San Agustín mounds were used for burials; within the earth mounds there were galleries and tomb chambers built of stone slabs, and the dead were placed in carved stone sacrophagi. The largest of the mounds had a diameter of 30 m (100 ft). San Agustín sculpture takes the form both of reliefs on boulders or cliff faces, and of columnar statues. The sculptures often portray humans whose grimacing mouths reveal crossed fangs (like the Chavín deities of Peru) and who carry clubs or play pan-pipes. Small "alter-ego" figures are often perched on the main figure's head, neck, or shoulders; the alter-egos, which probably represent spirit guardians, also occur in the art of La Tolita. The sites where the mounds and sculpture occur were apparently ceremonial centers; most of the San Agustín population lived in dispersed hamlets.

During the "Integration Period" spanning the years from A.D. 500 to the time of the Spanish conquest, regional cultures in Ecuador and Colombia coalesced to form larger units. Populations grew to their maximum size; they were organized into chiefdoms, with large central sites that contained temples, élite residences and tombs. The large numbers of people were supported by intensive agriculture, involving ridge and ditch systems in the lowlands, and terracing and small-scale irrigation in the highlands. Metal-working reached its peak during this period.

The San Agustín culture continued to flourish in the Integration period. The chiefdom centered at Manta also persisted, as the site reached its maximum size. This Manteño culture is notable for its towns, mass-produced pottery, copper tools, and stone sculptures, which often took the form of U-shaped seats supported by figures. T-shaped copper axes made by Manteño craftsmen are too thin to have served as tools; they must instead have been used as standardized units of exchange. Similar "money axes" have been found at sites in western Mexico, which strongly suggests that Ecuadorian traders were regularly sailing along the Pacific coast to Mexico in balsa rafts. This was probably the route by which metal-working was diffused to Mexico.

Copper money axes were even more common in the Milagro culture of the Guayas River basin, a neighbor and contemporary of the Manteño. The Milagro people built small mounds, to keep their houses above seasonal floods, but also platforms, as long as 100 m (330 ft) and as high as 10 m (30 ft), which were probably surmounted by temples or chiefs' residences. Burials, sometimes placed within tubes formed by stacked urns whose bottoms had been broken through, were deposited in mounds of intermediate size. Low, long ridges found north of Guayaquil suggest that the Milagro practiced an intensive form of agriculture that enabled them to maintain large numbers of people. The Milagro were highly skilled metal-workers, producing rings, ear-rings, nose-rings, bracelets and plumed crowns of gold and silver. Some burials were accompanied by large numbers of ornaments, indicating the high rank of the deceased.

Exceptional gold-work has been found, most often by looters, in graves and tombs of the Calima and Quimbaya cultures, in the southern highlands of Colombia. Gold artifacts, made by lost wax, casting, soldering, annealing, and hammering techniques, include masks, breast-plates, crowns, helmets, earrings and nose-rings. Particularly characteristic of Quimbaya gold-work are small pendants in animal or human form, and fluted, narrow-necked flasks made of gold or tumbaga. These flasks were probably used to hold lime, which was chewed along with narcotic coca leaves.

In the northeastern highlands of Colombia, the Tairona culture flourished from about A.D. 1000 to 1530. The population of this area during that time is estimated at about 300,000. Chiefs who controlled multi-village federations resided in Tairona towns, which were quite large: the site of Pueblito, for example, has stone foundations of about 3,000 circular houses. Some more elaborate structures at Pueblito may have been palaces or temples. Reservoirs, irrigation canals, and agricultural terraces on which maize was grown, were built in the vicinity of the town.

Fig. 100. Stone figure, San Agustín culture (height 1.8 m).

311

An unsettling reminder of the vagaries of archaeological preservation is presented by the case of the Chibcha (or Muisca). The Spanish conquistadors who arrived in 1537 reported large populations, palisaded towns and villages, palaces and temples, gold and emeralds. The Chibcha were divided into two chiefdoms: one chief, Zipa, had his capital at old Bogotá, the other, Zaque, lived in a town to the north, in the Tunja basin. Wars were being fought within the chiefdoms when the Spaniards arrived on the scene. The Chibcha worshipped the sun, and practiced human sacrifice. They traded emeralds to the Tairona, in exchange for gold, beads and sea shells. The investiture ceremony of the Chibcha chiefs, which involved the tossing of numerous golden ornaments into a lake, and the chief's immersion in the lake waters to wash off the gold dust with which he had been coated, gave rise to the legend of El Dorado, "The Golden One".

Until recently, archaeologists had found no traces of Chibcha settlements on the valley floors of the Bogotá and Tunja basins. However, a huge refuse deposit, perhaps 2 kilometers in extent, was discovered in the 1960s at La Ramada, in the Bogotá basin. Test excavations revealed the presence of post-holes in the clay that underlies the refuse deposit. This may well have been the site of the Chibcha capital, whose structures were built of poles and thatch, not stone. The few examples of Chibcha stone sculpture are far inferior to the sculptures of San Agustín. Their goldwork, although most sophisticated in technique than the crude appearance of their pendants would suggest, lacks the aesthetic appeal of Calima

Fig. 101. Coclé polychrome painted vessel; the design features crabs (diameter 32.4 cm).

312

and Quimbaya pieces. if we did not have Spanish accounts of the richness of the Chibcha chiefdoms, the archaeological record would belie their importance (Willey 1971, Feldman and Moseley 1983).

Chiefdoms were encountered by the conquistadors who arrived in Panama in 1519; these ranked societies seem to have developed after A.D. 500 (Helms 1979). Burials of a chiefly élite have been found at Sitio Conte, in central Panama, a cemetery which dates from A.D. 500 to 1000. Chiefs had been interred along with sacrificed wives and retainers. They were accompanied by gold and tumbaga ornaments and by intentionally broken pottery. The style of the crowns, breast-plates, ear and nose orna-ments and pendants is very similar to that of metal-work from the Quimbaya area of Colombia; and these pieces may well have originated in that region. The attractive polychrome painted pottery from Sitio Conte, in the style known as Coclé, includes plates that bear depictions of alligators, birds, humans and crabs (Cooke 1985).

CARIBBEAN CHIEFDOMS

As noted earlier, the first inhabitants of the Caribbean islands were coastal foragers, who began to arrive from Venezuela after 5000 B.C. Around A.D. 1, farming people from the lower Orinoco, who made Saladoid pottery and probably spoke Arawak, colonized the Lesser Antilles. By A.D. 120, their descendants had reached Puerto Rico. Apart from pottery, continuity in several types of stone and shell artifacts suggests that the previous inhabitants of the islands may have been absorbed by the new farming groups. On Puerto Rico, around A.D. 700, a new, simpler plain pottery developed from the painted Saladoid style. This ware, called Ostionoid, was carried from Puerto Rico to Hispaniola and Jamaica. Around A.D. 850, the Chicoid ceramic style, which featured incised and punctate decoration and adornos of monkey-like or human shape, developed from the Ostionoid style in Hispaniola, and was soon carried westward to Cuba and back east to Puerto Rico. Hundreds of Chicoid sites, mostly small middens with or without shells, are known in the Greater Antilles. The most impressive sites consist of middens adjoin-ing stone-lined plazas or ball-courts. Capá, in west-central Puerto Rico, is such a site. The largest site on the island, Capá contained nine stone-bordered enclosures. The biggest of these, measuring 50 by 35 m (160 by 120 ft) may have been a field on which was played the ball-game described by Spanish observers. A rubber ball was bounced into the air by players who, forbidden to use hands or feet, used their hips instead. Stone "collars" or belts found in Puerto Rico resemble the U-shaped stone yokes from the Veracruz region of Mexico, which are believed to have been worn on the hips of ball-players or else to be stone replicas of wooden devices of this sort. The Puerto Rican pieces probably had the same function. In view of the similarities both in the paraphernalia of the ball-game and its rules, as reported by Spanish observers in the 1500s, there can be little doubt that the Caribbean game was somehow derived from Mexico, where it had been known since Olmec times. However, it remains to be explained why the game should have been more elaborated in Puerto Rico than in the islands that lie farther west and closer to Mexico. Representations of *zemis*, ancestral spirits, were frequently carved on the Puerto Rican stone belts, which suggests that the ball-game had a religious aspect, as it did also in Mexico. Wood and stone zemis were also kept in each Taino household, and the chief's zemis were worshipped in a temple.

The Chicoid archaeological remains from Puerto Rico, Hispaniola and Cuba represent the material culture of the Taino, who were living on the islands when the Spaniards arrived (Willey 1971). The Spaniards observed towns with as many as 1,000 houses and 5,000 inhabitants. Slash and burn agriculture provided most of the food; bitter manioc was the primary crop, supplemented by sweet potatoes and maize. The Taino towns were ruled by local chiefs, who were subservient to a paramount chief; there were five such regional rulers in Hispaniola. The rulers and their retainers constituted a privileged aristocracy, set apart from commoners and slaves. As happened elsewhere in Central and South America, these complex societies quickly collapsed under the onslaught of European armies, diseases and exploitation.

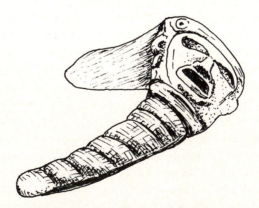

Fig. 102. Stone belt with carved face of a zemi, from Puerto Rico (length ca. 30 cm).

ANDEAN CIVILIZATIONS

Preceramic chiefdoms

Incipient agriculture had begun in the Andean highlands, or sierra, of Peru by 5500 B.C., perhaps even earlier. Meanwhile, the inhabitants of the narrow, arid coastal strip were becoming increasingly reliant on fish, shellfish and sea mammals. They also began to cultivate plants, which they acquired either from the highland peoples or the inhabitants of the tropical forests on the eastern side of the Andes. Cotton and gourds, which were used to make nets and floats for fishing, were particularly important; but remains of edible plants, such as squash, beans, achira root and guavas, have also been found in coastal middens dating from 2500 B.C. Archaeologists continue to argue about the relative contributions of marine resources and cultivated plants to the diet of the early coastal villagers. Around 2000 B.C., monumental structures were built at several coastal sites. Their size implies the coordination of a large number of workers, which could only have been achieved by a fairly complex social–political organization. Michael Moseley (1975a) has suggested that these complex societies represent the germ of Andean civilization, and he argues that the subsistence base of this nascent civilization was provided not by agriculture but by efficient harvesting of marine resources. If Moseley is correct, coastal Peru would appear to be a unique case of civilization developing from a non-agricultural subsistence base. However, the term "civilization" may not really be applicable to the coastal societies of 2000 B.C. The archaeological evidence – large, probably ceremonial structures, at centers with resident populations on the order of 1,500 people, surrounded by dispersed villages – seems to imply a chiefdom organization.

The biggest site of the Preceramic period (before 1800 B.C.) was El Paraíso, also known as Chuquitanta. It is located about 2 km from the ocean, in the Chillón valley, on Peru's central coast. The ruins of El Paraíso cover more than 50 hectares (125 acres), and consist of some six to nine mounds of collapsed masonry. These mounds were once large platforms that rose to heights of 3 to 6 m (9 to 20 ft); the largest measured 250 by 50 m (830 by 166 ft). The three main buildings formed a U-shaped complex, consisting of a temple and two protruding wings surrounding a patio that was open at the end opposite the temple. It has been estimated that 1,500 or more people might have lived at El Paraíso; however, not much domestic debris was found at the site, which suggests that it functioned primarily as a ceremonial center, with few permanent residents. Nevertheless, a sizeable work force must have been recruited to quarry and haul the 90,000 metric tons (100,000 tons) of rock that were used to

315

build the platforms. The laborers presumably came from small villages in the surrounding region, and they may have been rewarded with feasts and gifts provided by the chiefs and priests. This inferred corvée labor system has been seen as an embryonic form of the *mit'a* labor tax imposed by the Inca state on its subjects, 3,500 years later (Moseley 1975a, 1983a), but it

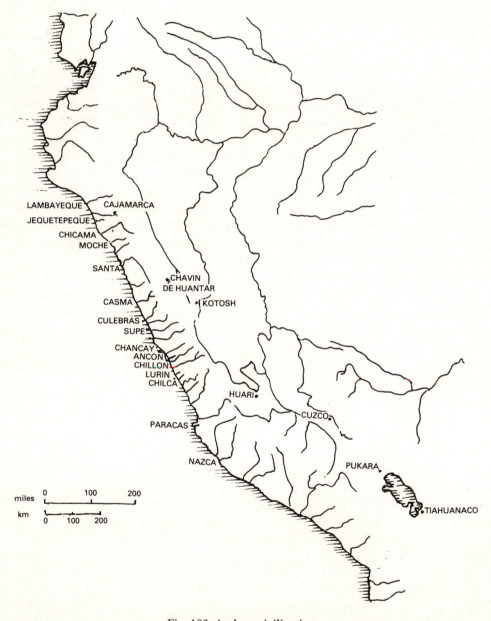

Fig. 103. Andean civilizations.

316

also seems analogous to the chiefdom-level organizations that were responsible for the Hopewell mounds and earthworks in the Ohio Valley.

El Paraíso was more than three times the size of the next largest Preceramic site, Aspero, which was located near the mouth of the Rio Supe. This 13-hectare site comprised six platforms, the largest of which was 10 m (30 ft) high, with rooms and courtyards built on top of them. Terraced platforms were also constructed at the nearby site of Piedra Parada. One feature of the latter site is a subterranean circular court, 20 m (65 ft) in diameter; similar courts occur at the Preceramic sites of Salinas de Chao and Alto Salaverry. Circular courts were still typical features of ceremonial buildings a thousand years later, in Early Horizon times, and rectangular sunken courts appeared even later, at highland sites of the Middle Horizon (A.D. 500–1000). A particularly impressive Preceramic mound dominated the site of Salinas de Chao: it was 24 m (80 ft) high.

The construction of ceremonial centers was not limited to the coast. At Kotosh, in the valley of the Rio Huallaga on the eastern slopes of the Andes, Japanese archaeologists have excavated two mounds, the larger one of which turned out to consist of 10 superimposed buildings. The lowest and earliest Mito phase was Preceramic, and dated to before 1800 B.C. This early structure was an 8 m- (26 ft-) high platform, upon which stood a room that measured 9 m (30 ft) on a side. Beneath a niche in one wall, a pair of crossed arms had been sculpted in bas-relief, in clay.

Fig. 104. One of the buildings at Chuquitanta (El Paraíso); it measures about 50 m on a side.

Another site with platforms, La Galgada, has recently been found in the Rio Santa drainage, mid-way between the coast and the sierra. This area is not very well suited for agriculture, so it seems likely that access to, or control of, an exchange or transhumance route was the primary reason for building the site there (Moseley 1983a). Obviously the inhabitants of these highland centers did not subsist on fish and shellfish: their diet included potatoes, quinoa, and other highland crops, with meat provided by guinea pigs and llamas.

The function of the Kotosh structure remains mysterious; for that matter, we really do not know exactly what went on on top of the coastal platforms. Were they temples or chiefs' residences? The existence of highland centers, as early as those of the coast, again suggests a parallel with Hopewell. Preceramic Peru also seems to have been an "interaction sphere", a network of chiefdoms linked in alliance and exchange relationships. Perhaps decorated twined textiles, such as the pieces found at Huaca Prieta, were prestige items exchanged by the élite. Many centuries later, the Incas collected woven textiles as a form of taxation; this shows that textiles had retained a special value in Andean economies, which they may have first acquired in Preceramic times.

The Initial Period

At about 1800 B.C., most of the Preceramic centers on the coast were abandoned, but similar sites soon appeared inland in the river valleys, near tracts of land where irrigation farming could be practiced. Archaeologists generally agree that this shift in settlement distribution reflected a re-orientation of the economy toward greater dependence on agriculture. However, while some authors (Patterson 1971, Cohen 1977b; but cf. Wilson 1981) have suggested that fast-increasing populations had exceeded the carrying capacity of the coastal resources, an alternative explanation cites tectonic (earthquake) activity (Moseley 1983a, 1983b). This may have caused the coastal land to rise, and the anchovy schools – a key resource, used to make storable fish paste – to retreat to deeper waters, farther offshore. The shifting of settlement to inland locations would, according to this model, have been a response to more difficult fishing conditions. In any case, basic continuity in architectural forms and other aspects of culture implies that the change was not a drastic one. The apparent ease of the transition to an agricultural economy might also suggest that river valley agriculture had already assumed more importance in Preceramic coastal economies than the maritime theory would allow.

At the same time that this change in settlement pattern occurred, a new technology was introduced to Peru. Pottery, which had been made in

Ecuador since 3000 B.C., began to be produced in the northern highlands of Peru around 1800 B.C. Ceramic techniques had presumably been borrowed from the Ecuadorians. Pottery has been of great importance to archaeologists in developing a chronological framework for ancient Peru, so it is understandable that its introduction has been seen as a beginning of sorts – thus 1800 B.C. is considered to be the start of the "Initial" period. Besides pottery, other important technological innovations of this period were the heddle loom, used for weaving, and techniques of metallurgy. Gold was being worked in the highlands before 1200 B.C.

The biggest ceremonial center of the Initial Period was La Florida, which now stands in the suburbs of Lima, 13 km (8 miles) inland from El Paraíso. Its main structure was a huge platform, 255 m (840 ft) long, 55 m (180 ft) wide, and 35 m (110 ft) high, which was built about 1750–1700 B.C. Las Haldas, situated between the Casma and Culebras valleys, was another important site of this period (Matsuzawa 1978). A village was established there by 1700 B.C., but the ceremonial complex, which covered an area of 600 by 60 m (2,000 by 200 ft) was built later, around 1200–900 B.C. There was little refuse associated with the mounds and plazas, which suggests that the ceremonial center was not permanently inhabited. At Caballo Muerto, in the Moche valley, there were at least eight major temple platforms. Construction began around 1500 B.C., and the most impressive structures were erected before 800 B.C. Another contemporary site was Cerro Sechín, in the lower Casma valley. This rather small site is noteworthy for its incised stone stelae, which were set against the outer wall of a low platform. The carvings depict, besides a few geometric forms and possible bundles of weapons, human figures. These include trophy heads; bare-headed men, wearing kilts, some of whom appear to have been hacked through the middle and to be falling, so that their long hair streams upward from their heads; and warriors with caps, painted faces and loincloths, who carry maces or scepters. These carvings presumably record the conquests of a local chief; in their theme, but not their style, they are strongly reminiscent of the "danzante" stelae of Monte Albán in the Mexican highlands.

Certain aspects of the Sechín carvings – the off-center eyeball, face paint, loincloths, and the long fingernails – suggest a connection with the art of the Chavín culture. The nature of this apparent relationship has long been obscured by uncertainties in the dating of Cerro Sechín and other coastal sites, and of the highland site of Chavín de Huantár. Recently derived C14 dates indicate that the earliest construction phase at Chavín de Huantár began around 850 B.C. (Burger 1981). Dates from coastal sites show that Cerro Sechín and the other sites where similarities to Chavín in iconography, architecture, and ceramic forms have been noted, are considerably earlier. It now appears that some of the basic ele-

319

ments of Chavín culture were borrowed from the cultures of the north-central coast.

CHAVÍN – THE EARLY HORIZON

The style which crystallized at Chavín spread rapidly throughout the northern highlands and the northern and central sections of the coast, and even affected the ceramics made on the southern coast. Archaeologists have interpreted this wide stylistic diffusion as a marker of some form of inter-regional social or political integration; they have referred to the phase of Chavín influence as the Early Horizon (900–250 B.C.).

Chavín de Huantár, the apparent center of the Early Horizon inter-action network, is situated about 3,200 m (10,600 ft) above sea level, in the Mosna valley of the northern highlands. The site consists of a civic center, with retaining walls and terraces covering 6 hectares (15 acres), and an attached residential area, encompassing 50 hectares (125 acres). The size of Chavín's resident population is debatable; some scholars believe that

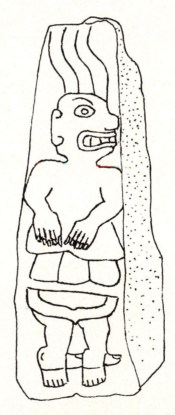

Fig. 105. A stela from Cerro Sechín. (After Willey 1971.)

the workers who built the monuments were recruited from the larger Santa valley, 50 km (31 miles) away. The main complex consists of a sunken, stone-paved court, 48 m on a side, with low platforms standing on its north and south sides, and a great terraced platform, called the Castillo, occupying its west side. The Castillo was made of earth and rock, with a retaining wall of dressed stones, some of which weighed more than a ton. Set into the wall were sculptures, depicting wrinkled human faces and jaguar-men. The platform measured 75 m (250 ft) on each side at its base, and reached a height of 13 m (43 ft). Several small buildings stood upon the summit, to which stairways ascended. However the main focus of activity must have been inside the Castillo, since about one-third of its interior was hollow. Long galleries led to small niche-like rooms, which were arranged in several levels, connected by ramps and stairways; an elaborate ventilation system provided air. Although no human remains were found in the Castillo, it seems most likely that it served as a funerary monument. The building's sacred character is indicated by a carved stela that still stands in one of the niche-rooms, at the center of the Castillo. Shaped like a giant tanged spear or knife, 4.5 m (15 ft) tall, this "Lanzón" stela depicts a grimacing, fanged jaguar-man, with an eccentric eye, long curved fingernails, and locks of hair in the form of snakes. This was presumably an important, if not the chief deity of the Chavín culture; because of his grimace, he has been called the "Smiling God". In other Chavín carvings, a being with similar attributes grasps staffs in either hand; he is therefore known as the "Staff God". Besides these feline–human deities, Chavín stone carvings featured birds of prey, snakes, fish, bats, crabs and crocodile-like monsters (Rowe 1967). The crabs imply contact with the coast, while the jaguar, snake and crocodile show that the Chavín people were familiar with the tropical rain forests that lay east of the Andes. These figures were carved, in very complicated designs that emphasized curved lines, on stelae, altars, friezes, lintels and round columns. The felinized human also appeared in designs on pottery, textiles, beaten gold, and wooden artifacts that were made throughout the northern highlands and on the northern and central coast of Peru. Chavín influence was not as strongly felt on the southern coast, where a distinctive ceramic tradition, called Paracas, prevailed during the Early Horizon; nevertheless some decorated Paracas vessels did incorporate Chavín-derived motifs.

The widespread distribution of the Chavín style poses the same sort of archaeological problem as does the occurrence of Olmec figurines and ceramics in the highlands of Mexico. What degree of economic, social, political or ideological unification is represented by the rapid diffusion of an art style? It has generally been assumed that the spread of Chavín art and temple architecture was the material reflection of the expansion of a

Fig. 106. The Lanzón stela. Chavín de Huantár. (After Willey 1971.)

religious cult centering on the "Staff God". Ceramic vessels and textiles bearing Chavín motifs do not appear to have been restricted to temples or major centers – they were also acquired by the inhabitants of small villages. Presumably, in each community, members of high-ranking lineages were in a position to obtain these luxury goods. If Chavín were the center of an empire, comparable to those established by military conquest during the Late and, probably, Middle Horizons, one would expect to find the ruins of forts or administrative centers; but none have actually been identified.

Several coastal sites of the Early Horizon may have been the centers of chiefdoms as powerful as that of Chavín de Huantár. Two sites in the Casma Valley are particularly impressive. At Sechín Alto, there were six terraced platforms, with temple–plaza complexes on their summits. The largest platform measured 250 by 300 m (825 by 980 ft) at its base, and rose to a height of 35 m (115 ft); in volume, it was 15 times the size of the Castillo (Moseley 1983a). The main structure at the site of Moxexe was a 30 m- (99 ft-) high platform, which measured 160 by 170 m (530 by 560 ft) at its base. Huge rectangular enclosures adjoined it. One of them contained hundreds of rooms, arranged along streets. These might have been workers' quarters, or perhaps store houses. Many of the room complexes stood on low platforms. Life-sized, painted clay figures, in Chavín style, were placed in niches in the retaining walls of the platforms. Moxexe seems to have been the center of a chiefdom, perhaps even a small state (Sanders and Marino 1970).

The Initial Period and Early Horizon in the southern highlands

In the basin surrounding Lake Titicaca, in the southern highlands, villages and towns were established around 1200 B.C. The villagers subsisted by cultivating tubers and quinoa, and herding llamas; those who lived near the lake also took fish from its waters. Some sites of the Wankarani culture, located south of Lake Titicaca, may have held as many as 3,900 people. This early culture is also noteworthy for evidence of smelting of copper ores. Dated at 1200 to 800 B.C., this is the earliest such industry in the Andes (Kolata 1983). At Chiripa, on the southern shore of Lake Titicaca, a mound was constructed at about 1300–1200 B.C. After 900 B.C., a stone retaining wall was built on three sides of the mound; between 500 and 100 B.C., a sunken court was installed on its summit, and carved stelae were set up within it. This sunken court is indicative of a stylistic and ideological connection with the chiefdoms of the northern coast and highlands, where such features already had a long history. Chiripa too was probably a chiefdom center.

323

The Early Intermediate Period, 200 B.C.–A.D. 600

Following the decline of Chavín around 200 B.C., the widely diffused style associated with it was replaced by more localized art styles. Despite the somewhat anti-climactic impression that is evoked by the label "Intermediate", the ensuing period was actually a time of cultural florescence. Cities and states developed; large-scale irrigation systems were constructed in the coastal valleys; populations reached their maximum size in many areas; and artisans turned out excellent ceramics, textiles and metal-work. The emergence of states also had its negative side: warfare became more common, and fortresses and fortified towns and cities appeared.

Mochica

On the north coast, the Mochica civilization flourished from A.D. 200 to 700. Mochica potters produced beautiful stirrup-spouted funerary vessels, on which they modelled and painted realistic depictions of gods, ceremonies, craft activities, hunting, fishing, farming, buildings, warfare, court rituals, crime and punishment, tribute collection, diseases and sexual acts. Based on changes in the shape of spouts, five stylistic phases in the development of pottery have been defined (Willey 1971). The style first appeared in the Moche and Chicama valleys, then spread into all the coastal valleys, from Jequetepeque in the north to Casma in the south, abruptly replacing the local styles of pottery. This replacement is generally interpreted as an indication of conquest, a conclusion which is supported by the construction of what appear to be provincial capitals and fortresses in the subjugated valleys.

The site of Moche, on the southern edge of the Moche valley, was evidently the capital of the Mochica state. It comprised two huge adobe structures – the Huaca del Sol and Huaca de la Luna – an immense plaza, and an extensive residential zone. The Huaca del Sol was a terraced platform, which measured 340 by 160 m (1,120 by 530 ft) at its base, and rose to a total height of 41 m (135 ft). Ramps provided access to the buildings on its summit. More than 130 million mold-made bricks were used in construction of this platform. The bricks that composed each section bore the same maker's marks, as distinct from other sections, which suggests that the bricks at each location had been set in place by work teams, recruited from one community and operating as a separate unit. If this interpretation is correct, it would seem that the Mochica state instituted a system of corvée (draft) labor for public projects, similar to the mit'a system of the later Inca empire (Moseley 1975b). The other major structure at Moche, the Huaca de la Luna, consisted of a massive, terraced multi-room

Fig. 107. Mochica pottery: (A) painted scene of warrior and stripped and bleeding captive; (B) stirrup-spout jar, sub-phase IV style; (C) portrait vessel (height 29.2 cm). (A after Disselhoff and Linné 1961; B and C after Willey 1971.)

complex, standing on the summit of a 23 m- (76 ft-) high platform. The summit buildings, decorated with brightly colored murals in the same style as the painted pottery, were kept clean. In contrast, trash heaps were found on top of the Huaca del Sol, suggesting that its summit may have served as élite living quarters.

Full-time craft specialists probably made the Moche pottery, some of which was mass-produced, using molds. The various metal-working techniques employed by the Mochica also imply specialization. Gold, silver, and copper were worked by hammering, repoussé, embossing, lost-wax and open-mold casting, soldering, welding, annealing, alloying, gilding and inlay. Not only ornaments but weapons and even farming tools were made of metal. The inference of specialization is confirmed by scenes on Mochica vessels, depicting craftsmen working under the direction of supervisors.

Distinctive modes of dress denoted other specialized positions in Mochica society: rulers, nobles, priests, warriors, slaves, messengers, servants, hunters, fishermen and farmers. Marked differences in the wealth of grave goods that accompanied burials suggest that Mochica society was stratified, and scenes on the painted pots offer clear proof of hierarchical organization. Rulers are shown being carried about in sedan chairs, sitting on canopied thrones, receiving tribute and presiding at the executions of war captives. Scenes of warfare are quite common, leaving little doubt that the Mochica state expanded into neighboring valleys by military conquest. The conquered valleys were then firmly tied to the state; messengers and goods travelled along inter-valley roads, garrisons stationed in fortresses prevented rebellion, and in each valley a provincial capital was built, with major structures modelled on the Huaca del Sol and Huaca de la Luna. The governors in charge of each valley are probably represented by the realistic Mochica portrait vessels. It is possible to recognize certain individuals whose faces recur on vessels from several sites in a single valley, but are limited to that valley alone; these may have been the provincial governors. The portraits of other individuals occur in several valleys; these men were quite probably the rulers of the Mochica state.

The capital at Moche seems to have been subjected to massive flooding when, some time around A.D. 400–500, the course of the Moche River was altered by earthquakes (Moseley 1983a, 1983b). After the flooding, sand dunes began to cover the site. The desertion of Moche at that time did not, however, mark the end of the coastal state. A new capital seems to have been established farther north, at the city of Pampa Grande in the Lambayeque Valley. This city extended over an area of at least 4.5 square kilometers (3 square miles). Its main platform mound measured 250 by

180 m (825 by 590 ft) and was 50 m (165 ft) high. The state centered at Pampa Grande seems to have lasted until about A.D. 600–700, when the north coast was absorbed into the Huari empire.

Nazca

The Nazca culture of the southern coast was contemporaneous with Moche. Nazca polychrome painted pottery developed out of the earlier Paracas tradition. Besides making attractive pottery, the Nazca wove fine textiles, but their most famous artistic creations are the Nazca lines (McIntyre 1975, Isbell 1978). These form huge designs, which are fully discernible only from an aerial perspective. The lines were made by removing small stones to expose the bare ground. Besides straight lines, there are spiral patterns, trapezoids, and giant animals, such as spiders, hummingbirds, monkeys and fish. These designs often extend for several hundred meters. The animal figures resemble those shown in Nazca pottery and textile designs, which allows us to attribute the lines to the same culture. It is quite certain, contrary to the well-publicized claims of

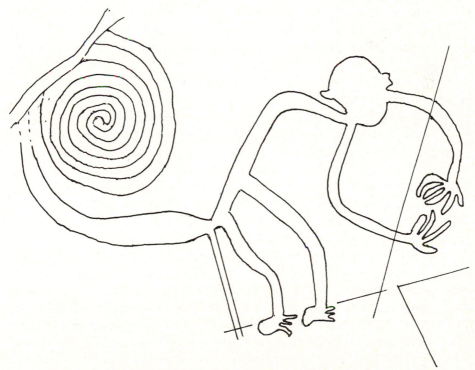

Fig. 108. Aerial view of giant monkey (95 m), Nazca.

Erich von Däniken, that the Nazca lines were not laid out to guide extra-terrestrial astronauts to their landing strips, but exactly what the lines were meant to be is less clear. Some of the straight lines may have been directed toward celestial positions, and may have had some sort of astro-nomical function or significance; however the animal figures could hardly have served as practical astronomical aids. Perhaps their makers hoped that divine beings, living in the sky, would be pleased when they gazed down upon the designs. On a more pragmatic level, idle peasants, when they were not planting, harvesting, or digging or cleaning irrigation canals, could have been kept busy making giant designs. The lines might have constituted a make-work project, analogous to the massive mounds of the north coast. Terraced temple platforms were not constructed in the Nazca region until late in the Early Intermediate period, when a multi-valley state seems to have emerged, with its center at Cahuachi. This site covered 1 square km, and contained a 20 m- (65 ft-) high terraced platform.

Early Intermediate developments in the southern highlands: Pukara

The site of Pukara, which lies 75 km (46 miles) northwest of the northern shore of Lake Titicaca, grew to the size of a true city between 100 B.C. and A.D. 100 (Kolata 1983). Its main structure was a temple, built on an arti-ficial terrace and consisting of a rectangular sunken court, enclosed by rooms on three sides. An extensive residential area lay in the plain below this acropolis. Pukara stone sculpture was highly developed: incised flat reliefs on stelae generally depicted animals – felines, lizards, serpents, fish – while sculptures in the round portrayed men, often shown wearing or holding trophy heads. Pukara decorated pottery utilized the same motifs that occurred in the stone sculptures. The polychrome vessels were painted in black and yellow on a red slip; incised lines separated the zones of color. Some vessels were made in the form of human heads; others were decorated with human or feline faces, modelled in relief. Both the decorative techniques and motifs, and vessel forms, of Pukara ceramics have parallels in the pottery from Tiahuanaco, near the southern end of Lake Titicaca – these similar ceramics at Tiahuanaco have recently been dated to between 400 B.C. and A.D. 100. Given the slight priority of the Tiahuanaco material, it seems that the people of Pukara may have developed their ceramics and sculpture under the influence of the Tiahuanaco culture. The contemporary Paracas pottery of the southern coast also shows a strong influence from the Tiahuanaco tradition, perhaps reflecting the establishment of Tiahuanaco colonial enclaves on the coast.

The Middle Horizon: Tiahuanaco and Huari

The ruins of Tiahuanaco stand 3,842 m (12,600 ft) above sea level, in the puna zone, 21 km (13 miles) southeast of Lake Titicaca. Archaeological surveys have shown that the site covered some 4 square km (1.5 square miles). The central core of monumental structures, occupying an area of 50 hectares (125 acres), was surrounded by an extensive residential zone. It is thus evident that Tiahuanaco was not a vacant ceremonial center but a true city, with a population estimated at anywhere from 20,000 to 40,000 people (Kolata 1983).

Most of the potatoes and other crops on which the city's inhabitants subsisted were grown in artificially drained fields. Some 80,000 hectares (200,000 acres) of lake-side marshes were reclaimed for agriculture, by means of a system of ditches and ridges which resembled the chinampas of Aztec Tenochtitlán. The lake also yielded fish, which helped meet the protein needs of the city's residents.

In the central precinct of Tiahuanaco, two wide avenues were lined by temples, standing on high or low platforms, élite residences, and tombs. The largest temple platform is called the Akapana. Each side of this platform was about 200 m (650 ft) long, and it was 15 m (50 ft) high. A lower, smaller platform, only 3 m (10 ft) high and measuring 126 by 118 m at its base, is known as the Kalasasaya. On its summit stood small shrines and a sunken court. Such courts were a typical feature of Tiahuanaco architecture; they show the local culture's debt to the Chavín tradition, which is also evident in Tiahuanaco iconography.

At the northwestern entrance to the Kalasasaya stood a carved monolith, known popularly as the Gateway of the Sun (despite the absence of any obvious solar symbolism). The central figure of the relief is a god who holds a staff in each hand. The staff in his left hand seems to be a condor-headed scepter; the other one might be a spearthrower with darts. The god wears a fan-shaped head-dress, ornamented with puma heads. On either side, 48 smaller figures run toward or kneel before him. This deity is obviously the same "Staff God" who was worshipped at Chavín de Huantár; but it is not known exactly how his cult was transferred from the north to this southern sierra locale where it was revived hundreds of years after its initial occurrence.

The image of the "Staff God" was one of the decorative motifs painted on Tiahuanaco pottery. Other motifs were pumas, human figurines and religious symbols. The designs were painted in white, black, yellow, grey and brown, on a red-slipped background. A characteristic Tiahuanaco vessel form was the drinking goblet, or *kero*. The same designs, which evidently had the official approval of the state, also were applied to textiles, wood carvings and metal ornaments.

The outstanding achievement of Tiahuanaco civilization was in the realm of stone architecture. The stone masons' skill is most evident in the temple platform of Puma-Punku, which was composed of huge stone blocks, perfectly fitted using no mortar. Some of the blocks weighed as much as 90 metric tons (100 tons). The stone sculptures of Tiahuanaco were done in a rather stiff, rectilinear style. Huge columnar statues stood as tall as 7.6 meters; they depicted human figures, wearing costumes like that of the "Staff God".

Tiahuanaco had been occupied as early as 400 B.C., and the city grew during the Early Intermediate period. Tiahuanaco's artwork and ideology diffused widely through the Central Andes after A.D. 375. This diffusion marks the beginning of the Middle Horizon, which lasted until A.D. 1000. On the south coast, the Tiahuanaco style fused with the Nazca style; it replaced the Early Intermediate style called Interlocking on the central coast, and it replaced Mochica on the north coast. A slightly variant style was adopted in the northern highlands. This stylistic diffusion, unlike the

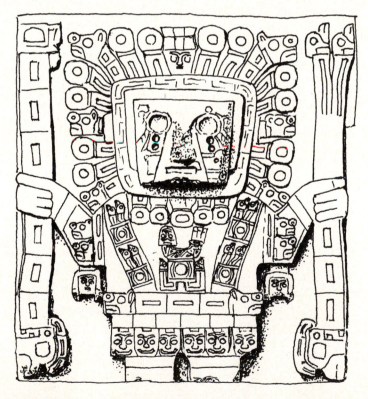

Fig. 109. Staff God, Gateway of the Sun, Tiahuanaco (height ca. 45 cm).

one that occurred during the Early Horizon, is generally believed to be a manifestation of the imperial expansion, by conquest, of the Tiahuanaco state.

On the southern shore of Lake Titicaca, two secondary centers, Luqurmata and Pajchiri, were established by the Tiahuanaco state; they probably housed administrators who oversaw the land reclamation projects in that area. Smaller sites, with terraced mounds, constituted a third level of settlement, and still smaller habitation mounds, presumably occupied by the peasants, formed the fourth level of the settlement hierarchy (Kolata 1983). We would expect to find such a four-level settlement system in an ancient state such as Tiahuanaco.

Tiahuanaco's region of control extended southward into the Atacama region of northern Chile, where economic colonies were established on the coast and in interior oases. These colonies were linked to Tiahuanaco and to one another by llama caravans. Textiles, gold keros and wooden snuff trays, decorated in the purest Tiahuanaco style, were deposited in graves in Chile; these pieces may have been imported from the capital city, to be used by colonial officials. Economic colonies were also set up on the edge of the eastern jungles. These lowland sites provided the highland centers with such items as coca, maize, peppers, tropical fruits, medicinal plants and dried fish. The history of Andean highland-based empires, from Tiahuanaco to the Incas, can be interpreted as essentially an effort by mountain-dwellers to ensure a steady supply of low-altitude products, that is, to achieve *vertical control* (Moseley 1983a).

While the archaeological evidence clearly demonstrates Tiahuanaco's imperial expansion to the south, west and east, the Middle Horizon political situation to the north of the Titicaca basin is more difficult to interpret. The picture is complicated by the presence of a major center in the Mantaro basin, near Ayacucho, some 725 km (450 miles) northwest of Tiahuanaco. This site, Huari, has not been very thoroughly excavated, but it was evidently quite a large city, covering 300 hectares (750 acres) at its peak, around A.D. 700. Its central core, containing at least one temple, was encircled by a massive wall; around the core sprawled a residential zone which contained thousands of multi-family dwellings. Some of the houses had more than one storey, and their walls were built of mud and roughly split stones, surfaced with mud stucco or gypsum plaster. Huari's growth seems to have been unplanned, for there is no evidence of an overall grid pattern. At a late stage in the city's development, huge compounds or enclosures were built, containing residences and open land.

Late in the Early Intermediate period, Huari had trade connections with the Nazca state, as shown by the incorporation of Nazca designs into the locally produced pottery of the style called Chakipampa A. Cultural influence from Tiahuanaco becomes evident at the beginning of the

Middle Horizon, around A.D. 500. At Conchopata, a site near Huari which seems to have been a religious shrine, large beaker-shaped urns were found which bore painted polychrome depictions of the Tiahuanaco "Staff God". These vessels appear to have been locally made; some of the designs were indigenous, and Conchopata-style pottery has not been found at Tiahuanaco itself. It seems most likely that Tiahuanaco priests introduced the cult and symbols of the "Staff God" to the people of Conchopata. The Conchopata style, and the cult in which the urns were used, soon spread to Huari and other sites in the area. New ceramic styles, Chakipampa B and Viñaque, resulted from this influence. The introduction of these wares into the Nazca valley, the northern sierra, and the central and northern coast, is probably a reflection of Huari's conquest of these regions, which may have occurred around A.D. 700. Besides introducing Viñaque-style pottery, the Huari conquerors were responsible for the construction of new architectural units in the coastal valleys – large, rectangular adobe-walled compounds. Large, planned, walled rectangular compounds were also built in the sierra, at Piquillacta in the Cuzco basin, and at Viracocha Pampa, near modern Huamachucho in the northern highlands. In each case a road ran through the middle of the compound. These traces of roads, along with a site that resembles later Inca *tambos*, or waystations, suggest that a network of roads may have connected Huari provincial centers. The compounds are assumed to have served some imperial administrative function, whether as garrisons, store houses, or governors' palaces (Isbell and Schreiber 1978).

The relationship of the Huari and Tiahuanaco states is unclear. Were these cities the centers of separate northern and southern-oriented empires, or dual capitals of a single empire (as Cuzco and Quito were in the later years of the Inca empire)? Some archaeologists recognize a break in ceramic style distributions which may mark the boundary between the northern and southern states; on the other hand, the regular plan of the compounds is more reminiscent of Tiahuanaco's architecture than of the contour-adjusted buildings at Huari. Moreover, recent excavations at Huari have revealed traces of Tiahuanaco-like dressed stone architecture underlying the level with mud and split stone walls. This raises the possibility that Huari may have begun as a colony of Tiahuanaco (Moseley 1983a).

The Late Intermediate period: Chimu

However Tiahuanaco and Huari may have been related, their decline and abandonment occurred at about the same time, roughly A.D. 1000. Tiahuanaco religious symbols soon disappeared from Andean artwork, marking the end of the Middle Horizon. In the Late Intermediate period that followed, distinct regional traditions re-appeared. This was a time of cultural regression in the central and southern highlands, where cities were deserted and the population dispersed into small rural hamlets. However, on the coast, the Late Intermediate saw the climactic developments of urban life and state organization.

As it had during Early Intermediate times, the Moche valley again emerged as the central focus of a multi-valley conquest state. The great site of Chan Chan, founded around A.D. 800 at the northern edge of the valley, became the capital of the Chimu empire. The Chimu started taking over the other coastal valleys around A.D. 1200, but they were conquered by the Incas in 1465. At their peak, the Chimu controlled all of the valleys from Tumbey in the north to Chancay in the south – a distance of 1,000 km (625 miles).

The capital at Chan Chan comprised a civic center, 6 square km in extent, and an additional 19 square km (11 square miles) of outlying buildings (Moseley and Mackey 1973). The central precinct contained nine huge adobe-walled compounds, measuring about 200 to 600 m (660 to 2,000 ft) on a side, and one compound that was somewhat smaller than the rest. Each of the compounds, except the small one (called the Tello enclosure), contained or was adjacent to a truncated pyramidal mound, which served as a burial platform. The compounds seem to have been built sequentially, construction of each commencing upon the ascendance of a new king. While he lived, the compound served as the ruler's palace; when he died, his body was laid within the platform, which was subsequently maintained as a shrine by his clan descendants. The platforms were looted long ago, but recent excavations in one of them revealed human skeletal remains in the rooms surrounding the T-shaped central chamber. These remains all belonged to young women; making an allowance for additional skeletons that had probably once been present in the disturbed rooms, it can be estimated that 200 or 300 young women,

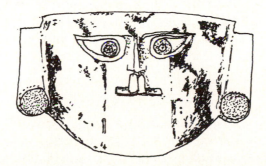

Fig. 110. Chimu funerary mask (gold, with red paint) (24 × 40 cm).

probably members of the royal harem, were sacrificed either at the time of the deceased ruler's funeral or at later commemorative ceremonies.

The Chimu royalty seem to have practiced split inheritance, a custom that the Incas borrowed from them. All of the deceased ruler's wealth – material possessions, lands and revenues – passed to his junior heirs, to be used for sacrifices at his shrine. The heir to the throne, inheriting only the king's political authority, had to build his own palace compound, and raise new revenues to finance his administration, whether by increasing labor taxes, reclaiming land for agriculture, or conquering more territory. Geoffrey Conrad's recent (1981) suggestion that the heirs' quest for new revenue sources was the primary driving force behind the expansion of both the Chimu and Inca empires has been sharply criticized by scholars (Isbell 1981, Paulsen 1981) who see the imperial conquests as responses to actual or potential environmental stress. Thus, Paulsen argues that the Inca and previous highland-based empires took shape during dry periods, when agricultural productivity in the highlands declined, and Isbell suggests that the centralized imperial administrative and redistributive systems of the Chimu and Incas served to counteract the effects of localized droughts, flooding, pests or blights.

The greatest project initiated by the Chimu was the digging of a canal that would bring water to fields in the Moche valley from the Chicama river, about 30 km (18 miles) to the north – however, this inter-valley canal was never finished. One proposed explanation is that tectonic uplift may have caused a change in the slope of the canal, forcing abandonment of the project (Ortloff et al. 1983). Another intriguing theory (Kus 1984) suggests that such a long canal could never have been practical, because three-quarters of the water it carried would have evaporated or been absorbed en route. Kus suggests that the Chimu rulers may have begun the project to demonstrate to their subjects that they were taking action to allay drought conditions; when the water shortage eased, work on the canal stopped. Recent surveys of the Chan Chan vicinity have shown that the canal network that surrounded the city gradually contracted after A.D. 1000 (Moseley 1983b). This evidence supports the idea that the inter-valley canal was a response to a perceived long-term water shortage, and also suggests that the expansion of the Chimu state occurred while, and perhaps because, its local resource base was shrinking.

Late Horizon: the Incas

The Cuzco Valley, in the southern highlands, had been a cultural back-water since the Initial period. The Huari state had briefly intruded, setting up the outpost of Piquillacta, but when Huari collapsed, the area had again become an isolated region of small villages. A small local chiefdom, the Incas, raided their neighbors repeatedly, but they did not win much territory. Around A.D. 1410 the semi-mythical emperor (Sapa Inca) Viracocha began to forge alliances with other groups. In 1438 his son, Yupanqui, who had assumed the name Pachakuti, or "Cataclysm", defeated the rival Chanca state. Having thus strengthened his grip on the area around his capital at Cuzco, Pachakuti sent his armies into the Titicaca basin, where they defeated the forces of the Colla and Lupaqa kingdoms. About 1463, Pachakuti's son, Topa, outflanked the Chimu by marching his army through the mountains to Quito, then attacked the coastal empire from the north. By defeating the Chimu, the Incas removed their last serious rival; and since they had already conquered the Titicaca basin, they now controlled the two historic centers of Andean civilization. Topa became emperor in 1471, and proceeded to enlarge his domain. He crushed a revolt in the Titicaca region, then sent troops through Bolivia, into northern Argentina, then across northern Chile as far as the Maule River. There the Inca army met fierce resistance from Araucanian tribesmen, so they advanced no farther. Topa's successor, Huayna Capac, conquered more territory in the upper Amazon region and in Ecuador, where he built a second capital at Quito. So, by 1525, the Inca empire stretched from northern Ecuador to south-central Chile, a distance of more than 4,000 km (2,500 miles). The empire's population is conservatively estimated to have numbered about six million, and a figure of 12 million is credible. The empire was called Tawantinsuyu, "The Land of the Four Quarters". Each quarter constituted a large province: Antisuyu (northeast), Collasuyu (southeast), Chinchasuyu (northwest), and Cuntisuyu (southwest). These were further divided into small provinces, whose boundaries sometimes corresponded to those of conquered kingdoms.

At the pinnacle of the political hierarchy stood the emperor, or Sapa Inca, who was believed to be descended from the Sun God, Inti. He was married to his sister, but also kept numerous concubines, who had been chosen from amongst the people for their beauty by special officials called *Apupanacas*. As mentioned earlier, the Incas adopted the royal Chimu custom of split inheritance. When a Sapa Inca died, his body was mummified and became the focus of a cult. His successor had to construct a new palace for himself, and had to develop new sources of revenue.

In theory at least, the Inca imperial bureaucracy was organized according to a decimal system, with a hierarchy of officials responsible for units of 10, 50, 100, 500, 1,000, 5,000 and 10,000 households (Julien 1982). These decimal officials were usually local provincial people. Higher officials of the empire were recruited from the royal lineage or from among the noble lineages of conquered peoples. Pachakuti is said to have begun the practice of selecting talented commoners as officials; they were

made "Incas by privilege" and were awarded estates on the outskirts of
Cuzco. A corps of special investigators scrutinized the behavior of the
provincial officials.

The Incas instituted several policies that were intended to ensure their
control of conquered territory, but that also had the effect of unifying the

Fig. 111. Maximum extent of the Inca empire.

empire culturally. Any native groups that were likely to cause trouble were sent off to distant areas, while loyal colonists called *mitima* were brought in to settle newly conquered lands. Although they generally left intact the local political hierarchy of a conquered state or chiefdom, the Incas required that the ruler's sons be sent to Cuzco, where they were educated at court in the Inca language, Quechua. Local religious beliefs were also respected, but conquered peoples were compelled to worship the Inca pantheon of nature gods: the Creator, the Sun (ancestor of the royal lineage), Thunder, and the Earth Mother. The chief god or sacred object of a conquered province was taken to Cuzco, where it was placed either in the Temple of the Sun or in a special shrine, where it was looked after by a priestly staff recruited from that province. Throughout the empire, human sacrifices were periodically performed. Selected boys and girls, about 10 years old, were taken from the provinces to Cuzco for a special ceremony; afterward, these *capacochas* were dispatched to shrines in the various provinces, where they were sacrificed (Rowe 1982).

A vast network of paved roads, with a total length of some 30,000 km (18,750 miles), linked the provincial centers to Cuzco, facilitating the movement of troops, transportation of luxury goods, and transmission of information. In hilly areas, the roads were cut out of bedrock; particularly steep slopes were traversed by means of stone steps or zigzags. Where the highways had to cross wide rivers, suspension bridges were built; cables made by braiding twigs and vines were strung between stone towers on either side. Relay runners were stationed along the roads, at intervals of about a kilometer; they memorized and transmitted government messages.

The administration of a far-flung empire, with more than six million subjects, obviously required efficient processing of a great amount of information. Surprisingly, the Incas never devised a system of writing, which we might consider a necessary administrative tool; instead, the Inca bureaucrats relied on sets of knotted strings, called *quipu* (*khipu*). A special hereditary group of state functionaries, the *Quipucamayocs*, memorized the history, myths and census statistics that were symbolized by the knots on the quipu strings, and recited them for state officials.

Inca commoners belonged to land-owning, endogamous patrilineal clans, called *ayllus*. The lands they farmed were divided into three sections, the produce from those divisions belonging to the temples, the Sapa Inca (or state), and the ayllu, respectively. Each commoner was obliged to devote some of his time and energy to working on the state-owned land. This labor tax was called *mit'a*. The portion of the crop claimed by the state was taken to state store houses; this food could be used to feed the army or drafted laborers working on roads or buildings, and it was also available to alleviate famines. The Incas developed a method of storing

the staple crop of the highlands, potatoes, by freeze-drying them to make
chuño. Much of the state-owned maize and other grain crops was brewed
to make *chicha* beer. Providing laborers with ample supplies of chicha
seems to have been one of the most important functions of the administrative centers. At one such center, Huanuco Pampa, excavators have
found tons of large jars, thought to have been used for chicha, in rooms
adjacent to plazas (Morris 1982). Culinary pottery and food remains were
also found in these rooms. This evidence suggests that redistributive
feasts were held in the plazas; a further implication is that, like a giant
chiefdom, the Inca state may have based its authority largely on its liberal
ceremonial redistribution of food, drink, and goods.

The most important of the goods doled out by the state were textiles.
These were woven for the state by women, youths and old men, whose
labor in weaving fulfilled their mit'a obligation. Ceramics and metal
objects were produced for the state by specialist craftsmen. Bronze
became more common than it had been in earlier Andean civilizations,
replacing stone tools for many functions; it was used to make crowbars,
chisels, axes, clubs, knives and tweezers. The Incas invented the *taclla*, or
"foot plow", which consisted of a pole with a bronze point, a foot rest near
the point, and a handle at the end. This tool was used to break up the
ground, dig holes for planting, and harvest potatoes; it is still used today
by native Andean farmers. Inca-style polychrome ceramics were concentrated at the focal points of state authority – provincial administrative
centers, temples, store houses, garrisons and waystations (*tambos*). Local
aristocrats seem to have eagerly acquired Inca vessels, and also used
imitative wares produced by local potters. The common people continued
to make rather crude versions of the traditional ceramics of their
respective regions.

Inca architecture was particularly impressive. Cut stone blocks were
fitted precisely into place, using no mortar. Small blocks were laid in
regular courses, in constructing the walls of temples and palaces; huge
polygonal stones were used for terraces and fortresses such as Sacsahuaman, near Cuzco. Minor buildings were constructed of rough
masonry, adobe bricks, or mud and split stones.

The Incas did not build cities. Even their capital, Cuzco, was occupied
only by members of the Sapa Inca's court and by priests. Cuzco seems to
have been laid out in the form of a giant stylized puma. Most of the
empire's inhabitants lived in villages or small towns, which seldom held
more than 1,000 residents. The non-urban character of Inca civilization
contrasts with Mesoamerica, where the contemporary Aztecs built the
huge city of Tenochtitlán. Markets and merchants, which played an
important role in long-distance trade in Mesoamerica, were also notably
absent from the Inca empire. Luxury goods were produced for, and dis-

tributed to the population by, the state, which required special licenses for the ownership of non-essential items (Lanning 1967, Bankes 1977).

In rapidly conquering so vast an empire, the Incas may have over-extended themselves. Internal stresses nearly caused the dissolution of the empire after Huayna Capac's death, probably due to smallpox, in 1525. One of his sons, Huascar, proclaimed himself Sapa Inca in Cuzco; but another son, Atahuallpa, the governor of Quito, also claimed the throne. Huascar, finding it difficult to develop new sources of revenue, had threatened to put an end to the royal ancestor cults, whose wealth he coveted. The nobles therefore backed Atahuallpa, who was also supported by disaffected subject peoples. Atahuallpa's armies ultimately defeated Huascar's forces in the protracted civil war that ensued; but as the victorious Atahuallpa approached Cuzco, he was informed that a small Spanish army had landed on the coast. Astonishingly, Pizarro's little force of 168 men succeeded in conquering an empire of six million people. Pizarro managed to cause panic in the usually formidable Inca army in the plaza of Cajamarca, and to take Atahuallpa prisoner there, promising to release him if a huge ransom of gold were paid. Atahuallpa obliged by ordering a large room filled with golden objects gathered from all corners of the empire, but Pizarro then ordered that he be executed by strangling. A year later, the Spanish army captured Cuzco. The Spaniards took control of the native bureaucracy, using it for their own purposes, and appointed a puppet Sapa Inca, Manco Capac. He led a rebellion in 1536, but it was crushed, and the Spaniards consolidated their conquest of the empire.

Fig. 112. Walls of the "fortress" (possibly a religious structure) at Sacsahuaman, near Cuzco.

7

Parallel worlds

As we near the conclusion of this survey of American prehistory, it is appropriate that we consider again the questions that have preoccupied theorists since Europeans' first encounter with the native Americans. How did civilizations, with their cities, stratified social classes, organized religions, markets, and other characteristics which the Spanish invaders could immediately recognize as analogues of their own, arise in Mexico and Peru? Why didn't societies of comparable size and complexity develop elsewhere in the Americas?

DIFFUSION RECONSIDERED

One explanation of Old World–New World parallelisms, which was suggested by the first writers to speculate about the matter, is that cultural traits were carried to America by prehistoric travellers from the Old World. Today, no one would seriously suggest that the Indians were simply displaced Israelites, Welshmen or Atlanteans. However, there are still a few archaeologists, such as George Carter (1977), Betty Meggers (1975), Paul Tolstoy (1974b) and Gordon Ekholm (1964), who contend that particular Old World cultures did have a significant impact on those of the New World, through such mechanisms as trade and religious proselytizing. Arguments for diffusion generally rest on the complexity and arbitrariness of the traits compared, the apparent suddenness with which they occur in the alleged recipient culture, their priority in the supposed donor area, and the existence of a practicable route of transmission.

In previous chapters, we have examined some of the controversies over transoceanic diffusion. In the case of the bottle gourd, the theory that it was carried to South America by canoe-paddling African fishermen–farmers will remain highly implausible until someone finds hitherto non-existent evidence of very early cultivation, both in West Africa and eastern South America. Meggers and Evans' argument for the introduction of pottery-making to the coast of Ecuador by Japanese fishermen was rather convincing, until earlier well-made pottery was unearthed from an underlying stratum at Valdivia. The similarity of numerous decorative motifs in Jomon and Valdivia pottery is still striking, but it is best to see this as simply illustrating the results that convergent development can sometimes achieve.

The seemingly abrupt florescence of the Olmec civilization on Mexico's Gulf Coast has also given rise to diffusionist theories (Jett 1983). A bearded, long-nosed figure, known as "Uncle Sam", who appears on a stele at La Venta, has struck some observers as Semitic-looking; this has inspired suggestions of Phoenician voyages across the Atlantic. Others point to the Olmec use of jade, their religious obsession with felines, and a few other traits, as indications of derivation from Shang China (Meggers 1975). Of course, one would expect, if Shang voyages across the Pacific were responsible for the rise of New World civilization, that the first American civilizations would be found not on the Gulf Coast but on the Pacific coast. In fact, the earliest large scale ceremonial centers *are* located on the Pacific coast of Peru, but these date to about 1900 B.C. – several hundred years too early for the Shang to have had any role in their creation. The intricate designs of the later (ca. 900 B.C.) Chavín art style are somewhat reminiscent of Shang and Chou bronzes, but there is every reason to suppose that the Chavín style arose from an indigenous artistic tradition, of which we have an early expression in the textile designs from Huaca Prieta.

Leaving aside the question of their origins, once the New World civilizations were thriving, might they have attracted the attention of Old World merchants or missionaries? It has been suggest that Buddhist missionaries might have introduced a number of artistic and architectural traits found in classic Mesoamerican civilizations, such as figures intertwined with water lilies, sitting figures with crossed legs, a monstrous mask from whose jaws plants spring, and corbelled niches (Ekholm 1964). Some scholars have pointed to apparent correspondences in the complex calendrical systems and cosmologies of Mesoamerica and India: the Indian game of pachisi, and the Aztec game, patolli, both of which had cosmological connotations, were strikingly similar, as Edward Tylor noted in 1896. However, no objects of indisputable South Asian origin have turned up in secure archaeological contexts in Mesoamerica, and *vice versa*. Lacking such evidence, suggestions of a trans-Pacific connection remain only intriguing but unlikely alternatives to explanations based on convergent development.

An obvious weakness of the trans-Pacific theories is the absence of any archaeological or ethnological trace of influence exerted by Indian or Chinese civilization on the sea-faring peoples of the Pacific Islands. If hypothetical Asian travellers repeatedly sailed straight across the Pacific in search of converts or trading partners, one would think they would have encountered the Polynesians *en route*. Alternatively, the voyagers might have hugged the coasts of northeastern Asia and northwestern America, in which case some evidence of their passage might be expected in the material remains or cultural traditions of the inhabitants of the coast. In fact, some scholars detect an Asiatic influence in the artwork of the Northwest Coast: its stylistic conventions for the depiction of animals are very similar to those used to portray animals in Shang bronzes. However, not only are different media involved (bronze vs. wood), but the Shang pieces are more than 3,000 years older than the Northwest Coast examples, most of which were carved after A.D. 1800.

Recently it was claimed that pierced stones found off the California coast could be identified as the anchors of ancient chinese merchant vessels; however, it has been shown that they were probably used by nineteenth-century Chinese–American fishermen (Frost 1982). If Asian sea-farers ever sailed along the coast of California, they established no ports or depots, left nothing behind, and had no discernible impact on the local inhabitants, who remained hunter–gatherers until their contact with Europeans. This fact raises a crucial point: diffusion can only have a significant effect on a recipient culture when it is predisposed to adopt the new objects or ideas that it is offered.

If American archaeologists have sometimes appeared overly anxious and stubborn about claims of trans-oceanic diffusion, their reactions can be explained as reflecting two predominant concerns. First, diffusionist theories have often rested, explicitly or implicitly, on the racist assumption that native Americans were backward savages, incapable of devising sophisticated cultures without the benevolent assistance of more advanced white-skinned tutors. This seems to explain the attention devoted in popular literature on Mesoamerican civilization to Quetzalcoatl, the mythical fair-skinned and bearded culture hero who was said to have brought civilization to the Mexicans and then sailed away. American archaeologists have felt compelled to counter such denigration of native Americans' abilities by demonstrating that complex societies developed independently in the New World. Anti-diffusionists have also had another, more philosophical motivation. If it can be shown that civilizations arose in the Americas in complete isolation from similar complex societies of the Old World, a strong case can be made for the argument that there is an inherent tendency for simple human societies to become progressively more complex under certain conditions, and that this process of cultural evolution is amenable to scientific generalization and even prediction. In other words, if complete isolation is assumed, the American continent can be seen as a sort of giant island laboratory, on to which a few humans have been cast ashore, allowing scientists to observe what kinds of societies and behavior patterns they generate, starting from scratch and receiving no external cues. On the contrary, diffusionists argue that demonstration of even a single trans-oceanic contact would puncture the illusion of independence and raise the possibility that civilization is but an accident, conceived of only once by some nameless genius, from whom the spark was then passed on to receptive minds in other societies.

It should be noted that Mexico and Peru are the only cases in which complete isolation of emergent civilizations from earlier civilized societies is a possibility. The centers of so-called "pristine" or primary civilization in the Old World – Mesopotamia, Egypt, the Indus Valley and China – all had at least indirect contact with other centers. A good illustration of this fact is the appearance of the horse-drawn chariot around 1700–1500 B.C. both in Egypt and China, the centers most distant from one another. Nevertheless, few Old World prehistorians would suggest today that civilization was exported wholesale from Mesopotamia to the other centers, where it emerged somewhat later. Instead, archaeologists believe that, in each case, local factors led to the development of complex societies. However, exactly what combination of population growth, agricultural intensification, trade, warfare, social stratification, etc., was involved in the development of the state and civilization in each instance is a matter for argument, speculation and further research.

While there is a general consensus with regard to trans-oceanic diffusion theories, the issue of diffusion vs. independent development is still unresolved where possible transmission of cultural traits *within* the Americas is concerned. There are several examples of this problem, from different periods. I have suggested that the fishtail points of Central and South America represent the diffusion, by migration, of the fluted point tradition from North America. However, Alan Bryan (1978) and other archaeologists contend that the South American points are the product of convergent, independent development by hunter–gatherers who had arrived in South America thousands of years earlier. We have reviewed the weak points of the case for Japanese introduction of pottery-making to the Americas; but the origins of the American ceramic traditions remain problematic. The earliest Valdivia pottery, at around 3000 B.C., is too well-made to be close to the experimental beginnings of the craft. The same is true of the Swasey pottery from the proto-Mayan site of Cuello, which may date as far back as 2000 B.C., if the radiocarbon dates for the site prove to be correct. It is possible that both of these ceramic traditions were ultimately derived from a single ancestral source in northern South America. This tradition may be represented at the site of Puerto Hormiga in Colombia, which has yielded the earliest pottery known in the Americas. It should also be recalled that the earliest pottery in the Mexican highlands occurs in the Purron phase of Tehuacan, around 2300 B.C. In the southeastern United States, fiber-tempered pottery appeared around 2500–2000 B.C. At some coastal sites, it was found in association with ring-shaped shell mounds. A similar mound was present at Puerto Hormiga, where the pottery was also fiber-tempered. Is this simply a matter of two isolated groups of coastal shellfish-collectors independently discovering that, as replicative experiments have shown, vegetal fibers make an excellent tempering agent (Peterson 1980)? Or can it be that the appearance of pottery in all these areas between 3000 and 2000 B.C. is not a coincidence, but instead shows that ceramic techniques diffused from a single source?

The diffusion of maize from the highlands of southern Mesoamerica, where it originated, probably as a mutant of teosinte, has been pretty well-established. Maize seems to have been carried southward as far as the Peruvian Andes before 3000 B.C. It appears to have been cultivated at Real Alto, on the coast of Ecuador, around 2500 B.C. (uncalibrated). Evidently, two species of squash of Mexican origin had been brought to the coast of Peru by 2500 B.C. The early diffusion of maize suggests that its potential as a food source had already been recognized by groups living outside Mesoamerica; this casts some doubt on the otherwise plausible theory that the rapid transition to sedentary village life in Mesoamerica after 1700 B.C. was a response to improvements in the yield of maize, such that it only then became more productive than wild plants. Maize may have been carried northward to New Mexico by 3500 B.C., if the dates for Bat Cave are correct. However, recent re-assessment of this site suggests that the maize may actually be as many as 3,000 years younger than originally thought (Lipe 1983). In the eastern U.S., Mexican-derived squash was being grown in Missouri and Kentucky before 2300 B.C. It is conceivable that techniques of pottery manufacture were transmitted to the Southeast through the same network that brought tropical cultigens to the region.

The early appearance of Mesoamerican cultigens in eastern North America raises the question of whether the emergence of ranked societies, first in the Ohio Valley (Adena and Hopewell), then in the Mississippi Valley, would have occurred if there had not been significant influences from the south. At present, the paucity of maize finds in Ohio and Illinois Hopewell sites suggests that cultivation of Mesoamerican crops was a minor part of the Hopewellian subsistence base. Few other traits of Hopewell culture appear to be specifically Mexican; copper ear-spools and pan-pipes might be markers of southern influence. On the contrary, many characteristic Hopewellian features, such as atlatl weights and gorgets, show a continuation of Late Archaic traditions. Most importantly, the elaborate ceremonial treatment of the dead can be traced from Hopewell, through Adena, back to the Late Archaic cultures of the eastern woodlands.

The case for diffusion of mound construction from Mexico looks somewhat better, however, when one considers Poverty Point. The massive complex of concentric earthworks and mounds there seems to be hundreds of years earlier (ca. 1200 B.C.) than the Adena burial mounds. This date makes Poverty Point contemporaneous with the Olmec site of San Lorenzo, where great quantities of earth were heaped up to alter the shape of the plateau on which the site stood. Both sites lie near the coast of the Gulf of Mexico, so that they might conceivably have been linked by canoe voyages. However, there is no precise Olmec prototype for the concentric ridges at Poverty Point; the figurines from the latter site bear only the faintest resemblance to Olmec pieces; there is little or no evidence of the cultivation of Mesoamerican plants at Poverty Point; and the lithic and ceramic assemblages from the Louisiana site clearly indicate its origins in the Southeastern Archaic cultural tradition. The extraordinary early florescence of Poverty Point apparently ought to be explained not in terms of its accessibility to hypothetical routes of Mexican influence, but as the result of its location in proximity to diverse and abundant riverine resources.

The later Mississippian societies (A.D. 700–1500) almost certainly had some contact, probably indirect, with Mesoamerican civilization. The Mississippians cultivated maize and squash and, after A.D. 1200, beans. There is an unmistakable Mexican flavor in Mississippian artwork. However, there are also carry-overs from the Hopewell artistic tradition. The practice of situating élite dwellings and temples on top of mounds, and arranging those mounds around central open plazas, has often been attributed to Mexican influence; but platform mounds seem to have first been built by Hopewell-influenced groups in the lower Mississippi Valley and in northern Florida. It is clear that there was no large-scale intrusion of Mesoamerican populations into the Mississippi Valley; perhaps a few far-ranging pochteca merchants may occasionally have reached Cahokia or other Mississippian centers.

Cahokia, judging by its size, was either a very large and complex chiefdom or a nascent state at its peak, around A.D. 1050 to 1250. It is intriguing that the most complex of the southwestern Pueblo cultures flourished in Chaco Canyon at roughly the same time; its climax came at about 1020 to 1120. It is conceivable that these periods of florescence might somehow be related to the establishment of the Toltec empire in Mexico, which lasted from the mid-tenth century until A.D. 1168. One can speculate that new ideas and organizational skills might have been carried northward by Mexican refugees, fleeing from the Toltec armies; or that the extension of Toltec control resulted in more secure trade routes, encouraging the pochteca to undertake more long-distance journeys. One school of Southwestern archaeologists sees the Chaco phenomenon as inspired by Mexican-based merchants, who travelled to the Southwest to acquire turquoise. From this perspective, cultural developments in the Southwest are viewed as reactions, in the peripheral sphere of influence of Mexican civilization, to events in the core region. Clear evidence of Mexican intrusion into the Southwest has been found at the site of Casas Grandes, in northern Chihuahua. A Mogollon-related settlement there was replaced around A.D. 1150 by a town whose architecture, including mounds and ball-courts, was entirely Mexican in style. Obviously, Chaco Canyon's climax cannot be directly related to this particular Mexican intrusion, since construction of Pueblo Bonito began more than 200 years before the Mexican take-over of Casas Grandes. Furthermore, the architecture, ceramics, and other traits of the Chaco Canyon pueblos are clearly based in earlier Anasazi traditions. On the other hand, Chacoan contact with Mexico is proven by finds of unquestionable imports, notably copper bells and macaws. These items must have been exchanged for some locally produced commodities, such as turquoise, which the Mexicans desired. Control of long-distance trade with Mexico may have enhanced the status of the Chaco Canyon élite; however, even if one makes allowance for perishable items that have not survived in the archaeological record, the quantity of imports found at Chacoan sites is simply not great enough to sustain the notion that that trade might have been the primary cause of the élite's formation. Instead, the developments in Chaco Canyon are best seen as an independent case of the emergence of complex social and political institutions as a result of water control, differential wealth and environmental circumscription.

We have examined numerous other situations where the relative importance of indigenous and exogenous factors has been a matter of controversy. Did the Olmec impose civilization on the peoples of the Mexican highlands, through trade and conquest? Or, did local élites arise independently, then borrow Olmec ideology to bolster their status? Were the Mayan cities established in areas of maximum agricultural potential, or at sites from which the flow of goods to and from Teotihuacán could be most effectively controlled? Was the collapse of those cities caused, directly or indirectly, by the decline of Teotihuacán, or by a local ecological–economic catastrophe? Considering the approximate contemporaneity of the Olmec in Mesoamerica and the Chavín civilization in Peru, one must wonder whether there was not some connection between these emergent civilizations. In fact, recent archaeological work in Ecuador suggests that prehistoric cultures there contributed traits to both Mesoamerica and the Andes.

Obviously, we must recognize that trade, conquest, migration and other mechanisms of diffusion have often significantly affected the course of development of prehistoric cultures; however, it is equally apparent that the successful transplantation of diffused traits depends on a pre-existent infrastructure of appropriate ecological, economic and socio-political conditions in the recipient culture.

PARALLELISMS IN CULTURAL EVOLUTION

Having rejected trans-oceanic diffusion as an adequate explanation of Old World–New World cultural similarities, it remains for us to explore the implications of the alternative perspective, from which American cultures are seen as recapitulating, in isolation, the same evolutionary process observed in the Old World.

We must first note the possible effects on cultural trajectories of two factors that are not independent in each case. First, there have been climatic changes during the late Pleistocene and Holocene that have had world-wide effects. We should therefore expect that unrelated cultures with similar ecological adaptations and economic and social organizations might have reacted similarly and contemporaneously to changes in temperature, sea level, floral and faunal communities, etc. Second, the first people to enter the Americas were anatomically modern humans, of the species *Homo sapiens sapiens*. They shared with their Old World relatives whatever drives, capabilities and mental and behavioral patterns are genetically inherent in that species. These inborn factors would include language capability, omnivorous dietary preferences, and a tendency to form families and bands, and to divide labor according to sex. Furthermore, the earliest American cultures can be linked to a specific, if very widespread, cultural tradition – the Upper Paleolithic of Eurasia. This connection is manifest in such material traits as punched blades, end-scrapers, bifacially chipped stone points, bone points, spearthrowers and tailored clothing. Less tangible links are harder to demonstrate archaeologically, but a good case can be made for the derivation of the complex of beliefs and behaviors known as shamanism from the Upper Paleolithic cultures of Eurasia. When we observe strangely similar traits on either side of the Pacific, such as dragons in China and feathered serpents in Mesoamerica, or animals depicted with their bodies splayed out on either side of their faces, in Shang bronzes and Northwest Coast wood carvings, we must entertain the possibility that these convergences arose either because the human mind is "pre-wired" so that it works in only so many ways (e.g. by creating binary oppositions) or because certain deep-seated psychological themes were established in the Upper Paleolithic cultures of Asia and continued to find expression periodically in descendant cultural traditions in Asia and America. In any case, we cannot refer to inherently similar human propensities to explain the diversity of New World cultures. Why did genetically related people, starting from the same cultural baseline around 9000 B.C., establish a series of empires in Peru, but continue to live in hunting bands in Tierra del Fuego?

The answer to this question clearly involves ecological differences. The polar regions are extreme cases of environmental limitation of cultural development; scarcity of plant and animal resources precluded the growth of human populations to a size where complex forms of organization were necessary. In the New World, as in the Old World, complex

a

b

Fig. 113. Split representation in the art of the Northwest Coast and early China: (A) Haida painting of a bear; the animal is shown split in two, the profiles joined at the middle; (B) bronze vessel, Shang dynasty, from An-Yang; a split animal mask in middle panel; small dragons, face to face and in profile, in upper panel. (After Lévi-Strauss 1967.)

societies developed in the tropical, sub-tropical and temperate regions, where resources were diverse and abundant. Marked variations in altitude, rainfall and vegetation, are particularly apparent in Mesoamerica and Peru, where the most complex American societies developed; this suggests that exchange and redistribution of resources among the inhabitants of densely packed, highly diverse ecozones may have been a critical factor in the emergence of civilizations. On the other hand, fine-tuned analysis of most environments will reveal some degree of resource diversity and patchiness. Archaic-level hunter–gatherers generally adapted to such situations by moving seasonally from one resource area to the next; why didn't societies in Peru and Mesoamerica stabilize at this adaptive level? The significance of environmental diversity as a critical factor in the emergence of complex societies is called into question by two contrasting examples in North America. On the one hand, early chiefdoms arose in the lower Mississippi and Ohio River valleys, areas of low topographic, climatic and biotic diversity. On the other hand, in California, despite its varied coastal, foothill and mountain ecozones, no large, complex chiefdoms or states ever developed.

Wittfogel, Steward and other scholars noted that early civilizations tended to occur in river valleys. In fact, in the Americas, chiefdoms did develop in the major river valleys, e.g., the Mississippi, Amazon, and Orinoco, but large-scale states arose in arid highland lake basins such as the Valley of Mexico and Lake Titicaca. These cases of state formation seem to support part of Wittfogel's hydraulic theory, in that construction and maintenance of extensive irrigation systems were necessary to support large populations in these arid regions. We should recall, however, the example of the Hohokam and their presumed descendants, the Pima, which shows that maintenance of an extensive irrigation system, even where it is circumscribed by an inhospitable arid environment, does not necessarily lead to state formation.

Archaeologists have generally assumed that complex socio-political institutions presuppose large populations, and that the latter can only be supported by intensive agriculture. Until recently, some scholars argued that the Maya seemed to contradict this generalization, since they practiced only non-intensive slash and burn agriculture; however, new evidence of terraces, canals, and other forms of intensification shows that the Maya were not exceptional in this regard. Recent surveys of Tikal and other Mayan centers have shown that they were large and densely populated enough to warrant the label "urban"; therefore, most archaeologists have abandoned the idea that the Maya were a unique example of a civilization without cities.

While the Maya can now be seen as dependent upon intensive agriculture, it remains a matter of debate whether the same was true of the early complex societies that built the ceremonial centers of the Peruvian coast. Might these apparent chiefdoms have been supported primarily by marine resources? Or does the proximity of sites like Chuquitanta to arable riverine areas imply an orientation toward agriculture? Ethnographic examples from the Northwest Coast show that ranking, redistributive economies and sophisticated artistic traditions can develop in the absence of agriculture. However, while the marine adaptations of the Northwest Coast offer apt analogues to coastal Peru, the Peruvian ceremonial centers, with their large scale structures, are not paralleled on the Northwest Coast. The earthworks of Poverty Point, Adena and Hopewell cultures may be cited as evidence that large-scale construction projects can be successfully undertaken by groups that rely primarily (though not entirely) on hunting and gathering. Clearly the Hopewellians did cultivate squash and gourds, and probably tobacco; maize has also been found at several sites. Nevertheless, as recent carbon isotope analyses have confirmed, maize was not a major item in the Hopewellian diet. It is likely that the Hopewellians transplanted and cultivated native seed-bearing plants; but archaeologists currently reconstruct their economic base as essentially broad-spectrum hunting and gathering, with only a minor agricultural component.

Assuming that this interpretation will not be undercut by future discoveries, we can tentatively juxtapose the Northwest Coast societies, the Poverty Point and Ohio Valley mound-builders, some California groups, and perhaps also the coastal Peruvian chiefdoms, as examples of a level of social evolution that seems to be unparalleled in the Old World. This stage, which may be termed the "Developed Archaic", comprises hunting–gathering–fishing societies in which ranking and other manifestations of complex organization are present.

Actually, it may be best to think of three alternative parallel trajectories followed by Archaic-level cultures in the Americas. First, in regions where natural resources were scarce – the Arctic, Sub-Arctic, and arid deserts like the Great Basin – small, mobile, highly dispersed groups maintained Archaic adaptations up to the time of European contact. In regions of greater biotic diversity and abundance, such as coasts and temperate forests, the development of efficient collecting strategies permitted the establishment of more permanent settlements, and the maintenance of larger and denser populations. In these areas, the second trajectory was followed, leading to a "Developed Archaic" climax in each instance. Among hunter–gatherers who occupied rich environments, a common strategy to offset potential resource fluctuations was periodic aggregation of dispersed groups for pooling and redistribution of food collected from a wide area. Redistribution was often handled by "big men", whose positions tended to become hereditary; this led to ranking on the basis of lineage. Redistribution feasts were necessary for ecological and economic reasons, but to ensure that they were held, they were cast in the form of supernaturally sanctioned rituals. These ritual feasts might initially be tied to natural cycles – e.g. first fruits rituals of increase ceremonies – but as ranking became more entrenched, rituals were increasingly associated with events in the life cycle of élite individuals, such as initiation, assumption of office, or death. As chiefs were given control over internal redistribution, they were also empowered to use the society's surplus resources for exchanges by which external alliances were forged and maintained. Obviously, this model of societies that followed the second, Developed Archaic trajectory is largely dependent both on ethnographic analogy and reasonable conjecture, but one can look in the archaeological record for distinctive traces of such societies. Among these would be large-scale structures, often funerary in nature, and exotic imported materials, which attest to the operation of widespread exchange networks. Exotic items will generally occur only in a limited number of élite residences and burials. Ultimately, the evolution of Developed Archaic societies was limited by the carrying capacities of their environments. No matter how efficient the collecting strategies employed, hunter–gatherers cannot sustain population densities comparable to those of farmers. The highest density reported for hunter–gatherers is 2.3 people per square km (6 people per square mile); this was the density of population in the most abundant environments in California at the time of contact.

The third trajectory was followed by the inhabitants of semi-arid or tropical regions, who developed or adopted agriculture. Initially, judging from the Tehuacan and Ayacucho sites, the adaptive strategies of the hunter–gatherers in these areas were hardly distinguishable from those of Archaic peoples elsewhere. Nevertheless, they were starting to transplant and tend certain plants which, after centuries of such manipulation, became domesticated cultigens, utterly dependent on humans for their propagation. Several thousand years after the beginnings of cultivation, permanent farming villages were established. This event marks the inception of what has traditionally been known as the Formative stage. Agriculture fostered population growth, and, by a positive feedback loop, increasing numbers of people could only be sustained by the adoption of more intensive farming methods, such as irrigation, terracing, and double-cropping. Agriculture allowed much higher population densities than hunting and gathering. Sedentism, population growth, redistribution and exchange, and warfare led to the emergence of agriculture-based chiefdoms in Formative Mesoamerica, northern South America, the Caribbean, the southeastern United States and possibly also in the Southwest. The most complex, state-organized societies evolved from chiefdoms in Mesoamerica and Peru only (although there were large and complex chiefdoms elsewhere, such as Cahokia, that came close to this level). Why the inhabitants of these two areas should have advanced farthest along the third developmental trajectory remains to be fully explained; perhaps their head start in the adoption of agriculture was an important factor.

The apparently different relationships of agriculture to sedentary life in the New and Old Worlds call for comment and explanation. In the Near East, permanent villages seem to have appeared at about the same time that the first steps in the domestication of plants and animals were taken, around 9000–8000 B.C. However, there are a few earlier finds, such as the grinding stones and sickle blades associated with a circular hut at Ein Gev in Israel, and dated at about 13,700 B.C., which suggest that selective harvesting of wild plants, and perhaps experimental cultivation, had begun long before 9000 B.C. If so, the Near Eastern sequence would more closely parallel what happened in the Americas. In Mesoamerica, thousands of years appear to have elapsed between the first agricultural experiments and the adoption of sedentary lifeways. On the other hand, hunter–gatherers had established permanent villages in coastal Peru and in the Illinois valley before 5000 B.C., and in California around 4000–3000 B.C. Why didn't the incipient farmers of Mexico become sedentary until 1500 B.C.? One possibility is that their lack of domesticated ungulates forced them to continue to rely on hunting to provide necessary high-quality proteins, which maize did not supply (Harris 1977). The continual pursuit of deer, rabbit, peccary, etc., required frequent movement, thus preventing the establishment of fixed settlements. Perhaps it was only when the regional human population had grown, or the available game had been depleted, to the extent that hunting no longer yielded enough meat to justify drawing labor away from intensive plant cultivation, that permanent villages were set up. The major flaw of this theory is that it does not explain why hunting and trapping should not have been delegated to task groups, making occasional forays out of permanent villages. Another explanation focusses on the gradual improvement of maize over the course of 3,000 years following its initial cultivation. Around 2000 B.C., the cobs had grown large enough to assure higher caloric yields from maize fields than from comparable stands of wild plants (Flannery 1973). Therefore, only then did it make sense to settle down next to one's maize fields instead of moving about between patches of sequentially ripening wild plants. This theory, while plausible, is weakened somewhat when one realizes that maize was already so much valued as a food source by 3000 B.C. that it had been spread far southward, through the Andes, and that by 2500 B.C., it was the staple crop that supported large villages in Ecuador. Of course, this might show that South American cultivators were able to develop better races of maize more rapidly. A third possibility is that village life depended on the creation of socio-political institutions that could counteract the tendency of hunter–gatherers to disperse as a way of solving group conflicts. Formal recognition of headmen as mediators and judges, the adoption of ideologies that supported their exercise of authority, as well as increased emphasis on the kinship and ceremonial ties between families, would have been involved in the social transformation that permitted year-round cohabitation. Of course, one must ask what people gained in return for this surrender of their autonomy, and this leads us back to the supposition that there was some unprecedented economic compulsion or reward that caused the rapid adoption of village life after thousands of years of nomadism.

Another obvious contrast between Old and New World sequences lies in the duration of the village farming stage. In the Near East, village farming was widespread by 7000 B.C., but the first temples were built in southern Mesopotamia around 4500 B.C., and the first cities appeared in the same area more than a thousand years later. A comparably long period separates the inception of village farming in India and China from the emergence of the first states in those regions. In contrast, only a few hundred years after villages began to dot the Mesoamerican landscape, monumental construction was already being undertaken by the Olmec chiefdoms of the Gulf Coast, and only 700 years later states began to appear in the highlands. In coastal Peru, some permanent marine-oriented villages (e.g. Paloma) were evidently established as early as 5500 B.C. It is possible that inundation of the coastline may account for the absence of village sites between this early period and about 2500 B.C., when sites such as Pampa and Huaca Prieta attest to widespread sedentism. Only a few centuries later, large-scale construction was under way at Chuquitanta (El Paraíso). In the Andean highlands, village life, based on a mixture of agriculture and camelid-herding, became established not long before 2000 B.C., when a ceremonial center was built at Kotosh. Large ceremonial centers had emerged in the highlands by 1000 B.C., and urban centers had taken shape in the Titicaca basin by 100 B.C. It seems that the shift to sedentism may have caused rapid population growth, both in Mexico and Peru. A thirty-fold increase, from 200 to 6,000 people, is reported to have occurred in the Ancón-Chillón region on the Peruvian coast, in the period from 2500 to 1750 B.C. This is the time when sedentism began and the center at Chuquitanta was built. In the eastern part of the Valley of Mexico, the population is estimated to have grown from 10,000, around 850–550 B.C., to 110,000 around 250 B.C.–A.D. 100. It is apparent that rapid population growth was linked, in each case, to increasing political centralization, but the causal mechanism has yet to be clarified.

Several differences in the development of Old and New World cultures may help to explain why, when they finally came into contact, the American civilizations collapsed before the onslaught of the European invaders. For one thing, the native Americans never made any practical use of the wheel. Finds of wheeled toys demonstrate that the basic principle was known to the ancient Mexicans; but as they lacked any domesticated animal larger than the dog, vehicles offered no obvious advantage over the human back as a mode of transport. In the Andes, the domesticated llama was used as a pack animal, like its Old World cousin, the camel. The steep mountain slopes would have rendered wheeled vehicles useless. In Europe, the wheel was the basic device from which all advanced technology involving pulleys, gears, cogs and screws was derived. However, despite the obvious advantage that the Spanish invaders held because of their crossbows, cannon, sailing ships, and other military hardware, the Aztecs successfully drove them out of Tenochtitlán. Superior wheel-based technology certainly contributed to the Spanish victory, but it was not the decisive factor.

Cortes' troops carried steel swords, and wore steel armor; the Aztec warriors wore cotton armor, and their swords were edged with sharp, but brittle, obsidian. Metal-working had not been introduced to Mexico until after A.D. 900. Gold and copper were used almost exclusively for non-utilitarian objects. The techniques of metal-working had probably diffused northward from the Andes, where copper smelting seems to have begun as early as 1200 B.C., in the southern Titicaca basin. At about the same time, gold was being worked in the central Andes. In Peru, some tools were made of copper and (by the time of the Incas) bronze; but, as in Mexico, metal was used primarily for ornaments and ceremonial objects. Iron smelting, which began in the Near East before 1000 B.C., was never developed by New World metal-workers. Again, as in the case of the wheel, the defeats suffered by Spanish forces at the hands of obsidian-armed Aztec warriors suggest that the natives' lack of iron or steel did not predetermine the outcome of their struggle with the Europeans.

The critical factor seems instead to have been the native Americans' lack of antibodies against Old World micro-organisms. Few, if any, infectious diseases were endemic in American populations. Several depictions in Mexican and Peruvian art of hunchbacks suggest that tuberculosis may have been present aboriginally, but if so, it was not a common ailment. A form of non-venereal syphilis also seems to have been known in Mesoamerica before contact. However, it was the arrival of the white man that first exposed the native Americans to the viruses that cause smallpox and measles, and the rickettsia that cause typhus. An infected black soldier in the army led by Cortes' rival, Narvaez, brought smallpox from Cuba to the Mexican coast. The disease was soon carried to Tenochtitlán, where it ravaged the defenders of the city; among the dead was Cuitlahuac, who had organized the successful uprising against the Spanish. Decimated and demoralized, the Aztecs could no longer hold off Cortes' army, and Tenochtitlán fell (Diaz 1963). Within five years, smallpox spread through Central America, and reached Peru in 1525. The death of the Inca ruler, which precipitated the civil war between his successors and thus facilitated Pizarro's conquest of the empire, was caused by smallpox. These devastating smallpox epidemics were followed by outbreaks, in Mexico and Peru, of measles in 1530, and of a disease that was probably typhus in 1546. The cumulative effect of these uncontrollable epidemics was a population loss of almost unimaginable dimensions (Ashburn 1947). Reasonable estimates of the native American population at the time of contact are on the order of 57 million; some 21 million people lived in Mesoamerica, about 7.5 million inhabited the Inca empire, and the population of the Intermediate area and Caribbean islands may have been 14–15 million (Denevan 1976). It is thought that disease had wiped out 90% of the population of the nuclear zone (Mesoamerica, Peru and the Intermediate area) by 1568; in other words, more than 39 million people had perished in less than 50 years following the initial outbreak of smallpox.

Why were there no American diseases to afflict the European invaders with equally terrible virulence? It has long been thought that syphilis was such a disease, because the first well-reported outbreak in Europe occurred shortly after Columbus' return from the New World. However, it now appears more likely that a non-venereal strain of syphilis had always been present in Europe. When Europeans, reacting to the colder weather of the Little Ice Age, began to wear more clothing indoors, thus hindering the usual skin-to-skin transmission of the spirochete bacillus, the microbe responded by taking the venereal route (McNeill 1976).

Syphilis is the only disease for which an American origin is even arguable. There are two possible explanations for the absence of endemic diseases in the New World. The first is that microbes like the smallpox virus can only become established in human populations that are dense enough to permit frequent transmission from one human host to another, and numerous enough for there always to be disease-resistant survivors in which the virus can reside until the next outbreak – in other words, these germs can only flourish in urban situations. Densely occupied cities appeared in the New World 3,000 years later than they did in the Old World; nevertheless, the first probable smallpox epidemic struck the Mediterranean region as late as the third century A.D. Evidently, even in a hospitable urban environment, a human virus may take a long time to evolve. Perhaps the 1,500 or 2,000 years of urban life in the Americas were not enough time for this process to occur. However, early references to pestilence in the literature of both Mesopotamia and Egypt show that some form of contagious disease was already present in the Near East by 2000 B.C., only 1,000 years after the beginnings of urbanism. So lack of time in the New World does not seem to be an adequate explanation of the absence of endemic diseases in such densely settled areas at the Valley of Mexico.

The absence of diseases in pre-Columbian America can be more convincingly attributed to the paucity of domesticated mammals. Most of the microbes that caused the Old World diseases seem to have originally infected animals, and then shifted to human hosts. Thus, smallpox was evidently derived from cowpox, measles from rinderpest, and influenza from a disease that affects pigs (McNeill 1976). For the same reasons that endemic human diseases require large, dense populations, microbes more often afflict herd animals than the more solitary species. As we have seen, the people of Mesoamerica never domesticated any herd animals. They did, of course, have the dog; but the dog, which lived in small packs in the wild, was not the primary host for diseases that would attack humans. This explanation therefore seems to be valid for Mexico, but it does not account very well for the Peruvian case. In Peru, llama-herding seems to have been practiced by 2000 B.C., and possibly began as early as 4000 B.C.; the raising of guinea pigs may be of comparable antiquity. So not only was there a long period during which the ancient Peruvians maintained close contact with large camelid herds, but they also kept domesticated rodents in their dwellings. In the Old World, of course, the dreaded bubonic plague was transmitted by fleas from rodents to humans. If we hope to explain the absence of infectious disease in the native human population of Peru, we must first ask why the domesticated animals did not suffer from diseases similar to those that afflicted their Old World counterparts. Unfortunately, no one has come up with a very good answer to this question.

We can only speculate about the possible outcome of the confrontation between the Old and New Worlds, had disease not played so crucial a role. Might the highly-organized Incas, and the less efficient but equally fierce Aztecs, have successfully resisted the European invasion? Japan was never subjugated by the Europeans, and although China and India fell under Western domination for a century or two, the colonizers were ultimately driven out. Similarly, white colonists were ultimately forced to cede most of Africa to the native populations, retaining only the southern tip of the continent. In contrast, only tiny remnants of the native population survived the wave of European colonization that swept over North America and much of South America. In the nuclear zone, a few million native people were left alive when the epidemics subsided. They abandoned the gods who had failed them in their time of need, and adopted the god of the Catholic priests. Unable to offer effective resistance, they generally resigned themselves to political domination and economic exploitation, although rebellions against the Spanish élite did flare up from time to time. Although the native ideologies and political systems were obliterated by the conquest, many aspects of aboriginal culture, including some of the ancient languages, persisted among the rural villagers. After centuries of dominance, Hispanic culture has become so firmly entrenched, and the commingling of the native and alien races has proceeded so far, that full restoration of the indigenous traditions is impossible. Nevertheless, there has been a recent resurgence of interest and pride in the achievements of the Indian ancestors. This trend was nicely exemplified by the decision to demolish several seventeenth- and eighteenth-century buildings in the heart of Mexico City, in order that the central pyramid of Tenochtitlán might be excavated and restored.

References

Adams, R. E. W., ed. 1977. *The origins of Maya civilization*. Albuquerque, University of New Mexico Press

Adams, R. M. 1966. *The evolution of urban society*. Chicago: Aldine

Adovasio, J. M. 1979. Comment (on Madsen 1979). *American Antiquity* 44 (4): 723–30

Adovasio, J. M., J. D. Gunn, J. Donahue, and R. Stuckenrath 1977. Progress report on the Meadowcroft rockshelter – a 16,000 year chronicle. In *Amerinds and their paleoenvironments in northeastern North America*, edited by W. S. Newman and B. Salwen, Annals of the New York Academy of Sciences, vol. 288

  1978. Meadowcroft rockshelter, 1977: an overview. *American Antiquity* 43 (4): 632–51

Adovasio et al., J. E. Guilday and K. Volman 1980. Yes Virginia, it really is that old: a reply to Haynes and Mead. *American Antiquity* 45 (3): 588–95

Aikens, C. M. 1970. *Hogup Cave*. University of Utah Anthropological Papers, no. 93

  1978. Archaeology of the Great Basin. *Annual Review of Anthropology* 7: 71–87

  1983. The Far West. In *Ancient North Americans*, edited by J. D. Jennings, pp. 149–201. San Francisco: Freeman

Ames, K. M. 1981. The evolution of social ranking on the Northwest Coast of North America. *American Antiquity* 46 (4): 789–805

Anderson, D. D. 1968. A stone age campsite at the gateway to America. *Scientific American* 218 (6): 24–33

Andrews, G. F. 1975. *Maya cities*. Tulsa: University of Oklahoma Press

Anonymous 1984. Life in ice age Chile. *Mammoth Trumpet* 1 (1): 1

Anton, F., and F. J. Dockstader 1968. *Pre-Columbian art and later Indian tribal arts*. New York: Abrams

Arundale, W. H. 1981. Radiocarbon dating in eastern Arctic archaeology: a flexible approach. *American Antiquity* 46 (2): 244–71

Asch, D. L., K. B. Farnsworth, and N. B. Asch 1979. Woodland subsistence and settlement in west central Illinois. In *Hopewell archaeology: the Chillicothe conference*, edited by D. S. Brose and N. Greber, pp. 80–5. Ohio: Kent State University Press

Ascher, R. 1961. Analogy in archaeological interpretation. *Southwestern Journal of Anthropology* 17 (4): 317–25

References

Ashburn, P. M. 1947. *The ranks of death: a medical history of the conquest of America*. New York: Coward-McCann

Bader, O. 1970. The boys of Sungir. *Illustrated London News*, vol. 256, 7 March, pp. 24–5

Ball, J. W. 1977. The rise of the northern Maya chiefdoms: a socioprocessual analysis. In *The origins of Maya civilization*, edited by R. E. W. Adams, pp. 101–32. Albuquerque: University of New Mexico Press

Bandi, H. 1969. *Eskimo prehistory*. College, Alaska: University of Alaska Press

Bankes, G. 1977. *Peru before Pizarro*. Oxford: Elsevier

Beadle, G. W. 1977. The origins of Zea mays. In *Origins of agriculture*, edited by C. A. Reed, pp. 615–37. The Hague: Mouton

Bean, L. J. and T. F. King, eds. 1974. *'ANTAP: California Indian political and economic organization*. Ballena Press Anthropological Papers, no. 2

Bender, B. 1985. Emergent tribal formations in the American midcontinent. *American Antiquity* 50 (1): 52–62

Bender, M. M., D. A. Baerreis, and R. L. Steventon 1981. Further light on carbon isotopes and Hopewell agriculture. *American Antiquity* 46 (2): 346–53

Bernal, I. 1969. *The Olmec World*. Berkeley and Los Angeles: University of California Press

Bettinger, R. L. and M. A. Baumhoff 1982. The Numic spread: Great Basin cultures in competition. *American Antiquity* 47 (3): 485–503.

Binford, L. R. 1968. Post-Pleistocene adaptations. In *New Perspectives in archeology*, edited by S. R. Binford and L. R. Binford, pp. 313–41. Chicago: Aldine

  1978. *Nunamiut ethnoarchaeology*. New York: Academic Press

Bird, J. 1938. Before Magellan. *Natural History* 41 (1): 16–28

  1963. Pre-ceramic art from Huaca Prieta, Chicama Valley. *Nawpa Pacha* 29–34

Birdsell, J. B. 1951. The problem of the early peopling of the Americas as viewed from Asia. In *Papers on the physical anthropology of the American Indian*, edited by W. Laughlin. New York: Viking Fund

  1981. *Human evolution*, 3rd edition. Boston: Houghton Mifflin

Bischof, H. and J. V. Gamboa 1972. Pre-Valdivia occupations on the southwest coast of Ecuador. *American Antiquity* 37 (4): 548

Blanton, R. E. 1976. The origins of Monte Albán. In *Cultural change and continuity: essays in honor of James Bennett Griffin*, edited by C. E. Cleland, pp. 223–32. New York: Academic Press.

  1978. *Monte Albán: settlement patterns at the ancient Zapotec capital*. New York: Academic Press.

  1980. Cultural ecology reconsidered. *American Antiquity* 45 (1): 145–51

Blanton, R. E. and S. Kowalewski 1981. Monte Albán and after in the Valley of Oaxaca. In *Supplement to the handbook of Middle American Indians: Archaeology*, edited by J. A. Sabloff, pp. 94–116. Austin: University of Texas Press

Boas, F. 1940. Changes in bodily form of descendants of immigrants. *American Anthropologist* 42: 183–9

Bordes, F. 1968. *The old stone age*. London: World University Library

Braidwood, R. J. and G. Willey, eds. 1962. *Courses toward urban life*. Chicago: Aldine

Brain, J. P. 1978. Late prehistoric settlement patterning in the Yazoo Basin and

Natchez Bluffs regions of the lower Mississippi Valley. In *Mississippian settlement patterns*, edited by B. D. Smith, pp. 331–68. New York: Academic Press

Brennan, L. A. 1974. The lower Hudson: a decade of shell middens. *Archaeology of Eastern North America* 2 (1): 81–93

Brose, D. S., J. A. Brown and D. W. Penney 1985. *Ancient art of the American Woodland Indians*. New York: Abrams

Brose, D. S. and N. Greber, eds. 1979. *Hopewell archaeology: the Chillicothe conference*. Ohio: Kent State University Press

Brown, K. L. 1980. A brief report on Paleoindian–Archaic occupation in the Quiche basin, Guatemala. *American Antiquity* 45 (2): 313–24

Broyles, B. J. 1971. *Second preliminary report: the St. Albans site, Kanawha county, West Virginia*. West Virginia Geologic and Economic Survey, Report of Investigations, no. 3

Brumfiel, E. M. 1983. Aztec state making: ecology, structure, and the origin of the state. *American Anthropologist* 85 (2): 261–84

Bryan, A. L., ed. 1978. *Early man in America from a circum-Pacific perspective*. Edmonton: University of Alberta Press

Bryan, A. L., et al. 1978. An El Jobo mastodon kill at Taima-Taima, Venezuela. *Science* 200: 1275–7

Burger, R. L. 1981. The radiocarbon evidence for the temporal priority of Chavín de Huantár. *American Antiquity* 46 (3): 592–602

Butzer, K. W. 1974. *Environment and archaeology*, 2nd edition. Chicago: Aldine-Atherton

Byers, D. S. and R. S. MacNeish, eds. 1967–76. *The prehistory of the Tehuacan Valley*, 5 vols. Austin: University of Texas Press

Caldwell, J. R. 1964. Interaction spheres in prehistory. In *Hopewellian studies*, edited by J. R. Caldwell and R. L. Hall, pp. 133–43. Springfield: Illinois State Museum Scientific Papers no. 12

Calnek, E. E. 1982. Patterns of empire formation in the Valley of Mexico, Late Postclassic period, 1200–1521. In *The Inca and Aztec states 1400–1800*, edited by G. A. Collier, R. I. Rosaldo and J. D. Wirth, pp. 43–62. New York: Academic Press

Campbell, B. 1982. *Humankind emerging*, 3rd edition. Boston: Little Brown

Campbell, J. M. 1968. Territoriality among ancient hunters: interpretation from ethnography and nature. In *Anthropological archaeology in the Americas*, edited by B. J. Meggers, pp. 1–21. Washington, D.C.: Anthropological Society of Washington

Campbell, J. M. and L. S. Cordell 1975. The Arctic and Subarctic. In *North America*, edited by S. Gorenstein, pp. 36–73. New York: St Martin's Press

Canby, T. Y. 1979. The search for the first Americans. *National Geographic* 156 (3): 330–63

1982. The Anasazi. *National Geographic* 162 (5): 554–92

Carlisle, R. C. and J. M. Adovasio, eds. 1982. *Meadowcroft: collected papers on the archaeology of Meadowcroft rockshelter and the Cross Creek drainage*. Prepared for symposium at 47th annual meeting of Society for American Archaeology, Minneapolis, 4–17 April 1972

Carneiro, R. 1970. A theory of the origin of the state. *Science* 169: 733–8

Carter, G. F. 1977. A hypothesis suggesting the possibility of a single origin of agriculture. In *Origins of agriculture*, edited by C. A. Reed, pp. 89–133. The Hague: Mouton

Caso, A. 1932. Reading the riddle of ancient jewels. *Natural History* 32 (5): 464–80

Chard, C. S. 1974. *Northeast Asia in prehistory*. Madison, Wisconsin: University of Wisconsin Press

Chomko, S. A. and G. W. Crawford 1978. Plant husbandry in prehistoric eastern North America: new evidence for its development. *American Antiquity* 43 (3): 405–8

Clark, D. W. and A. M. Clark 1980. Fluted points at the Batza Tena obsidian source, northwestern interior Alaska. In *Early Native Americans*, edited by D. Browman, pp. 141–59. The Hague: Mouton

Coe, J. L. 1964. *The formative cultures of the Carolina piedmont*. Philadelphia: Transactions of the American Philosophical Society 54 (5)

Coe, M.D. 1962. *Mexico*. New York: Praeger

1966. *The Maya*. New York: Praeger

1968a. *America's first civilization*. New York: American Heritage

1968b. San Lorenzo and the Olmec civilization. *Proceedings, Dumbarton Oaks Conference on the Olmec*, edited by E. P. Benson, pp. 41–78. Washington, D.C.: Dumbarton Oaks

1977. Olmec and Maya: a study in relationships. In *The origins of Maya civilization*, edited by R. E. W. Adams, pp. 183–95. Albuquerque: University of New Mexico Press

1981. San Lorenzo Tenochtitlán. In *Supplement to the handbook of Middle American Indians: Archaeology*, edited by J. A. Sabloff, pp. 117–46. Austin: University of Texas Press

Coe, M. D. and K. V. Flannery 1964. Microenvironments and Mesoamerican prehistory. *Science* 143 (3607): 650–4

Coe, W. R. 1975. Resurrecting the grandeur of Tikal. *National Geographic* 148 (6): 792–811

Cohen, M. N. 1977a. *The food crisis in prehistory*. New Haven: Yale University Press

1977b. Population pressure and the origins of agriculture: an archaeological example from the coast of Peru. In *Origins of agriculture*, edited by C. A. Reed, pp. 135–77. The Hague: Mouton

Coles, J. M. and E. S. Higgs 1969. *The archaeology of early man*. London: Penguin

Collins, D. 1976. *The origins of Europe*. New York: Crowell

Conrad, G. W. 1981. Cultural materialism, split inheritance, and the expansion of ancient Peruvian empires. *American Antiquity* 46: 3–26

Cook, S. F. 1946. Human sacrifice and warfare as factors in the demography of precolonial Mexico. *Human Biology* 18: 81–102

Cooke, R. G. 1985. Ancient painted pottery from central Panama. *Archaeology* 38 (4): 33–9

Cowgill, G. 1975. On the causes and consequences of ancient and modern population changes. *American Anthropologist* 77: 505–25

Cowgill, U. M. 1962. An agricultural study of the southern Maya lowlands. *American Anthropologist* 64: 273–86

Culbert, T. P. 1973. (editor) *The Classic Maya collapse*. Albuquerque: University of New Mexico Press

1974. *The lost civilization: the story of the Classic Maya*. New York: Harper and Row

1983. Mesoamerica. In *Ancient North Americans*, edited by J. D. Jennings, pp. 495–555. San Francisco: Freeman

Curran, M. L. 1984. The Whipple site and Paleoindian tool assemblage variation: a comparison of intrasite structuring. *Archaeology of Eastern North America* 12: 5–40

Dahlin, B. A. 1984. A colossus in Guatemala: the preclassic Maya city of El Mirador. *Archaeology* 37 (5): 18–25

Damp, J. 1984. Architecture of the early Valdivia village. *American Antiquity* 49 (3): 573–85

Davies, N. 1973. *The Aztecs*. Norman: University of Oklahoma Press

Davis, W. 1978. So-called jaguar–human copulation scenes in Olmec art. *American Antiquity* 43 (3): 453–7

DeBoer, W. R. 1974. The archaeological evidence for manioc cultivation: a cautionary note. *American Antiquity* 39: 419–33

Deetz, J. 1965. *The dynamics of stylistic change in Arikara ceramics*. Urbana: Illinois Studies in Anthropology 4

1967. *Invitation to archaeology*. Garden City, New York: Natural History Press

Dekin, A. A., Jr. 1976. The Arctic small tool horizon: a behavioral model of the dispersal of human population into an unoccupied niche. In *Eastern Arctic prehistory: Paleoeskimo problems*, edited by M. S. Maxwell, pp. 156–63. Society for American Archaeology Memoir no. 31

Denevan, W. M., editor 1976. *The native population of the Americas in 1492*. Madison: University of Wisconsin Press

Diaz, Bernal 1963. *The history of the conquest of New Spain*, translated by A. P. Maudsley. Baltimore: Pelican

Dickson, D. B. 1981. The Yanomamo of the Mississippi Valley? Some reflections on Larson (1972), Gibson (1974), and Mississippian period warfare in the southeastern United States. *American Antiquity* 46 (4): 909–16

Diehl, R. A. 1981. Tula. In *Supplement to the handbook of Middle American Indians: Archaeology*, edited by J. A. Sabloff, pp. 277–95. Austin: University of Texas Press

Dikov, N. N. and E. E. Titov 1984. Problems of the stratification and periodization of the Ushki sites. *Arctic Anthropology* 21 (2): 1–68

Dillehay, T. D. 1984. A late ice-age settlement in southern Chile. *Scientific American* 251 (4): 106–19

Dincauze, D. F. 1976. *The Neville site: 8000 years at Amoskeag*. Cambridge, Mass.: Peabody Museum Monograph 4

Disselhoff, H. and S. Linné 1961. *The art of ancient America*. New York: Crown

Doyel, D. E. 1979. The prehistoric Hohokam of the Arizona desert. *American Scientist* 67 (5): 544–54

Dragoo, D. W. 1964. The development of Adena culture and its role in the formation of Ohio Hopewell. In *Hopewellian studies*, edited by J. R. Caldwell and R. L. Hall. Springfield: Illinois State Museum Scientific Papers 12

1976a. Adena and the eastern burial cult. *Archaeology of Eastern North America* 4: 1–9

1976b. Some aspects of eastern North American prehistory: a review 1975. *American Antiquity* 41 (1): 3–27

Drucker, P. 1963. *Indians of the Northwest Coast*. Garden City, New York: Natural History Press

Dumond, D. E. 1961. Swidden agriculture and the rise of Maya civilization. *Southwestern Journal of Anthropology* 17 (4): 301–16

1980. The archeology of Alaska and the peopling of America. *Science* 209 (44600): 984–91

1983. Alaska and the Northwest Coast. In *Ancient North Americans*, edited by J. D. Jennings, pp. 69–113. San Francisco: Freeman

Eddy, F. W. 1974. Population dislocation in the Navaho Reservoir district, New Mexico and Colorado. *American Antiquity* 39 (1): 75–84

Ekholm, G. F. 1964. Transpacific contacts. In *Prehistoric man in the New World*, edited by J. D. Jennings and E. Norbeck, pp. 489–510. Chicago: University of Chicago Press

Elsasser, A. B. 1978. Development of regional prehistoric cultures. In *California*, vol. 8, *Handbook of North American Indians*, edited by R. F. Heizer, pp. 37–57. Washington, D.C.: Smithsonian Institution

Emmerich, A. 1977. *Sweat of the sun and tears of the moon*. New York: Hacker

Farb, P. 1968. *Man's rise to civilization as shown by the Indians of North America from primeval times to the coming of the industrial state*. New York: Dutton

Farnsworth, P., J. E. Brady, M. J. DeNiro and R. S. MacNeish 1985. A re-evaluation of the isotopic and archaeological reconstructions of diet in the Tehuacan Valley. *American Antiquity* 50 (1): 102–16

Feldman, R. A. and M. E. Moseley 1983. The northern Andes. In *Ancient South Americans*, edited by J. D. Jennings, pp. 179–239. San Francisco: Freeman

Fell, B. 1976. *America B.C.* New York: Quadrangle/New York Times Book Co.

Fitting, J. E. 1977. Social dimensions of the Paleoindian adaptation in the northeast. In Newman and Salwen, eds., *op. cit.*, pp. 369–74

Fitzhugh, W. 1976. Paleoeskimo occupations of the Labrador coast. In Maxwell, ed., *op. cit.*, pp. 89–102

Fladmark, K. R. 1979. Routes: alternate migration corridors for early man in North America. *American Antiquity* 44 (1): 55–69

Flannery, K. V. 1968a. Archaeological systems theory and early Mesoamerica. In *Anthropological archaeology in the Americas*, edited by B. J. Meggers, pp. 67–87. Washington, D.C.: Anthropological Society of Washington

1968b. The Olmec and the Valley of Oaxaca: a model for inter-regional interaction in Formative times. In *Proceedings, Dumbarton Oaks Conference on the Olamec*, edited by E. P. Benson, pp. 79–110. Washington, D.C.: Dumbarton Oaks

1972. The origins of the village as a settlement type in Mesoamerica and the Near East: a comparative study. In *Man, settlement and urbanism*, edited by P. J. Ucko, R. Tringham and G. W. Dimbleby. London: Duckworth

1973. The origins of agriculture. *Annual Review of Anthropology* 2: 271–310

1976. (editor) *The early Mesoamerican village.* New York: Academic Press

Flannery, K. V., J. Marcus and S. Kowalewski 1981. The Preceramic and Formative of the Valley of Oaxaca. In *Supplement to the handbook of Middle American Indians*, edited by J. A. Sabloff, pp. 48–93. Austin: University of Texas Press

Flenniken, J. J. 1978. Reevaluation of the Lindenmeier Folsom: a replication experiment in lithic technology. *American Antiquity* 43 (3): 473–9

Flinn, L., C. G. Turner II and A. Brew 1976. Additional evidence for cannibalism in the Southwest: the case of LA 4528. *American Antiquity* 41 (3): 308–18

Ford, J. A. 1969. *A comparison of Formative cultures in the Americas: diffusion or the psychic unity of man?* Washington, D.C.: Smithsonian Institution Contributions to Anthropology, 2

Ford, L. T. 1976. Adena sites on Chesapeake Bay. *Archaeology of Eastern North America* 4: 63–89

Ford, R. I. 1974. Northeastern archaeology: past and future directions. *Annual Review of Anthropology* 3: 385–413

1979. Gathering and gardening: trends and consequences of Hopewell subsistence strategies. In *Hopewell Archaeology*, edited by D. Brose and N. Greber, pp. 234–8. Ohio: Kent State University Press

Fowler, M. L. 1971. Agriculture and village settlement in the North American East: the central Mississippi Valley area, a case history. In *Prehistoric agriculture*, edited by S. Struever, pp. 391–403. Garden City, New York: Natural History Press

1975. A Pre-Columbian urban center on the Mississippi. *Scientific American* 233 (2): 93–101

1978. Cahokia and the American Bottom: settlement archaeology. In *Mississippian settlement patterns*, edited by B. D. Smith, pp. 455–78. New York: Academic Press

1980. The temple town community: Cahokia and Amalucan compared. In *Early Native Americans*, edited by D. L. Browman, pp. 391–400. The Hague: Mouton

Fowler, M. L. and R. L. Hall 1978. Late prehistory of the Illinois area. In *Northeast*, vol. 15, *Handbook of North American Indians*, edited by B. G. Trigger, pp. 560–8. Washington, D.C.: Smithsonian Institution

Freidel, D. A. 1979. Culture areas and interaction spheres: contrasting approaches to the emergence of civilization in the Maya lowlands. *American Antiquity* 44 (1): 36–54

Fried, M. H. 1967. *The evolution of political society.* New York: Random House

Frison, G. C. 1978. *Prehistoric hunters of the high plains.* New York: Academic Press

Frison, G. C. and G. M. Zeimens 1980. Bone projectile points: an addition to the Folsom cultural complex. *American Antiquity* 45 (2): 231–7

Frost, F. J. 1982. The Palos Verdes Chinese anchor mystery. *Archaeology* 35 (1): 22–8

Funk, R. E. 1976. *Recent contributions to Hudson Valley prehistory*. Albany: New York State Museum Memoir 22

  1978. Post-Pleistocene adaptations. In *Northeast*, vol. 15, *Handbook of North American Indians*, edited by B. G. Trigger, pp. 16–27. Washington, D.C.: Smithsonian Institution

  1983. The northeastern United States. In *Ancient North Americans*, J. D. Jennings, ed., pp. 303–71. San Francisco: Freeman

Furst, P. T. 1968. The Olmec were-jaguar motif in the light of ethnographic reality. In *Proceedings, Dumbarton Oaks Conference on the Olmec*, edited by E. P. Benson, pp. 143–78. Washington, D.C.: Dumbarton Oaks

Galinat, W. C. 1971. The evolution of corn and culture in North America. In *Prehistoric agriculture*, edited by S. Struever, pp. 534–43. Garden City, New York: Natural History Press

Gardner, W. M. 1977. Flint Run Paleoindian complex and its implications for eastern North American prehistory. In Newman and Salwen, eds., *op. cit.*, pp. 257–64

Gibson, J. L. 1974a. Poverty Point: the first North American chiefdom. *Archaeology* 27 (2): 97–105

  1974b. Aboriginal warfare in the protohistoric Southeast: an alternative perspective. *American Antiquity* 39: 130–3

Giddings, J. L. 1954. Early man in the Arctic. *Scientific American* 190 (6): 82–8

Goodyear, A. C. 1982. The chronological position of the Dalton horizon in the southeastern United States. *American Antiquity* 47 (2): 382–5

Gorman, F. 1972. The Clovis hunters: an alternative view of their environment and ecology. In *Contemporary archaeology*, edited by M. Leone, pp. 206–21. Carbondale: Southern Illinois University Press

Gowlett, J. A. J. 1984. *Ascent to civilization: the archaeology of early man*. New York: Knopf

Graham, R. W., C. V. Haynes, D. L. Johnson and M. Kay 1981. Kimmswick: a Clovis–mastodon association in eastern Missouri. *Science* 213: 1115–17

Gramly, R. M. 1977. Deerskins and hunting territories: competition for a scarce resource of the northeastern woodlands. *American Antiquity* 42: 601–5

  1982. *The Vail site: a Paleo-Indian encampment in Maine*. Buffalo, New York: Bulletin of the Buffalo Society of Natural Sciences, no. 30

  1984. Kill sites, killing ground, and fluted points at the Vail site. *Archaeology of Eastern North America* 12: 110–21

Green, F. E. 1963. The Clovis blades: an important addition to the Llano culture. *American Antiquity* 29: 145–65

Greengo, R. E. 1964. *Issaquena: an archaeological phase of the Yazoo Basin in the lower Mississippi Valley*. Memoirs of the Society for American Archaeology, no. 18

Grenne-Ravits, R. and G. Coleman 1976. The quintessential role of Olmec in the central highlands of Mexico: a refutation. *American Antiquity* 41: 196–205

Griffin, J. B. 1960. Some prehistoric connections between Siberia and America. *Science* 131 (3403): 801–12

  1983. The Midlands. In *Ancient North Americans*, edited by J. D. Jennings, pp. 243–301. San Francisco: Freeman

Grimes, J. R., et al. 1984. Bull Brook II. *Archaeology of Eastern North America* 12: 159–83

Grove, D. C. 1968. Chalcatzingo, Morelos, Mexico: a reappraisal of the Olmec rock carvings. *American Antiquity* 33 (4): 486–91

    1981. The Formative period and the evolution of complex culture. In *Supplement to the Handbook of Middle American Indians: Archaeology*, edited by J. A. Sabloff, pp. 373–91. Austin: University of Texas Press

Grove, D. C., K. C. Hirth, D. E. Buge and A. M. Cyphers 1976. Settlement and cultural development at Chalcatzingo. *Science* 192: 1203–10

Guidon, N. and G. Delibrias 1986. Carbon-14 dates point to man in the Americas 32,000 years ago. *Nature* 321: 769–71

Haberman, T. W. 1984. Evidence for aboriginal tobaccos in eastern North America. *American Antiquity* 49 (2): 269–87

Hall, R. L. 1980. An interpretation of the two-climax model of Illinois prehistory. In *Early Native Americans*, edited by D. L. Browman, pp. 401–62. The Hague: Mouton

Hamblin, R. L. and B. L. Pitcher 1980. The Classic Maya collapse: testing the class conflict hypothesis. *American Antiquity* 45: 246–67

Hammond, N. 1977. The earliest Maya. *Scientific American* 236 (3): 116–33

    1982a. *Ancient Maya civilization*. New Brunswick, New Jersey: Rutgers University Press

    1982b. Unearthing the oldest known Maya. *National Geographic* 162 (1): 126–40

Hammond, N. et al. 1979. The earliest lowland Maya: definition of the Swasey phase. *American Antiquity* 44 (1): 92–110

Hariot, T. 1590. *A briefe and true report of the new found land of Virginia*. London

Harner, M. 1977. The ecological basis for Aztec sacrifice. *American Ethnologist* 4 (1): 117–35

Harp, E. 1983. Pioneer cultures of the Sub-Arctic and the Arctic. In *Ancient North Americans*, edited by J. D. Jennings, pp. 115–47. San Francisco: Freeman

Harris, M. 1968. *The rise of anthropological theory*. New York: Crowell

    1977. *Cannibals and kings*. New York: Random House

    1979. *Cultural materialism: the struggle for a science of culture*. New York: Random House

Harrison, P. D. and B. L. Turner II, editors 1978. *Pre-Hispanic Maya agriculture*. Albuquerque: University of New Mexico Press

Hassan, F. 1980. *Demographic archaeology*. New York: Academic Press

Haury, E. W. 1976. *The Hohokam, desert farmers and craftsmen: excavations at Snaketown 1964–1965*. Tucson: University of Arizona Press

Haviland, W. A. 1969. A new population estimate for Tikal, Guatemala. *American Antiquity* 34 (4): 429–33

Haynes, C. V. 1980. Paleoindian charcoal from Meadowcroft rockshelter: is contamination a problem? *American Antiquity* 45 (3): 582–7

    1982. Were Clovis progenitors in Beringia? In *Paleoecology of Beringia*, edited by D. M. Hopkins et al., pp. 383–98. New York: Academic Press

Haynes, C. V., D. J. Donahue, A. J. T. Jull and T. H. Zabel 1984. Application of accelerator dating to fluted point Paleo-Indian sites. *Archaeology of Eastern North America* 12: 184–91

Heizer, R. F. 1968. New observations on La Venta. In *Proceedings, Dumbarton Oaks Conference on the Olmec*, edited by E. P. Benson. Washington, D.C.: Dumbarton Oaks

1978. (editor) *California*, vol. 8, *Handbook of North American Indians*. Washington, D.C.: Smithsonian Institution

Heizer, R. F. and A. B. Elsasser 1980. *The natural world of the California Indians*. Berkeley: University of California Press

Helms, M. W. 1979. *Ancient Panama: chiefs in search of power*. Austin: University of Texas Press

Henderson, J. S. 1981. *The world of the ancient Maya*. Ithaca: Cornell University Press

Heyerdahl, T. 1971. *The Ra expeditions*. Garden City, New York: Doubleday

Hopkins, D. M., J. V. Matthews, Jr., C. E. Schweger and S. B. Young, editors 1982. *Paleoecology of Beringia*. New York: Academic Press

Howells, W. W. 1973. *Cranial variation in man: a study by multivariate analysis of patterns of difference among recent human populations*. Papers of the Peabody Museum, no. 67

Irwin, H. T. 1975. The far west. In *North America*, edited by S. Gorenstein, pp. 133–64. New York: St Martin's Press

Irwin-Williams, C. 1967. Picosa: the elementary Southwestern culture. *American Antiquity* 32 (4): 441–55

1968. (editor) *Early man in western North America*. Eastern New Mexico University Contributions in Anthropology 1 (4)

Isaac, E. 1970. *Geography of domestication*. Englewood Cliffs, New Jersey: Prentice-Hall

Isbell, W. H. 1978. The prehistoric ground drawings of Peru. *Scientific American* 239 (4): 140–53

1981. Comment on Conrad. *American Antiquity* 46 (1): 27–30

Isbell, W. H. and K. J. Schreiber 1978. Was Huari a state? *American Antiquity* 43 (3): 372–90

Jefferson, T. 1801. *Notes on the state of Virginia*. London: John Stockdale (reprinted, Chapel Hill: University of North Carolina Press, 1954)

Jennings, J. D. 1974. *Prehistory of North America*, 2nd edition. New York: McGraw-Hill

1983a. (editor) *Ancient North Americans*. San Francisco: Freeman

1983b. (editor) *Ancient South Americans*. San Francisco: Freeman

Jett, S. C. 1983. Precolumbian transoceanic contacts. In *Ancient North Americans*, edited by J. D. Jennings, pp. 557–613. San Francisco: Freeman

Julien, C. J. 1982. Inca decimal administration in the Lake Titicaca region. In *The Inca and Aztec states 1400–1800: anthropology and history*, edited by G. A. Collier, R. I. Rosaldo and J. D. Wirth, pp. 119–51. New York: Academic Press

Kaplan, L. 1971. Archeology and domestication in American *Phaseolus* (beans). In *Prehistoric agriculture*, edited by S. Struever, pp. 516–33. Garden City, New York: Natural History Press

Kauffman, B. E. 1977. Preliminary analysis of seeds from the Shawnee-Minisink site. MS, American University

Kay, M., F. B. King and C. K. Robinson 1980. Curcurbits from Phillips Spring: new evidence and interpretations. *American Antiquity* 45 (4): 806–22

Kidder, A. V. 1924. *An introduction to the study of Southwestern archaeology, with a preliminary account of the excavations at Pecos.* New Haven: Yale University Press

King, C. 1978. Protohistoric and historic archaeology. In *California*, edited by R. F. Heizer, pp. 58–79. Washington, D.C.: Smithsonian Institution

King, L. 1969. The Medea Creek cemetery (LAn–243): an investigation of social organization from mortuary practices. *UCLA Archaeological Survey Annual Report* 11: 23–68

King, T. F. 1976. *Political differentiation among hunter–gatherers: an archaeological test.* Unpublished Ph.D. thesis, University of California, Riverside

1978. Don't that beat the band? Non-egalitarian political organization in prehistoric central California. In *Social archaeology, beyond subsistence and dating*, edited by C. Redman et al., pp. 77–112. New York: Academic Press

Klein, R. G. 1974. Ice age hunters of the Ukraine. *Scientific American* 230 (6): 96–105

Kolata, A. L. 1983. The South Andes. In *Ancient South Americans*, edited by J. D. Jennings, pp. 241–85. San Francisco: Freeman

Kowaleski, S. A. 1980. Population–resource balances in period I of Oaxaca, Mexico. *American Antiquity* 45: 151–65

Kraft, H. C. 1977. Paleoindians in New Jersey. In Newman and Salwen, eds., *op. cit.*

Krieger, A. D. 1964. Early man in the New World. In *Prehistoric man in the New World*, edited by J. D. Jennings and E. Norbeck, pp. 23–84. Chicago: University of Chicago Press

Kroeber, A. L. 1925. *Handbook of the Indians of California.* Bureau of American Ethnology Bulletin no. 78

Kus, J. S. 1984. The Chicama-Moche canal: failure or success? An alternative explanation for an incomplete canal. *American Antiquity* 49 (2): 408–15

La Barre, W. 1972. *The ghost dance.* New York: Delta

La Fay, H. 1975. The Maya, children of time. *National Geographic* 148 (6): 729–67

Lahren, L. and R. Bonnichsen 1974. Bone foreshafts from a Clovis burial in southwestern Montana. *Science* 186: 147–50

Lanning, E. P. 1967. *Peru before the Incas.* Englewood Cliffs, New Jersey: Prentice-Hall

1974a. Western South America. In *Prehispanic America*, edited by S. Gorenstein, pp. 65–86. New York: St Martin's Press

1974b. Eastern South America. In Gorenstein, ed., *op. cit.*, pp. 87–109

Larson, L. H. 1971. Archaeological implications of social stratification at the Etowah site, Georgia. In *Approaches to the social dimensions of mortuary practices*, edited by J. A. Brown. Memoirs of the Society for American Archaeology, no. 25

1972. Functional considerations of warfare in the Southeast during the Mississippian period. *American Antiquity* 37: 383–92

Lathrap, D. W. 1958. The culture sequence at Yarinacocha, eastern Peru. *American Antiquity* 23 (4): 379–88

1970. *The upper Amazon*. New York: Praeger

1977. Our father the cayman, our mother the gourd: Spinden revisited, or a unitary model for the emergence of agriculture in the New World. In *Origins of agriculture*, edited by C. A. Reed, pp. 713–50. The Hague: Mouton

Lathrap, D. W., J. G. Marcos and J. Zeidler 1977. Real Alto: an ancient ceremonial center. *Archaeology* 30 (1): 2–13

Laughlin, W. S. 1966. Eskimos and Aleuts: their origin and evolution. In *New roads to yesterday*, edited by J. R. Caldwell, pp. 247–67. New York: Basic Books

Lee, R. B. and I. De Vore, editors 1968. *Man the hunter*. Chicago: Aldine

Lévi-Strauss, C. 1967. *Structural anthropology*. New York: Doubleday

Lightfoot, K. G. and G. M. Feinman 1982. Social differentiation and leadership development in early pithouse villages in the Mogollon region of the American Southwest. *American Antiquity* 47 (1): 64–86

Lipe, W. D. 1983. The Southwest. In *Ancient North Americans*, edited by J. D. Jennings, pp. 421–93. San Francisco: Freeman

Lippi, R. N., R. M. Bird and D. M. Stemper 1984. Maize recovered at La Ponga, an early Ecuadorian site. *American Antiquity* 49 (1): 118–24

Llagostera Martinez, A. 1979. 9,700 years of maritime subsistence on the Pacific coast of Chile. *American Antiquity* 44: 309–24

Longacre, W. A. 1964. Archaeology as anthropology: a case study. *Science* 144 (3625): 1454–5

Lyman, R. L. 1984. Broken bones, bone expediency tools, and bone pseudotools: lessons from the blast zone around Mount St. Helens, Washington. *American Antiquity* 49 (2): 315–33

Lynch, T. F. 1980. *Guitarrero cave: early man in the Andes*. New York: Academic Press

1983. The Paleo-Indians. In *Ancient South Americans*, edited by J. D. Jennings, pp. 87–137. San Francisco: Freeman

MacDonald, G. F. 1968. *Debert: a Paleo-Indian site in central Nova Scotia*. Ottawa: National Museum of Canada Anthropological Papers no. 16

MacGowan, K. and J. A. Hester 1962. *Early man in the New World*. New York: Doubleday

MacNeish, R. S. 1964. Ancient Mesoamerican civilization. *Science* 143: 531–7

1971. Early man in the Andes. *Scientific American* 224 (4): 36–46

1972. The evolution of community patterns in the Tehuacan Valley of Mexico and speculations about the cultural processes. In *Man, settlement and urbanism*, edited by P. Ucko, R. Tringham and G. Dimbleby. London: Duckworth

1977. The beginning of agriculture in central Peru. In *Origins of agriculture*, edited by C. A. Reed. The Hague: Mouton

1978. *The science of archaeology?* Scituate, Massachusetts: Duxbury Press

Madsen, D. B. 1975. Dating Paiute-Shoshone expansion in the Great Basin. *American Antiquity* 40 (1): 82–6

1979. The Fremont and the Sevier: defining prehistoric agriculturalists north of the Anasazi. *American Antiquity* 44 (4): 711–22

Madsen, D. B. and M. S. Berry 1975. A reassessment of northeastern Great Basin prehistory. *American Antiquity* 40 (4): 391–405

Mangelsdorf, P. C., R. S. MacNeish and W. C. Galinat 1964. Domestication of corn. *Science* 143 (3606): 538–45

Marcus, J. 1983. Lowland Maya archaeology at the crossroads. *American Antiquity* 48 (3): 454–88

Marshall, S. B. 1986. Paleo-Indian artifact form and function. In *The Shawnee-Minisink site: archaeology in the Delaware Valley*, edited by C. W. McNett. New York: Academic Press

Martin, P. S. 1973. The discovery of America. *Science* 179: 969–74

1982. The pattern and meaning of Holarctic mammoth extinction. In *Paleo-ecology of Beringia*, edited by D. M. Hopkins et al., pp. 399–408. New York: Academic Press

Martin, P. S. and H. E. Wright, editors 1967. *Pleistocene extinctions*. New Haven: Yale University Press

Martin, P. S. and F. Plog 1973. *The archaeology of Arizona*. Garden City, New York: Natural History press

Matheny, R. T. 1976. Maya lowland hydraulic systems. *Science* 193: 639–46

Matos Moctezuma, E. 1980. New finds in the Great Temple. *National Geographic* 158 (6): 767–75

Matsuzawa, T. 1978. The Formative site of Las Haldas, Peru: architecture, chronology, and economy (translated by I. Shimada). *American Antiquity* 43 (4): 652–73

Maxwell, M. S. 1976. editor *Eastern Arctic prehistory: Paleoeskimo problems*. Society for American Archaeology Memoir no. 31

1980. Archaeology of the Arctic and Subarctic zones. *Annual Review of Anthropology* 9: 161–85

McDowell, B. 1980. The Aztecs. *National Geographic* 158 (6): 704–52

McEwen, G. F. and D. B. Dickson 1978. Valdivia, Jomon fishermen, and the nature of the North Pacific: some nautical problems with Meggers, Evans, and Estrada's (1965) transoceanic contact hypothesis. *American Antiquity* 43 (4): 362–71

McGhee, R. 1976. Paleoeskimo occupations of central and high Arctic Canada. In *Eastern Arctic prehistory: Paleoeskimo problems*, edited by M. S. Maxwell, pp. 15–39. Society for American Archaeology Memoir no. 31

1984. Contact between native North Americans and the medieval Norse: a review of the evidence. *American Antiquity* 49 (1): 4–26

McGhee, R. and J. A. Tuck 1976. Un-dating the Canadian Arctic. In *Eastern Arctic prehistory: Paleoeskimo problems*, edited by M. S. Maxwell, pp. 6–14. Society for American Archaeology Memoir no. 31

McIntyre, L. 1975. Mystery of the ancient Nazca lines. *National Geographic* 147 (5): 716–28

McNeill, W. H. 1976. *Plagues and peoples*. Garden City, New York: Anchor Press

McNett, C. W., S. B. Marshall and E. E. McDowell 1975. Second season of the upper Delaware Valley early man project (report for National Geographic Society and National Science Foundation)

McNett, C. W., J. Evans and R. J. Dent 1977. Third and fourth seasons of the upper Delaware Valley early man project 1976–7 (Report for National Geographic Society and National Science Foundation)

References

Mead, J. I. 1980. Is it really that old? A comment about the Meadowcroft rock-shelter "overview". *American Antiquity* 45 (3): 579–81

Meggers, B. J. 1971. *Amazonia: man and culture in a counterfeit paradise*. Chicago: Aldine

1975. The transpacific origins of Mesoamerican civilization: a preliminary review of the evidence and its theoretical implications. *American Anthropologist* 77 (1): 1–27

1979. Climatic oscillation as a factor in the prehistory of Amazonia. *American Antiquity* 44: 252–66

Meggers, B. J. and C. Evans 1969. A transpacific contact in 3000 B.C. *Scientific American* 214 (1): 28–35

1983. Lowland South America and the Antilles. In *Ancient South Americans*, edited by J. D. Jennings, pp. 287–335. San Francisco: Freeman

Meyers, J. T. 1971. The origins of agriculture: an evaluation of three hypotheses. In *Prehistoric agriculture*, edited by S. Struever, pp. 101–21. Garden City, New York: Natural History Press

Michael, H. N. 1984. Absolute chronologies of Late Pleistocene and Early Holocene cultures of northeastern Asia. *Arctic Anthropology* 21 (2): 69–80

Millon, R. F. 1967. Teotihuacán. *Scientific American* 216 (6): 38–48

1973. *Urbanization at Teotihuacán, Mexico, vol. 1, the Teotihuacán map*. Austin: University of Texas Press

1981. Teotihuacán: city, state, and civilization. In *Supplement to the handbook of Middle American Indians: Archaeology*, edited by J. A. Sabloff, pp. 198–243. Austin: University of Texas Press

Mochanov, Y. 1977. *Drevneishie etapy Zaseleniia chelonekom severovostochnoi Azii*. Novosibirsk: Nauka

1980. Early migrations to America in the light of a study of the Dyuktai Paleolithic culture in Northeast Asia. In *Early Native Americans*, edited by D. Browman, pp. 119–31. The Hague: Mouton

Molina Montes, A. F. 1980. The building of Tenochtitlán. *National Geographic* 158 (6): 753–65

Morgan, L. H. 1877. *Ancient society*. New York: Henry Holt

Morlan, R. E. and J. Cinq-Mars 1982. Ancient Beringians: human occupation in the late Pleistocene of Alaska and the Yukon territory. In *Paleoecology of Beringia*, edited by D. M. Hopkins et al., pp. 353–81. New York: Academic Press

Morris, C. 1982. The infrastructure of Inka control in the Peruvian central highlands. In *The Inca and Aztec states 1400–1800: anthropology and history*, edited by G. A. Collier, R. I. Rosaldo and J. D. Wirth, pp. 153–71. New York: Academic Press

Moseley, M. E. 1975a. *The maritime foundations of Andean civilization*. Menlo Park, California: Cummings

1975b. Prehistoric principles of labor organization in the Moche Valley, Peru. *American Antiquity* 40: 191–6

1983a. Central Andean civilization. In *Ancient South Americans*, edited by J. D. Jennings, pp. 179–239. San Francisco: Freeman

371

1983b. The good old days *were* better: agrarian collapse and tectonics. *American Anthropologist* 85 (4): 773–99

Moseley, M. E. and C. Mackey 1973. Chan Chan: Peru's ancient city of kings. *National Geographic* 152: 319–45

Muller, J. 1983. The Southeast. In *Ancient North Americans*, edited by J. D. Jennings, pp. 373–419. San Francisco: Freeman

Müller-Beck, H. 1967. On migrations of hunters across the Bering land bridge in the Upper Pleistocene. In *The Bering land bridge*, edited by D. M. Hopkins, pp. 373–408. Stanford, California: Stanford University Press

1982. Late Pleistocene man in northern Eurasia and the mammoth-steppe biome. In *Paleoecology of Beringia*, edited by D. M. Hopkins et al., pp. 329–52. New York: Academic Press

Munson, P. J., P. W. Parmalee and R. A. Yarnell 1971. Subsistence ecology of Scovill, a terminal Middle Woodland village. *American Antiquity* 36: 410–31

Murra, J. V. 1982. The mit'a obligations of ethnic groups to the Inka state. In *The Inca and Aztec states 1400–1800: anthropology and history*, edited by G. A. Collier, R. I. Rosaldo and J. D. Wirth, pp. 237–62. New York: Academic Press

Myers, T. P., M. R. Voorhies and R. G. Corner 1980. Spiral fractures and bone pseudotools at paleontological sites. *American Antiquity* 45 (3): 483–9

Nelson, D. E., R. E. Morlan, J. S. Vogel, J. R. Southon and C. R. Harrington 1986. New dates on northern Yukon artifacts: Holocene not Upper Pleistocene. *Science* 232 (4751): 749–50

Newman, W. S. and B. Salwen, editors 1977. *Amerinds and their paleoenvironments in northeastern North America*. Annals of the New York Academy of Sciences vol. 288

Nichols, D. L. 1982. A Middle Formative irrigation system near Santa Clara Coatitlan in the Basin of Mexico. *American Antiquity* 47 (1): 133–44

Niederberger, C. 1979. Early sedentary economy in the Basin of Mexico. *Science* 203: 131–46

O'Brien, P. J. 1972. Urbanism, Cahokia, and Middle Mississippian. *Archaeology* 25 (3): 188–97

Ortiz, A., editor 1979. *Southwest*, vol. 9, *Handbook of North American Indians*. Washington, D.C.: Smithsonian Institution

Ortloff, R., M. E. Moseley and R. A. Feldman 1983. The Chicama-Moche inter-valley canal: social explanations and physical paradigms. *American Antiquity* 48 (2): 375–89

Palerm, A. 1955. The agricultural basis of urban civilization in Mesoamerica. In *Irrigation civilizations: a comparative study*, edited by J. Steward, pp. 28–42. Washington, D.C.: Pan American Union, Social Science Monographs 1

Parsons, J. J. and W. M. Denevan 1967. Pre-Columbian ridged fields. *Scientific American* 217: 92–100

Parsons, M. 1970. Preceramic subsistence on the Peruvian coast. *American Antiquity* 35: 292–303

Patterson, T. C. 1971. The emergence of food production in central Peru. In *Prehistoric agriculture*, edited by S. Struever, pp. 181–207. Garden City, New York: Natural History Press

Paulsen, A. C. 1981. The archaeology of the absurd: comments on "Cultural materialism, split inheritance, and the expansion of ancient Peruvian empires". *American Antiquity* 46 (1): 31–7

Peebles, C. S. 1971. Moundville and surrounding sites: some structural consider-ations of mortuary practices, II. In *Approaches to the social dimensions of mortuary practices*, edited by J. A. Brown. Society for American Archaeology Memoir no. 25

1978. Determinants of settlement size and location in the Moundville phase. In *Mississippian settlement patterns*, edited by B. D. Smith, pp. 369–416. New York: Academic Press

Peterson, D. A., Jr. 1980. The introduction, use, and technology of fiber-tempered pottery in the southeastern United States. In *Early Native Americans*, edited by D. Browman, pp. 363–73. The Hague: Mouton

Pickersgill, B. and C. B. Heiser 1977. Origins and distribution of plants domesti-cated in the New World tropics. In *Origins of agriculture*, edited by C. A. Reed, pp. 803–35. The Hague: Mouton

Powers, W. R., editor 1975. Current research: Siberia. *American Antiquity* 40 (3): 370–2

Pozorski, T. 1980. The Early Horizon site of Huaca de los Reyes: societal impli-cations. *American Antiquity* 45 (1): 100–10

Price, B. J. 1971. Prehispanic irrigation agriculture in nuclear America. *Latin American Research Review* 6 (3): 3–60

Price, J. E. 1978. The settlement pattern of the Powers phase. In *Mississippian settle-ment patterns*, edited by B. D. Smith, pp. 201–32. New York: Academic Press

Proskouriakoff, T. 1960. Historical implications of a pattern of dates at Piedras Negras, Guatemala. *American Antiquity* 25 (4): 454–75

1961. The lords of the Maya realm. *Expedition* 4 (1): 14–21

1968. Olmec and Maya art: problems of their stylistic relation. In *Proceedings, Dumbarton Oaks Conference on the Olmec*, edited by E. Benson, pp. 119–34. Washington, D.C.: Dumbarton Oaks

Prufer, O. H. 1964. The Hopewell cult. *Scientific American* 211: 90–102

Quilter, J. and T. Stocker 1983. Subsistence economies and the origins of Andean complex societies. *American Anthropologist* 85 (3): 545–62

Quirarte, J. 1977. Early art styles of Mesoamerica and Early Classic Maya art. In *The origins of Maya civilization*, edited by R. E. W. Adams, pp. 249–83. Albuquerque: University of New Mexico Press

Rathje, W. L. 1971. The origin and development of lowland Classic Maya civiliz-ation. *American Antiquity* 36 (3): 275–85

Raymond, J. S. 1981. The maritime foundations of Andean civilization: a recon-sideration of the evidence. *American Antiquity* 46 (4): 806–21

Rick, J. W. 1980. *Prehistoric hunters of the high Andes*. New York: Academic Press

Ritchie, W. A. 1965. *The archaeology of New York state*. Garden City, New York: Natural History Press

Roosevelt, A. C. 1980. *Parmana: prehistoric maize and manioc subsistence along the Amazon and Orinoco*. New York: Academic Press

Rothschild, N. A. 1979. Mortuary behavior and social organization at Indian Knoll and Dickson Mounds. *American Antiquity* 44 (4): 658–75

Rounds, J. 1982. Dynastic succession and the centralization of power in

Tenochtitlán. In *The Inca and Aztec states 1400–1800*, edited by G. A. Collier, R. I. Rosaldo and J. D. Wirth, pp. 63–89. New York: Academic Press

Rouse, I. 1962. Southwestern archaeology today. Introduction to Kidder *op. cit.*, 2nd edition, pp. 1–53. New Haven: Yale University Press

Rowe, J. H. 1967. Form and meaning in Chavín art. In *Peruvian archaeology: selected readings*, edited by J. H. Rowe and D. Menzel, pp. 72–103. Palo Alto, California: Peek

1982. Inca policies and institutions relating to the cultural unification of the empire. In *The Inca and Aztec states 1400–1800*, edited by G. A. Collier, R. I. Rosaldo and J. D. Wirth, pp. 93–118. New York: Academic Press

Rowlett, R. M. 1982. 1,000 years of New World archaeology. *American Antiquity* 47 (3): 652–4

Ruz-Lhuillier, A. 1953. The pyramid tomb of a prince of Palenque. *Illustrated London News* 223 (5967): 321–3

Sabloff, J. A. and W. L. Rathje 1975. The rise of a Maya merchant class. *Scientific American* 233 (4): 73–82

Sanders, W. T. 1977. Environmental heterogeneity and the evolution of lowland Maya civilization. In *The origins of Maya civilization*, edited by R. E. W. Adams, pp. 287–98. Albuquerque: University of New Mexico Press

1981. Ecological adaptation in the Basin of Mexico, 23,000 B.C. to the present. In *Supplement to the handbook of Middle American Indians: Archaeology*, edited by J. A. Sabloff, pp. 147–98. Austin: University of Texas Press

Sanders, W. T. and J. Marino 1970. *New World prehistory: archaeology of the American Indian*. Englewood Cliffs, New Jersey: Prentice-Hall

Sanders, W. T., J. R. Parsons and R. J. Santley 1979. *The Basin of Mexico: ecological processes in the evolution of a civilization*. New York: Academic press

Sanders, W. T. and B. J. Price 1968. *Mesoamerica: the evolution of a civilization*. New York: Random House

Santley, R. S. 1980. Disembedded capitals reconsidered. *American Antiquity* 45: 132–45

Sauer, C. O. 1952. *Agricultural origins and dispersals*. New York: American Geographical Society

Scarborough, V. L. 1983. A Preclassic Maya water system. *American Antiquity* 48 (4): 720–44

Schaafsma, P. and C. F. Schaafsma 1974. Evidence for the origins of the Pueblo Katchina cult as suggested by Southwestern rock art. *American Antiquity* 39 (4): 535–45

Schoenwetter, J. 1974. Pollen records of Guila Naquitz cave. *American Antiquity* 39 (2): 292–303

Service, E. R. 1962. *Primitive social organization*. New York: Random House
1975. *Origins of the state and civilization*. New York: Norton

Sherratt, A., editor 1980. *The Cambridge encyclopedia of archaeology*. New York: Crown

Silverberg, R. 1968. *Mound builders of ancient America: the archaeology of a myth*. Greenwich, Connecticut: New York Graphic Society

Smith, B. D., editor 1978. *Mississippian settlement patterns*. New York: Academic Press

Snarskis, M. J. 1979. Turrialba: a Paleo-Indian quarry and workshop site in eastern Costa Rica. *American Antiquity* 44 (1): 125–38

Snow, D. R. 1976. *Archaeology of North America*. New York: Viking
  1980. *The archaeology of New England*. New York: Academic Press

Stanford, D. 1979. Bison kill by ice age hunters. *National Geographic* 155 (1): 114–21

Stark, B. L. 1981. The rise of sedentary life. In *Supplement to the Handbook of Middle American Indians: Archaeology*, edited by J. A. Sabloff, pp. 48–93. Austin: University of Texas Press

Stark, B. L. and B. Voorhies, editors 1978. *Prehistoric coastal adaptations*. New York: Academic Press

Steponaitis, V. 1978. Location theory and complex chiefdoms: a Mississippian example. In *Mississippian settlement patterns*, edited by B. D. Smith, pp. 417–54. New York: Academic Press

Steward, J. H. 1938. *Basin–Plateau aboriginal socio-political groups*. Bureau of American Ethnology Bulletin no. 120
  1955. *Theory of culture change*. Urbana: University of Illinois Press

Stocker, T., S. Meltzoff and S. Armsey 1980. Crocodilians and Olmecs: further interpretations in Formative period iconography. *American Antiquity* 45 (4): 740–58

Stoltman, J. B. 1978. Temporal models in prehistory: an example from eastern North America. *Current Anthropology* 19 (4): 703–6

Stoltman, J. B. and D. A. Baerreis 1983. The evolution of human ecosystems in the eastern United States. In *Late Quaternary environments of the United States*, vol. 2, *The Holocene*, edited by H. E. Wright, pp. 252–68. Minneapolis: University of Minnesota Press

Stothert, K. E. 1985. The preceramic Las Vegas culture of coastal Ecuador. *American Antiquity* 50 (3): 613–37

Struever, S. 1962. Implications of vegetal remains from an Illinois Hopewell site. *American Antiquity* 27 (4): 584–7
  1964. The Hopewell interaction sphere in riverine–western Great lakes culture history. In *Hopewellian studies*, edited by J. Caldwell and R. Hall. Springfield: Illinois State Museum Scientific Papers no. 12

Struever, S. and F. A. Holton 1979. *Koster: Americans in search of their past*. New York: Anchor/Doubleday

Struever, S. and K. D. Vickery 1973. The beginnings of cultivation in the Midwest–riverine area of the United States. *American Anthropologist* 75 (5): 1197–220

Stuart, G. E. 1972. Who were the Mound Builders? *National Geographic* 142 (6): 783–802
  1975. Riddle of the glyphs. *National Geographic* 148 (6): 768–91

Suttles, W. 1968. Coping with abundance: subsistence on the Northwest Coast. In *Man the hunter*, edited by R. B. Lee and I. DeVore, pp. 56–68. Chicago: Aldine

Swanson, E. H., W. Bray and I. Farrington 1975. *The New World*. Elsevier: Phaidon

Tainter, J. A. 1980. Behavior and status in a Middle Woodland mortuary population from the Illinois Valley. *American Antiquity* 45 (2): 308–12

Taylor, R. E., et al. 1985. Major revisions in the Pleistocene age assignments for North American human skeletons by C-14 accelerator mass spectrometry: none older than 11,000 C-14 years B.P. *American Antiquity* 50 (1): 136–40

Thomas, D. H. 1973. An empirical test of Steward's model of Great Basin settlement patterns. *American Antiquity* 38: 155–76

Tolstoy, P. 1974a. Mesoamerica. In *Prehispanic America*, edited by S. Gorenstein, pp. 29–74. New York: St Martin's Press

    1974b. Transoceanic diffusion and nuclear America. In *Prehispanic America*, edited by S. Gorenstein, pp. 124–44. New York: St Martin's Press

    1979. The Olmec in the central highlands: a non-quintessential approach. *American Antiquity* 44 (2): 333–7

Tuck, J. A. 1970. An Archaic Indian cemetery in Newfoundland. *Scientific American* 222 (6): 112–21

    1975. *An Archaic sequence from the Strait of Belle Isle, Labrador*. National Museum of Man Mercury Series, Archaeological Survey of Canada, no. 34

    1976a. *Ancient people of Port au Choix: the excavation of an Archaic Indian cemetery in Newfoundland*. Memorial University of Newfoundland Social and Economic Studies no. 17

    1976b. Paleoeskimo cultures of northern Labrador. In *eastern Arctic prehistory: Paleoeskimo problems*, edited by M. S. Maxwell, pp. 89–102. Society for American Archaeology Memoir no. 31

    1978a. Regional cultural development, 3000 to 300 B.C. In *Northeast*, vol. 15, *Handbook of North American Indians*, ed. B. G. Trigger, pp. 28–43. Washington, D.C.: Smithsonian Institution

    1978b. Northern Iroquoian prehistory. In *Northeast*, vol. 15, *Handbook of North American Indians*, ed. B. G. Trigger, pp. 322–33. Washington, D.C.: Smithsonian Institution

Tuck, J. A. and R. McGhee 1976. An Archaic Indian burial mound in Labrador. *Scientific American* 235 (5): 122–9

Turner, C. G. II 1978. Dental caries and early Ecuadorian agriculture. *American Antiquity* 43 (4): 694–7

    1983. Dental evidence for the peopling of the Americas. In *Early Man in the New World*, edited by R. Shutler, pp. 147–58. Beverley Hills: Sage Publications

    1986. Dentochronological separation estimates for Pacific Rim populations. *Science* 232 (4754): 1140–2

Vivian, R. G. 1970. An inquiry into prehistoric social organization in Chaco Canyon, New Mexico. In *Reconstructing prehistoric Pueblo societies*, edited by W. A. Longacre, pp. 59–83. Albuquerque: University of New Mexico Press

Wallace, W. J. 1978. Post-Pleistocene archeology, 9000–2000 B.C. In *California*, vol. 8, *Handbook of North American Indians*, edited by R. F. Heizer, pp. 25–36. Washington, D.C.: Smithsonian Institution

Walthall, J. A. 1980. *Prehistoric Indians of the Southeast: archaeology of Alabama and the Middle South*. University, Alabama: University of Alabama Press

Washburn, D. K. 1975. The American Southwest. In *North America*, edited by S. Gorenstein, pp. 103–32. New York: St Martin's Press

Webb, C. H. 1968. The extent and content of Poverty Point culture. *American Antiquity* 33: 297–331

Webb, S. D., J. Milanich, R. Alexon and J. S. Dunbar 1984. A *Bison antiquus* kill site, Wacissa River, Jefferson County, Florida. *American Antiquity* 49 (2): 384–92

Webb, W. S. 1946. *Indian Knoll site, Oh 2, Ohio County, Kentucky*. University of Kentucky Reports in Archaeology and Anthropology 4 (3): 115–365

Webster, D. L. 1977. Warfare and the evolution of Maya civilization. In *The origins of Maya civilization*, edited by R. Adams, pp. 335–71. Albuquerque: University of New Mexico Press

Wedel, W. R. 1961. *Prehistoric man on the Great Plains*. Norman: University of Oklahoma Press

    1983. The prehistoric Plains. In *Ancient North Americans*, edited by J. D. Jennings, pp. 203–41. San Francisco: Freeman

West, F. H. 1980. Late Paleolithic cultures in Alaska. In *Early Native Americans*, edited by D. Browman, pp. 162–87. The Hague: Mouton

Wheat, J. B. 1972. *The Olsen-Chubbuck site: a Paleo-Indian bison kill*. Society for American Archaeology Memoir no. 26

Willey, G. R. 1966. *An introduction to American archaeology*, vol. 1, *North and Middle America*. Englewood Cliffs, New Jersey: Prentice-Hall

    1971. *An introduction to American archaeology*, vol. 2, *South America*. Englewood Cliffs, New Jersey: Prentice-Hall

Willey, G. R. and P. Phillips 1958. *Method and theory in American archaeology*. Chicago: University of Chicago Press

Willey, G. R. and J. Sabloff 1980. *A history of American archaeology*, 2nd edition. San Francisco: Freeman

Wilmsen, E. N. 1968. Lithic analysis in paleoanthropology. *Science* 161: 982–7

    1974. *Lindenmeier: a Pleistocene hunting society*. New York: Harper and Row

Wilson, D. 1981. Of maize and men: a critique of the maritime hypothesis of state origins on the coast of Peru. *American Anthropologist* 86 (2): 358–68

Wing, E. 1977. Animal domestication in the Andes. In *Origins of agriculture*, edited by C. A. Reed, pp. 837–59. The Hague: Mouton

Winters, H. D. 1968. Value systems and trade cycles of the Late Archaic in the Midwest. In *New Perspectives in archeology*, edited by S. R. Binford and L. R. Binford, pp. 175–221. Chicago: Aldine

Wissler, C., editor 1909. *The Indians of greater New York and the lower Hudson*. Anthropological Papers of the American Museum of Natural History, vol. 3

Wittfogel, K. A. 1957. *Oriental despotism*. New Haven: Yale University Press

Woodbury, R. B. and E. B. W. Zubrow 1979. Agricultural beginnings, 2000 B.C.– A.D. 500. In *Southwest*, vol. 9, *Handbook of North American Indians*, edited by A. Ortiz, pp. 43–60. Washington, D.C.: Smithsonian Institution

Workman, W. B., editor 1980. Current research (northern interior Canada). *American Antiquity* 45 (1): 194

Yarnell, R. A. 1965. Early Woodland plant remains and the question of cultivation. *Florida Anthropologist* 18 (2): 78–81

1977. Native plant husbandry north of Mexico. In *Origins of agriculture*, edited by C. A. Reed, pp. 861–75. The Hague: Mouton

Yi, S. and G. Clark 1983. Observations on the Lower Paleolithic of Northeast Asia. *Current Anthropology* 24 (2): 181–202

1985. The "Dyuktai culture" and New World origins. *Current Anthropology* 26 (1): 1–20

Zeitlin, R. N. 1984. A summary report on three sessions of field investigations into the Archaic period prehistory of lowland Belize. *American Anthropologist* 86 (2): 358–68

Zevallos, M. C. et al. 1977. The San Pablo corn kernel and its friends. *Science* 196 (4288): 385–89

Author index

Adams, R. M., 305
Adovasio, J. M., 53, 67, 110, 125
Aikens, C. M., 116, 118–22, 124, 126, 127
Ames, K. M., 114, 130
Anderson, D. D., 143
Andrews, G. F., 288
Arundale, W. H., 145
Asch, D. L. and N. B., 110
Ashburn, P. M., 355

Bader, O., 31
Baerreis, D. A., 235
Ball, J. W., 282
Bankes, G., 339
Baumhoff, M., 124, 177
Beadle, G. W., 171
Bean, L. J., 137
Bender, B., 97
Bender, M. M., 235
Berry, M. S., 115, 121
Bettinger, R. L., 124, 177
Binford, L. R., 18, 164
Bird, J., 43, 188, 191
Bird, R. M., 180
Birdsell, J. B., 40, 42
Bischof, H., 182
Blanton, R. E., 269
Boas, F., 41
Bonnichsen, R., 71
Brennan, L. A., 93
Brose, D. S., 244
Brown, K. L., 80
Brumfiel, E. M., 303
Bryan, A. L., 81, 343
Burger, R. L., 319
Butzer, K. W., 46
Byers, D. S., 166

Calnek, E. E., 303
Campbell, J. M., 70, 144, 146, 154
Canby, T. Y., 64, 71, 210, 212, 214, 219
Carlisle, R. C., 53, 67, 110
Carneiro, R., 227, 248, 282
Carter, G. F., 161, 340
Caso, A., 300
Chard, C. S., 35
Chomko, S. A., 107, 110
Cinq-Mars, J., 52, 58
Clark, A. M., 57

Clark, D., 57
Clark, G., 35
Coe, J. L., 66, 108
Coe, M. D., 262, 264–9, 276, 279, 284, 285, 298, 303
Cohen, M. N., 95, 163, 164, 189, 190, 192, 318
Coleman, G., 271
Coles, J. M., 36
Conrad, G. W., 334
Cook, S. F., 306
Cooke, R. G., 313
Cordell, L. S., 144, 146, 154
Corner, R. G., 52
Cowgill, G., 95
Cowgill, U., 280
Crawford, G. W., 107, 110
Culbert, T. P., 284, 294
Curran, M. L., 64

Dahlin, B. A., 286
Damp, J., 180
Davies, N., 303
Davis, W., 265
DeBoer, W. R., 193
Deetz, J., 259
Delibrias, G., 79
Denevan, W. M., 200, 355
DeVore, I., 49, 70
Diaz, B., 355
Dickson, D. B., 182, 248, 251
Diehl, R. A., 296
Dikov, N. N., 38
Dillehay, T. D., 79
Dincauze, D. F., 66, 91
Disselhoff, H., 325
Doyel, D. E., 205
Dragoo, D. W., 97, 231, 233, 234
Drucker, P., 132
Dumond, D. E., 37, 58, 128, 143, 154, 280

Ekholm, G. F., 340, 341
Elsasser, A. B., 133, 134
Emmerich, A., 299
Evans, C., 182, 196–8, 340

Farb, P., 250
Farnsworth, K. B., 110
Farnsworth, P., 171
Feinman, G. M., 207

Feldman, R. A., 309, 313
Fell, B., 21
Fladmark, K. R., 47
Flannery, K. V., 171, 172, 174, 179, 260, 266, 267, 352
Flenniken, J. J., 56
Flinn, L., 210
Ford, J. A., 106
Ford, L. T., 234
Ford, R. I., 110, 234, 236, 243
Fowler, M. L., 249, 251
Freidel, D. A., 282
Fried, M. H., 16, 227
Frison, G. C., 74, 77, 139
Frost, F. J., 342
Funk, R. E., 64, 256
Furst, P. T., 265

Galinat, W. V., 171
Gamboa, J. V., 182
Gibson, J. L., 111, 229, 248, 251
Goodyear, A. C., 88
Gorenstein, S., 63
Gorman, F., 68
Gowlett, J. A. J., 23, 25, 46
Graham, R. W., 64
Gramly, R. M., 64, 256
Greber, N., 244
Green, F. E., 54
Greengo, R. E., 244
Grenne-Ravits, R., 271
Griffin, J. B., 63, 231, 232
Grimes, J. R., 64
Grove, D. C., 265–7
Guidon, N., 79

Haberman, T. W., 110
Hall, R. L., 249, 255
Hamblin, R. L., 294
Hammond, N., 179, 282
Hariot, T., 5
Harner, M., 175, 307
Harp, E., 147
Harris, M., 17, 175, 306, 352
Harrison, P. D., 281
Hassan, F., 95
Haury, E. W., 203
Haynes, C. V., 53, 64
Heiser, C. B., 162
Heizer, R. F., 134, 135, 137
Helms, M. W., 313

Henderson, J. S., 277–9, 284–6, 289, 292, 295
Hester, J. A., 41
Heyerdahl, T., 21
Higgs, E. S., 36
Holton, F. A., 90, 94, 98, 240
Hopkins, D. M., 46
Howells, W. W., 41

Irwih, H. T., 127
Irwin-Williams, C., 54, 120
Isaac, E., 161
Isbell, W. H., 327, 332, 334

Jefferson, T., 3
Jennings, J. D., 96, 119, 211, 258
Jett, S. C., 161, 341
Julien, C. J., 335

Kaplan, L., 175
Kauffman, B. E., 67
Kay, M., 110
Kidder, A. V., 8
King, F. B., 110
King, L., 133
King, T. F., 134, 135, 137
Klein, R. G., 28
Kolata, A. L., 323, 328, 329, 331
Kowalewski, S. A., 269, 270
Krieger, A. D., 51
Kroeber, A. L., 137, 224
Kus, J. S., 334

La Barre, W., 73
Lahren, L., 71
Lanning, E. P., 197, 339
Larson, L. H., 248
Lathrap, D. W., 161, 182, 195
Laughlin, W. S., 25, 30, 142
Lee, R. B., 49, 70
Lévi-Strauss, C., 348
Lightfoot, K. G., 207
Linné, S., 325
Lipe, W. D., 127, 219, 344
Lippi, R. N., 180
Llagostera Martinez, A., 157
Lynch, T. F., 52, 81, 157, 179, 186

MacGowan, K., 41
Mackey, C., 333
MacNeish, R. S., 52, 65, 166, 168, 170, 176, 187
Madsen, D. B., 115, 121
Marcos, J. G., 182
Marcus, J., 287, 290
Marino, J., 323
Marshall, S. B., 67
Martin, P. S., 59–61, 207, 219
Matos Moctezuma, E., 304
Matsuzawa, T., 319
Maxwell, M. S., 145, 147, 152
McEwen, G. F., 182
McGhee, R., 93, 145, 153
McIntyre, L., 327
McNeill, W. H., 355, 356

McNett, C. W., 67
Mead, J. I., 53
Meggers, B. J., 182, 193, 196–8, 200, 340, 341
Michael, H. N., 33, 36, 38
Millon, R. F., 275, 278
Mochanov, Y., 35, 36
Molina Montes, A. F., 304
Morgan, L. H., 6
Morlan, R. E., 52, 58
Morris, C., 338
Moseley, M. E., 192, 309, 313, 315, 316, 318, 323, 324, 326, 331–4
Muller, J., 111, 229, 243, 244, 247
Müller-Beck, H., 27
Munson, P. J., 236
Myers, T. P., 52

Nelson, D. E., 52
Newman, W. S., 71
Nichols, D. L., 203, 271
Niederberger, C., 178

O'Brien, P. J., 249
Ortiz, A., 216
Ortloff, R., 334

Palerm, A., 303
Parmalee, P. W., 236
Parsons, J. J., 200
Parsons, J. R., 272, 273, 275, 280, 303
Patterson, T. C., 188, 318
Paulsen, A. C., 334
Peebles, C. S., 252, 254
Peterson, D. A., 106, 344
Phillips, P., 81
Pickersgill, B., 162
Pitcher, B. L., 294
Plog, F., 207, 219
Price, B. J., 226
Price, J. E., 247
Proskouriakoff, T., 288
Prufer, O. H., 235, 237, 243

Quilter, J., 192
Quirarte, J., 285

Rathje, W. L., 282, 301
Raymond, J. S., 192
Rick, J. W., 185
Ritchie, W. A., 101, 104, 106, 108, 109, 256
Robinson, C. K., 110
Roosevelt, A. C., 193, 198, 199
Rothschild, N. A., 100
Rounds, J., 303
Rowe, J. H., 321, 337
Rowlett, R. M., 1
Ruz-Lhuillier, A., 289

Sabloff, J. A., 301
Salwen, B., 71
Sanders, W. T., 226, 272, 273, 275, 280, 282, 303, 323

Santley, R. S., 269, 272, 273, 275, 280, 303
Sauer, C. O., 160
Scarborough, V. L., 286
Schaafsma, C. F. and P., 222
Schoenwetter, J., 173
Schreiber, K. J., 332
Service, E., 16, 115, 215, 224, 227
Sherratt, A., 46
Silverberg, R., 3
Smith, B. D., 247
Snarskis, M. J., 80
Snow, D. R., 89, 90, 93, 101, 102, 106, 108, 109
Stanford, D., 73
Stark, B. L., 179
Stemper, D. M., 180
Steponaitis, V., 250
Steventon, R. L., 235
Steward, J., 16, 114
Stocker, T., 192, 265
Stothert, K. B., 157, 180
Struever, S., 90, 94, 98, 240
Stuart, G. E., 292
Swanson, E. H., 274

Taylor, R. E., 44
Thomas, D. H., 115
Titov, E. E., 38
Tolstoy, P., 271, 340
Tuck, J. A., 93, 106, 145, 256
Turner, B. L., 281
Turner, C. G., 11, 45, 180

Vickery, K. D., 110
Vivian, R. G., 215
Voorhies, B., 179
Voorhies, M. R., 52

Walthall, J. A., 89, 108, 109, 241
Webb, C. H., 111
Webb, S. D., 64
Webb, W. S., 98
Webster, D. L., 282
Wedel, W. R., 139, 256, 257, 259
Wheat, J. B., 75
Willey, G. R., 80, 81, 102, 103, 127, 128, 150, 151, 157–9, 199, 200, 211, 268, 277, 309, 313, 314, 320, 322, 324, 325
Wilmsen, E. N., 74
Wilson, D., 192, 318
Winters, H. D., 100
Wissler, C., 7
Wittfogel, K., 226
Woodbury, R. B., 203
Wright, H. E., 60, 61

Yarnell, R. A., 110, 236
Yi, S., 35

Zeidler, J., 182
Zeitlin, R. N., 179, 282
Zevallos, M. C., 180
Zubrow, E. B. W., 203

Subject index

Abejas phase, 172, 178
Acheulian, 23, 27, 51
Acoma pueblo, 216, 220
Acosta, Jose de, 2, 39
Adena, 112, 344, 345, 350,
    228–34, 235, 239
Adovasio, James, 53, 54
Afontova Gora, 36
Agate Basin phase, 138
Ainu, 40
Ajalpan phase, 172, 179
Ajuereado phase, 167, 173
Akapana, 329
Akmak, 143
Alberta phase, 138
Aldan River sites, 24, 35, 36, 37
Aleut language, 142
Aleutian prehistory, 143, 153,
    154
Algonquians, 106, 141, 153
Alma Plain pottery, 206
Altar de Sacrificios, 261, 283,
    285, 292
Altithermal, 119, 120, 144
Alto Salaverry, 317
Amargosa phase, 124
American Bottom, 249
Amvrocievkaya, 24, 32
Ananatuba phase, 196, 197
Anangula, 140, 143, 153
Anasazi, 20, 125, 126, 202,
    207–22, 346
Ancón-Chillón sites, 189–92
Anzick, 50, 71–2, 91
Arauquinoid pottery, 199
Arawakan languages, 197, 313
Archaic stage, 16, 18, 53, 55, 67,
    68, 69, 77, 79, 82–159 passim,
    163, 165, 207, 223, 224, 229,
    234, 282, 345, 349, 350, 351
Arctic Small Tool tradition, 146,
    147, 148, 149, 152, 153
Arenal complex, 189
Arikara, 259
Aruã culture, 199
Aspero, 317
Assawompsett II, 8, 88, 104
Atahuallpa, 339
Athapaskans, 141, 142, 144, 154
Atwater, Caleb, 3

Augustine mound, 234
Aurignacian, 29, 30, 35
Australia, peopling of, 29–30, 47
Australopithecus, 22
Avingak complex, 148
Ayacucho complex, 77, 187;
    sequence, 86, 155, 156, 185,
    187–90, 194, 351
Ayampitín points, 155, 157, 158
Ayers Mound, 232
Azcapotzalco, 8, 302
Aztalan (Wisconsin), 247
Aztec Ruins (New Mexico), 202,
    211
Aztecs, 2, 8, 176, 226, 278, 301–8,
    341, 354
Aztlan, 301

Bahía phase, 309
Bajada phase, 113, 120
Ball, J., 282
bannerstones, 66, 102
Banwari Trace, 156, 158
Bare Creek phase, 123
Bare Island points, 101
Barrancoid pottery, 195, 196, 198
Basketmaker culture, 207–9
Bat Cave, 344, 201, 202
Batza Tena, 50
Becan, 261, 286
Belize, 80, 164, 179, 282, 295
Berelekh, 34, 38
Beringia, 37, 45–7, 58, 82
Berlin, H., 288
Betatakin, 202, 219
bifurcate-base points, 89, 90
Big Sandy points, 101
Binford, Lewis R., 17, 18, 164
Bird, Junius, 80, 191
Bird Jaguar, 288, 293
Birnirk culture, 140, 152
Bison antiquus, 48, 64
Blackwater Draw, 48, 50, 54, 57,
    63, 65
Blanton, R., 269–70
Bluefish Cave, 1, 50, 58, 143
Boas, Franz, 6, 8, 14, 16, 41
Bonampak, 261, 284, 291, 295
Bonfire Shelter, 50, 74, 75
Borax Lake phase, 135

Border Cave, 24, 29
Boucher de Perthes, J. 4–5
bow and arrow, 127, 146, 159,
    206, 208, 243
Boylston Street weir, 88, 102
Brewerton complex, 101
Bryan, A., 343
Buchanan Reservoir, 000
budares, 193
Buikstra, J., 240
Bull Brook, 50, 57, 63, 64, 69, 73

Caballo Muerto, 319
Cachi phase, 188–9
Cahokia, 225, 249–52, 255, 345,
    352
Caiambé, 194, 199
Calakmul, 261, 287
calendar, Mesoamerican, 269,
    284
California Indians, 10, 18, 40, 44,
    108, 114, 124, 130, 162, 223,
    224, 234, 342, 350, 351, 352
Calima culture, 194, 311, 312
calpulli, 305
Campbell tradition, 121
Canaliño culture, 132–3
Canario phase, 190
Capá, 194, 313
capacocha sacrifices, 337
carbon 14 dating, 11–13, 145
Caribs, 197
Carneiro, Robert, 227, 282
Carter, George, 340
Casas Grandes, 202, 213–14, 346
Cascade phase, 120, 127, 128, 129
Casper, 50, 75
Castillo, 321, 323
Central Plains tradition, 230, 258
Cerro Mangote, 156, 157
Cerro Sechín, 319, 320
Cerros, 261, 286
Chaco Canyon, 21, 202, 209,
    210–17, 227, 345, 346
Chakipampa pottery, 332
Chalcatzingo, 261, 265, 266, 267,
    284
Chalchuapa, 261, 283
Chan-Bahlum, 289
Chan Chan, 308, 333–4

381

Charleston points, 89
charmstones, 133, 134
Chavín culture, 310, 319–23, 324, 329, 341, 346; Chavín de Huantár (type-site), 319–23
Chesowanja, 24, 25
Chiapa de Corzo, 284
Chibcha, 194, 312–13
Chichén Itzá, 261, 298–301
Chichimecs, 298, 301, 302
Chicoid culture, 313–14
chiefdoms, 131, 137, 200, 215, 223–6, 227, 245, 249–52, 254, 255, 260, 264, 267, 272, 282, 285, 287, 308–14, 315–19, 323, 345, 349, 351
Chihua phase, 188
Childe, V. G., 16, 160
Chimi, 154
Chimu, 332–5
chinampas, 273, 303, 329
Chinookan languages, 127
Chiricahua stage (Cochise culture), 120, 201
Chiripa, 323
Chobshi Cave, 155, 156
Cholula, 261, 279–80, 296
Choris complex, 140, 148, 149
Chorrera culture, 308
Choukoutien, 24, 25, 26; Upper Cave skeletons, 30, 40
Chumash, 132–3
Chuquitanta (El Paraíso), 191, 315–17, 319, 350, 353
Cienega Creek, 201
Cliff Palace, 218–19
Clovis culture, 51, 56–9, 61, 62–73, 74, 80, 116, 117, 143; fluted points, 48, 51, 54, 56, 57, 58, 59, 62, 64, 65, 67, 68, 71, 73, 80, 88, 116, 138, 343
Coalescent culture, 259
Coastal Archaic, 101
Coba, 261, 289
Cochise culture, 117, 120, 201
Coclé, 225, 312, 313
Cocom dynasty, 300–1
Cody phase, 138
Coe, Michael, 265, 267
Coles Creek culture, 250
Colha, 261, 282
Colima dogs, 175
Colonial period (Hohokam), 204
Columbus, Christopher, 1
Conchas phase, 191
Conchopata, 332
Conrad, G., 334
Cook, S. F., 306
Cooper Hopewellian, 230, 241
Copan, 261, 287
Copena, 230, 241
Corbina phase, 190
Cordilleran ice sheet, 46, 47
Corozal phase, 198, 199
Cortes, Hernan, 2, 354

Cosumnes phase, 133, 136
Coxcatlan phase, 169, 170, 173
Coyolxauhqui (Aztec goddess), 304
Cresap Mound, 231
cross-dating, 7
Cuello, 179, 282, 285, 343
Cueva Blanca, 173
Cuicuilco, 261, 272, 273
Cuitlahuac, 355
cultivation of plants, 81, 86, 109–10, 125, 136, 158, 159, 160–222 *passim*, 232, 235–6, 245, 246, 247, 256, 257, 260, 262, 270, 280, 294, 303, 315, 318, 344, 350, 352–3
Cumberland points, 64
Curl Snout, 278

Dalles, of Columbia River, 113, 118, 128
Dalton points, 88, 89, 90
Danger Cave, 113, 114, 115, 118, 119, 120
Darwin, Charles, 4, 5, 6, 47
Debert, 50, 73
Deetz, J., 259
Del Mar skull, 44
Delmarva Adena, 230, 234
Denbigh flint complex, 144–6, 148
dendrochronology, 10
Dent, 50, 68
Desert Archaic, 55, 67, 112–26, 165, 177, 350
Desert side-notched points, 124
diffusion, 20–1, 106–9, 111–12, 150, 153, 180–2, 212, 228–9, 245–6, 256, 259, 285, 321, 340–7
direct historical approach, 11
diseases, effects on native Americans, 354–6
Dogan Point, 88, 93
Dolni Věstonice, 24, 31
domestication of animals: camelids, 189, 353–4, 356; dogs, 81, 91, 119, 175, 176, 263, 307; guinea pigs, 188, 306; turkeys, 175
Dorset culture, 142, 145, 147, 148, 152
Double Adobe, 113, 117
Douglass, A. E., 10
Dutchess Quarry Cave, 50, 64
Dyuktai culture, 34, 35, 36, 37, 38, 58, 143
Dzibilchaltún, 261, 285, 296

Eayam phase, 129
Eden points, 138, 139
Ekholm, Gordon, 340
El Abra rockshelter, 155, 156
El Inga, 55, 78, 80
El Jobo, 78, 81

El Mirador, 261, 285, 286
El Riego phase, 118, 167–9, 171, 176
Elko points, 122, 123
Ellesmere Island, 140, 152–3
Encanto phase, 190
Encinitas tradition, 121, 132
Englefield Island, 156, 157, 159
Eskimos, 1, 19, 25, 31, 36, 39, 40, 70, 73, 92, 94, 102, 108, 141–55
ethnographic analogy, 19–20; examples, 68, 70, 72–3, 94, 114–15, 119, 129, 130–1, 133, 200, 207, 208, 215, 216–17, 223–5, 234, 242, 249–52, 254
Etowah, 230, 252, 254, 255
Eva, 88, 91, 94, 96, 97, 101
Evans, Clifford, 181, 182, 197
Eynan (Natufian site, Israel), 178
Ezhantsy, 34, 35

False Face society (Iroquois), 224
Fell, Barry, 21
Fell's Cave, 43, 49, 77, 78, 80, 156, 158
Figgins, J. D., 48
Firstview points, 76
Filimoshki, 33, 34
Fishtail points, 80–1, 158
Flannery, Kent, 18, 174, 260
Flint Mine Hill, 69
Flint Run, 50, 57, 69
Floral Park ware, 285
"Flowery Wars", 306
fluted points, *see* Clovis, Cumberland, Dalton, Fishtail, Folsom, Hardaway, Quad
Folsom points, 5, 41, 48, 56, 62, 73, 74, 74, 138; sites, 5, 41, 48, 50, 62, 70, 74–5, 138
Fort Center, 230, 244
Ford, James, 9–10
Formative stage, 16, 18, 260, 351
Fort Rock Cave, 50, 54, 55, 113, 116
founder effect, 40
Freidel, David, 282
Fremont culture, 114, 125, 126, 127, 177
Fried, Morton, 16, 227
Frontenac Island, 88, 100–1
functionalism, 14–15

Gamio, M., 8
Gatecliff Shelter, 113, 122
Gaviota phase, 191–2
Gilliland site, 209
Glacial Kame culture, 229, 230
Goodall culture, 230, 241
gourds, 109, 161–2, 173
Grasshopper, 216, 220
Grave Creek Mound, 230, 231
Greenland, 1, 140, 142, 145, 147, 152, 153
Guila Naquitz, 173

Guitarrero Cave, 77, 78, 79, 81, 86, 155, 156, 165, 185, 186, 188
Gulf of Georgia stage, 130
Gypsum Cave, 116

Hakataya culture, 136, 202
Hardaway points, 88, 89, 90
Harder phase, 127, 128
Harner, Michael, on Aztec cannibalism, 175, 307
Harness, 230, 236
Harris, C. W., site, California, 113
Harris, Marvin, 17, 175, 306–7
Harrisena site, 89
Healy Lake, 140, 144
Hell Gap, 50, 138
Heyerdahl, Thor, 21
Hogup Cave, 113, 115, 118, 119, 120, 121, 126
Hohokam culture, 203–5, 349
Hokan languages, 134
Holly Oak, engraved mammoth, 71
Holmes, W. H., 5, 7
Homo erectus, 23, 25, 26, 27, 30, 33, 44
Homo habilis, 23
Homo sapiens, 27, 29, 30, 31, 42, 347
Hooton, E. A., analysis of Pecos skulls, 41
Hopewell culture, 110, 112, 163, 226, 235–44, 245, 247, 256–7, 344, 345, 350; decline, 243–4; expansion of interaction sphere, 241–3
Hopi, 202, 216, 220, 221
Horner kill site, 139
Houx phase, 135
Hrdlička, Aleš, 5, 7, 47, 48
Hsihoutou, 23, 24
Huaca de la Luna, Moche, 324, 326
Huaca de Sol, Moche, 308, 324, 326
Huaca Prieta, 188, 191, 194, 341
Huanta phase, Ayacucho, 187
Huanuco Pampa, 338
Huari, 316, 327, 331–2, 334
Huascar, 339
Huayna Capac, 335, 339
Hueyatlaco, 54, 55
Huff site, 258
human sacrifice, 225; Aztec, 176, 302, 303, 304, 306–8; Cahokia, 225, 251–2; Chimu, 333–4; Coclé (Sitio Conte), 225, 313; Inca, 337; Kaminaljuyú, 225, 284; Kolomoki, 225, 245; Maya, 289, 291, 292, 306; Monte Albán, 268; Moundville, 254; Natchez, 251, 254; Olmec, 265, 306; Real Alto,

183; Tlatilco, 270; Toltec, 297, 298, 299, 306, 307
Humboldt Lakebed sites, 122
Jupa-Iya phase, 195, 198

Ikhine II, 34, 35
Illinois Hopewell, 239–41
Inca Cueva, 4, 155
Incas, 226, 227, 308, 334–9, 354, 355, 356
Independence I culture, Greenland, 140, 145
Indian Knoll burials, 88, 96, 98–100
Inupik language, 142
Ipiutak, 140, 149, 150
Iroquois, 2, 10, 104, 183, 217, 224, 256
Irwin-Williams, C., 55
Isbell, W., 334
Issaquena culture, 244
Itzcoatl, 302
Izapan style, 284–5, 287

Jaguar Cave, 119
Jauarí, 197
Java, 23, 24
Jay phase, 113, 120
Jaywa phase, Ayacucho, 187, 198
Jefferson, Thomas, excavation of burial mound, 3
Jomon pottery, 181, 182
Jones-Miller site, 50, 73, 75, 138
Judge, James, 215
Juxtlahuaca Cave, Olmec style paintings, 266

kachinas, origin of, 222
Kahroak, 140, 146
Kalasasaya, Tiahuanaco, 329
Kaminaljuyú, 225, 261, 277–8, 283–4
Kanawha points, 89, 90
Kansas City Hopewell, 256–7
Karatau, 24, 26
Kavik, 154
Kayenta region Anasazi, 219–20
Kettle Rock, 93
Khotylevo, 24, 28
Kidder, Alfred, 8, 207
Kiet Siel, 202, 219
Kimmswick, 50, 64–5
Kinishba, 202, 220
Kirk points, 89, 90
kivas, 20, 207, 209, 210, 212, 216, 217, 219, 220, 222
Klo-kut, 140, 154
Knorosov, Y., 288
Kodiak Island, 153–4
Kokorevo, 34, 36
Kolomoki, 225, 230, 244–5
Koster, 88, 90, 91, 94, 95, 96, 97–8, 110, 162, 178
Kotosh, 195, 316, 317–18
Kow Swamp, Australia, 24, 30

Kowalewski, S., 270
Kroeber, Alfred, 9
Kukhtuy III, 34, 38
Kuksu cult, California, 224, 234
Kumara, 34, 35
!Kung San (Bushmen), 61, 162
Kus, J. S., 334

La Florida, 319
La Galgada, 318
La Ponga, 180
La Sueva rockshelter, 155
La Tolita, 194, 308, 309
La Venta, 260, 261, 263, 264, 265, 266, 267, 268, 341
Lagoa Santa, 5
Laguna Beach skull, 44
Lake Forest Archaic, 97, 100, 101
Lake Mungo, Australia, skeletal remains, 24, 29
Lake Titicaca, 323, 328, 329, 331, 349, 353, 354
Lake Turkana, Kenya, hominid remains, 23, 24
Lamanai, 261, 285
Lamoka Lake site, 88, 96, 104; Lamoka points, 101
L'Anse Amour, burial mound, 88, 93, 94
L'Anse aux Meadows, Viking settlement, 140, 153
Lantien, China, 23, 24
Lanzón, Chavín de Huantár, 321, 322
Las Bocas, 266
Las Haldas, 319
Las Vegas midden, 157, 180
Lascaux, 65
Lathrap, Donald, 195, 197
Laurentian tradition, 101, 102
Laurentide ice sheet, 46, 53
Lauricocha caves, 185
Le Croy points, 89, 90
Lebenstedt, 24, 28
Lehner, 50, 63, 68
Lerma points, 55, 65, 81
L'Escale, 24, 25
Levi rockshelter, 50, 77
Lewisville, 50, 51
Libby, W. F., 11, 12
Lime Creek, 50, 77
Lind Coulee, 113, 118
Lindenmeier, 50, 74–5
Little Salt Spring, 50, 64
Llano Estacado, 56
Locarno Beach phase, Strait of Georgia, 113, 129
Lochnore-Nesikep, 113, 128
Loma Torremote, 272
Long Sault Island, Adena mounds, 234
Los Toldos, 77, 78, 79, 81
Lovelock Cave, 113, 122
Luqurmata, 331
Luz complex, 189

Machalilla culture, 180, 308
MacNeish, Richard S., 65, 77, 166, 169, 170, 171, 172, 173, 187
Madden Lake, Panama, 78, 80
Magellan sequence, Tierra del Fuego, 158
maize, cultivation of: in eastern woodlands, 110, 228, 235, 247, 255, 256; in Ecuador, 180, 352; in Mesoamerica, 166–72, 173–5, 179, 260, 262, 280, 305, 352; on Middle Orinoco, 193, 198; by Omagua and Tapajós (in Amazonia), 200; in Peru, 184–7, 338; in Plains, 257; in Southwest, 125, 201, 203, 206, 207, 208
Malambo culture, 194, 195
Malinowski, B., 14
Mal'ta, 24, 34, 36, 58
Manacupurú, 194, 199
Manco Capac, 339
Mangelsdorf, Paul, 166, 169–71
manioc, cultivation and preparation, 193, 195, 198, 199, 200
Manitoba mounds, 257
Manta, 194, 309–10; Manteño culture, 310
Mapa, China, 24, 27
Marajó Island, 194, 196–9
Marajoara culture, 198–9
Marksville, Hopewellian culture, 230, 231–43
Marmes Rockshelter, 43, 113, 118
Marpole phase, 113, 129–30
Martin, Paul S., "overkill" theory, 59, 60, 65
Marx, Karl, 17
Maxtla, 302
Maya, 179, 260, 278, 280–96, 298–301, 349; collapse of Peten centers, 294–6
Mayapán, 261, 300–1
Meadowcroft Rockshelter, 50, 53, 54, 58, 66, 67
Medea Creek, proto-historic Chumash cemetery, 133, 137
Medicine Lodge Creek, 50, 77, 113
megafauna, extinction of, 51, 59–62, 81, 82, 116, 117, 163–4, 167, 185
Meggers, Betty, 181, 197, 198, 199, 340
Menlo phase, 121–3
Mesa Verde, 202, 217–19, 220
Mexico, Basin of, 55, 267, 270–80, 301, 302, 303, 306, 307
Middle Missouri tradition, 230, 258–9
Midland phase, 138; skull, 41, 42, 43

Midwestern Taxonomic Method, 11
migration, 32–3, 47, 49, 51, 81, 142, 146, 152, 153, 197, 256
Milagro culture, 194, 310
Miller culture, 230, 241
Milliken, 113, 118
milpa cultivation, 280, 281
Mimbres culture, 202, 213–14
mirrors, Olmec, 265–7
Mississippian tradition, 245–55, 257, 258, 345
mi'ta (Inca corvée labor), 316, 324, 337
Mixe-Zoquean languages, 260
Mixtecs, 300, 306
Moche, 308, 324, 326, 333
Moche–Chicama canal, 334
Mochica culture, 66, 324–7, 330
Moctezuma I, 302, 306
Moctezuma II, 303, 304
Mogollon tradition, 125, 205–7, 208, 209, 213, 220, 346
Mojos region, Bolivia, 194, 200
Mongolia, Paleolithic of, 27, 28, 35
Mongoloids, 25, 36, 39, 40, 42, 45, 142
Monks Mound, Cahokia, 249
Montagnais-Naskapi, 73
Monte Albán, 261, 268–70, 275
Monte Verde, 78, 79–80
Moorehead complex, 101
Morgan, Lewis Henry, 6
Morlan, Richard, 52
mortuary practices, 71–2, 91, 93–4, 98–101, 105–6, 108, 127, 130, 132, 133–4, 135, 136, 183, 199, 200, 205, 213, 216, 220, 225, 229, 231–41, 244, 251–4, 257, 267, 270, 272, 278, 284, 289, 293, 300, 309–11, 313, 321, 333–4, 344
Morrow Mountain points, 91, 92
Moseley, Michael, 192, 315
Mound City, 230, 236
Moundville, 230, 246, 252, 254, 255
Mousterian industry, 27, 28, 29, 31, 35, 36, 58
Moxexe, 323
Muaco, 77, 78
Mummy Cave, 113, 138
Murray Springs, 50, 63

Naco, 50, 68
Nahuatl language, 65, 276
Namu, 113, 129
Natchez, 230, 250–1, 254, 255
Native Americans, physical traits of, 39, 42, 142; early skeletons, 41–4, 47, 96
Nazca culture, 316, 327–8, 330, 331, 332; lines, 327–8

Neanderthals, 27–30, 42, 44, 45
Nelson, Nels, 8
Neville site, 88, 91, 92; points, 91, 92, 94
"New" Archaeology, 17–18
Nez Percé, 127
Niah Cave, Borneo, 24, 29
Northern Archaic, 144, 147
Northwest Coast, 18, 71, 86, 114, 128–32, 143, 162, 163, 223, 347, 348, 350
Norton culture, 148–9
Numic languages, 123, 124, 125, 126, 221
Numipu phase, 127
Nunamiut, 18, 70, 153

Oaxaca, 260, 261, 266–70, 275
Ocean Bay tradition, 154
Ocos culture, 308
Ogden-Fettie site, 239
Okvik culture, 149–52
Old Bering Sea culture, 149–52
Old Copper culture, 88, 101, 103
Old Crow, bone artifacts from, 50, 52, 58, 143
Oldowan tools, 23
Olduvai Gorge, 23, 24
Olmec, 111, 112, 176, 260–7 *passim*, 268, 269–70, 271, 314, 321, 341, 345, 346, 353
Olorgesailie, 23
Olsen-Chubbuck kill site, 50, 61, 75–6, 138
O'Malley shelter, 113, 122
Omagua, 200
Ona, 19, 70, 158–9
Onion Portage, 140, 143–4
Orient culture, 229
Ostionoid cultures, 313
Otter Creek points, 101
"overkill" theory of Pleistocene extinctions, 60–2
Owasco culture, 256
Ozette site, 113, 130

Pacaicasa complex, 77, 187
Pacal, 288–90
Pachakuti, 335
Pachamachay, 185, 189
Paiján points, 155, 157
Paijanense culture, 155
Pajchiri, 331
Palenque, 261, 287–9, 294
Paleo-arctic tradition, 37, 58, 143–4, 146
Paleo-Indians, 19, 22, 37, 39–81 *passim*, 146, 158, 159, 167, 187, 223
Palisades complex, 144
Palli Aike, 43
Paloma, 190, 353
Pampa, 190–1
Pampa Grande, 326–7

Paracas ceramic tradition, 321, 328
Paredão, 194, 199
Parmana, 194, 198
Pastaza phase, 197
Paulsen, A., 334
Penutian languages, 127, 134
Perigordian industry, 31
Peten, 281–3, 285–7, 291, 294, 301
Phillips, P., 16, 87
Piki phase, Ayacucho, 187–8, 189, 190
Pikimachay, 51, 52, 77, 78, 187
Pima, 205, 349
Pinto Basin phase, 124; Pinto points, 122, 123
Pioneer period (Hohokam), 203–4
Piquillacta, 332, 334
Piqunin phase, 127, 128
Pizarro, Francisco, 2, 355
Plains Village cultures, 257–9
Plains Woodland cultures, 256–7
Plainview points, 74, 75, 77, 138
Plano culture, 61, 62, 70, 73, 74, 75, 76, 120, 138; points, 54, 61, 74, 75, 76, 90, 138
Plaquemine culture, 230, 250
Playa Hermosa phase, 191
Pleistocene, 26, 28, 30, 32, 33, 35, 43, 45–50, 59, 60, 64, 65, 68, 79, 82, 87, 90, 92, 112, 116, 163–5, 347
Plenge site, 50, 57
pochteca, Aztec merchants, 213, 246, 267, 345
Point of Pines, 202, 220
Point St George, 135
Polychrome ceramic tradition, Amazonia, 198, 199
population pressure, 32–3, 84, 95, 152, 163–5, 190, 203, 221, 227, 247, 269–70, 271, 283, 351
Port au Choix, Maritime Archaic cemetery, 72, 88, 105, 140
Portage complex, 144
Porter culture, 230, 241
Portrero Nuevo, 262, 263
pottery, origins of, 343–4; Arctic, 148; eastern woodlands, 106–9; Peru, 318–19; Puerto Hormiga, 106, 195, 197; Purron (Tehuacan Valley), 172; Southwest, 203, 206, 208; Swasey (Cuello), 179; Valdivia, 180–2
Poverty Point, 88, 111, 345, 350
Powell, J. W., 4
Powers phase, 230, 247
Preceramic period, Peru, 315–18
Pre-Dorset culture, 145–8
pre-projectile horizon, 51; sites, 50, 51, 52, 77, 79, 116

Price, Barbara, 226
Prince Rupert Harbor, 113, 130
Proskouriakoff, Tatiana, 288
Pueblo Alto, 217
Pueblo Bonito, 210–11, 213, 215–16, 346
Puente phase, Ayacucho, 187, 189
Puerto Hormiga, 106, 180, 182, 194, 195, 197, 198, 343–4
Pukara, 316, 328
Puma-Punku, Tiahuanaco, 330
Punuk culture, 151–2
Purron phase, Tehuacan, 172, 343
Putnam, F., 5
Peru, 43, 155

Qafzeh, Israel, early *Homo sapiens*, 29
Quad site, 50, 63
Quaquacuiltin, 307
Quebrada las Conchas, 156, 157
Quechua language, 159, 337
Quereo, 155, 156
Quetzalcoatl, 20, 222, 265, 298–9, 342
Quiani, 156, 157
Quimbaya culture, 194, 311, 313
quipu (khipu), 337

Radcliffe-Brown, A., 14
Rathje, William, on emergence of Maya civilization, 282
Real Alto, 180, 182–4, 194, 308, 344
Richmond Hill, 88, 89
Rio Grande pueblos, 202, 221
Ritchie, William, 86
Riverine Archaic, 97–9
Riverton, 88, 96, 110
Roadcut site, 118
Roosevelt, Anna, 193, 198, 199
Rose Spring phase, 124
Ruz-Lhuillier, A., 289

Sacsahuaman, 338, 339
Sahaptin languages, 127
St Albans points, 89, 90
Saladoid pottery, 196, 198
Salinas de Chao, 317
Salishan languages, 127, 130, 131
Salmon Ruins, 202, 211, 217
Salts Cave, 110
San Agustín culture, 194, 309–11, 312
San Cristobal pueblo, 8
San Dieguito complex, 81, 113, 117, 118, 120, 121, 124
San Jon points, 76
San Lorenzo, 260–6, 345
San Pedro Cochise, 201, 206
San Pedro pottery, Valdivia, 182
Sanders, William, 226, 282

Santa Marta Cave, 166
Santa Rosa culture, 230, 244
Santa Rosa Island, California, 50, 51–2
Santarém, 194, 199–200
Santley, R., on Monte Albán, 269–70
Sauer, Carl, 160
Scioto Valley (Ohio) Hopewell culture, 230, 235–9 *passim*
Scovill site, 236
sea level changes, 45–6, 82, 92, 96, 102, 104, 157, 164, 353
Sechín Alto, 323
Sedentary period (Hohokam), 204
Seip mounds, 230, 238
Selby-Dutton site, 50, 52
seriation, 9–10
Serpent Mound, 230, 231
Service, Elman, 16, 115, 215, 224, 227
setaria, 169, 171, 174
Shabik'eschee, 209
shamanism, 72, 73, 149, 224
Shang, 341, 342, 347, 348
Shawnee-Minisink, 50, 57, 66, 67
Shoop, 50, 51, 66, 69
Shoshoni, 73, 114, 115, 122, 124, 126, 162, 177, 223
Showlow pueblo, 10
Shui-tung-kou, 24, 28
Siberia, 33–8, 44, 45, 58, 143, 146, 148, 149, 150, 152
Sitio Conte, Panama, 194, 313
Skhul, Israel, early *Homo sapiens*, 29
Skraelings, Viking term for native Americans, 1, 153
Smith, Grafton Elliot, 21
Smith, Joseph, 3
Smithsonian Institution, 4
Snaketown, 202, 203
Southern Cult, 252–5
Southwest, village farming cultures of, 125–7, 201–22 *passim*
spearthrower (atlatl), 33, 65, 66, 102, 119, 128, 239, 243, 344, 347
Spier, L., 9
Spiro Mound, 72, 73, 230, 248, 254, 255
squash, 21, 109, 110, 160, 167, 168, 173, 178, 190, 191, 201, 203, 247, 257, 280, 344
Squier, E. G., and E. H. Davis, study of mounds, 4
Squibnocket points, 101
Staff God, Chavín and Tiahuanaco, 321, 329, 330, 332
Stallings Island, early pottery, 88, 106
Stanford, Dennis, 52

Stanfield-Worley Bluff Shelter, 88, 90
Stanly points, 91, 92
Stark points, 91, 92
steatite vessels, 107–9
Steward, Julian, 15, 16, 114, 115, 349
Stormy Sky, 278–9
Strong, William D., 11
Struever, Stuart, 98
SU site, 202, 207
Sudden Shelter, 113, 122
Sulphur Springs stage, Cochise culture, 117, 120
Surprise Valley, 94, 113, 121, 122
Susquehanna broad points, 108
Swasey pottery, Cuello, 179, 343
Swift Creek culture, 230, 241
Sylvan Lake, side-notched and stemmed points, 101, 103

Taber child, 44
Taconic points, 101
Tagua Tagua, 78, 81
Taima Taima, 77, 78
Taino, 314
Tairona, 194, 311
talud-tablero facades, 276–8
Talus Village, 202, 207
Tamaulipas, early cultivation in, 166, 173, 174
Tapajos, 200
Tehuacan Valley, 65, 86, 118, 166–73 *passim*, 176–9, 185, 187, 201, 343, 351
Tenochtitlán, 302–6, 338, 354, 355, 357
Tenochtitlán (Olmec site), 262–3
teosinte, possible maize ancestor, 170, 171, 173, 178
Teotihuacán, 8, 20, 226, 227, 261, 272–80, 295, 296, 298, 308, 346
Tepexpan skeleton, 43
Tequixquiac, 50, 55, 71
Terra Amata, 24, 25
Texcoco, 302, 303
Thomas, Cyrus, 4, 7, 227
Thomas, David H., 115, 122
Thule culture, 142, 152–4
Thunderbird site, 50, 69, 94
Tiahuanaco, 316, 328, 329–32
Tikal, 226, 249, 261, 278, 279, 281, 284–9, 293–5, 308, 349

Tingtsun, 24, 27
Tlaloc, 20, 265, 275, 276, 279, 303
Tlapacoya, 50, 55
Tlatelolco, 302, 303, 305
Tlatilco, 261, 266, 267, 270–1
Tlaxcala, 306
Toca do Boqueirao do Sitio da Pedra Furada, 79
Tolstoy, Paul, 340
Toltecs, 296–301, 307, 345
Topa, 335
Topiltzin, 298–300
Torralba and Ambrona (Spain), 23
Transitional (Terminal) Archaic, 106, 109
Trempealeau culture, 230, 241
Tremper, 236
Trenton Gravels, 5
Tres Zapotes, 260, 261, 265, 269, 284
Trinil, Java, 23
Trois Freres, France, 73
Troyville culture, 244
Tucannon phase, 127
Tuktu, 140, 144
Tula, 261, 296–301
Tularosa Cave, 201, 202
Tule Springs, 116
Tupians, 197
Turner mound, 236, 238
Turrialba, 78, 80
Tutishcainyo, 194–8
Tylor, Edward, 341
tzompantli (skull rack), 298, 299, 303, 307

Uaxactún, 261, 285, 287
Ulalinka, 33, 34
Upper Paleolithic cultures, 29–33, 35, 36, 54, 71, 73, 96, 347
Ushki, 34, 38
Ust Kan, 34, 35
Ust Mil II, 34, 35
Utes, 124, 126
Uxmal, 261, 296

Vail, 50, 57, 64, 65
Valdivia culture, 180–4, 194, 195, 308, 341
Valsequillo, 50, 54, 55, 58, 71
Varvarina Gora, 34, 35
várzea, 193
Ventana Cave, 113, 116, 117

Vergennes phase, 101
Verkhne-Troitskaya, 34, 37
Vikings, 1, 153
Viñaque pottery, 332
Vinette I pottery, 109
Viracocha Pampa, 332
Virú Valley, Willey's study of settlement patterns of, 15
Vivian, Gwynn, 215
Vogelherd, Germany, 24, 30
Vosburg complex, 101, 103

Wacissa River, bison kill site, 50, 64
Wading River points, 101
Walakpa complex, 140, 148, 149
Wankarani, 323
Wapanucket sites, 50, 51, 69, 88, 96, 104, 107
Webster, D., 282
Weeden Island culture, 230, 244–5
Weidenreich, Franz, 40
West Athens Hill, 50, 69
Wheat, Joe Ben, 76
wheels, 176, 354
Whipple site, 50, 64
White, John, paintings of Virginia Indians and Britons, 5
White, Leslie, 16
Willey, Gordon, 15, 16, 87
Williamson site, 50, 69
Wilmsen, Edwin, 74
Wilson Butte Cave, 50, 55, 113, 116
Windmiller phase, 133–4
Windust phase, 66, 113, 118, 120
Wisconsin glaciation, 27, 28, 46, 47
Wittfogel, Karl, 15, 349
Wiyot, 128, 135
Works Progress Administration (WPA) archaeology, 11

Xipe Totec, 265, 303, 306

Yaxchilán, 261, 288, 293
Yupik languages, 142
Yurok, 128, 135

zemis, 314
Zohapilco, 178, 270
zoned hachure pottery, 196, 197
Zuni pueblo, 202, 216